WELFARE REFORM

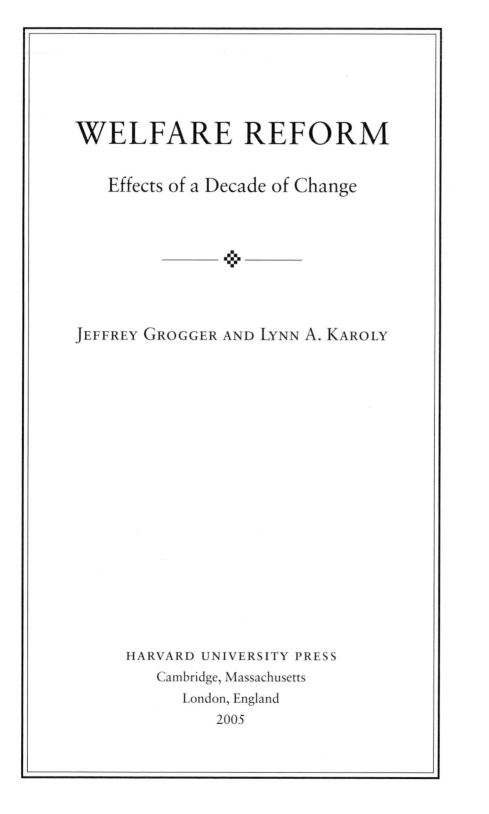

WELFARE REFORM

Effects of a Decade of Change

JEFFREY GROGGER AND LYNN A. KAROLY

HARVARD UNIVERSITY PRESS

Cambridge, Massachusetts

London, England

2005

Library of Congress Cataloging-in-Publication Data

Grogger, Jeff.
Welfare reform : effects of a decade of change / Jeffrey Grogger
and Lynn A. Karoly.
p.   cm.
Includes bibliographical references and index.
ISBN 0-674-01891-5 (alk. paper)
1. Public welfare—United States.   2. Welfare recipients—United States.
I. Karoly, Lynn A., 1961–   I. Title.
HV95.G743 2005
361.6′8—dc22   2005046125

Contents

Figures

Tables

❖

Preface

The Personal Responsibility and Work Opportunity Reconciliation Act (PRWORA) of 1996 fundamentally changed the cash welfare system in the United States. It eliminated the Aid to Families with Dependent Children (AFDC) program, replacing it with Temporary Assistance for Needy Families (TANF). It abolished the entitlement status of welfare, provided states with strong incentives to impose time limits, and tied funding levels to the states' success in moving welfare recipients into work.

By now much has been written about some of the apparent consequences of welfare reform. It is well known that caseloads plummeted during the 1990s and that employment rates of single mothers—the primary recipients of welfare in the United States—rose almost as fast. What remains controversial is how much of that transformation really stemmed from policy changes and how much resulted from other influences such as the boom economy of the late 1990s. We evaluate the evidence both on these questions and on other critical topics such as the effects of welfare reform on earnings, income, family structure, and the well-being of children.

The initial impetus for our work came in 2000 when the U.S. Department of Health and Human Services (DHHS) asked the RAND Corporation to review all of the studies that analyzed the causal effects of welfare reform. In the course of that project we made two key realizations that eventually led to this book. The first was that the policy changes stemming from welfare reform greatly expanded our opportunities to understand how low-income families respond to economic incentives. Under AFDC, the main difference among the states' welfare programs was the basic level of generosity (that is, the size of the cash grant). Economic theory predicts that behavior should vary with the level of generosity, and a fair amount of research was directed toward testing that prediction. Under TANF, state welfare programs vary to a much greater degree. Differences in generosity remain, but they are now accompanied by differences in time limits, work requirements, and other aspects that we explore in this book. These new policy differences enable researchers to test new dimensions of behavior. As a result, they put economic theory to a more demanding test. Our second key realization was that economic theory was largely up to that test, a point that we elaborate on at length.

In the course of this project we have incurred intellectual debts to a number of people who deserve particular thanks. The first is Jacob Klerman, who coauthored the DHHS report with us, authored Chapter 8 of this book, and provided extensive comments and suggestions on the entire manuscript. Two anonymous reviewers also provided detailed comments which greatly improved the manuscript's exposition and cohesion.

Howard Rolston deserves special acknowledgment, both for the role he played in guiding and overseeing the DHHS project and for encouraging us to take what we had learned from that effort and use it to write this book. A number of researchers provided input on the DHHS report that also shaped our thinking here. They include John Adams, Gordon Berlin, Rebecca Blank, Jeanne Brooks-Gunn, Greg Duncan, David Ellwood, David Fein, Steve Haider, Ron Haskins, Susan Mayer, Lawrence Mead, Bruce Meyer, Robert Moffitt, LaDonna Pavetti, Elaine Reardon, Isabel Sawhill, Robert Schoeni, John Karl Scholz, Steve Trejo, and Sheila Zedlewski.

Lynn received partial support from the RAND Corporation for the preparation of this book, and Judy Lewis at RAND provided valuable guidance with its publication.

Finally, our greatest thanks go to our families, without whose willingness to forgo our company for days and even weeks at a time, this book would not have been written.

Acronyms

ABC	A Better Chance (Delaware)
ACF	Administration for Children and Families (DHHS)
ADC	Aid to Dependent Children
AFDC	Aid to Families with Dependent Children
AFDC-UP	AFDC Unemployed Parent
AWWDP	Arkansas Welfare Waiver Demonstration Project
BPI	Behavioral Problems Index
CEA	Council of Economic Advisors
COS	Child Outcomes Study (NEWWS)
CPS	Current Population Survey
CWPDP	California Work Pays Demonstration Project
DHHS	U.S. Department of Health and Human Services
EITC	Earned Income Tax Credit
EMPOWER	Employing and Moving People Off Welfare and Encouraging Responsibility (Arizona)
FAP	Family Assistance Plan
FDP	Family Development Program (New Jersey)
FIP	Family Investment Program (Iowa)
FPL	Federal poverty line
FSA	Family Support Act of 1988
FTP	Family Transition Program (Florida)
GAIN	Greater Avenues for Independence (California)
GAO	General Accounting Office
HCD	Human Capital Development
IA	Income Assistance (Canada)
IMPACT	Indiana Manpower Placement and Comprehensive Training Program
JOBS	Job Opportunities and Basic Skills Training program

LFA	Labor Force Attachment
MFIP	Minnesota Family Investment Program
MFIP-IO	Minnesota Family Investment Program–Incentives Only
NEWWS	National Evaluation of Welfare-to-Work Strategies
NLSY	National Longitudinal Survey of Youth
NSAF	National Survey of America's Families
OBRA	Omnibus Budget Reconciliation Act of 1981
PBJI	Program for Better Jobs and Incomes
PIP	Preschool Immunization Project (Georgia)
PPI	Primary Prevention Initiative (Maryland)
PPVT-R	Peabody Picture Vocabulary Test–Revised
PRWORA	Personal Responsibility and Work Opportunity Reconciliation Act
PSID	Panel Study of Income Dynamics
SIME/DIME	Seattle/Denver Income Maintenance Experiments
SIPP	Survey of Income and Program Participation
SPD	Survey of Program Dynamics
SSP	Self-Sufficiency Project (Canada)
TANF	Temporary Assistance for Needy Families
TSMF	To Strengthen Michigan Families
UI	Unemployment Insurance
VIEW	Virginia Initiative for Employment Not Welfare
VIP/VIEW	Virginia Independence Program/Virginia Initiative for Employment Not Welfare
WIN	Work Incentive program
WRP	Welfare Restructuring Project (Vermont)
WRP-IO	Welfare Restructuring Project (Vermont)–Incentives Only

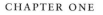

CHAPTER ONE

Introduction

In 1935 the United States implemented its first federal welfare program. Soon to become known as Aid to Families with Dependent Children, or AFDC, its goal was to alleviate need among single-parent families by raising their living standards without requiring single mothers to enter the labor market. That goal reflected contemporary social realities: few women worked outside the home, opportunities to do so were limited, and women who had lost their husbands—predominantly widows—were hard-pressed to support their children as a result.

Over time, those realities changed. One important change was the movement of women into the workforce. Between 1950 and 2000, the proportion of women with children who were working rose from 18 percent to 71 percent (O'Neill 2003). As social norms about work changed, policymakers attempted to reform the welfare system.

Starting in the 1960s, the rules of the AFDC program were altered to promote work. It was hoped that these reforms would stimulate employment and reduce welfare dependency. Despite these changes, however, caseloads remained high and employment among welfare recipients remained low.

By the 1980s welfare increasingly became associated with even greater social ills. Because it was available primarily to single parents, it was blamed for the increase in both divorce and out-of-wedlock childbearing. Whether the AFDC program was truly responsible for those problems was debated by researchers. Nevertheless, by the early 1990s, the perception that AFDC caused more problems than it solved was widespread among both policymakers and the public.

About that time, states began implementing statewide changes to their welfare programs under waivers from the AFDC program. Most of these waiver-based reforms were incremental. Some states increased the extent to which recipients could keep their benefits as they went to work. Others strengthened work requirements. Toward the mid-1990s, a few states

1

imposed time limits. Eventually over half the states reformed their welfare program under waivers.

The waiver era culminated in the passage of the federal Personal Responsibility and Work Opportunity Reconciliation Act of 1996 (PRWORA). Like previous reforms, PRWORA's goals were to reduce dependency and promote work. PRWORA, however, went much further than any previous reform effort. The act abolished AFDC, replacing it with the Temporary Assistance for Needy Families (TANF) program. In so doing, it ended the entitlement status of welfare, that is, it ended the government's obligation to provide benefits to all eligible families. It also strengthened and introduced new behavioral requirements. TANF requires most recipients to work or participate in so-called work-related activities. It imposes time limits on the receipt of federally funded benefits. It also allows states to use financial incentives to encourage work.

PRWORA also sought to promote marriage, maintain two-parent families, and reduce out-of-wedlock childbearing. To reduce the perceived disincentive to marriage, many states relaxed eligibility rules that made it difficult for married couples to receive welfare. To reduce the perceived childbearing incentive, many states imposed so-called family caps, which prevent benefits from rising when new babies are born to mothers already receiving welfare. To reduce the incidence of unwed-teen childbearing, many states required minor parents to live with their own parent or guardian. The states also implemented other measures designed to encourage parental responsibility more generally.

At the same time that these dramatic changes in welfare policy were taking place, welfare-related behavior was changing in a similarly dramatic manner. After reaching its all-time peak of 5 million families in 1994, the welfare caseload fell precipitously. By 2001 only 2.1 million families were receiving welfare. As a proportion of the total population, this represented the lowest level since 1964.

Other aspects of welfare-related behavior changed at the same time. The employment rate of single mothers, the primary adult recipients of welfare, was 69 percent in 1993. In 1999 it stood at 83 percent. Over this same period, single mothers' annual weeks of work rose from 29.5 to 36.7 and their earnings, expressed in terms of 1998 dollars, rose from $12,300 to $16,600. Fertility-related behavior changed, too. The proportion of children born out of wedlock, which had risen steadily since at least 1950, began to level off in 1994.

Interest in the link between the policy changes and the concomitant behavioral changes has been great. The simple association is striking. As reform was being carried out, welfare-related behavior was changing, and for the most part, it was changing for the better.

It is risky, however, to draw causal inferences from coincident trends. At the same time welfare was being reformed, other changes were occurring that could have had similar effects on behavior. The economy expanded for an unprecedented length of time. The expansion ultimately raised the wages paid to low-skill workers, for the first time in twenty years (Council of Economic Advisers 1999a). The Earned Income Tax Credit (EITC) became more generous between 1993 and 1996, providing further incentives for low-income families to work.

Isolating the effects of welfare reform has been the goal of a number of scientific studies. These include experimental analyses, which were used to evaluate many reforms carried out during the waiver era, and observational studies based on administrative data or nationwide surveys. Although the waiver era began only in the early 1990s, and PRWORA was passed even more recently, the number of studies that have been conducted is substantial. We count fifty-nine, which undoubtedly excludes some that have only recently been released.

These numerous studies, however, have appeared in a wide variety of outlets. The studies are addressed to different audiences; many are technical and use the jargon of various academic disciplines. Moreover, the two research strategies—experimental and observational—each have their own strengths and weaknesses, although previous reviews rarely consider the results from the two strategies together. One of our goals in writing this book is to assemble and evaluate the results from this large and diverse literature, with a focus on the welfare-related outcomes of greatest interest to researchers and policymakers: welfare use, employment and earnings, income and poverty, marriage and fertility, and child well-being.[1] We aim to summarize the literature for analysts who are doing their own research on the topic. We also seek to guide policymakers to the research results that they need to make informed policy choices.

Beyond assembling the results from a diverse body of literature, we have two further objectives in writing this book. The first is to determine whether the body of results from the welfare reform literature is consistent with an economic model of behavior. That is, we investigate whether the evidence from the relatively large number of studies, taken as a whole, is consistent with the predictions from a model that assumes that consumers are rational agents who maximize their well-being subject to the constraints imposed by the new welfare system.

Answering this question is important for several reasons. First, a simple economic model has guided policymakers' thinking about the welfare program since the mid-1960s (Berkowitz 1991). An important feature of that model was that many of its predictions were largely consistent with the data (Moffitt 1992). That model provided the motivation for some of the important reforms that were implemented during the 1990s, in part because it fit the data reasonably well.

Second, to the extent that the model still fits the data—at least after we extend the model to account for the policy changes implemented under welfare reform—it can help to "fill in" between the experiments, that is, to predict how behavior should change in response to new policy proposals that have not yet been studied empirically. Two examples help illustrate this point. Recent legislation reauthorizing PRWORA sought to increase the number of hours that recipients would have to work in order to satisfy their work requirements. At the same time, various groups proposed policy changes that would allow recipients to stop their time-limit clocks while working, effectively extending the amount of time that they could spend on aid.

Neither of these proposals has received any empirical study. Hour requirements are fairly uniform across the states, and only one state (Illinois) stops the time-limit clock once recipients find a job. Thus there is little data available to predict how these proposals might affect behavior.

However, if we have a model that is consistent with data that are available, then we can use that model to predict how families might respond to the proposed changes. The model may predict qualitatively how behavior should respond, in which case outside data might be available to quantify that prediction. Even when the model offers ambiguous qualitative predictions, it may provide guidance on the types of outside information one would need to make a useful prediction. The better the model fits the data that one has, the greater confidence one can have in such predictions.[2]

Our final objective is to assess the extent to which recent welfare reforms achieve the traditional policy objectives of promoting work, reducing dependency, and raising the living standards of the poor. Although these three objectives have factored into debates over welfare reform since at least the 1960s, they are not entirely compatible with one another. As the economic model of Chapter 3 predicts, and as much of the empirical work confirms, raising living standards too much reduces recipients' need to work and raises the risk of dependency. Welfare policy entails trade-offs among these (and other) competing objectives, and much of the debate and disagreement over the years has concerned the weight that each objective should receive.

Judging from the history of prolonged and sometimes heated debate over the welfare program, it seems unlikely that we will ever reach an enduring consensus that the welfare system has been perfected. As the history of AFDC shows, even when the welfare system remains unchanged, public support for it may change as society changes around it. Therefore we expect that there will always be interest in reforming the welfare program.

Although the objectives of the next era of reform may differ from those of the past, it seems likely that they will involve some mix of promoting work, reducing dependency, and alleviating need. As compared with earlier eras of reform, the most recent era involved a much broader array of policy innovations, which gives us the opportunity to observe how behavior responds to a much richer set of policy choices. Assessing how those choices achieve the traditional goals of the welfare program, and observing where important trade-offs arise among them, should help inform policy debates in the future.

Our Approach

Our analysis proceeds in three steps. First, we extend the traditional economic model of welfare incentives to analyze the effects of recent reforms on outcomes such as welfare use, employment, labor supply, and income. Some reforms, such as financial work incentives, can be analyzed using the traditional model. Others, such as work requirements, require fairly simple extensions. Time limits necessitate a more elaborate extension, requiring us to embed the traditional model within an intertemporal decision-making framework. Further extensions are required to consider the impact of these and other reforms on marriage, fertility, and child well-being. For each policy-outcome combination, where possible, we derive predictions from the extended model.

The economic approach yields the clearest predictions for two dimensions of behavior: welfare use and labor market activity. For these aspects of welfare-related behavior, we compare the predictions of the model with the results from the literature. For other welfare-related outcomes, including income, marriage, fertility, and child well-being, the theoretical predictions from the extended model are more often ambiguous. In these cases, the empirical evidence, while informative, does not offer a direct test of the theory. In many cases, however, the evidence still speaks to whether recent policy changes promote the traditional goals of welfare reform.

Our second step is to assemble the empirical evidence. We begin by cataloging the literature. We list the relevant studies and their key characteristics. We classify the experimental studies according to their major reform or bundle of reforms. We categorize the observational studies according to their key methodological features. Where possible, we put the results on a common scale.

The third step is to assess the quality of the evidence. All of the studies that we review seek to assess the causal effect of at least one reform policy on at least one aspect of welfare-related behavior. All of these studies must grapple with the problem that other policy changes, or the economy, could be responsible for the changes in behavior that analysts have attributed to welfare reform. All the studies we review attempt to control for such potentially confounding factors, but not all are equally successful.

The experimental studies would seem to have a natural advantage along these lines, because they employ random assignment to ensure that their results can be tied to the experimental policy. Yet experiments can suffer from design or implementation problems that limit the interpretation of their results. Conversely, although observational studies generally employ less compelling controls for confounding factors than the experiments, they sometimes offer other countervailing advantages. When we review the empirical estimates, we discuss how methodological issues bear on the interpretation of results from specific studies.

Organization of the Book

This chapter and the next provide motivation and background. Chapter 2 provides useful context for interpreting the results in subsequent chapters. It begins with a brief history of welfare reform, putting the recent era in perspective. It summarizes the policy reforms enacted by the states, first under waivers and then under TANF. It provides a further review of recent trends in welfare-related behavior. Finally, it briefly summarizes what is known about families that have recently left welfare.

Chapters 3 and 4 cover theory and methods. Chapter 3 reviews the economic model of welfare incentives under AFDC. It extends the model to derive predictions about the effects of important classes of reforms for welfare use, labor market behavior, and income. Some of the material in this chapter is already familiar. To the best of our knowledge, however, this is the first time that financial work incentives, work requirements, and time limits have been discussed in one place. Moreover, Chapter 3 appears to provide one of the first systematic discussions of the effects of welfare sanctions.

In Chapter 4 we focus on methodological issues. This discussion covers issues that are relevant throughout the book. We examine the major approaches to dealing with confounding factors, discussing the advantages and disadvantages associated with both experimental and observational studies. We also describe in some detail the studies whose results constitute the basis of the chapters that follow.

Chapters 5, 6, and 7 focus on the consequences of welfare reform for welfare use, labor market behavior (that is, employment, labor supply, and earnings), and income. As mentioned above, the economic model makes clear predictions, for the most part, for these aspects of behavior. Furthermore, these outcomes are related to the welfare policy goals of reducing dependency, increasing work, and raising living standards. Chapter 5 covers welfare use; Chapter 6 covers employment, labor supply, and earnings; and Chapter 7 covers income and poverty. Throughout these chapters, we compare the empirical estimates with the predictions from the model in Chapter 3. We also relate them to the traditional goals of welfare programs.

Marriage, childbearing, and children are the focus of Chapters 8 and 9. Because marriage and childbearing arguably are more complex forms of behavior than welfare use and work, the models used to analyze them are more complex as well. We begin Chapter 8 by discussing those models and their predictions regarding the effects of recent reforms. We then present evidence from recent studies.

How welfare reform should affect the well-being of children is a topic not directly addressed by most economic models. Yet it bears importantly on the long-run success of welfare reform. In Chapter 9 we provide an economic framework for understanding how different policy changes may affect different domains of child well-being, after which we present the results of several empirical studies.

In Chapter 10, we examine the results of the previous chapters as a whole. We look across all policy reforms and all outcomes to assess the evidence regarding the causal impact of reform. We consider both the quantity and the significance of the evidence that addresses each policy-outcome combination. Where possible, we determine whether the evidence is consistent with the model. We point out the trade-offs among competing objectives that different policy reforms entail. To conclude, we draw attention to the areas where little or no research is available, which suggests a lengthy agenda for future work.

Some important limitations to our approach should be acknowledged at the outset. Most of these limitations stem from the fact that there is a fixed number of studies available to analyze, that they sometimes focus on a limited set of policy reforms, and that reform was implemented under special, and unusually favorable, conditions.

First, all of the experiments that we review, along with many of the observational studies, focus on reforms that were carried out under waivers from the AFDC program. Most of those reforms were incremental in nature, involving either financial incentives or work requirements, for example. Most experiments were small in scale, involving recipients in at most a few counties. Small-scale studies involving incremental reforms can provide a sound basis for understanding the effects of those reforms. Whether they extrapolate to the TANF environment is open to question.

When the states implemented TANF, they generally imposed a number of reforms at once. The changes were large-scale in nature, involving the entire state's welfare delivery system. In many states, these changes took place in a political environment characterized by widespread and often vocal opposition to AFDC. When a number of reforms are imposed at once, they may interact in ways that are difficult to capture. Likewise, widespread political sentiment against welfare may reinforce the effects of reform in ways that incremental policy experiments do not. A few experiments and a number of observational studies focus on the effects of TANF and TANF-like bundles of reform without isolating the specific reforms that TANF entailed. These may provide a reasonable estimate of the overall effects of wide-ranging reforms carried out in a volatile political climate. By design, however, they are not informative about the effects of specific reforms.

The result is that we have a number of studies that provide information about the effects of specific reforms when those reforms are implemented in isolation. We also have a set of studies that is broadly informative about the effects of widespread changes. We have only a few studies that provide insights into the effects of specific reforms carried out as part of a set of sweeping changes instituted in an environment of political opposition to the welfare system.

In a related vein, almost all of the studies we review focus on a period of substantial economic growth. Beginning around 1993, the U.S. economy began expanding in ways that reduced unemployment to its lowest levels in thirty years and raised the wages of low-skill workers for the first time in decades. As a result, all the conclusions that we draw pertain to the effects of welfare reform in a favorable economic environment. There is reason to think that reform may have worked out differently in a less robust economy. Precisely because the economy was so strong for so long, there is little evidence on the interaction between the economy and the effects of welfare reform.

As a result of these limitations, this book cannot be characterized as describing the effects of specific policy changes carried out specifically under TANF. Likewise, we make no claim that the results presented here would obtain in a weaker labor market. The studies we review are capable of revealing how certain important policy reforms affect behavior under favorable economic conditions. Such estimates are useful for testing theories of behavior and for assessing the extent to which such policy reforms achieve certain policy goals. Although they cannot answer all of the questions that one might have regarding the effects of PRWORA per se, they provide valuable information about the effects of welfare programs on behavior and expand our understanding of important policy trade-offs more generally.

———— ❖ ————

CHAPTER TWO

Background

The changes in welfare policy that were implemented during the 1990s represent both an extension of and a departure from past policy. To set the stage for the theoretical and empirical analysis to follow, we begin this chapter with a brief history of federal welfare policy and previous reform efforts.[1] The discussion focuses on some of the motivations for reform and some of the shifts in emphasis among the goals of reform. We then describe the reforms undertaken during the 1990s. After that, we discuss changes in welfare-related behavior that took place during the 1990s, some of which may be attributable to welfare reform. We then discuss other recent policy changes that may have independently influenced welfare-related behavior. Finally, we describe the circumstances of the families that left welfare during the 1990s and the characteristics of those who remain on the rolls.

Brief History of Federal Welfare Policy

The AFDC program replaced by TANF in 1996 had its origins in the New Deal era, when it was designed to serve a specialized population deemed especially needy. Changes in women's labor force participation and in family structure later prompted a series of incremental reforms. On the eve of the most recent era of welfare reform, AFDC was a program whose unintended consequences made it unpopular with policymakers, the public, and recipients alike.

The Original Program

The AFDC program, originally known as Aid to Dependent Children, was implemented as part of the Social Security Act of 1935. The stated purpose of the program was to provide financing to the states in order to provide support for children "deprived of parental support or care by reason of death, continued absence from the home, or physical or mental incapacity of the parent." Despite the broad language, the program was understood at the time to represent an extension to the "mother's pensions" or "widow's pensions" that operated in some states and localities. The objective of the program was to provide financial assistance for children whose fathers had died. The assistance was intended to enable the mother to stay at home and care for her children. In an era when few mothers worked outside the home, this was seen as a superior alternative to having the mother work, leaving the children to fend for themselves or risk being sent into foster care (Berkowitz 1991).

The program was jointly administered by the states and the federal government. The federal government paid part of the costs via matching grants and established the "categorical" eligibility criteria: only single-parent families with dependent children were eligible for aid. Although a separate program for jobless two-parent families was established in 1961, single-parent families overwhelmingly remained the primary beneficiaries of the AFDC program until it was dismantled in 1996. The states set benefit levels, which determined income-eligibility limits. The states operated the program and, within the limits of the categorical criteria, retained substantial control in determining eligibility.

Because the states were free to set their own level of benefits, benefit levels varied widely. This remained true until the program ended, as seen in Table 2.1. As of 1996, monthly benefits for a family of three with no other income ranged from $923 in Alaska to $596 in California to $120 in Mississippi. Such variation is far greater than what might be attributable to cost-of-living differences. The state programs differed substantially in the extent to which they raised the living standards of poor, single-parent families.

The states also varied in their eligibility rules. Many states passed "fit parent" or "suitable home" provisions to limit payments to families whose behavior satisfied the authorities. Such rules were especially prevalent, and their enforcement was especially vigorous, in the South. The practical effect of such rules was that many otherwise eligible blacks were denied benefits.

Despite variation in benefit levels and eligibility rules, federal law required all states to treat recipients' earnings uniformly. Working recipients had their grants reduced dollar-for-dollar as their earnings rose. From today's perspective, this 100 percent tax rate provided a substantial disincentive to work. In an era when all but a few mothers stayed home with their children, this was a matter of little import. The notions of promoting work and reducing dependency that enter the policy debates of the future did not come into play in 1935. The program was designed to raise the living standards of deserving families who had be-

Table 2.1   Monthly AFDC benefits by state for a family of three with no other income, 1996

State	Benefit	State	Benefit
Alabama	$164	Montana	$438
Alaska	923	Nebraska	364
Arizona	347	Nevada	348
Arkansas	204	New Hampshire	550
California	596	New Jersey	424
Colorado	356	New Mexico	389
Connecticut	636	New York	577
Delaware	338	North Carolina	272
District of Columbia	415	North Dakota	431
Florida	303	Ohio	341
Georgia	280	Oklahoma	307
Hawaii	712	Oregon	460
Idaho	317	Pennsylvania	421
Illinois	377	Rhode Island	554
Indiana	288	South Carolina	200
Iowa	426	South Dakota	430
Kansas	429	Tennessee	185
Kentucky	262	Texas	188
Louisiana	190	Utah	416
Maine	418	Vermont	633
Maryland	373	Virginia	354
Massachusetts	565	Washington	546
Michigan	459	West Virginia	253
Minnesota	532	Wisconsin	517
Mississippi	120	Wyoming	360
Missouri	292		

Source: Committee on Ways and Means (2000), table 7-7.

come poor by no fault of their own. The program was intended to keep mothers out of the labor market, and to do so until their children had left home.

Changes in Women's Employment and the Policy Response

The program operated largely as intended for roughly the first two decades of its existence, drawing little attention from policymakers or the public. Caseloads were low; until 1950, the program never served more than 2 million people. Indeed, caseloads fell twice over this time, during World War II and again between 1950 and 1955 (Berkowitz 1991). By the 1960s, however, satisfaction with the program began to wane, largely as a result of far-reaching changes in society.

One of the most important changes involved the increasing role of women in the labor market. Figure 2.1 plots employment rates for women. Starting in the 1960s, employment rates rose substantially.

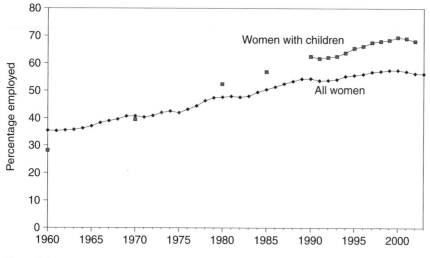

Figure 2.1
Female employment rates, 1960–2003. *Source:* All women: Bureau of Labor Statistics, Series LNU02300002Q, 2003; women with children: U.S. Census Bureau, *Statistical Abstract of the United States,* various years.

Whereas only 36 percent of women worked outside the home in 1960, 48 percent were employed in 1980. Only in the 1990s, after approaching 60 percent, did the female employment rate stop rising. Perhaps most important, employment rose among women with children. As Figure 2.1 shows, while only 28 percent of women with children worked outside the home in 1960, that number rose to 40 percent by 1970. By the 1990s, nearly 70 percent of women with children worked for pay. In contrast, employment rates among welfare recipients peaked at 16 percent in 1973 and then fell, even as employment among non-welfare mothers rose substantially (Committee on Ways and Means 1996, table 8-28).

The movement of large numbers of mothers into the labor market raised concerns about idleness on the part of welfare mothers, who rarely sought employment. The increase in working mothers "invalidated the fundamental assumption that welfare served a useful social function because it permitted women a dignified alternative to the labor force" (Berkowitz 1991, 95). The result was a number of attempts to reform the welfare program in order to promote work; many of these efforts were motivated by economic models of welfare incentives (Berkowitz 1991).

Policy reforms enacted in 1967 included both "carrots" and "sticks" to promote employment. The carrot took the form of the AFDC program's first financial work incentive. The so-called $30-and-a-third policy "disregarded" the first $30 dollars of the recipient's earnings, plus one-third of the remainder, in calculating her benefit. In other words, employed welfare recipients were allowed to keep the first $30 of their monthly earnings and one-third of the rest, reducing the effective tax rate on earnings. It was argued that reducing the "benefit-reduction rate" from 100 percent to 67 percent should stimulate employment, as the economic model discussed in the next chapter predicts, even though the 67 percent marginal tax rate remained high.

The 1967 reforms also introduced the Work Incentive (WIN) program. WIN required states to register nonexempt recipients for work-related activities that focused on training and education. But the legislation exempted recipients with children under age six, and they accounted for a substantial fraction of the caseload. As a result, relatively few recipients registered, and even fewer took part in the programs. Of the 3.3 million family heads on the rolls at the end of 1974, only 1.3 million were registered with the program, and only 250,000 actually participated (Berkowitz 1991).

The limited effectiveness of the 1967 reforms meant little change in employment among recipients. There was also little change in the size of the caseload, which, for reasons discussed below, had grown substantially. The result was further attempts at reform by both the Nixon and Carter administrations.

The Nixon administration proposed an ambitious reform that arguably provided some balance between the competing goals of raising living standards and promoting work. The proposed Family Assistance Plan (FAP) included a guaranteed income for families with children that would have been uniform nationwide. Although the income guarantee would have reduced benefits in the most generous states, it would have substantially raised grant levels and living standards in low-benefit states. To promote work, the proposal included financial work incentives that were substantially more generous than AFDC. It also included work requirements for some family heads.

After the Nixon plan failed in Congress, the Carter administration was the next to try its hand at reform. Like the Nixon plan, Carter's Program for Better Jobs and Incomes (PBJI) involved a financial work incentive and work requirements for some recipients. Like Nixon's FAP, PBJI failed to win congressional approval.

Although neither FAP nor PBJI became law, their failures highlight the difficulties that arise from the conflicting goals of welfare programs. Both proposals were opposed by both liberals and conservatives. Liberals argued that the plans focused too much on promoting work and not enough on raising living standards of the poor. During debates over both bills, liberals argued for higher benefits. Conservatives, in contrast, contended that the plans did not go far enough to promote work and argued for stricter work requirements (Weaver 2000). Conflict over the goals of welfare reform resulted in a policy impasse during the 1970s.

In 1981 the Reagan administration sought to reduce the welfare rolls. To do so, the Omnibus Budget Reconciliation Act (OBRA) of 1981 eliminated the AFDC financial work incentive after the recipient's first four months of work. After four months, recipients would face a 100 percent tax rate, as they did before 1967. This policy change reduced the rolls by roughly 400,000 recipients. It also represented a departure from the previous policy trend of using financial incentives and work requirements to promote work.

The trend was restored by the Family Support Act of 1988 (FSA). The key feature of the FSA was the JOBS (Job Opportunities and Basic Skills Training) program, which replaced WIN. To promote the transition from welfare to work, JOBS required the states to run work-related activity programs and meet target levels for participation in those programs. FSA gave states considerable flexibility in designing their JOBS programs, with activities ranging from job-skills training to community work experience. The law also introduced sanctions for those who failed to meet JOBS requirements (DHHS 1997). The sanction involved reducing the recipient's grant by the amount paid to the noncompliant individual, usually the adult. Sanctions generally applied until the recipient came into compliance, but could be even longer for second-, third-, or higher-order sanctions. FSA also limited exemptions, including the key age-related exemption. Whereas WIN had exempted mothers with children under age six, JOBS reflected the general increase in employment rates of mothers with young children by exempting only recipients with children under age three (or age one at state option). In principle, the JOBS work requirement and associated sanctions applied to a much larger proportion of the caseload than the previous work incentives under WIN.

As a balance against the stricter work requirements, FSA also required the states to provide child care and other support services such as medical care when such services were deemed necessary for the recipient to participate in the JOBS program. Funding for such services, however, generally went wanting as the recession of the early 1990s strained state budgets. Moreover, the target participation rate for JOBS was just 20 percent of nonexempt recipients (as of fiscal year 1995), and in practice states were never penalized when they failed to meet this modest standard (DHHS 1997). As a result, JOBS served many fewer recipients than the supporters of FSA envisioned.

Other Changes in Society and the Welfare Program

As important as the changes in female employment were for stimulating efforts to reform AFDC, other changes in society also played a critical role in setting the stage for the reforms of the 1990s. At the same time that women were entering the workforce in unprecedented numbers, equally unprecedented changes in family structure were taking place. Together with changes in eligibility rules, these changes transformed the welfare population and caused great concern about the unintended consequences of AFDC.

Beginning in the 1960s, divorce rates began to rise. Figure 2.2 shows that, in 1960, there were 2.2 divorces per 1,000 population. That figure rose to 2.5 in 1965, then accelerated. The divorce rate peaked in 1981 at 5.3 per 1,000. It fell thereafter, reaching 4 per 1,000 in 2001.[2]

At the same time, the share of out-of-wedlock births rose, most of which involved never-married women. Figure 2.3 shows that in 1960, births to unwed mothers accounted for only about 5 percent of all births. They grew steadily over the next three decades, accounting for 10.7 percent of births in 1970 and nearly one out of five births in 1980. By 1994, when the trend leveled off, they accounted for nearly one-third of U.S. fertility.

The result of these trends in family structure was that many more children were being raised in single-parent families where the mother was

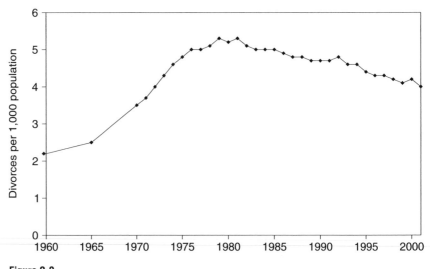

Figure 2.2
Divorce rates, 1960–2001. *Source:* U.S. Census Bureau, *Statistical Abstract of the United States, 2003,* Table 83.

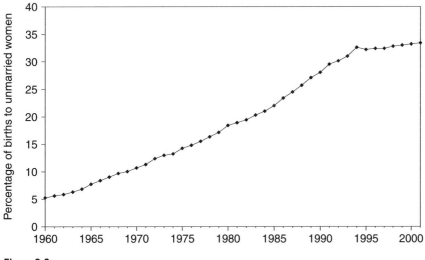

Figure 2.3
Share of births to unmarried women, 1960–2001. *Source:* DHHS (1985), table I-3; U.S. National
Center for Health Statistics (2002), table D; and Martin, Park, and Sutton (2002), table C.

not a widow. In 1960, only 4 percent of single mothers had never married; 26 percent were widows. By 1994, 36 percent of single mothers had never married; only 4 percent were widows (U.S. Census Bureau 1960, 1994). These trends in marriage and fertility resulted in a new class of families that satisfied the categorical eligibility criteria of the AFDC program. In conjunction with changes in other eligibility criteria, they dramatically changed the size and composition of the AFDC population.

Eligibility criteria became more lenient in the mid-1960s, when the Supreme Court issued a series of rulings striking down the "suitable home" rules that many states had used to limit access to AFDC. At the same time, a growing welfare rights movement increased public awareness of the program and pressured local welfare offices to expand the rolls. Some of the Johnson administration's War on Poverty efforts may have had similar effects (Piven and Cloward 1971).

These changes in family structure and program eligibility requirements transformed the nature of the AFDC population. The caseload more than tripled in just over a decade, increasing from 3 million persons in 1960 to 4.3 million in 1965 to 10.1 million in 1971. The program's cost also rose rapidly (Weaver 2000).[3] Because many divorced and never-married mothers struggled financially, they made up an increasing fraction of the caseload. In the late 1930s most families had received aid by virtue of the father's death; by 1988 the majority of adult recipients were never-married mothers (Committee on Ways and Means 1996, table 8-28). Because restrictive eligibility rules had been particularly prevalent in the South, their elimination raised the proportion of African Americans receiving aid. Only 14 percent of recipients were black in 1936; by 1973, blacks accounted for 46 percent of the caseload (Gilens 1999).

Evidence of substantial levels of dependency caused further concern about AFDC. In 1983 Mary Jo Bane and David Ellwood reported that roughly 14 percent of all welfare spells would last at least ten years (Bane and Ellwood 1983). Because long-term recipients remained on aid while others came and left, such long-term recipients accounted for nearly half of the welfare population at any point in time. Bane and Ellwood (1994) later extended the analysis to account for the fact that many former recipients eventually returned to the rolls. This increased the evidence of dependency even further: accounting for multiple spells, Bane and Ellwood found that almost one-quarter of all recipients would spend at least a decade on aid. This evidence of substantial dependency, in conjunction with the trends in the composition of the caseload, left many policymakers with the impression that what had started as a program to support widows and their children had become a program that primarily supported divorced and never-married women, most of whom did not work, and many of whom would spend long periods on aid.

As important as these changes were, even more important was the change in the way policymakers came to think about the link between the program and social trends. Rather than being seen as a solution to social problems, welfare increasingly was seen as a cause of those problems. Changes in eligibility and family structure had been viewed as contributing to the "welfare mess" of the early 1970s, but by the 1980s the welfare program was increasingly portrayed as the *cause* of adverse trends in family structure. The notion that welfare was undermining the traditional family became the most controversial issue in welfare policy discussions (Ellwood 1988).

Some of the evidence for this view came from social experiments. The Seattle and Denver Income Maintenance Experiments (SIME/DIME) provided randomly selected low-income households with an income guarantee and compared their behavior with that of a randomly selected control group. Results from the experiment showed that the program raised divorce rates substantially (Groeneveld, Hannan, and Tuma 1983). Although researchers took issue with the interpretation of the evidence (Cain 1986), the initial results were quickly picked up by policymakers (Weaver 2000).

The most forceful proponent of the idea that welfare was causing the decline in family structure, however, was Charles Murray, who took to an extreme the economic model of fertility that we discuss in Chapter 8.

He argued that the welfare system had structured incentives in such a way as to "make it profitable for the poor to behave in the short term in ways that were destructive in the long term" (Murray 1984, 9). The result was out-of-wedlock childbearing, poverty, and the transmission of welfare dependence from one generation to the next. He concluded that it would benefit the poor to eliminate welfare altogether, rather than to perpetuate a system that trapped them in a life of poverty and dependence. Although his methods and conclusions were harshly criticized, his view gained currency at a time when President Ronald Reagan had declared that "government is not the solution to our problem, government is the problem."

Thus, between the mid-1930s and the early 1990s, both the welfare program and the terms of the policy debate had been transformed. A program that had started as a means of raising the living standards of what was viewed as a particularly disadvantaged and deserving segment of the population was now viewed as serving a large and increasingly undeserving group characterized by idleness, dependency, and unwed childbearing. The dominant policy focus had moved from raising living standards, to promoting work and reducing dependency, to reversing the decline of the traditional family. The nail in the AFDC coffin came in the early 1990s, when the caseload began to rise sharply, much as it had in the mid-1960s. At that point, pressure for substantial reform became irresistible.

Policy and Program Changes during the 1990s

The push for further reform came first from the states, which sought waivers from the rules of the AFDC program. As the AFDC caseload reached an all-time high, the FSA was viewed as increasingly ineffective. Candidate Bill Clinton pledged to "end welfare as we know it" and the Republican "Contract with America" sought to overhaul the welfare system. Policymakers achieved welfare reform at the national level when the Personal Responsibility and Work Opportunities Reconciliation Act was signed into law in August 1996.

State Waivers

Since 1962, section 1115 of the Social Security Act granted authority to the secretary of health and human services to waive the rules and regulations governing AFDC. Under this provision, states could petition the U.S. Department of Health and Human Services (DHHS) to implement experimental, pilot, or demonstration projects they believed would result in a more effective welfare program. These experiments were required to be cost-neutral and to include a rigorous evaluation, usually involving random assignment.

Although a few states took advantage of this provision prior to 1990, these waiver-based reforms became the mechanism by which the states reformed their AFDC programs in advance of a consensus leading to national reform. Between 1987 and 1992, fifteen waiver applications in fourteen states were approved during the Reagan administration and another fifteen applications from twelve states were approved during the Bush administration (Harvey, Camasso, and Jagannathan 2000). As reform efforts accelerated during the first term of the Clinton administration, the federal government approved eighty-three waivers representing forty-three states and the District of Columbia. In total, all but five states received approval for one or more waivers.[4] Twenty-nine of the waivers involved statewide reforms, all of which were implemented between 1992 and 1996. In the discussion that follows, we focus on statewide waivers enacted between 1992 and 1996.[5]

The waiver-based reforms encompassed a wide range of changes to the traditional AFDC program, many of which were later incorporated into PRWORA. In some cases, the reforms built on early policy changes; others represented new strategies. States experimented with changes to the financial work incentives embodied in the AFDC program, with stricter requirements for work or related activities, and with tougher sanctions for noncompliance. Reforms introduced in this period also included time limits and caps on the benefit increase associated with having another child while on welfare, known as "family caps." Other, more minor reforms, often bundled with these changes, included changes in the rules that governed eligibility (for example, those associated with the level of assets held by the family, and those associated with one- versus two-parent families) and the availability of other benefits, such as medical care, as families transitioned off of welfare.

Under FSA, the high implicit tax rate, equal to 100 percent after four months of work, discouraged welfare recipients from working.[6] Waivers were used to provide an incentive for greater work effort by allowing AFDC recipients to keep more of their earnings while on welfare (see Table 2.2). In order to "make work pay," states either increased the earned-income disregard (the initial portion of earned income that is excluded before benefits are reduced), reduced the tax rate on remaining earnings, or extended the period during which earnings were disregarded. For example, Utah raised the initial disregard to $100 and lowered the tax rate to 50 percent. In January 1996, Connecticut implemented the most generous financial incentive, exempting 100 percent of earnings up to the

Table 2.2 Statewide financial-incentive waivers, 1992–1996

State	Approval date	Implementation date	Earned income disregard rule
New Jersey	7/92	Never	N.A.
Michigan	8/92	10/92	$200 and 20%
California	10/92	12/92	$120 and 33%
Utah[a]	10/92	1/93	$100 and 50%
Wisconsin	10/92	7/94	$200 and 50% (applicants under age 20)
Vermont	4/93	7/94	$150 and 25%
Iowa	8/93	10/93	20% initially; 50% after all deductions
Illinois	11/93	11/93	67%
Georgia	6/94	Never	N.A.
Connecticut	8/94	1/96	100% up to FPL
Nebraska[a]	2/95	10/95	60%
Montana[a]	4/95	2/96	$200 and 25% (recipients in unsubsidized jobs)
Delaware[a]	5/95	10/95	Fill the gap budgeting (recipients only)
Virginia[a]	7/95	7/95	100% up to FPL (recipients only)
Massachusetts	8/95	11/95	$120 and 50% (nonexempt recipients only)
Ohio	3/96	7/96	$250 and 50% for 12 months
New Hampshire	6/96	Never	50%
Tennessee	7/96	9/96	$134
Hawaii	8/96	2/97	20% then $200 then 36% of remainder
Maryland	8/96	10/96	20%

Source: Crouse (1999), table W-3; DHHS (1997), table IV.

Note: N.A.= not available; FPL = federal poverty line. Only statewide waivers with approval dates before PRWORA passage in August 1996 are listed.

a. Waiver policy phased into statewide coverage over time. Implementation date is when phase-in began.

federal poverty line. In total, by the time of PRWORA's passage, twenty states had approval for implementing a revised financial work incentive.

Dissatisfied with the JOBS work requirement, states applied for waivers to strengthen the mandate for work and sanctions for noncompliance. One focus was to expand the portion of the caseload subject to work requirements. Table 2.3 shows that there were twenty-four states with statewide waivers to change the age-related exemption from work requirements. Most states reduced the age-exemption threshold, expanding the JOBS mandate to recipients with younger children. A few states actually raised the age-exemption threshold. Balancing against more expansive work mandates, waivers related to work requirements also often included a list of exceptions that would exempt individuals viewed as more deserving of aid (see DHHS 1997). One state, however, eliminated all JOBS exemptions, leaving caseworkers to determine which recipients did not have to participate.

Weakness in previous work requirements also stemmed from the lenient sanctions levied against those who did not comply. Thus another focus of waiver-based reforms was the penalty associated with noncom-

Table 2.3 Statewide age-related exemption waivers, 1992–1996

State	Approval date	Implementation date	Exempt when youngest child is under age:
New Jersey	7/92	10/92	2 years
Oregon	7/92	2/93	3 months
Vermont	4/93	7/94	16 weeks
Iowa	8/93	10/93	3 months
Hawaii	6/94	2/97	6 months
Connecticut	8/94	1/96	1 year
Michigan	10/94	10/94	No exemption
Indiana	12/94	5/95	3 years if family cap does not apply; 12 weeks otherwise
Nebraska[a]	2/95	5/95	12 weeks
Montana[a]	4/95	2/96	1 year
Delaware[a]	5/95	10/95	12 weeks
Virginia[a]	7/95	7/95	18 months
Massachusetts	8/95	11/95	6 years
Wisconsin	8/95	1/96	1 year
Illinois	9/95	Never	N.A.
North Carolina	2/96	7/96	5 years
Texas	3/96	6/96	5 years
South Carolina	5/96	Never	1 year
Florida	6/96	Never	6 months
Maine	6/96	Never	2 years
New Hampshire	6/96	Never	13 weeks if child conceived on AFDC; 1 year otherwise
Tennessee	7/96	9/96	16 weeks
Idaho	8/96	Never	12 weeks
Maryland	8/96	10/96	12 weeks

Source: Crouse (1999), tables W-2 and W-2a; DHHS (1997), table I.A.

Note: N.A. = not available. Age-related exemptions apply to requirement to participate part-time in a work-related activity. Some states also had waivers that changed the age-related exemption for full-time participation. Only statewide waivers with approval dates before PRWORA passage in August 1996 are listed.

a. Waiver policy phased into statewide coverage over time. Implementation date is when phase-in began.

pliance. In total, twenty-six states received approval for reforms to their sanctions policy between 1992 and the passage of PRWORA (see Table 2.4). In many states, the sanction policy under JOBS, which only partially reduced the family's benefit, was replaced by what became known as the full-family sanction, whereby the family's full grant was eliminated, either for a fixed period of time or until compliance was attained.[7] Other waivers extended the duration of sanctions. In some states, the sanction associated with the first violation was stiffened; other states increased the severity associated with the maximum sanction possible after repeated instances of noncompliance. States that stiffened their sanctions early in the reform era tended to increase the severity of their sanctions to a lesser degree than states that acted later.

Whereas waiver-based reforms that affected financial work incentives, work requirements, and sanctions could be viewed as variations on past policies, waivers that introduced time limits on the receipt of benefits represented a substantial departure from past policy (see Table 2.5). Under AFDC, welfare receipt was an entitlement: individuals were entitled to benefits as long as they remained eligible for the program. Starting in 1993, a handful of states, led by Iowa, received approval to begin introducing limits on the amount of time recipients could receive benefits. Among the sixteen states with waivers approved prior

Table 2.4 Statewide JOBS sanction waivers, 1992–1996

State	Approval date	Implementation date	Initial sanction	Final sanction
New Jersey	7/92	10/92	20% for 1 month[a]	Adult portion for 3 months[a]
Oregon[b]	9/92	2/93	N.A.	N.A.
Vermont	4/93	7/94	Cash grant tied to hours worked	
Iowa	8/93	10/93	Adult portion for 3 months	Full family for 6 months
Georgia	11/93	1/94	Adult portion for 1 month	Adult portion for 6–24 months
South Dakota	3/94	6/94	[c]	
Connecticut	8/94	1/96	20% for 3 months	Full family for 3 months
Michigan	10/94	10/94	25%	Full family
Indiana	12/94	5/95	JOBS for 2 months[a]	JOBS for 36 months[a]
Nebraska[b]	2/95	10/95	Full family for 1 month[a]	Full family for life
Montana[b]	4/95	2/96	Adult portion for 1 month	Adult portion for 12 months
Delaware[b]	5/95	10/95	33% until compliance	Full family for life
Arizona	5/95	11/95	JOBS for 1 month[a]	
Virginia[b]	7/95	7/95	Full family for 1 month[a]	Full family for 6 months[a]
West Virginia	7/95	2/96	Adult portion for 3 months[a]	Full family for 6 months[a]
Massachusetts	8/95	11/95	Adult only	Full family
Wisconsin	8/95	1/96	Hours not participated valued at minimum wage	
Illinois	9/95	10/95		Full family for 6 months[a]
North Carolina	2/96	7/96	$50 for 3 months	$75 for 12 months
Texas	3/96	6/96	Adult portion until compliance	
Ohio	3/96	7/96	Adult portion for 1 month[a]	Full family for 6 months[a]
South Carolina	5/96	Never	Adult portion until compliance	Full family until compliance
New Hampshire	6/96	Never	JOBS for 1 month[d]	Full family
Tennessee	7/96	9/96	Full family until compliance	Full family for 3 months[a]
Idaho	8/96	Never	Full family for 1 month[a]	Full family for life
Maryland	8/96	10/96	Full family until compliance	Full family for 1 month[a]

Source: Crouse (1999), table W-3; DHHS (1997), table I.B.

Note: N.A. = not available. Sanctions policies apply for noncompliance with JOBS requirements for work or related activities. Some states had sanction policies that applied to other behavior, such as refusal of a job offer or a voluntary quit. Only statewide waivers with approval dates before PRWORA passage in August 1996 are listed.

a. Indicates that the unit is sanctioned for the specified number of months or until the sanctioned individual complies with the activity requirements, whichever is longer.

b. Waiver policy phased into statewide coverage over time. Implementation date is when phase-in began.

c. Waiver sanction policy was the same as JOBS except for the sanction associated with voluntary quits, equal to a full family sanction for three months.

d. Indicates that the unit is sanctioned for the specified number of months or until the sanctioned individual complies with the activity requirements, whichever is shorter.

Table 2.5   Statewide time-limit waivers, 1992–1996

State	Approval date	Implementation date	Time limit; portion of grant affected
Iowa	8/93	10/93	Individually based time frame for self-sufficiency; full family
Indiana[a]	12/94	5/95	Lifetime 24 months; adult only
Nebraska[a]	2/95	10/95	24 out of 48 months; full family
Delaware[a]	5/95	10/95	Lifetime 24 months; full family
Arizona	5/95	11/95	24 out of 60 months; adult only
Virginia[a]	7/95	7/95	Lifetime 24 months; full family
Washington	9/95	1/96	48 out of 60 months; 10 percent reduction for every 12 months past 48 months
Illinois	9/95	2/96	Limited scope[b]
Connecticut[a]	12/95	1/96	Lifetime 21 months; full family
North Carolina	2/96	7/96	24 months, then ineligible for 36 months; full family
Ohio	3/96	7/96	36 out of 60 months; full family
Texas[a]	3/96	6/96	12, 24, or 36 months (depending on job readiness), then ineligible for 60 months; adult only
Oregon	3/96	7/96	24 out of 84 months; full family
South Carolina	5/96	Never	Lifetime 24 months; full family
Tennessee[a]	7/96	10/96	18 months, then ineligible for 3 months, lifetime 60 months; full family
Hawaii	8/96	2/97	Lifetime 60 months; full family

Source: Crouse (1999), table W-1; DHHS (1997), table II.B.

Note: Only statewide waivers with approval dates before PRWORA passage in August 1996 are listed.

a. Waiver policy phased into statewide coverage over time. Implementation date is when phase-in began.

b. Twenty-four-month time limit applies only to cases with youngest child age 13 and above, and only months without earnings count toward the time limit.

to the passage of PRWORA, the length of the time limits varied from twenty-one to sixty months. Some states imposed lifetime limits, after which the family was ineligible for further aid, while others imposed intermittent limits, specifying a number of months during which recipients could receive aid within a particular window of time. For example, Nebraska's time limit allowed recipients to receive welfare for only twenty-four out of every forty-eight months. A few states implemented adult-only time limits, through which only the adult's portion of the grant was terminated once the family reached the limit. Most states included provisions for extending benefits for good cause or other types of exceptions.

Motivated by the perception that welfare had contributed to the trend toward increased single parenthood, especially out-of-wedlock births, New Jersey became the first state to implement a family cap (see Table 2.6). AFDC had provided higher benefits for larger families, so having a baby while on aid would raise the family's income. Family-cap waivers were used to either freeze the benefit level or provide for a smaller increase when a new child was born. By the time of PRWORA's passage, nineteen states had received approval for a family-cap waiver, although not all of them implemented the cap.

In addition to the waiver-based reforms summarized in Tables 2.2 to 2.6, states received approval for an array of other changes to the AFDC program (see DHHS 1997). These included delayed work requirements, which mandate work after a certain period on aid; higher asset limits (for example, on savings accounts, automobiles) used to determine eligibility for AFDC; changes in eligibility rules affecting two-parent families; extensions of noncash benefits such as Medicaid and child care subsidies to families leaving welfare; and responsibility requirements requiring parents to immunize their children and ensure they attend school.

The Personal Responsibility and Work Opportunities Reconciliation Act

The era of waiver-based reforms set the stage for an emerging consensus that substantial reform at the national level was needed.

Table 2.6 Statewide family-cap waivers, 1992–1996

State	Approval date	Implementation date	Family cap policy
California	7/92	Never[a]	No increase in benefits
New Jersey	7/92	10/92	No increase in benefits
Georgia	11/93	1/94	No increase in benefits
Arkansas	4/94	7/94	No increase in benefits
Wisconsin	6/94	1/96	No increase in benefits
Indiana	12/94	5/95	Partial increase in form of voucher
Nebraska[b]	2/95	10/95	No increase in benefits
Delaware[b]	5/95	10/95	No increase in benefits
Arizona	5/95	11/95	No increase in benefits
Virginia	7/95	7/95	No increase in benefits
Massachusetts	8/95	11/95	No increase in benefits
Maryland	8/95	3/96	Increase in form of voucher
Mississippi	9/95	10/95	No increase in benefits
Illinois	9/95	12/95	No increase in benefits
Connecticut	12/95	1/96	Partial increase in benefits
North Carolina	2/96	7/96	No increase in benefits
South Carolina	5/96	Never	Increase in form of a voucher
Florida	6/96	Never	Partial increase in benefits
Tennessee[b]	7/96	9/96	No increase in benefits

Source: Crouse (1999), table W-5; DHHS (1997), table III.

Note: Only waivers with approval dates before PRWORA passage in August 1996 are listed.

a. California eventually adopted a family cap through a waiver approved in August 1996 and implemented in September 1997.

b. Waiver policy phased into statewide coverage over time. Implementation date is when phase-in began.

Building on the idea of personal responsibility in return for opportunity provided by the government, a signature theme of both the 1992 Clinton presidential campaign and the 1994 Contract with America, political forces converged to bring about a dramatic transformation of the welfare program (Heclo 2001). At the same time many state governors, buoyed by their experience under waivers, joined those at the national level to support major reform, pushing for block-grant funding of AFDC and a devolution of responsibility for designing the welfare system from the federal to the state level.

The debate that culminated in PRWORA in August 1996 illustrates the policy trade-offs that have long been embedded in the design of the U.S. welfare system. On the one hand, reformers sought changes that would reduce or eliminate the perceived incentives associated with the AFDC program for idleness, single parenthood, and out-of-wedlock childbearing. These advocates placed a priority on temporary assistance, where the transition to work would be a primary objective and where the formation and maintenance of two-parent families would be encouraged. On the other hand, more cautious voices raised concerns about the adequacy of a safety net that was not permanent, especially for individuals who faced significant barriers, such as a lack of marketable skills, physical and mental health problems, substance abuse, and exposure to domestic violence. Children in such families were viewed as especially vulnerable if their adult caretakers faced a lifetime limit on benefits. Ultimately the reform bill that was crafted contained the elements desired by those advocating for greater personal responsibility, while allowing states to exempt particularly at-risk segments of the caseload and maintaining historically high funding levels. In addition, along most policy dimensions, states were allowed the flexibility they desired to craft their welfare programs according to their own objectives.

PRWORA's multiple policy goals are reflected in its preamble. It aimed to:

increase the flexibility of States in operating a program designed to:

1. provide assistance to needy families so that children may be cared for in their own homes or in the homes of relatives;
2. end the dependence of needy parents on government benefits by promoting job preparation, work, and marriage;
3. prevent and reduce the incidence of out-of-wedlock pregnancies and establish annual numerical goals for preventing and reducing the incidence of these pregnancies; and
4. encourage the formation and maintenance of two-parent families.

(PL 104-193, 1996)

In implementing these objectives, PRWORA eliminated many federal requirements for state welfare programs. Most notably, the entitlement status of welfare was abolished and federal funding of the AFDC and JOBS programs was consolidated into a single Temporary Assistance for Needy Families block grant.[8] Each state's block grant was funded at the annual spending level corresponding to fiscal years 1992 to 1995. States were required to contribute at least 75 percent of their funding in fiscal year 1994 for programs replaced by TANF, including related programs such as child care.[9]

During the year following the passage of PRWORA, almost all states started the process of replacing their AFDC programs with their TANF program. Table 2.7 shows the implementation dates for state TANF programs, which range from September 1996 for Massachusetts, Michigan, and Vermont to January 1998 for California. In most states, the changes

Table 2.7 Implementation of state TANF programs

State	Date	State	Date
Alabama	11/96	Montana	2/97
Alaska	7/97	Nebraska	12/96
Arizona	10/96	Nevada	12/96
Arkansas	7/97	New Hampshire	10/96
California	1/98	New Jersey	7/97
Colorado	7/97	New Mexico	7/97
Connecticut	10/96	New York	11/97
Delaware	3/97	North Carolina	1/97
District of Columbia	3/97	North Dakota	7/97
Florida	10/96	Ohio	10/96
Georgia	1/97	Oklahoma	10/96
Hawaii	7/97	Oregon	10/96
Idaho	7/97	Pennsylvania	3/97
Illinois	7/97	Rhode Island	5/97
Indiana	10/96	South Carolina	10/96
Iowa	1/97	South Dakota	12/96
Kansas	10/96	Tennessee	10/96
Kentucky	10/96	Texas	11/96
Louisiana	1/97	Utah	10/96
Maine	11/96	Vermont	9/96
Maryland	12/96	Virginia	2/97
Massachusetts	9/96	Washington	1/97
Michigan	9/96	West Virginia	1/97
Minnesota	7/97	Wisconsin	9/97
Mississippi	7/97	Wyoming	1/97
Missouri	12/96		

Source: Crouse (1999), table A.

Note: In some states, the actual implementation date was after the official implementation date. In those cases, we record the actual date.

that resulted from the devolution of welfare policy from the federal to the state exceeded what was required by TANF (Gais et al. 2001). As a result, welfare programs that once varied across states primarily by the size of the welfare grant now vary along dozens of dimensions. Table 2.8 summarizes key TANF policies by state in place as of July 2000, based on the Urban Institute's Welfare Rules Databook (Rowe and Roberts 2004).[10]

TANF placed no restrictions on financial incentives, either on earned-income disregards or benefit-reduction rates. Although four states have essentially retained the AFDC incentive structure in their TANF plans, most states have implemented more generous incentives in order to promote work (see Table 2.8). For example, thirteen states have disregards of $150 or more and twenty-seven have benefit-reduction rates of 50 percent or less, at least for a period of time. Connecticut continues to have the most generous financial incentive in the country, allowing recipients to keep their entire benefit until their earnings exceed the federal poverty line (FPL).

Requirements to work or engage in work-related activities such as education, training, or job search remain an important component of TANF, which links state funding levels to "work-participation targets" that specify the proportion of the caseload that must either work or take part in approved work-related activities for a minimum number of hours. TANF removed most federal requirements regarding exemptions and required services, although it specified which activities counted toward the participation targets. In addition, most states adopted a deadline for work activity that was shorter than the twenty-four months required by PRWORA, in some cases requiring welfare recipients to participate in work or related activities immediately upon receiving benefits. In most states, the allowable exemptions from work requirements were narrowed. For example, six states do not allow an automatic exemption based on the youngest child's age, and another forty have age-related exemptions that range from three to twelve months. Often these exemptions can be used only once in the recipient's lifetime (see Table 2.8).

Table 2.8 shows that, under TANF, states still vary in the severity of their sanctions for failing to comply with work requirements. Eight states have continued to use the sanction policy in place under AFDC/JOBS, at least for the first instance of noncompliance. Most states now have a policy of graduated sanctions, whereby sanctions become more severe with repeated violations. Thirty-six states have policies that eventually allow for full-family sanctions. Fourteen impose full-family sanctions at the first violation. Seven states may eventually disqualify the family for life from receiving benefits.

Table 2.8 State TANF policies for single-parent recipient units, July 2000

State	Earned-income disregards[b]	Age-related exemption[c]	Initial sanction[d] Amount reduction	Initial sanction[d] Time (in months)	Most severe sanction[d] Amount reduction	Most severe sanction[d] Time (in months)	Time limit[e] Months	Time limit[e] Adult only	Family cap[f]
Alabama	100% (3 mos.); 20% (4+ mos.)	36	25%	3+	100%	6	60		
Alaska	$150, 33.3% (12 months); percentage declines gradually to 10% by months 49–60	12[l]	Adult portion	C	Adult portion	12+	60		
Arizona[a]	$90, 30%	No exemption	25%	1	100%	1+	24 out of 60	Yes	Yes
Arkansas	No disregards (flat grant)	3[l]	25%	C	25%	C	24		Yes
California	$225, 50%	12[m]	Adult portion	C	Adult portion	6+	60	Yes	Yes
Colorado	$120, 33.3% (4 mos.); $120 (8 mos.); $90 (9+ mos.)	12[m]	25%[m]	1[m]	100%[m]	3+[m]	60		
Connecticut	100% of FPL	12	20%	3+	Case is closed	3; must reapply	21		Yes
Delaware	$120, 33.3% (4 mos.); $120 (8 mos.); $90 (9+ mos.)	13 weeks	33.3%	2−	100%	Permanent	36		Yes
D.C.	$100, 50%	12	Adult portion	C	Adult portion	6+	60		
Florida	$200, 50%	3[n]	100%	C	100%	3+	48; 24 out of 60 or 36 out of 72[s]		Yes
Georgia	$120, 33.3% (4 mos.); $120 (8 mos.); $90 (9+ mos.)	12[l]	25%	3−	100%	Permanent	48		Yes
Hawaii	20%, $200, and the variable percentage rate[g]	6	100%	C	100%	3+	60		
Idaho	40%	No exemption	100%	1+	100%	Permanent	24		
Illinois	66.7%	12	50%	C	100%	3+	60		Yes
Indiana	No disregards (flat grant)	3	Adult portion	2+	Adult portion	36+	24	Yes	Yes

Table 2.8 *(continued)*

State	Earned-income disregards[b]	Age-related exemption[c]	Initial sanction[d] Amount reduction	Initial sanction[d] Time (in months)	Most severe sanction[d] Amount reduction	Most severe sanction[d] Time (in months)	Time limit[e] Months	Time limit[e] Adult only	Family cap[f]
Iowa	20% and 50% of remainder	No exemption	100%	C	100%	6	60		
Kansas	$90, 40%	12	100%	C	100%	2+	60		
Kentucky	100% (2 mos.);[h] $120, 33.3% (4 mos.); $120 (8 mos.), $90 (15+ mos.)	12[l]	Pro rata portion[o]	C	100%	C	60		
Louisiana	$1,020 (6 mos.); $120 (7+ mos.)	12[l]	Adult portion	3	Case is closed	C	60; 24 out of 60		
Maine	$108, 50%	12[l]	Adult portion	C	Adult portion	6+	None		
Maryland	35%	12[l]	100%	C	100%	C for 30 days	60	Yes	Yes
Massachusetts[a]	$120, 50%	No exemption	Warning only	—	100%	C for 2 weeks	24 out of 60		Yes
Michigan	$200, 20%	3	100%[p]	1+	100%	1+	None		
Minnesota	38%	12	10%	1+	Vendor payment and 30%	1+	60		
Mississippi	100% (6 mos.);[h] $90 (7+ mos.)	12[l]	100%	2+	100%	Permanent	60		Yes
Missouri	66.7%, $90 (12 mos.); $90 (13+ mos.)[i]	12	25%	C	25%	3+	60		
Montana[a]	$200, 25%	No exemption	Adult portion	1	Adult portion	12+ and must renegotiate contract	60[q]		
Nebraska[a]	20%	3	100%	1+	100%	Up to 12	60; 24 out of 48		Yes
Nevada	100% (3 mos.); 50% (4–12 mos.); max ($90, 20%) (13+ mos.)	12[l]	Max (33.3%, pro rata share)	1+	100%	Permanent	60; 24 followed by 12 ineligible		
New Hampshire[a]	50%	24	Adult portion	1+	66% of benefit less adult portion	1+	60		

Table 2.8 *(continued)*

State	Earned-income disregards[b]	Age-related exemption[c]	Initial sanction[d] Amount reduction	Initial sanction[d] Time (in months)	Most severe sanction[d] Amount reduction	Most severe sanction[d] Time (in months)	Time limit[e] Months	Time limit[e] Adult only	Family cap[f]
New Jersey	100% (1 mo.);[h] 50% (2+ mos.)	3	Adult portion	1+	100%	3	60		Yes
New Mexico	All earnings in excess of 29 hours per week; $150, 50% (24 mos.); $150, 50% (25+ mos.)	12[l]	25%	C	Case is closed	6+	60		
New York	$90, 47%	12[l]	Adult portion	C	Pro rata portion	6+	60[r]		
North Carolina[a]	100% (3 mos. of employment);[h] 27.5% thereafter	12[l]	25%	3	100%	3+	60; 24 followed by 36 ineligible		Yes
North Dakota	Max ($90, 27%) and additional amount computed from formula[j]	4	Adult portion	1+	100%	3+	60		Yes
Ohio	$250, 50% (18 mos.)	12	Adult portion	1+	100%	6+	60; 36 followed by 24 ineligible		
Oklahoma	$120, 50%	3[l]	100%	C	100%	C	60		Yes
Oregon	50%	3	$50	2−	Case is closed	C	24 out of 86		
Pennsylvania	50%	12[l]	Adult portion	1+	100%	Permanent	60		
Rhode Island	$170, 50%	12	Adult portion	C for 2 weeks	140% of adult portion	C for 2 weeks	60	Yes	
South Carolina	50% (4 mos.); $100 (5+ mos.)	12[l]	100%	C for 1 month and reapply	Case is closed	C for 1 month and reapply	60; 24 out of 120		Yes
South Dakota	$90, 20%	3	Warning only	—	Case is closed	1+ and reapply	60		
Tennessee	$150	4	100%	C for 2 weeks	100%	3+	60; 18 followed by 3 ineligible		Yes

Table 2.8   *(continued)*

State	Earned-income disregards[b]	Age-related exemption[c]	Initial sanction[d] Amount reduction	Initial sanction[d] Time (in months)	Most severe sanction[d] Amount reduction	Most severe sanction[d] Time (in months)	Time limit[e] Months	Time limit[e] Adult only	Family cap[f]
Texas	$120, 90% (up to $1,400 for 4 of 12 mos.); $120 thereafter	36	Adult portion	1+	Adult portion	6+	60; 12, 24, or 36 followed by 60 ineligible[s]	Yes	
Utah	$100, 50%[k]	No exemption	$100	C	100%	C	36		
Vermont	$150, 25%	18[n]	Adult portion	C	Adult portion	6+	None		
Virginia[a]	$120, 33.3% (4 mos.); $120 (8 mos.); $90 (9+ mos.)	18[l]	100%	1+	100%	6+	60; 24 followed by 24 ineligible		Yes
Washington	50%	3[l]	Adult portion	C up to 1 month	Max (adult portion, 40%)	C for 2 weeks	60		
West Virginia	60%	12[l]	33.3%	3	100%	6+	60		
Wisconsin	No disregards (flat grant)	3	Min wage × hours nonparticipation	C	100%	Permanent	60		
Wyoming	$200	3[l]	100%	C	100%	C	60		Yes

Source: Rowe and Roberts (2004), table L4 (earned-income disregards), table L6 (age-related exemptions), table III.B.3 (sanctions), tables IV.C.1 and IV.C.2 (time limits), table L10 (family caps).

Note: C = until compliance; FPL = federal poverty line.

+Indicates that the unit is sanctioned for the specified number of months or until the sanctioned individual complies with the activity requirements, whichever is longer.

−Indicates that the unit is sanctioned for the specified number of months or until the sanctioned individual complies with the activity requirements, whichever is shorter.

a. Other segments of the caseload may face other rules (including being exempt if they meet certain criteria). See Rowe and Roberts (2004) for additional detail.

b. Only earned-income disregards that apply to single-parent families are described in the table. Child-care disregards and other special disregards, such as deductions for time-limited units or family-capped units, are not included. When no duration is specified for the disregards, they remain for the entire period of receipt.

c. Recipient is exempt if age of youngest child in months is less than indicated number.

d. Initial and most severe sanctions for noncompliance with work requirements for single-parent unit head. "Adult portion" of benefit describes the portion of the benefit the sanctioned individual would have received. Since the table only represents sanctions for single-parent adults, in all cases the sanctioned individual is an adult.

e. Records lifetime time limit that applies and, where applicable, any intermittent time limits. Also indicates if time limits apply only to adult portion of the benefit.

Table 2.8 *(continued)*

f. Records whether benefit increases are capped with the addition of another child to the assistance unit. Additional details on state family cap policies are found in Rowe and Roberts (2004).

g. The variable percentage rate is a percentage that allows a household to earn up to the standard of need and still retain eligibility. This rate is around 36 percent.

h. 100% disregard is limited to certain months and conditions related to employment status. See Rowe and Roberts (2004) for details.

i. This disregard only applies to recipients who become employed while receiving TANF. Applicants and those recipients who gained employment before receiving TANF are allowed to disregard $120 and 33.3% of remainder for first four months, $120 next eight months, $90 thereafter.

j. The formula equals A*(A/B)*.5, where A = min[earnings after initial disregard, B] and B = Employment incentive limit.

k. To be eligible for the 50 percent disregards, the recipient must have received benefits in at least one of the previous four months.

l. Limited or one-time exemption. See Rowe and Roberts (2004) for details.

m. May vary by county. Applies to county in state with largest welfare population.

n. May be required to engage in certain activities (for example, attend classes).

o. The pro rata portion of the benefit is equal to the total monthly benefit divided by the number of members in the unit.

p. The entire benefit is removed if noncompliance occurs within the first two months of assistance. If noncompliance occurs after the initial two months of receipt, the benefit is reduced by 25 percent.

q. Recipients initially face a twenty-four-month limit in the Pathways program. After recipients reach the twenty-four-month limit, they enter the Community Service Program for the remainder of their sixty months of eligibility.

r. After sixty months the unit is still eligible to receive noncash assistance through the state's Safety Net Assistance program.

s. Longer limits apply to least-job-ready recipients. See Rowe and Roberts (2004) for details.

Waiver-based experimentation with time limits on benefit receipt opened the door for this most radical of reforms to be incorporated into PRWORA. Although PRWORA prohibits the use of federal funds to pay for more than sixty months of benefits for an adult recipient, states are free to set more restrictive time limits.[11] Eight states have implemented time limits of less than sixty months (see Table 2.8). Another thirteen have imposed intermittent time limits. Six states have adult-only time limits. A handful of states have indicated that they will pay for adult and child benefits in excess of sixty months from state-only funds.

PRWORA leaves to state discretion a number of other policies that were formerly the focus of wavier-based experimentation. For example, there is no requirement that benefit levels be related to family size, leaving states with the option of establishing a family cap, an option applied in twenty-one states as of 2000 (see Table 2.8). Asset limits that affect TANF eligibility and eligibility rules for two-parent families are also left to state discretion.[12]

In addition to changing the formal policies that structure states' welfare systems, PRWORA has changed the way that many welfare offices function at operational and informal levels as well. PRWORA's emphasis on work provides an important example. Motivated by both work-participation targets and pre-PRWORA research findings, many states have altered the focus of the welfare-to-work programs by which recipients satisfy their work-related activity requirements. Whereas earlier work programs generally emphasized skills development, offering education and training classes designed to raise skills and eventual wages, many states now run placement-oriented programs that stress a "work first" message, encouraging recipients to quickly find and take essentially any job in order to generate earnings.

Early research indicated that placement-oriented programs achieved greater employment results more quickly than skills-oriented programs (Freedman, Friedlander, and Riccio 1993). As a result, a number of waiver-era reforms involved side-by-side comparisons of the two approaches. We discuss these comparisons in the chapters that follow. Beyond changing the services received by welfare recipients, the work-first approach has resulted in a "culture change" in many welfare offices, transforming the delivery of services in other ways that are often difficult to quantify (Gais et al. 2001).

Finally, PRWORA differs from previous law in a way that has important implications for the nature of the studies that we review in this book. Section 1115 of the Social Security Act generally required waiver-based reforms to be evaluated rigorously. In the 1990s, this meant that many such reforms were implemented as random-assignment experiments. In contrast, PRWORA does not require states to evaluate their reforms. As a result, there are no experimental studies of states' TANF programs.

Welfare-Related Outcomes in the 1990s

All of the policy and program changes of the 1990s were motivated by the desire to change the behavior of families on welfare or at risk of entering welfare. Reduced dependency would be reflected in lower caseloads, and economic self-sufficiency would translate into greater work effort and perhaps even higher earnings and income. If the reforms were successful, they would also produce changes in childbearing and family formation. Indeed, as noted in Chapter 1, the trends in many of these outcomes did change as the states changed their welfare programs. Here we focus more closely on recent trends in welfare-related behavior. We also discuss economic trends and trends in other policy areas that also may have contributed to the decline in the welfare caseload. Finally, we discuss the circumstances of families who left the welfare rolls during the 1990s and the characteristics of those who remain.

Recent Trends in Welfare-Related Behavior

Figure 2.4 presents data for the period 1970 to 2001 on the rate of welfare receipt, defined as the proportion of the U.S. population re-

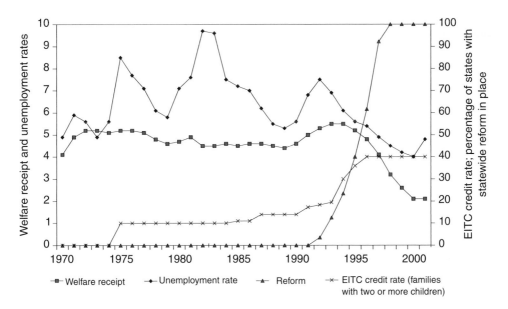

Figure 2.4
Welfare receipt, unemployment, the EITC, and statewide reform, 1970–2001. *Source:* Caseload:
DHHS (2001b); unemployment rate: BLS (2002); EITC credit rate: Hotz and Scholz (2003); state-
wide reform: authors' tabulations of data from CEA (1999b).

ceiving cash aid under either AFDC or TANF. For most of this period,
the rate of welfare receipt was fairly stable. Between 1988 and 1994,
however, it increased substantially. After peaking at 5.5 percent in 1993,
the welfare rate started falling. By 2000 it had reached 2.1 percent, a
thirty-five-year low.

Figure 2.5 plots the employment rate, annual earnings, and annual income of single mothers for the period 1980–1999. Since single mothers
are the primary adult recipients of welfare, the effects of welfare reform should be particularly apparent in measures of their labor market
behavior. All three measures in Figure 2.5 show the effects of the recession of the early 1980s and the expansion that followed. In the early
1990s, all three measures stayed roughly constant. Thereafter, all rose.
The post-1993 increase in employment was especially rapid. Income
rose more slowly than earnings (at an average annual rate of 3.5 percent
versus 5.1 percent), because for many single mothers, welfare payments
fell as earnings increased.

Although the average incomes of single mothers increased over the
1990s, what cannot be seen in Figure 2.5 is that some low-income families lost ground over at least part of the period. Average incomes among
the lowest fifth of single mothers fell between 1995 and 1997 (Primus et
al. 1999). Recent data from the Census Bureau's annual March Current

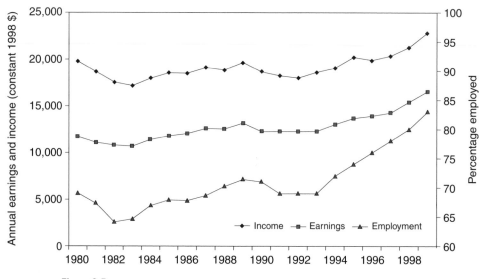

Figure 2.5
Employment, earnings, and income for female-headed families, 1980–1999. *Source:* Authors' tabulations of March CPS data.

Population Survey (CPS) indicate that some of those losses have been recouped (Haskins 2001), but data from the Census Bureau's Survey of Income and Program Participation (SIPP) do not show any evidence of improvement (Bavier 2001).

Recent trends in family structure also suggest another effect of welfare reform. Figure 2.3 showed that the share of nonmarital births stopped rising about 1994, as welfare reform was getting under way. Figure 2.6 shows that the proportion of children living in two-parent families stopped falling at about the same time. Furthermore, there is evidence that these changes have been more pronounced for families with lower income or less education, precisely the groups that are more likely to be affected by welfare reform (Acs and Nelson 2001; Dupree and Primus 2001; Bavier 2001).

Other Factors Influencing Welfare-Related Behavior

In addition to showing the rate of welfare receipt, Figure 2.4 also plots the unemployment rate, a conventional summary measure of economic conditions. Prior to 1990, changes in the welfare rate were weakly associated with changes in the unemployment rate, as evidenced by the small increases in the welfare rate during the 1975 and 1980 recessions. Some have suggested that the 1981 OBRA eligibility restrictions explain why caseloads did not rise much as unemployment ap-

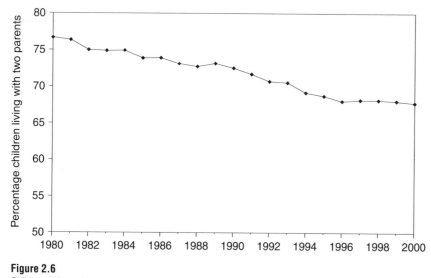

Figure 2.6
Children living with two parents, 1980–2000. *Source:* U.S. Bureau of the Census (2001b).

proached 10 percent in the early 1980s, although the welfare rate also rose little during the earlier recession in the mid-1970s. In contrast, since 1990, changes in the rate of welfare receipt have closely tracked changes in the unemployment rate. Both increased sharply during the early 1990s and decreased sharply thereafter. In 2001, in a softening economy, the unemployment rate rose to almost 6 percent. At the same time, the rate of welfare receipt stopped falling.

Figure 2.4 also plots the credit rate available to low-income workers with two or more children from the Earned Income Tax Credit. For the lowest-income families, the EITC acts as a wage subsidy, augmenting each dollar of earnings by the program's credit rate. Thus in 1990 such families received 14 cents for each dollar they earned. Starting in 1991, families with two or more children enjoyed a higher credit rate than families with a single child. Figure 2.4 shows that the credit rate for families with two or more children increased substantially after 1993, reaching 40 percent in 1996.[13] Economic theory predicts that employment should increase as the subsidy rises; a higher subsidy could lure welfare recipients, or would-be recipients, into the labor market and off the rolls. The increase in the EITC thus provides another potential explanation for falling caseloads and rising employment among single mothers.

Finally, Figure 2.4 also plots the cumulative percentage of states that had implemented statewide welfare reform in each year, under either waivers or TANF. As discussed above, the first statewide waivers were implemented in 1992, and by 1998 all states had implemented their TANF plans. The implementation of welfare reform coincides with the decline in welfare receipt, but it also coincides with the decline in unemployment and the increased generosity of the EITC.

The figure highlights the central problem facing analysts who attempt to estimate the effects of welfare reform: reform took place at the same time that the economy improved dramatically and the EITC was expanded. Expansions of public health coverage for low-income families and increases in the minimum wage also could have contributed to the observed changes in welfare-related behavior.[14] Disentangling the effects of the economy and other policy changes from the effect of welfare reform is one of the central challenges to analysts who seek to estimate the effects of welfare reform. Moreover, this central problem is not only an issue for studies attempting to explain the decline in welfare use. It equally affects studies that aim to explain changes in the labor market behavior of single mothers.

The Circumstances of Families Who Leave Welfare

Whether or not the decline in the caseload can be attributed to welfare reform, the caseload fell dramatically, and the circumstances of the families who left welfare during the 1990s provide further invaluable context for the analysis that follows.[15] Such contextual information comes from so-called welfare-leaver studies. These studies track families leaving the welfare rolls. They provide no information about the causal effects of welfare reform, since they provide no indication of how families leaving welfare would have behaved if welfare reform had not been implemented. Nevertheless, these studies provide useful information about the labor markets in which former welfare recipients participate and some insights into their behavior.

To begin, the leaver studies document that not all welfare exits are permanent. Although most welfare leavers remain off the rolls for at least one year, 23 to 35 percent return within twelve months of their exit. However, most of those who return do not stay for long: 71 percent leave again within a year of rejoining the rolls.

Most of those who stay off welfare succeed in finding jobs, but they tend to be of short duration and are often part-time. Roughly 60 to 75 percent of welfare leavers gain employment at some time during the first year after exiting welfare, but only about 40 percent are employed in each of their first four quarters off welfare. Only 13 percent work full-time for the entire year.

Across the various leaver studies, monthly earnings among employed welfare leavers average roughly $600 to $1,100 in their first quarter off the rolls. There is some evidence of earnings growth, but it is small. By their fourth quarter off welfare, leavers with earnings typically make between $700 and $1,300 a month (DHHS 2001a).

Low earnings growth could stem either from low wage growth or from intermittent work. Recent research suggests that the wages of low-income women rise with work experience in a manner that is comparable to that of other workers when experience is measured as actual hours of previous work (Gladden and Taber 2000; Loeb and Corcoran 2001). This finding suggests that low earnings growth is due to sporadic employment.

The household income of welfare leavers, which includes the earnings of the parent, other adults in the household, food stamp payments, and other public and private transfers, tends to be low both shortly after the family leaves welfare (that is, within six to eight months) and after more time has passed (twenty-six to thirty-four months). In both cases, incomes range from $1,000 to $1,500 per month (DHHS 2001a).

Bavier (2001) reports that leavers have about the same household income after leaving welfare, on average, as they had while they were on welfare. The sources of income are different, with earnings accounting for a larger proportion and transfer payments a smaller one, but on average, the total level of income is about the same. This fact has probably had an important, if not widely acknowledged, effect on the post-PRWORA debate over welfare policy.

Before PRWORA was passed, there were widespread fears that the combination of time limits and work requirements would cause many families to leave the rolls and endure great hardship as a result. To say that families leaving welfare have incomes of $12,000 to $18,000 a year hardly suggests that their lives are free of hardship. However, to say that their postwelfare incomes are similar to their incomes while on welfare suggests that the deprivation that many observers feared has not been as acute as expected. If it had turned out that welfare leavers' postexit incomes were only a fraction of their incomes while on welfare, the entire tenor of post-PRWORA discussions over welfare reform would likely be quite different. Whether these relatively optimistic trends will hold in the face of a soft labor market, or persist once large numbers of recipients reach the time limit, remains to be seen.

Characteristics of Welfare Recipients in the Postreform Era

Given the unprecedented decline in welfare caseloads since 1993, a natural question to ask is, Who remains on aid? Table 2.9 provides a description of the welfare population in 2001, the most recent year for

Table 2.9   Characteristics of AFDC/TANF recipients, 1992–2001

	1992	1994	1996	1998	2000	2001
Total cases (1,000s)	4,769	5,046	4,553	3,176	2,269	2,121
Race/ethnicity (%)[a]						
White	39	37	36	33	31	30
Black	37	36	37	39	39	39
Hispanic	18	20	21	22	25	26
Average age of adults	30	31	31	31	31	31
Age of youngest child (%)[b]						
Age 5 or less	63	62	60	56	54	54
Age 6 or above	36	36	39	42	44	45
Employed (%)	7	8	11	23	26	27

Source: DHHS (2003), section X, exhibit II.
Note: Years refer to fiscal years.
a. Columns do not add to 100 percent due to other racial groups and "unknown" cases.
b. Columns do not add to 100 percent due to "unknown" cases.

which data are available. For purposes of comparison, the table also reports recipient characteristics for earlier years.

Along with the change in the caseload has come a change in the racial and ethnic composition of welfare recipients. Whites made up 39 percent of the caseload in 1992; in 2001 they accounted for only 30 percent. The share of African Americans on the rolls has remained roughly constant, rising only from 37 to 39 percent of the caseload. The main growth has been among Hispanics, who now account for 26 percent of welfare rolls, as compared with only 18 percent in 1992.

The average age of adult recipients has remained roughly constant since 1992, but the age distribution of children receiving welfare has changed quite a bit. In 1992, the youngest child in 63 percent of welfare families was age five or younger. By 2001 that share had fallen to 54 percent. The share of families with older children had risen accordingly.

Perhaps the largest change involves the employment of welfare recipients. In 1992 only 6.6 percent of adult recipients worked for pay. By 2001 that number had risen to 26.7 percent. In light of TANF's work requirements, such growth may be less surprising than the fact that workers still remain in the minority among welfare recipients. Among employed welfare recipients, average monthly earnings have grown substantially. Whereas employed recipients typically earned $466 in 1996, by 2000 average earnings had grown to $686 per month (DHHS 2003).

One way to interpret such changes is to note that, prior to welfare reform, many observers expressed concern that the postreform caseload would consist increasingly of recipients who had the least skills and the remotest chances of achieving self-sufficiency. Although the data in Table 2.9 do not speak directly to these issues, the trend in racial composition reinforces such concerns. Minority recipients are often more disadvantaged than white recipients, so the increase in minority recipients, particularly among Hispanics, who may experience language barriers, is at least roughly consistent with concerns that the post-PRWORA caseload would contain increasing concentrations of low-skill and high-barrier recipients.

However, other trends suggest otherwise. Childcare issues are generally greatest for women with young children, but women with young children make up a smaller share of the caseload than they did before. Likewise, welfare recipients are now much more likely to work than they used to be, and those who work earn more. These trends would seem to bode well for eventual self-sufficiency.

We conclude that recent trends in recipient characteristics are mixed. They offer ambiguous support for the notion that the postreform caseload would result in increasing concentrations of increasingly disadvantaged recipients. The data are neither wholly consistent with this hypothesis, nor do they completely repudiate it.

❖

CHAPTER THREE

An Economic Model

With some background in hand, we turn to the first step of our analysis. We present the conventional economic model of welfare incentives under AFDC and extend it as necessary to predict the effects of three major categories of reforms: financial work incentives, requirements for work or related activities (and sanctions for noncompliance), and time limits. Of all the policy reforms implemented under PRWORA, these three are among the most important, and are likely to have consequences for welfare use, labor market behavior, and income. Indeed, the model suggests that these reforms may entail trade-offs among the traditional policy goals of reducing dependency, promoting work, and alleviating need. Studying other aspects of behavior, such as marriage, fertility, and child well-being, requires more complex models, which we discuss in later chapters.

We begin with an exposition of the leisure-consumption model used to analyze behavior under AFDC. We then extend the model to accommodate in turn the three key policy changes that have been implemented under PRWORA. We derive predictions from the model regarding the effects of each of the policies on each of the outcomes. It is these predictions, summarized in the final section of this chapter, which we compare in subsequent chapters to the results of numerous empirical analyses.

AFDC and the Standard Economic Model

Although some of the reforms implemented under PRWORA represent changes in kind from AFDC, others are better thought of as changes in degree. Time limits, as we have seen, were a fundamental change, whereas financial work incentives and work requirements have their roots in earlier reforms. Therefore it is useful to review the standard model used to analyze behavior under AFDC before discussing the reforms implemented under waivers and TANF.

Figure 3.1 displays the leisure-income diagram long used to analyze welfare incentives. Underlying the figure and the model it represents are a number of assumptions. The first is that welfare and work represent the only potential sources of income. The second is that there are no fixed costs of work. Relaxing these assumptions complicates the analysis without affecting the qualitative predictions of the model. The third assumption is that the consumer is free to choose her hours. This may be a reasonable assumption when the labor market is strong, jobs are relatively easy to come by, and the consumer can adjust her hours by changing jobs. In a weak labor market, when jobs are harder to get, this assumption may be less realistic. The fourth assumption is utility maximization. Interpreted strictly, utility maximization implies that all families eligible for welfare should sign up for benefits. Since this runs contrary to fact, some analysts have added stigma or transaction costs to the model (Moffitt 1983; Currie and Grogger 2002). Again, elaborating the model in this way complicates the discussion without affecting the qualitative results. To keep the analysis as simple as possible, we maintain all of these assumptions.

In Figure 3.1, leisure, denoted by L, is defined as all time not spent working for a wage, and increases to the right along the x-axis. The point $\bar{L}$ represents the total time available to be allocated between work and leisure, such as the 720 hours in a typical month. Income, denoted by I, is measured along the y-axis. The point $\bar{I}$ represents the amount of income that the consumer could earn if she could somehow devote all of her time to working for the wage w. The line $\bar{I}\bar{L}$ is the consumer's no-welfare budget constraint, indicating the range of feasible combinations of leisure and income that the consumer could choose among in the absence of a welfare system. Its slope is equal to $-w$.

The consumer maximizes her utility at the point x, where her budget constraint is tangent to the indifference curve labeled U_x. Since leisure is defined as all time not spent working for a wage, the choice of leisure determines both the choice of employment (whether to work at all) and the choice of labor supply (how many hours to work). Hours of work, denoted by h, can be measured along the x-axis moving to the left from the point $\bar{L}$. At the no-welfare optimum, the consumer works h_0 hours.

As discussed in Chapter 2, the original AFDC program allowed each state to set its maximum welfare grant, that is, the benefit payable to families with no other income. In all states, benefits for working families were reduced by a dollar for each dollar of earnings. Thus the implicit tax on earnings was 100 percent.

Figure 3.1 illustrates the effect of introducing a welfare system with a maximum grant of G and a tax rate of 100 percent.[1] With a 100 percent tax on earnings, the break-even point, that is, the point at which the con-

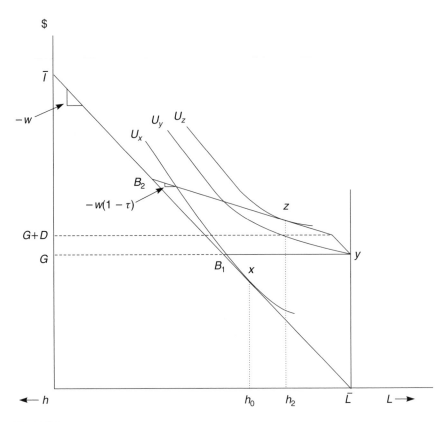

Figure 3.1
The consumer's choice problem under AFDC

sumer becomes income-ineligible for welfare, occurs at point B_1, where income is still G. The consumer's total budget constraint is given by two segments: the diagonal segment $\bar{I}B_1$, and the horizontal segment B_1y. She chooses the point along this budget constraint where her utility is highest. Figure 3.1 illustrates the choice of a consumer for whom the maximum occurs at point y, where she receives welfare, foregoes employment, and receives utility U_y.

We can also think of this consumer as solving her problem in a slightly different way that involves two steps. In the first step, she makes two calculations. She first calculates the maximum utility that she could achieve along the no-welfare budget constraint, $\bar{I}L$, then calculates the maximum utility she could achieve along the welfare budget constraint, B_1y. In the second step, she chooses whether to use welfare or not so as to achieve the higher optimum. Thus she compares the maximum utility she could get while on welfare with the maximum utility she could get while off of welfare, points y and x, respectively. Since $U_y > U_x$, she chooses point y, which is to say, she chooses welfare. This two-step approach to the problem emphasizes that the consumer is always free to choose the no-welfare option if it leaves her better off. Because this fact proves useful in analyzing the effects of work requirements and time limits, we adopt this approach for the rest of the chapter.

With a 100 percent tax rate on earnings, it is not surprising that the consumer forgoes employment while receiving welfare. Her income is the same at any point between B_1 and y, but her leisure is greatest at y. Working reduces leisure without any compensating gain in income.

The work disincentive inherent in such a system led Congress to introduce the $30-and-a-third policy as a financial incentive in 1967. As discussed in Chapter 2, the monthly earnings disregard under $30-and-a-third was $30 and the tax rate was 67 percent. Thus for earnings in excess of $30 a month, the recipient could keep one of every three dollars she earned.

Figure 3.1 illustrates the effects of such a financial incentive. The kinked line B_2y illustrates the consumer's welfare budget constraint with a disregard of D and a benefit-reduction rate of τ. The segment to the right of the kink has slope $-w$ given the zero tax rate on the first D dollars of earnings. The segment to the left of the kink has slope $-w(1 - \tau)$, which is the consumer's after-tax wage on earnings in excess of D. The point B_2 represents the new break-even point.

We consider how a financial incentive should affect the behavior of three different groups of consumers: (1) welfare recipients who were not working prior to the financial incentive; (2) welfare recipients who were working prior to the financial incentive; and (3) nonrecipients at risk of entering welfare. The consumer located at point y in Figure 3.1 represents a consumer who was not working prior to the financial incentive. For these consumers (group 1), lower tax rates, effected by either increases in D or decreases in τ, should increase employment and labor supply. The incentive causes the consumer in Figure 3.1 to move from point y to point z. She continues to receive welfare, but now combines welfare with employment, working h_2 hours.

Once working, such recipients may stay on welfare longer than they would have otherwise because the higher break-even threshold allows them to remain eligible and receive a larger benefit at higher levels of earnings. The expanded financial incentive provides no incentive for recipients to leave welfare altogether, although it should decrease the fraction of the caseload that remains on welfare without working.

The financial incentive may cause welfare payments to either rise or fall, depending on how one measures them. In any given month, welfare payments to working recipients are lower than payments to recipients who are not working. In Figure 3.1, the welfare payment to a nonworking recipient is G, whereas the payment to a working recipient is equal to the vertical distance between the welfare budget constraint and the no-welfare budget constraint. However, because the financial incentive may lead welfare recipients to stay on welfare longer than they would have otherwise, the sum of welfare payments over a period longer than one month could rise. Whether aggregate payments rise or fall, the recipient's income rises, because she is allowed to keep more of her welfare benefit at any level of earnings.

Group 2 consists of welfare recipients who were working even before the incentive was implemented. Because they were already working, the financial incentive is unlikely to affect this group's employment status. The labor supply response of this group cannot be predicted by the model. Expanding the financial incentive increases the return to work, which by itself should increase hours of work. However, the expanded incentive also raises the recipient's income for a given level of labor supply. Assuming that leisure is a normal good, that is, that consumers desire greater leisure as their incomes rise, this should decrease hours of work. Thus these two effects, known as the "substitution effect" and the "income effect," respectively, work in opposite directions. As a result, the net effect of a financial incentive on the labor supply of initially working welfare recipients is ambiguous. Logically, the substitution effect must dominate the income effect at low wages, since at some wage the consumer enters the labor market (that is, she moves from zero hours to positive hours). Nevertheless, the income effect can dominate at higher income levels.

The model predicts that the expanded financial incentive should cause welfare use to rise among group 2. The reasons are essentially the same for this group as for the first group of welfare recipients who were not working initially. How the incentive should cause monthly payments to change cannot be predicted, because the answer would depend on the change in recipients' labor supply. For the same reason, the model cannot predict how the financial incentive should affect the incomes of initially working welfare recipients.

Group 3 consists of consumers who are initial nonrecipients. Because the financial incentive increases the break-even level from B_1 to B_2, consumers initially situated between B_1 and B_2 become eligible for welfare.[2] The model predicts that those consumers should enter the welfare system as a result.

The financial incentive should also decrease the labor supply of initial nonrecipients, since it lowers these workers' after-tax wage while raising their income at a given labor supply. Thus the income and substitution effects reinforce each other, reducing hours of work. The effect of the incentive on the incomes of initial nonrecipients cannot be predicted, because it depends on the magnitude of their labor supply reduction.

Therefore in the total population, accounting for both recipients and initial nonrecipients, an expanded financial incentive would be expected to increase welfare use, although its effects on welfare payments cannot be predicted. Employment is predicted to rise, but the effect on labor supply is uncertain. For recipients not working initially, labor supply should increase. Initially working recipients, however, may reduce their labor supply, as would initial nonrecipients who enter the program. The full effect of the incentive on income is ambiguous, because any increase in income among recipients not working initially could be offset by a decrease in income among initially working recipients and initial nonrecipients.

Financial Work Incentives

For the most part, the states' financial work incentives under TANF differ from those under AFDC in degree rather than in kind. Most states have implemented financial incentives that are more generous than the $30-and-a-third policy, although a few states have implemented policies that may be less generous, depending on the recipient's labor supply and work history.

In evaluating the results of random-assignment experiments involving financial incentives, the most relevant predictions from the theory are those pertaining to welfare recipients, since most consumers participating in the experiments were receiving welfare to begin with. In evaluating the results of observational studies, predictions regarding the behavior of initial nonrecipients are also relevant. Observational studies typically involve general samples of low-income families rather than more restrictive samples of welfare recipients, and thus in such investigations it is possible, at least in principle, to observe entry effects among initial nonrecipients.

Such entry effects may be mitigated, however, by the way that many states have structured their financial incentives. Under TANF, many states have implemented dual break-even thresholds, with a lower threshold for initial applicants and a higher threshold for ongoing recipients (Rowe and Roberts 2004). Figure 3.1 can be used to illustrate. Under a dual-threshold scheme, the state retains the original break-even point B_1 for new applicants, but its financial incentive results in a break-even point of B_2 for recipients. Families must have incomes below B_1 to qualify for aid when applying for welfare initially, but then can increase their incomes to B_2 by working without becoming ineligible for aid. Such dual-threshold schemes allow the state to provide the financial incentive for those on welfare without expanding eligibility to those not initially on welfare.

Requirements for Work or Related Activities

We begin the analysis of work requirements by discussing the effects of a perfectly enforced work-related activity mandate. By perfect enforcement, we mean that otherwise-eligible consumers can receive benefits only if they comply with the mandate. The assumption of perfect enforcement implies complete compliance. This assumption is unrealistic, but it simplifies the analysis. We discuss the more realistic case of imperfect enforcement below, when we discuss sanctions for noncompliance.

The behavioral effects of work-related activity mandates can be analyzed using Figure 3.2. For the sake of simplicity, we have set $D = 0$, so the welfare budget constraint is given by the segment By, the slope of which is $-w(1 - \tau)$. In the absence of a work requirement, the consumer is free to locate anywhere along that segment while participating on welfare. In the case illustrated, she maximizes her utility at the point y, where she forgoes employment.

Consider first the effects of a mandate that requires the recipient to work at least $\bar{h}_1$ hours at a wage-paying job. This restricts the welfare budget constraint to the segment Bz_1; locating at the point y is ruled out. Given the new constraint, the consumer's utility is maximized by locating at point z_1, where she just satisfies the work requirement. She remains on welfare, but the work requirement has indeed caused her to become employed.

A more stringent work requirement, stipulating $\bar{h}_2$ hours of work, would not only cause her to become employed, but would also cause her to leave welfare. Under that requirement the consumer would maximize her utility along the new welfare budget constraint Bz_2 by locating at point z_2. However, the indifference curve passing through z_2 lies beneath the indifference curve labeled U_x, which represents the maximum utility the consumer can achieve along the no-welfare budget constraint. Thus the consumer would do better by forgoing welfare altogether, locating at point x, the no-welfare optimum.[3]

A mandate that is satisfied by wage-paying work should reduce welfare payments, since the benefit payable to a working recipient is less than that payable to a nonworking recipient. The effect of the mandate on income depends on both the stringency of the mandate and the tax rate. If the tax rate is less than 100 percent, as illustrated in Figure 3.2, then a lenient mandate, such as a requirement to work $\bar{h}_1$ hours, should

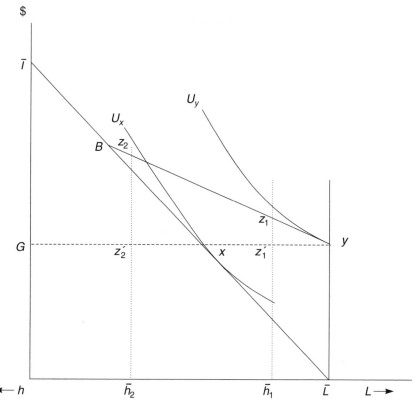

Figure 3.2
The consumer's choice problem with requirements for work or related activities

increase income. If the tax rate is 100 percent, then the same mandate would leave income unchanged. The gain in earnings would be counteracted by an equal decrease in benefits. If the mandate causes consumers to leave welfare, as would the requirement to work $\bar{h}_2$ hours, it reduces both welfare payments and income.

If we assume that the disutility of participating in work-related activities is the same as the disutility of working, then we can also use Figure 3.2 to analyze the effect of a perfectly enforced work-related activity mandate that is satisfied by an unpaid activity such as job-search training. In this case, if the consumer stays on welfare, her income will be the same (equal to G) regardless of how much time she devotes to the activity. Thus remaining on welfare would involve locating along the segment Gy rather than the segment By. That is, the mandate would cause the consumer to reduce her leisure without increasing her income.

In response to a requirement to participate in unpaid activities for $\bar{h}_1$ hours, the consumer would locate at point z_1'.[4] Doing so would neither increase her employment nor decrease her welfare use. A requirement that stipulated $\bar{h}_2$ hours would again induce her to locate at point x, since she would attain greater utility by leaving welfare and becoming employed rather than satisfying the more stringent work-related activity mandate.

In the case where the mandate is satisfied by unpaid activities, welfare payments fall only to the extent that consumers leave welfare. Likewise, income may fall among those who leave welfare, but it stays constant among those who remain on the rolls.

This analysis suggests that we should expect different types of welfare-to-work programs to have different effects on behavior. Although the ultimate goal of most programs is to increase recipients' employment, different programs take different approaches to achieve that goal. Placement-oriented programs provide assistance with resumes and job-search techniques, whereas skills-oriented programs aim to enhance recipients' basic skills, with an eye toward improving their eventual wage offers.

In terms of Figure 3.2, one can think of placement-oriented programs as seeking to move recipients onto the budget segment Bz_1 as quickly as possible. In contrast, skills-oriented programs may move them first onto segment Bz_1, where they gain skills before moving into work along segment Bz_1. As a result, one should expect placement-oriented welfare-to-work programs to have larger short-run effects on employment.

Whether work-related activity mandates are satisfied via placement- or skills-oriented welfare-to-work programs, they reduce recipients' utility. Thus we would not expect recipients to comply with them voluntarily. Moreover, efforts to induce compliance via enforcement are unlikely to succeed completely. Despite the existence of legally mandated requirements, we would expect to find some consumers at disallowed locations on the budget set, such as point y.

In order to increase compliance with the mandates, states generally impose sanctions for noncompliance. The theory discussed in the last chapter predicts that the level of compliance should be inversely related to the certainty and severity of sanctions (Becker 1968). Beyond affecting compliance, sanctions may affect welfare use and employment. To illustrate, it is useful to think in terms of polar cases. Sanctions that are sufficiently certain and severe would give rise to complete compliance, the effects of which have been analyzed above. In the complete absence of sanctions, work-related activity mandates would be meaningless, and the consumer in Figure 3.2 would continue to locate at point y. From this we deduce that, for any particular work requirement, stronger sanctions should lead to greater changes in behavior (that is, greater increases in employment and labor supply and greater reductions in welfare use); weaker sanctions should result in lesser changes. Of course, in addition to affecting recipients' behavior, sanctions may reduce the caseload mechanically when noncompliant recipients are detected and dropped from the rolls.

In principle, the need for sanctions could be avoided by tying financial incentives in the form of earnings supplements to voluntary hours-of-work requirements. Although such policies have not been adopted in states' TANF plans, two of the experiments that we discuss in later chapters fall into this category. Simplified versions of such programs can be characterized by the minimum hours threshold required to qualify for the supplement, a target, or "benchmark," level of earnings, and a benefit-reduction rate. The benchmark earnings level and the benefit-reduction rate determine the earnings supplement as a function of the consumer's earnings.

For a program with an hours requirement of $\bar{h}$, a benchmark earnings level of T, and a benefit-reduction rate of $\tau < 1$, the consumer's budget constraint under the supplement program would be the segment B_2z in Figure 3.3, the slope of which is $1 - \tau$. Of course, since the program is voluntary, the consumer may choose to receive welfare instead. With a welfare program that involves a grant of G and a 100 percent tax rate, this means that she could locate along the segment B_1y.

Like the effects of a pure financial incentive, the effects of the earnings supplement that is tied to work may vary across different groups of consumers. For those originally receiving welfare without working, who were located at point y when the program was introduced, the model predicts that the program should decrease the use of welfare by inducing some consumers to abandon the welfare program for the supplement program by taking employment and working at least $\bar{h}$ hours. The supplement decreases welfare payments to initially nonworking welfare recipients, although it increases supplement payments. It should also increase incomes.

Among consumers who initially were not on welfare and were meeting the program's hours requirement, such as those who were located at point x in Figure 3.3, the supplement provides an incentive to reduce hours (though not below $\bar{h}$). The reason is that the program raises such consumers' income at any level of labor supply in excess of $\bar{h}$ and effectively reduces their after-tax wage. Thus the income and substitution effects reinforce each other, much like the effect of a financial incentive on initial nonrecipients. As in the case of financial incentives, the effects of the supplement on the incomes of workers not initially receiving welfare will depend on the extent of their labor supply reduction.

Finally, the effects of the earnings supplement on consumers who were initially combining work and welfare (not illustrated) may be complex.

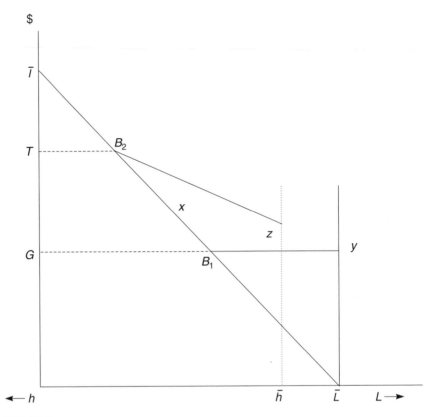

Figure 3.3
The consumer's choice problem with a voluntary earnings supplement tied to hours of work

The supplement program may induce some such consumers to abandon the welfare program in favor of the supplement program, reducing welfare use. However, those workers' labor supply could either rise or fall in the process, depending on whether they were initially working enough to satisfy the supplement program's hours requirement. Likewise, their incomes could either rise or fall.

Time Limits

Time limits may affect welfare receipt in two distinct ways. The most obvious effect is mechanical: welfare use (and payments) are eliminated once recipients exhaust their benefits. However, time limits may also have behavioral effects, causing consumers to reduce their welfare receipt before they reach the limit.

Analyzing the behavioral, or anticipatory, effects of time limits requires us to incorporate the future consequences of the consumer's current welfare use into her time-allocation problem. Her choices today will explicitly affect her constraints tomorrow. By using welfare excessively early on, the consumer may forgo the option of using welfare in the future.

Incorporating the future consequences of current behavior requires some additional notation.[5] Let the consumer's stock of benefits at time t, denominated in months of welfare use, be given by S_t. Let the maximized expected value of the consumer's lifetime utility, starting at date t, be given by $EV_t(S_t)$. Lifetime expected utility is an increasing function of S_t, because the larger is S_t, the lower is the probability that the consumer will have exhausted her benefits at a time when she would otherwise wish to use them. The factor that the consumer uses to discount the future is ρ. If $\rho = 0$, the consumer completely disregards the future in making her current decisions. If $\rho = 1$, she gives the future the same weight as the present. Generally, we expect that $0 < \rho < 1$.[6]

The consumer's problem under time limits is depicted in Figure 3.4.[7] As in the case without time limits, we can think of the consumer as solving her problem in two steps. In the first step, she maximizes her current-period utility, first along the no-welfare budget constraint $\bar{I}L$ and then

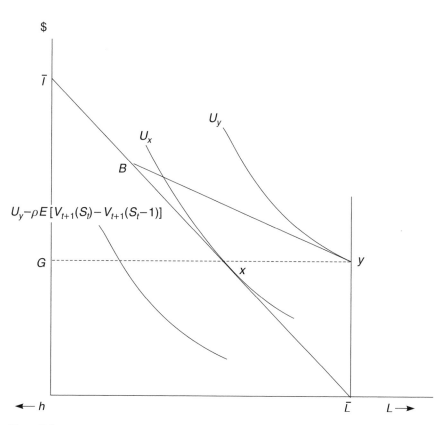

Figure 3.4
The consumer's choice problem with time limits

along welfare budget constraint By. The respective optima are x, yielding current-period utility U_x, and y, yielding current-period utility U_y.

In the second step, the consumer chooses whether to use welfare on the basis of which point yields her the highest level of utility. Unlike the previous cases, however, the consumer must now consider more than just the current-period utility associated with each choice. She must also consider how her welfare use today affects her lifetime expected utility beginning tomorrow.

The key to analyzing the future consequences of the consumer's current welfare use is to note that a consumer with a stock of S_t units of welfare benefits at date t will have a stock of either S_t or $S_t - 1$ units at date $t + 1$. If she forgoes welfare today, she will have S_t units tomorrow. In that case, $S_{t+1} = S_t$, and the expected value of lifetime utility beginning tomorrow is $EV_{t+1}(S_t)$. If she uses welfare today, then $S_{t+1} = S_t - 1$, and the expected value of lifetime utility beginning tomorrow is $EV_{t+1}(S_t - 1)$. In other words, if the consumer uses welfare today, she enjoys greater current-period utility (U_y versus U_x), but the expected value of her lifetime utility starting in the next period (discounted to the present) falls from $\rho EV_{t+1}(S_t)$ to $\rho EV_{t+1}(S_t - 1)$. Thus in the presence of time limits, the decision to use welfare involves not just a comparison between U_x and U_y, but rather a comparison between $U_x + \rho EV_{t+1}(S_t)$ and $U_y + \rho EV_{t+1}(S_t - 1)$, or equivalently, between U_x and $U_y - \rho E[V_{t+1}(S_t) - V_{t+1}(S_t - 1)]$. If the future cost of today's welfare use is high enough, the consumer will forgo welfare today, even though she reduces her current-period utility by doing so. Figure 3.4 depicts a consumer who would choose to use welfare in the absence of time limits, but chooses to forgo welfare in their presence.

Not surprisingly, this model predicts that time limits should lead consumers to reduce their welfare use and increase their employment and labor supply. It also predicts that these effects should be greatest among families with the youngest children. Families become ineligible for welfare once their youngest child turns eighteen, which means that families with the youngest children have the longest horizon over which to draw benefits. Since the value of the welfare option is greatest among consumers with the longest horizon over which to execute it, time limits should lead to the greatest reductions in welfare use (and welfare payments) among families with the youngest children. It is interesting to note that this prediction accords with the data in Table 2.9, which showed that families with young children made up a smaller proportion of the caseload in the post-PRWORA period.

One potential objection to the model described above is that it implicitly assumes that consumers are forward looking and have time-consistent preferences. If consumers are short-sighted or otherwise have pres-ent-biased preferences, then this model may not be applicable. If the effects of time limits failed to follow the pattern predicted by the model above, one might seek to generalize the model to allow for time-inconsis-tent preferences.

Summarizing the Predictions

For ease of reference in the discussion that follows, we summarize the predictions from the model in Table 3.1. The table takes the form of a matrix, with the reform policies arrayed along the rows and the various aspects of welfare-related behavior, or outcomes, arrayed along the col-umns. The entry in each cell, which represents a policy-outcome combi-nation, indicates the predicted effect of the policy on the outcome.

The first row shows that, all else equal, financial work incentives are predicted to increase welfare use and employment. Their effects on wel-fare payments, labor supply, and income are ambiguous. The ambiguity arises for two reasons: the possibility of dominant income effects among initially employed welfare recipients, and the possibility of entry effects among initial nonrecipients.

There is less ambiguity regarding the effects of work (or work-related activity) requirements. They should decrease welfare use and payments while generally increasing employment and labor supply. Their effects on income may be either positive or negative, depending on whether they raise earnings by enough to offset the reduction in welfare payments. Sanctions reinforce the effects of work requirements and thus have simi-lar effects.

Time limits are similar. They are predicted to decrease welfare use and welfare payments while increasing employment and labor supply. Be-cause earnings may rise while benefit payments fall, their effect on in-

Table 3.1 Predicted effects of selected policy reforms on selected outcomes

Policy reforms	Outcomes				
	Welfare use	Welfare payments	Employment	Labor supply	Income
Financial work incentives	+	+/−	+	+/−	+/−
Work requirements	−	−	+	+	+/−
Sanctions	−	−	+	+	+/−
Time limits	−	−	+	+	+/−

come could be either positive or negative. Sanctions reinforce the effects of work requirements and thus have similar effects.

Table 3.1 highlights some of the potential trade-offs among the goals of decreasing dependency, increasing employment, and alleviating need. Financial work incentives should increase recipients' employment, and may increase their income, but at the expense of increasing their welfare use. In contrast, work requirements and time limits should decrease welfare use while increasing employment, but they may reduce income at the same time. Of course, whether these policies actually reduce income is an empirical question, since the predictions from the theory are ambiguous. The empirical trade-offs among different policy goals is an important focus of the chapters that follow.

Also in later chapters, we will expand Table 3.1 to include columns for other outcomes, such as marriage, fertility, and child well-being. We will also add rows for policies primarily designed to affect those outcomes, such as family caps, and for various combinations of policies that appear in the experimental literature. In Chapter 10, we will again return to the matrix as a means of organizing the evidence. In the next chapter, we discuss key characteristics of the studies that provide this evidence.

———————— ❖ ————————

CHAPTER FOUR

Methodological Issues

The model from the last chapter makes ceteris paribus predictions about the effects of welfare reform. Put differently, it makes predictions about the causal effects of different reforms. Thus comparing the theory to the data requires estimates of the causal effects of reform.

In this chapter we focus on the two principal methodologies used in the literature to isolate the effects of welfare reform policies: random assignment experiments and observational studies. We identify the strengths and weaknesses associated with each approach. We also highlight a number of other methodological issues that are relevant for research in this area. One conclusion from this discussion is that no single methodology—let alone single study—is likely to provide definitive, comprehensive answers about the effects of welfare reform. Rather, one needs to draw insights and conclusions from the entire body of methodologically sound studies. We summarize key features of those studies at the end of this chapter.

Before proceeding, we note that not all studies of welfare reform have sought to estimate the causal effects of reform. A number of qualitative studies have interviewed small numbers of at-risk families to provide a detailed picture of how recent policy changes have affected their lives (Quint et al. 1999; Scott, London, and Edin 2001; Scott et al. 2001). Implementation studies have been conducted to learn how those policy changes are implemented within welfare offices and other agencies that deliver services to the poor (Nathan and Gais 1999; Sandfort 1999; Fink and Widom 2001). The leaver studies discussed in Chapter 2 have tracked the progress of former recipients as they exit the rolls and enter the workforce. All of these studies provide useful context for interpreting the effects of reform. They do not, however, address the causal effects of those reforms.

Causal effects are important because they allow us to assess whether the model from the last chapter fits the data generated by recent policy changes. They are also important because they answer a key policy question: how behavior changes in response to changes in policy. Because the causal effects of reform are important both in general and for our specific purposes, we focus in the next section on approaches to estimating them.

Methods of Causal Inference in Studies of Welfare Reform

Estimating the causal effects of reform requires the analyst to compare the behavior that is observed when reform takes place with the behavior that would have been observed if reform had not taken place, holding everything else constant. The behavior that would have been observed in the absence of reform is referred to as the counterfactual. The fact that the counterfactual is unobserved is the main obstacle to drawing causal inferences.

The research challenge is to devise a strategy that predicts what outcomes would have been observed under the counterfactual. If the researcher fails to hold constant other factors that could independently influence the outcome, such as the economy, then the resulting estimates of the effects of reform may be invalid, that is, biased or inconsistent. They may reflect not only the effect of the policy of interest but also the effects of the other factors that were not held constant. Such estimates are not useful for testing the theory, since a proper test requires estimates of the ceteris paribus effect of the policy reform. Furthermore, such estimates fail to inform policymakers how behavior changes as a result of the policy change.

Analysts have adopted two general research strategies for controlling for confounding factors, that is, for factors that could independently affect welfare-related behavior and potentially invalidate the estimated effects of reform: random assignment experiments and econometric analyses of observational data. Both have strengths and weaknesses.

Random Assignment

One approach to the problem of confounding factors is random assignment.[1] Rather than relying on existing variation in policies or programs, the analyst induces random variation. To test a new program, a study population is chosen, typically persons receiving or applying for welfare at a particular time. Then each member of the study population is assigned either to the control group, which is subject to the preexisting policy environment, or the treatment group, which is subject to the new policy environment. The assignment is determined by the logical equivalent of a coin toss.

In principle, random assignment holds everything constant except the policy whose effect the analyst seeks to estimate. Since individuals assigned to the new program differ from those assigned to the existing program only by a flip of a coin, confounding influences, such as the economy, should be identical for the two groups. If randomization is implemented properly, there should be no systematic differences across the two groups other than those attributable to the different policy environments. Thus the average effect of the policy, which is referred to as the "treatment effect" or the "impact" of the policy, can be estimated by the difference in mean welfare-related outcomes between the treatment group and the control group.[2]

Such experiments can be a powerful evaluation tool. The importance of controlling for confounding factors and the potential of random assignment for doing so led the federal government to require random assignment evaluations as a component of many section 1115 waivers.[3] In reality, not all waivers were evaluated, especially those that were approved shortly before the passage of the 1996 PRWORA legislation, either because the waiver-based reforms were never implemented or there was not sufficient time to get an evaluation under way (Harvey, Camasso, and Jagannathan 2000). Many of the evaluations implemented high-quality experimental designs, in some cases with follow-up periods that extended up to five years after randomization.[4] We review many of the studies emerging from such waiver evaluations in the chapters that follow.

However, despite their advantages, random assignment studies have a number of disadvantages. First, random assignment is expensive and often difficult to implement. As a result, not all programs are experimentally evaluated.

Second, random assignment evaluations miss initial entry effects. Because these studies focus on individuals who were receiving or applying for welfare at the start of the program, experiments miss changes in behavior among individuals at risk of entering welfare. As discussed in the last chapter, financial work incentives may promote entry by raising the income eligibility threshold. Other reforms, such as work requirements and time limits, may deter entry. Random assignment evaluations will miss both types of entry effects. This is important, because recent evidence suggests that about half of the recent decline in the welfare caseload resulted from reductions in entry rates, particularly reductions in initial entries (Haider, Klerman, and Roth 2001; Grogger, Haider, and Klerman 2003).

Third, random assignment experiments may not reproduce the results of universally implemented programs. Experiments may be implemented in locations with above-average management capability; more generally, large-scale program changes may tax managerial capabilities to a greater extent than small-scale changes. Broader implementations may also affect labor markets by raising the supply of low-skill workers. Thus similar reforms may yield different results when implemented as a local pilot program than when implemented as a statewide program.

Fourth, random assignment studies are not immune from problems that can bias their findings. For example, experimental contamination may result when treatment group members "cross over" by moving to a location that is not part of the evaluation. Cross-over may also occur when control group members become eligible to receive program services. Such cross-over will cause the experiment to underestimate the true effect of the program. In addition, sample attrition for follow-up data collection may be nonrandom and therefore bias the estimated treatment effects. Depending on the nature of the attrition, the bias can be either positive or negative (Heckman, Smith and Taber 1998).

A further important problem involves participants' perceptions of the rules that apply to them. In several of the random assignment studies that we review, members of the treatment group were confused about which of the new policies applied to them. In others, members of the control group incorrectly believed that they were subject to the new reforms. This latter form of confusion is a particular concern in exceptional-control evaluation designs, where almost all the population is assigned to the new "treatment" rules, and only a small fraction of the study population is assigned to the old "control" rules. In an environment where most recipients are subject to welfare reform and welfare reform receives considerable public and media attention, it may be difficult to persuade the controls that they are not subject to the new rules themselves.[5] Consequently the control group may behave more like the treatment group, biasing the estimated program impacts toward zero. Exceptional-control designs became more common toward the end of the waiver period.

Because of these problems, we conclude that the experimental approach is probably better suited for evaluating incremental policy changes than for evaluating the far-reaching changes associated with TANF. TANF was implemented statewide, which probably imposed greater management challenges than localized programs. It may have changed the supply of low-wage workers in the labor market as well. Confusion about TANF's new rules was widespread, at least during the period immediately after its implementation. Finally, the political climate surrounding PRWORA may have changed the "message" received by recipients regarding welfare, affecting recipients' expectations about future welfare availability and their motivation to find work in ways that small-scale experiments could not have done.

For these reasons, we view the waiver-based experiments as useful for learning about the effects of particular reforms, or bundles of reforms, in isolation. As such, they are particularly valuable for testing the theory laid out in Chapter 3. With a few exceptions that we note below, the experiments are less useful for evaluating the effects of sweeping policy changes. Fortunately, this limitation of the experimental approach is one of the strengths of the observational studies.

Econometric Methods for Observational Data

In observational studies, the analyst compares outcomes across different states and time periods where different policies are in place. As discussed in Chapter 2, prior to the 1990s, the U.S. welfare system had been largely uniform across states, with the exception of varying benefit levels. By the eve of PRWORA, however, the program exhibited substantial state-to-state variation because of waiver-based reforms. Moreover, states implemented their reforms, under waivers and TANF, at different times. This variation in the timing and nature of reform provides a "natural experiment" that has the potential, using appropriate statistical techniques, to isolate the causal impact of welfare reform on welfare-related behavior. Such observational studies are one component of the literature we draw from in the chapters that follow.

Observational studies typically analyze administrative data or nation-wide survey data. An advantage of observational analyses is that they can capture entry effects—unlike conventional experiments—by studying the entire population at risk of welfare. They may also be better suited to capturing, if not isolating, the effects of a change in the "message" that accompanies a sweeping reform.

The key problem with the observational approach is that welfare policy is not all that varies across states and time periods. Many potentially confounding factors vary as well, as we saw in Chapter 2. The key challenge for observational studies is to convincingly hold all else equal.

Regression analysis is the standard approach to this problem. To control for the effect of the economy, for example, observational studies usually include the local unemployment rate as an independent variable in a linear regression model. In this way, standard regression methods control for observable confounding factors.[6]

But many of the factors influencing welfare-related outcomes are difficult, or even impossible, to measure. Thus the principal challenge facing observational studies is controlling for unmeasurable, or unobservable, confounding influences. Now even more than before PRWORA, states determine their welfare programs. States differ in many ways besides their welfare programs, however, and some of those differences—in general attitudes or political sentiment, for example—may affect both welfare-related behavior and welfare policy in the state. If such unobservable differences are not somehow controlled for, then the analyst may erroneously attribute to changes in welfare policy changes in welfare-related behavior that are, in fact, the result of the unobserved factors. This problem of unobservable influences, or "unobservables," goes by many names, including "unobserved heterogeneity," "policy endogeneity," "omitted variable bias," and "spurious correlation." It is the central threat to the validity of observational studies.

This problem can be illustrated by way of a regression model that is similar to some of those estimated in the observational literature. The model can be written as:

$$y_{ist} = R_{st}\beta + Z_{st}\gamma + X_{ist}\delta + \alpha_{st} + \varepsilon_{ist} \tag{4.1}$$

In equation (4.1), y_{ist} is the welfare-related outcome, such as welfare receipt or employment, of the ith household in the sth state in year t. R_{st} is a variable or vector of variables characterizing welfare reform in the sth state in year t; Z_{st} is a vector of other state-level characteristics that vary from year to year, such as the maximum welfare benefit or the state unemployment rate. The vector X_{ist} captures household-level characteristics that predict welfare-related behavior, such as the mother's age, race, education, and number of children. The regression framework explicitly controls for the observable factors included in Z_{st} and X_{ist}. The terms β, γ, and δ are parameters to be estimated. The effect of welfare reform is given by β.[7]

There are two types of unobservables that influence welfare-related behavior: those that vary at the state level over time, captured by α_{st}, and those that vary idiosyncratically across households, given by ε_{ist}. The policy endogeneity problem arises if the unobservables that vary across states over time influence welfare reform in the state, that is, if α_{st} is correlated with R_{st}.[8]

A common approach to this problem is to assume that α_{st} can be decomposed into three components: a "state effect" that varies across states, but is invariant over time; a "year effect" or "period effect" that varies over time, but is the same across all states; and a residual component that is uncorrelated with welfare reform. An example of a state-specific, time-invariant unobservable might be the state's general political leaning. An example of an economywide, time-varying unobservable might be the Federal Reserve's macroeconomic policy choices. We can write

$$\alpha_{st} = \mu_s + \tau_t + v_{st} \tag{4.2}$$

where μ_s is the state effect, τ_t is the year effect, and v_{st} is the residual component. Substituting equation (4.2) into equation (4.1) yields a model that can be estimated by adding state dummies and year dummies to the other variables on the right-hand side of the regression equation. This model is commonly referred to as the state-fixed effects estimator. Because it utilizes before-and-after changes across different states to estimate the effects of welfare reform, it is also sometimes referred to as the (generalized) difference-in-difference estimator.[9] Under the assumption that v_{st} is uncorrelated with R_{st}, this estimator provides consistent estimates of the effects of welfare reform.[10]

This assumption has been questioned by numerous analysts, who argue that it is unlikely to hold in the turbulent policy environment of the 1990s, when the economy moved rapidly from bust to boom and welfare caseloads fell rapidly after reaching historic highs. To provide at least partial controls for time-varying, state-specific unobservables, some analysts have generalized the state-fixed-effects approach by adding state-specific time trends (both linear and quadratic) to their models. Such trends may capture smoothly trending unobservables within a state.

Other researchers have generalized the model by adding to the analysis data from individuals who should not have been affected by welfare reform, such as families with incomes too high to qualify for aid (or with education levels usually associated with such incomes). For a group of such unaffected families, equation (4.1) can be written as

$$y_{ist} = Z_{st}\gamma + X_{ist}\delta + \alpha_{st} + \varepsilon_{ist} \tag{4.3}$$

Equation (4.3) reflects the notion that, among families not affected by welfare reform, $\beta = 0$. In this approach, data from such unaffected families are pooled with data from potentially affected families. In effect, the unaffected families serve as a comparison group for the affected families, which serve as a treatment group. This approach is sometimes referred to as the difference-in-difference-in-difference, or triple-difference, approach, because it utilizes between-group differences in before-and-after changes across different states to estimate the effects of welfare reform.

A question concerning the triple-difference approach is whether the comparison group provides an adequate counterfactual for the treatment group, that is, whether the comparison group provides a valid estimate of how the treatment group would have behaved if reform had not been implemented. A closely related question is whether the other factors in the model—the Z and X vectors—affect the treatment and comparison groups similarly. To some extent this question can be addressed by allowing the coefficients of those vectors to vary between the two groups. As with the other approaches discussed above, however, there is always the possibility that some omitted factor, whose effects on welfare-related behavior vary between groups, may result in biased estimates.

Measuring the Policy Environment

The analysis from Chapter 3 derived the qualitative effects of several specific reform policies. But when implemented, these reforms can vary from one setting to another. For example, some financial work incentives are more generous than others and some sanctions are more stringent than others. Such variations raise concerns about how the reforms are measured. These issues differ between the experimental and observational studies. We discuss each case in turn.

Characterizing the Policy Environment in Random Assignment Studies

Random assignment studies are designed to measure the impact of the "treatment," that is, the program features that differ between the experimental and control groups. The experimenter controls the policy environment being evaluated through the design of the program. In the case of welfare reform evaluations, these program features include financial incentives to encourage work, requirements to participate in work or related activities, time limits, parental responsibility requirements, and so on.

In some of the random assignment studies we consider, the treatment consists of a single policy reform, such as a financial work incentive. Two studies employ dual-treatment designs. Both dual-treatment experiments involve two experimental groups (in addition to the control group), one of which experiences a financial work incentive and the other of which is subject to both the financial incentive and mandated work or related activities. The dual-treatment design provides information about the effects of financial work incentives, the dual-reform bundle, and the incremental effect of the work-related activity mandate.

Most of the experiments, however, were implemented to evaluate multifaceted state waiver programs rather than specific reform policies.

Therefore most studies involve a single treatment group that is subject to multiple policy reforms. We refer to this as "policy bundling." Such designs shed light on the effects of reform as a bundle, although the experimental impact estimates from such programs do not identify the effects of specific reforms.

Program implementation is another issue that affects experimental studies. Programs that appear similar on paper may be implemented differently in different places. Insight into such differences is sometimes provided by a process study involving analyses of program records, a caseworker survey, or a recipient survey.

Characterizing the Policy Environment in Observational Studies

Whereas random assignment studies generate their own policy variation, observational studies make use of the variation that exists between states and over time. This approach requires the analyst to characterize the welfare policies that are in place in each state in each year. This has proved to be a difficult undertaking, in part because there are so many policies to characterize and in part because a single policy can vary along several dimensions. Moreover, those dimensions may be difficult to quantify. It is also difficult to measure how they were implemented.[11]

The approach taken by many analysts is to characterize a policy change in terms of the date on which the policy (or policy bundle) was adopted. The analyst constructs a dummy variable that is equal to one after the policy is in place and equal to zero beforehand.[12] The analyst then includes that dummy variable in her regression model. In the context of a difference-in-difference regression (or its generalizations, as discussed above), the coefficient attached to such a variable indicates how much the welfare-related outcome changed in the states that adopted the policy once the policy was adopted.

This methodology raises the question of when the policy change actually occurred. For example, by using adoption dates, the assumption is that the policy was in place once it was passed into law and that behavior would change from that point forward. Others assume that the policy was in place (and hence behavior would change) once it was officially implemented. In practice, the appropriate date may be even later, when the program is fully implemented and the new rules are well understood by potential recipients. Such on-the-ground implementation dates are difficult to determine, which explains why they have never been used in observational studies. If it takes time for a policy to become effective once it is officially adopted, then dummy variables based on official adoption dates (or even official implementation dates) may underestimate the effects of reform.

Fortunately, even if this question is difficult to resolve conceptually, it may be resolvable empirically. Analysts may disagree about whether the legal adoption date or the official implementation date best characterizes the date on which the policy was put in place, but one can test whether the difference affects the estimated effects of reform. In principle, a similar comparison could be made between official implementation dates and dates that better reflect the actual process of implementation.

An important drawback of restricting attention to official adoption or implementation dates is that they capture only one dimension of policy variation. They merely divide the sample into pre- and postreform periods, telling us how behavior changes after reform. They provide no information about other dimensions of variation that might have important effects on behavior, such as the extent of an enhanced earnings disregard or the magnitude of a reduction in age-related exemptions from work requirements.

Restricting attention to enactment dates may also result in a specification that is particularly susceptible to bias from unobservable trends. Dummy welfare reform variables tend to equal zero in the early part of the sample period and equal one at the end of the sample period. Thus they are correlated with trends or, more precisely, in the context of difference-in-difference regressions, with state-specific trends that deviate from national trends. If the analyst fails to control for such trends, the results may be biased estimates of the effects of reform, since the reform dummy is correlated with the trends.

Furthermore, policy bundling poses problems for observational studies, much as it poses problems for the experiments. Some of these policy bundling problems arise from the way that states implemented welfare reform. In many cases, states implemented waivers that changed their welfare system in several different ways at the same time. When policies are adopted together, there is less variation along each policy dimension to separately measure the effect of individual policies. Likewise, when reforms are implemented simultaneously, testing for interactions between them becomes difficult. The limited number of postreform data points available for study, resulting both from the recency of the reforms and from the lags in data release, exacerbate these problems.

The analytical problems posed by the timing of reforms and policy bundling are displayed graphically in Table 4.1, which summarizes some of the information presented in Tables 2.2 to 2.6. For each year between 1992 and 1996, there are five cells for each state. Each cell corre-

Table 4.1 Timing and bundling of specific reforms under waivers, 1992–1996

	1992	1993	1994	1995	1996
Alabama					
Alaska					
Arizona				S T FC	
Arkansas			FC		
California	FI				
Colorado					
Connecticut					FI A S T FC
District of Columbia					
Delaware				FI A S T FC	
Florida					
Georgia			S FC		
Hawaii					
Idaho					
Illinois		FI		S FC	T
Indiana				A S T FC	
Iowa		FI A S T			
Kansas					
Kentucky					
Louisiana					
Maine					
Maryland					FI A S FC
Massachusetts				FI A S FC	
Michigan	FI		A S		
Minnesota					
Mississippi				FC	
Missouri					
Montana					FI A S
Nebraska				FI A S T FC	
Nevada					
New Hampshire					
New Jersey	A S FC				
New Mexico					
New York					
North Carolina					A S T FC
North Dakota					
Ohio					FI S T
Oklahoma					
Oregon		A S			T
Pennsylvania					
Rhode Island					
South Carolina					
South Dakota			S		
Tennessee					FI A S T FC
Texas					A S T
Utah		FI			
Vermont			FI A S		
Virginia				FI A S T FC	
Washington					T
West Virginia					S
Wisconsin			FI		A S FC
Wyoming					

Source: Implementation dates from Tables 2.2 to 2.6.

Note: A = age-related work exemption; FC = family cap; FI = financial work incentive; S = work-requirement sanction; T = time limit.

sponds to one of the major reforms carried out under waivers: financial work incentives, changes to age-related exemptions from work requirements, work-requirement sanctions, time limits, and family caps. Cells are shaded in the year in which the indicated (statewide) policy reform was implemented in the indicated state. Thus we see that Arkansas implemented a family cap in 1994; California implemented a financial work incentive in 1992.

Most important, the table highlights the timing and bundling issues that observational studies must confront. Only three states implemented statewide waivers in 1992; only four implemented statewide waivers the following year. Most of the waivers were implemented in 1995 and 1996. With relatively few exceptions, policy reforms were implemented in bundles. In some cases, the number of policies included in the bundle was small, such as in Georgia, which implemented stricter sanctions and a family cap in 1994. In many other cases, however, the bundles included four or five simultaneous policy reforms, such as in Delaware in 1995 and Connecticut in 1996. Furthermore, in only a handful of cases did a state implement two different bundles in two different years, which in principle would allow the analyst to distinguish the effect of the first bundle from that of the second. Taken as a whole, these timing and bundling issues make it extremely difficult to estimate the effects of specific reform policies on the basis of qualitative (dummy) variables.

One approach to this problem is to characterize the reforms more completely. Rather than simply relying on the timing of a reform to identify its effect, it is sometimes possible to measure the intensity of the reform (for example, the generosity of a financial work incentive). Exploiting such quantitative variation in policy reforms has several advantages. First, it measures a more policy-relevant effect: not merely the effect of the average financial incentive, but the effect of incentives of varying sizes. Second, there may be less correlation among quantitative measures of bundled policies than among qualitative measures, since the intensity of reforms varies even among states that implemented the same mix of reforms. Thus the use of quantitatively varying regressors may reduce collinearity and improve the precision of the estimates of specific reforms. Third, the additional implication that the effect should vary with the strength of the reform can be tested, at least in principle.

Some analysts have adopted this approach and characterized policy changes in ways that allow their effects to vary along important dimensions. In addition to capturing the strength of financial work incentives, several studies allow the effects of time limits to vary by the age of the youngest child in the family. Others allow the effects of sanctions to vary according to the perceived severity of the sanction.

Of course, defining other dimensions of policy variation is not always simple. Financial incentives vary by the magnitude of their earnings disregard, their tax rate, and in some states, both the disregard and the tax rate vary with the recipient's work history. Time limits vary in their length, in the magnitude of the benefit reduction once the limit is reached, and in the availability of exemptions and extensions. Sanctions vary greatly, as seen in Chapter 2, and that variation has led to disparities in classifications by different analysts.

Four different sets of analysts have attempted to characterize the sanction policies that states enacted shortly after the implementation of TANF. All four coded each state's sanctions as lenient, intermediate, or stringent. The characterizations are shown in Table 4.2. The aspects of state policies used to rate the different states vary between analysts; as a result, the summary ratings vary to a considerable extent. Pennsylvania is a case in point. Its sanction policies are rated as lenient by one set of analysts, intermediate by two others, and stringent by another. Indeed, the four sets of ratings are in agreement for only twenty-eight of the fifty-one states, making it difficult to compare results across studies. If analysts cannot agree on what a strict sanction policy is, the effects of a "strict" sanction policy may vary across studies for reasons that have more to do with measurement than with real behavior.

Moreover, none of the rankings incorporates information about the monetary value of the sanctions. This omission is important, because a partial-family sanction in a high-benefit state may result in the same financial penalty as a full-family sanction in a low-benefit state. Likewise, none of the rankings incorporates information about the rate at which sanctions are imposed, which is shown in the last two columns of the table.[13] Since the theory discussed in Chapter 3 predicts that both the severity of the sanction and the probability of detection should affect behavior, any characterization of sanctions that omits information about the likelihood of detection is incomplete.

In the same way that official adoption or implementation dates may not reflect the actual timing of policy implementation, more detailed measures of policy characteristics usually only capture variation in official statutes and regulations. However, the de facto variation in implementing a statute may be as important as the de jure variation in the actual statutes. For example, states with the same full-family sanction policy have varying numbers of people who have actually been sanctioned; states with similar time-limit policies vary in the proportion of

Table 4.2 Four characterizations of states' sanction policy

State	Study				All measures agree? (5)	Percentage under full-family sanction (6)	Percentage under any sanction (7)
	CEA (1999b) (1)	GAO (2000) (2)	Burke and Gish (1998), as cited by Rector and Youssef (1999) (3)	Pavetti and Bloom (2001) (4)			
Alabama	Intermed.	Intermed.	Intermed.	Stringent			7.4
Alaska	Lenient	Lenient	Lenient	Lenient	Yes	0.2	3.0
Arizona	Intermed.	Intermed.	Intermed.	Intermed.	Yes	1.6	5.7
Arkansas	Stringent	Lenient	Stringent	Lenient		2.4	4.5
California	Lenient	Lenient	Lenient	Lenient	Yes	0.0	0.9
Colorado	Intermed.	Intermed.	Intermed.	Intermed.	Yes	0.9	5.5
Connecticut	Intermed.	Intermed.	Intermed.	Intermed.	Yes	0.3	1.8
Delaware	Stringent	Intermed.	Intermed.	Stringent		0.8	15.3
D.C.	Lenient	Lenient	Lenient	Lenient	Yes	0.0	5.6
Florida	Stringent	Stringent	Stringent	Stringent	Yes	5.1	5.1
Georgia	Stringent	Intermed.	Stringent	Stringent		0.0	0.9
Hawaii	Lenient	Stringent	Lenient	Stringent			0.0
Idaho	Stringent	Stringent	Stringent	Stringent	Yes	4.7	4.7
Illinois	Intermed.	Intermed.	Intermed.	Intermed.	Yes	4.5	9.8
Indiana	Intermed.	Lenient	Lenient	Lenient		1.2	6.0
Iowa	Intermed.	Stringent	Intermed.	Stringent		0.8	3.2
Kansas	Stringent	Stringent	Stringent	Stringent	Yes	2.3	2.3
Kentucky	Intermed.	Intermed.	Lenient	Intermed.		0.1	5.3
Louisiana	Intermed.	Stringent	Intermed.	Stringent		0.1	2.3
Maine	Lenient	Lenient	Lenient	Lenient	Yes	0.0	4.3
Maryland	Stringent	Stringent	Intermed.	Stringent		1.4	12.3
Massachusetts	Intermed.	Intermed.	Intermed.	Stringent		0.3	3.2
Michigan	Intermed.	Intermed.	Intermed.	Stringent		0.4	3.2
Minnesota	Lenient	Lenient	Lenient	Lenient	Yes	0.0	6.3
Mississippi	Stringent	Stringent	Stringent	Stringent	Yes	2.0	2.0
Missouri	Lenient	Lenient	Lenient	Lenient	Yes	0.0	11.3
Montana	Lenient	Lenient	Lenient	Lenient	Yes	0.3	7.6
Nebraska	Stringent	Stringent	Stringent	Stringent	Yes	0.5	0.6
Nevada	Stringent	Intermed.	Intermed.	Intermed.		0.0	2.2
New Hampshire	Lenient	Lenient	Intermed.	Lenient		0.0	4.0
New Jersey	Intermed.	Intermed.	Intermed.	Stringent		1.0	8.0
New Mexico	Intermed.	Intermed.	Intermed.	Intermed.	Yes	0.0	0.0
New York	Lenient	Lenient	Lenient	Lenient	Yes		0.0
North Carolina	Lenient	Intermed.	Lenient	Intermed.		0.5	29.1
North Dakota	Intermed.	Intermed.	Intermed.	Stringent		0.2	5.7
Ohio	Stringent	Stringent	Stringent	Stringent	Yes	2.2	2.2
Oklahoma	Stringent	Stringent	Stringent	Stringent	Yes	2.7	3.1
Oregon	Intermed.	Intermed.	Intermed.	Intermed.	Yes	0.7	0.7
Pennsylvania	Stringent	Intermed.	Lenient	Intermed.		0.0	5.4
Rhode Island	Lenient	Lenient	Lenient	Lenient	Yes		1.0
South Carolina	Stringent	Stringent	Stringent	Stringent	Yes	2.8	8.0
South Dakota	Intermed.	Intermed.	Intermed.	Stringent		1.1	1.1
Tennessee	Stringent	Stringent	Stringent	Stringent	Yes	0.3	0.3
Texas	Lenient	Lenient	Intermed.	Intermed.		0.0	15.5

Table 4.2 *(continued)*

State	Study				All measures agree? (5)	Percentage under full-family sanction (6)	Percentage under any sanction (7)
	CEA (1999b) (1)	GAO (2000) (2)	Burke and Gish (1998), as cited by Rector and Youssef (1999) (3)	Pavetti and Bloom (2001) (4)			
Utah	Intermed.	Intermed.	Intermed.	Stringent		0.6	3.3
Vermont	Intermed.	Intermed.	Lenient	Intermed.		0.0	0.0
Virginia	Stringent	Stringent	Stringent	Stringent	Yes	0.9	0.9
Washington	Lenient	Lenient	Lenient	Lenient	Yes	0.0	4.8
West Virginia	Stringent	Intermed.	Intermed.	Intermed.		0.0	0.0
Wisconsin	Stringent	Stringent	Stringent	Stringent	Yes	4.6	22.8
Wyoming	Stringent	Stringent	Stringent	Stringent	Yes	7.0	7.0
Total/Average					28 yes	1.2	5.1

Note: Columns (6) and (7) are from GAO (2000) and pertain to 1998. The terminology used to describe the severity of sanctions differs among authors. Our "lenient" category corresponds to the categories described as "partial/partial" by CEA (1999b); "partial" by GAO (2000); "weak" by Rector and Youssef (1999); and "lenient" by Pavetti and Bloom (2001). Our "intermediate" category corresponds to the categories described as "partial/full" by CEA (1999b); "graduated" by GAO (2000); "moderate" or "delayed full-check" by Rector and Youssef (1999); and "moderate" by Pavetti and Bloom (2001). Our "stringent" category corresponds to the categories described as "full/full" CEA (1999b); "full-family" by GAO (2000); "initial full-check" by Rector and Youssef (1999); and "stringent" by Pavetti and Bloom (2001).

people who receive extensions when they reach the time limit. Some of this variation is probably due to heterogeneity in the case mix, but much of it appears to be due to variation in how nominally similar programs are implemented.

Finally, estimating the effects of specific policy reforms carried out under TANF may be even more difficult than estimating their effects under waivers. Whereas statewide waivers were implemented over a four-year period, TANF was implemented throughout the country over a period of just eighteen months. The brevity of this period greatly limits the number of post-TANF data points available to disentangle the effects of specific reforms, exacerbating problems associated with timing and bundling. As a result, observational studies have typically been more successful in estimating the effects of reforms-as-a-bundle than in estimating the separate effects of individual reforms.

Data Sources for Welfare Outcomes

Both randomized trials and observational studies require data on welfare-related outcomes. In this section, we review commonly used data sources and discuss their utility. We also discuss sample sizes and statistical power, issues that are relevant for both observational and experimental analyses.

Data Sources

Tables 4.3 and 4.4 summarize the major sources of administrative and survey data, respectively. Randomized trials usually abstract their own data from administrative records and often field their own surveys. Observational studies usually analyze existing sources of data.

Table 4.3 Sources of administrative data for analysis of welfare reform

Data source	Outcomes	Coverage	Notes
State reports to DHHS	Caseload	All states, pre- and post-TANF	Aggregate program counts; some aggregate information on distribution of caseload by demographic group
State reports to DHHS	Work activities; participation rate	All states, post-TANF	Aggregate data only on total work activities and participation rates, and numbers in specific program components; some JOBS data available
State-specific welfare program data	Caseload; welfare payments; sanctions; program activities	Within a single state; availability of historical data varies widely	Issues of data quality; systems are not consistent across states, making cross-state comparisons difficult
Unemployment insurance data	Employment; earnings	Within a single state; availability of historical data varies widely	Gaps in coverage; data relatively comparable across states and some cross-state efforts have been mounted; limited numbers of covariates (difficult to identify at-risk population)
Other social welfare program administrative data	Participation in Food Stamp Program, Medicaid, subsidized housing, child-care subsidies, foster care, child support, etc.	Within a single state; availability of historical data varies widely	
Other administrative data (e.g., birth certificates)	Births; etc.	Nationwide (e.g., births) or state-specific; historical data varies	Welfare recipients not identified

Table 4.4   Sources of survey data for analysis of welfare reform

Data source	Outcomes	Coverage	Notes
Current Population Survey (CPS)	Program participation and income/poverty status in previous calendar year; employment and earnings at interview and in previous calendar year; family structure	Nationwide, relatively consistent cross-sectional survey content back to 1968	Sample size: about 55,000 households in repeated cross-sections; increasing in March 2001 and beyond
Survey of Income and Program Participation (SIPP) and Survey of Program Dynamics (SPD)	Longitudinal data for same outcomes as CPS, plus (monthly) program entry and exit	Nationwide, relatively consistent panel survey content back to 1984; each panel is followed for about two-and-a-half years	Sample size: varies by panel, about 30,000 households at any point in time
Panel Study of Income Dynamics (PSID)	Longitudinal data for same outcomes as CPS, plus program entry and exit and measures of child well-being	Nationwide, relatively consistent panel survey content back to 1968	Sample size: about 4,800 families in original 1968 cohort augmented by splits to 8,000 families in 2001
National Longitudinal Survey of Youth (NLSY)	Longitudinal data for same outcomes as CPS, plus program entry and exit and measures of child well-being	Nationwide, relatively consistent panel survey content back to 1979	Sample size: about 11,500 youth in original 1979 cohort plus the children of the original cohort of young women followed since 1986
National Survey of America's Families (NSAF)	Data for similar outcomes as CPS, plus hardship, housing, health status and health-care use, attitudes, knowledge of service availability	Representative population in thirteen states; relatively consistent cross-sectional survey content in 1997 and 1999	Sample size: about 44,000 households in repeated cross-sections
Experimental evaluation surveys	Vary	Treatment and control groups	Details vary across evaluations

As seen in Table 4.3, administrative data cover many of the outcomes of interest, and, for welfare program participants, they cover the entire caseload at a given time. The drawbacks of administrative data are that they lack information about nonparticipants and provide limited data on individual socioeconomic characteristics. Certain outcomes, such as measures of child well-being, are not typically available from administrative data sources. There is also considerable variation in state-level data systems and in their suitability for research.

The major sources of survey data shown in Table 4.4 also cover many of the welfare-related outcomes of interest. These databases are typically rich in socioeconomic information, and they usually cover both program participants and nonparticipants. Some surveys track respondents over time so that behavior can be studied over both short and long horizons. The limitations of these databases include relatively small samples of welfare recipients; survey nonresponse; attrition from panel surveys; and reporting errors (Bavier 2001). Administrative databases can find locating and tracking those no longer on welfare to be problematic.

Statistical Power

Whether the available data are sufficient to generate precise estimates is the subject of some discussion in the literature (see, in particular, Adams and Hotz 2001). The observational studies discussed in this book almost all use generalized difference-in-difference methods. As such, they require that outcomes be consistently measured across time, both before and after reform, and across states, and that there be enough observations in each state-year cell to construct an estimate of the outcomes of interest in the population of interest.

These seemingly simple requirements make most conventional data sources unsuitable for observational analyses. The requirement of consistent data across states rules out state-specific administrative data. The requirement of consistent data across years rules out most single-interview studies and studies that began after reform was under way. The need to construct a rough estimate of the outcomes in the population of interest rules out almost all other data sources. Such disqualifications occur because welfare use is relatively rare from a statistical perspective. At the 1994 peak, 5.5 percent of the population was on welfare. This figure means that even a moderate-sized random sample of 10,000 households is likely to yield only a few hundred households with any welfare recipients. The resulting state-specific estimates of the rate of welfare receipt will be "noisy" due to classical sampling variability. That is, much of the variation across states will be due to variation in who happens to be sampled, rather than variation in the true number of people receiving welfare.

Very few surveys satisfy all of the requirements needed to carry out a difference-in-difference analysis. The CPS and the SIPP have been used to estimate the effects of reform as a bundle. Analysts have had some success in using them to estimate the effects of specific reforms. Attempts to use the Panel Study of Income Dynamics (PSID) and the National Longitudinal Survey of Youth (NLSY), which are substantially smaller, appear to have been less successful.

Finally, it is worth noting that power issues may also arise in the experimental evaluations, especially in the analysis of population subgroups. Even when the total sample in treatment and control groups is sufficiently large to detect a meaningful effect with a high probability, the likelihood of detecting similar effects within smaller subgroups generally will be much smaller. Thus detecting impacts in subgroups will require larger and more costly samples. Furthermore, some experimental sites are simply not large enough to support the required sample sizes. One approach to address this issue is to pool results across studies and then consider subgroup differences (see, for example, Michalopoulos and Schwartz 2000; H. Bloom, Hill, and Riccio 2001; and Greenberg et al. 2001).

Summary of Studies Included in the Analysis

To better understand the experimental and observational studies on which our analysis draws, we review their key features.

Features of Random Assignment Studies

Tables 4.5 and 4.6 summarize the features of the experimental evaluations that we review and provide a reference for the chapters that follow.[14] Table 4.5 describes features of each experiment, such as whether it was part of a statewide reform, the population it served, the period of randomization and length of the follow-up, sample sizes, the policy environment for the controls (typically AFDC/JOBS), and contextual information in the form of the unemployment rate and welfare benefit level. Table 4.6 provides details on the policy reforms applicable to the treatment group.

The studies are divided into five groups in both tables according to their central reform or reforms. The grouping of studies, and the order of studies within groups, serves as the organizing principle in the chapters that follow. The first group, shown in Panel A of Table 4.5, consists of three experiments that focused on financial work incentives: California's Work Pays Demonstration Program (CWPDP), the Incentives-Only components of the Vermont Welfare Restructuring Project (WRP-IO), and the Minnesota Family Investment Program (MFIP-IO). WRP-IO and MFIP-IO were parts of dual-treatment experiments where the Incentives-Only groups were given financial work incentives. The other experimental groups were subject to work-related activity mandates as well.

The next group of studies, shown in Panel B, consists of programs that imposed or strengthened requirements for mandatory work or related activities. These studies include Los Angeles Jobs-First GAIN (Greater Avenues for Independence), the Basic Track of the Indiana Manpower Placement and Comprehensive Training Program (IMPACT), and the eleven programs included in the National Evaluation of Welfare-to-Work Strategies (NEWWS).

Table 4.5   Selected design features of experimental studies

Name	State	Sites	Demo part of statewide reform?	Cases served	RA period Start	RA period End
A. Programs that focus on financial work incentives						
California Work Pays Demonstration Project (CWPDP)	CA	3 counties	No	Single-parent recipients[b]	Oct. 92	Dec. 92
Welfare Restructuring Project–Incentives Only (WRP-IO)	VT	6 welfare districts	Yes	Single-parent recipients and applicants[b]	Jul. 94	Jun. 95
Minnesota Family Investment Program–Incentives Only (MFIP-IO)	MN	3 urban counties	No	Urban single-parent long-term (> 24 mos. in last 36 mos.) recipients	Apr. 94	Mar. 96
	MN	3 urban counties	No	Urban single-parent recent applicants	Apr. 94	Mar. 96
B. Programs that focus on mandatory work or related activities						
LA Jobs-1st GAIN	CA	Los Angeles County	No	Single-parent recipients and applicants[b]	Apr. 96	Sep. 96
Indiana Manpower Placement and Comprehensive Training Program (IMPACT) Basic Track	IN	Statewide	Yes	Recipients and applicants, less job ready	May 95	Dec. 95[j]
Atlanta Labor Force Attachment (LFA)	GA	Atlanta	No	Recipients and applicants	Jan. 92	Jan. 94
Grand Rapids Labor Force Attachment (LFA)	MI	Grand Rapids	No	Recipients and applicants	Sep. 91	Jan. 94
Riverside Labor Force Attachment (LFA)	CA	Riverside	No	Recipients and applicants	Jun. 91	Jun. 93
Portland	OR	Portland	No	Recipients and applicants; no cases with substantial barriers	Feb. 93	Dec. 94
Atlanta Human Capital Development (HCD)	GA	Atlanta	No	Recipients and applicants	Jan. 92	Jan. 94
Grand Rapids Human Capital Development (HCD)	MI	Grand Rapids	No	Recipients and applicants	Sep. 91	Jan. 94
Riverside Human Capital Development (HCD)	CA	Riverside	No	Recipients and applicants, low education	Jun. 91	Jun. 93
Columbus Integrated	OH	Columbus	No	Recipients and applicants	Sep. 92	Jul. 94

Table 4.5 *(continued)*

| FU length | Sample sizes | | | Controls | Initial conditions in state (for RA start year) | | Cites |
	Total	T	C		U rate (%)	Max $ grant[a]	
42 mos.	7,841	5,211	2,630	AFDC/JOBS	9.3	663	Becerra et al. (1998); Hu (2003)
42 mos.	2,196	1,087	1,109	AFDC/JOBS	4.7	638	Bloom et al. (1998); Hendra and Michalopoulos (1999); Bloom, Hendra, and Michalopoulos (2000)
thru 6/98	1,769	835	934	AFDC/JOBS	4.0	532	Miller et al. (1997); Miller et al. (2000); Gennetian and Miller (2000)
thru 6/98	3,113	980	2,133	AFDC/JOBS	4.0	532	Miller et al. (1997); Miller et al. (2000); Gennetian and Miller (2000)
24 mos.	15,683	11,521	4,162	AFDC/JOBS plus Work Pays[d]	7.2	607	Freedman, Knab et al. (2000)
2 yrs.[k]	3,856	3,090	766	AFDC/JOBS	4.7	288	Fein et al. (1998)
5 yrs[e]	2,938	1,441	1,497	AFDC/JOBS plus "fill-the-gap" budgeting[f]	7.0	280	Freedman, Friedlander et al. (2000); McGroder et al. (2000); Hamilton et al. (2001)
5 yrs.[g]	3,012	1,557	1,455	AFDC/JOBS	9.3	474	Same as above
5 yrs.	6,726	3,384	3,342	AFDC/JOBS plus Work Pays after late 1993[d]	7.7	694	Same as above
5 yrs.	4,028	3,529	499	AFDC/JOBS	7.3	460	Same as above
5 yrs.[e]	2,992	1,495	1,497	AFDC/JOBS	7.0	280	Same as above
5 yrs.[g]	2,997	1,542	1,455	AFDC/JOBS	9.3	474	Same as above
5 yrs.	4,938	1,596	3,342	AFDC/JOBS plus Work Pays after late 1993[d]	7.7	694	Same as above
5 yrs.[h]	4,672	2,513	2,159	AFDC/JOBS	7.3	334	Same as above

Table 4.5   *(continued)*

Name	State	Sites	Demo part of statewide reform?	Cases served	RA period Start	RA period End
Columbus Traditional	OH	Columbus	No	Recipients and applicants	Sep. 92	Jul. 94
Detroit	MI	Detroit	No	Recipients and applicants	May 92	Jun. 94
Oklahoma City	OK	Oklahoma City	No	Applicants	Sep. 91	May 93

C. Programs that tie financial work incentives to hours of work or related activities

Name	State	Sites	Demo part of statewide reform?	Cases served	RA period Start	RA period End
Welfare Restructuring Project (WRP)	VT	6 welfare districts	Yes	Single-parent recipients and applicants[b]	Jul. 94	Jun. 95
To Strengthen Michigan Families (TSMF)	MI	4 local service offices	Yes	Single-parent recipients[b]	Oct. 92	Oct. 92
	MI	4 local service offices	Yes	Single-parent applicants[b]	Oct. 92	Sept. 95
Family Investment Program (FIP)	IA	9 counties	Yes	Recipients	Sept. 93	Sept. 93
	IA	9 counties	Yes	Applicants	Oct. 93	Mar. 95
Minnesota Family Investment Program (MFIP)	MN	3 urban counties[i]	No	Urban single-parent long-term (> 24 mos. in last 36 mos.) recipients[b]	Apr. 94	Mar. 96
	MN	3 urban counties[i]	No	Urban single-parent recent applicants[b]	Apr. 94	Mar. 96
Self-Sufficiency Project (SSP)[c]	Canada (BC, NB)	Province-wide	No	Single-parent recipients	Nov. 92	Mar. 95
Self-Sufficiency Project Plus (SSP-Plus)[c]	NB	Lower NB	No	Single-parent recipients	Nov. 94	Mar. 95
Self-Sufficiency Project Applicants (SSP-A)[c]	BC	Vancouver and lower British Columbia	No	Single-parent applicants (no IA for at least 6 months prior to RA)	Feb. 94	Feb. 95
New Hope	WI	2 areas of Milwaukee	No	Poor families employed FT at RA	Jul. 94	Dec. 95
	WI	2 areas of Milwaukee	No	Poor families not employed FT at RA	Jul. 94	Dec. 95

Table 4.5 *(continued)*

FU length	Sample sizes			Controls	Initial conditions in state (for RA start year)		Cites
	Total	T	C		U rate (%)	Max $ grant[a]	
5 yrs.[h]	4,729	2,570	2,159	AFDC/JOBS	7.3	334	Same as above
5 yrs.[i]	4,459	2,226	2,233	AFDC/JOBS	8.9	459	Same as above
5 yrs.[e]	8,677	4,309	4,368	AFDC/JOBS	6.7	341	Same as above
42 mos.	4,376	3,267	1,109	AFDC/JOBS	4.7	638	Bloom et al. (1998); Hendra and Michalopoulos (1999); Bloom, Hendra, and Michalopoulos (2000)
4 yrs.	8,739[m]	4,462	4,277	Until 10/94: AFDC/JOBS; after 10/94: modified AFDC/JOBS	8.9	459	Werner and Kornfeld (1997)
1 to 2 yrs.	6,042[m]	3,017	3,025	Until 10/94: AFDC/JOBS; after 10/94: modified AFDC/JOBS	8.9	459	Werner and Kornfeld (1997)
14 qtrs[bb]	6,684	4,461	2,223	AFDC/JOBS	4.0	426	Fraker and Jacobson (2000)
8 qtrs[bb]	6,009	3,973	2,036	AFDC/JOBS	4.0	426	Fraker and Jacobson (2000)
thru 6/98	1,780	846	934	AFDC/JOBS	4.0	532	Miller et al. (1997, 2000); Gennetian and Miller (2000)
thru 6/98	4,049	1,916	2,133	AFDC/JOBS	4.0	532	Miller et al. (1997, 2000); Gennetian and Miller (2000)
54 mos.	5,729	2,880	2,849	Trad. IA	BC: 10.5 NB: 12.8	BC: 1,131 NB: 747	Michalopoulos et al. (2000, 2002); Morris and Michalopoulos (2000)
18 mos.	596	293	303	Trad. IA	N.A.	N.A.	Quets et al. (1999)
30 mos.	2,852	1,422	1,430	Trad. IA	N.A.	N.A.	Michalopoulos, Robins, and Card (1999)
thru 12/98[aa]	418	218	200	No New Hope benefits	4.7	518	Bos et al. (1999); Bos and Vargas (2001); Huston et al. (2003)
thru 12/99[aa]	935	459	476	No New Hope benefits	4.7	518	Bos et al. (1999); Bos and Vargas (2001); Huston et al. (2003)

Table 4.5   *(continued)*

Name	State	Sites	Demo part of statewide reform?	Cases served	RA period Start	RA period End
D. Programs that focus on TANF-like bundle of reforms						
Employing and Moving People Off Welfare and Encouraging Responsibility (EMPOWER)	AZ	3 in Phoenix; 1 on Navajo reservation	Yes	Recipients (including those receiving TMA)	Oct. 95	Oct. 95[s]
A Better Chance (ABC)	DE	5 pilot offices	Yes	Single parent recipients and applicants[x]	Oct. 95	Sept. 96[y]
Indiana Manpower Placement and Comprehensive Training Program (IMPACT) Placement Track	IN	Statewide	Yes	Recipients and applicants, more job ready	May 95	Dec. 95[j]
Virginia Independence Program (VIP) and Virginia Initiative for Employment Not Welfare (VIEW)[u]	VA	3 cities: Lynchburg, Petersburg, and Portsmouth[v]	Yes	Recipients[w]	Jul. 95	Jul. 95
Family Transition Program (FTP)	FL	Escambia County	No	Recipients and applicants	May 94	Feb. 95
Jobs First	CT	Manchester New Haven	Yes	Recipients and applicants	Jan. 96	Feb. 97
E. Programs that focus on other reforms						
Arkansas Welfare Waiver Demonstration Project (AWWDP)	AR	10 counties	N.A.	Recipients and applicants	N.A.	N.A.
Family Development Program (FDP)[n]	NJ	10 counties[o]	Yes	Recipients	Oct. 92	Oct. 92
	NJ	10 counties[o]	Yes	Applicants	Oct. 92	Dec. 94
Primary Prevention Initiative (PPI)	MD	6 welfare offices (4 urban, 2 rural)	Yes	Recipients and applicants	Jun. 92	Aug. 95
Preschool Immunization Project (PIP)	GA	Muscogee County	Yes	Recipients[q]	Nov. 92	Nov. 92

Note: BC = British Columbia; C = control; FT = full time; FU = follow-up; IA = Canadian Income Assistance; N.A. = not available; NB = New Brunswick; RA = random assignment; T = treatment; TMA=transitional medical assistance; U = unemployment.

a. For one adult and two children.

b. Evaluation also includes sample of two-parent families with results reported separately.

Table 4.5   *(continued)*

FU length	Sample sizes			Controls	Initial conditions in state (for RA start year)		Cites
	Total	T	C		U rate (%)	Max $ grant[a]	
36 mos.[t]	2,934	1,476	1,458	AFDC/JOBS	5.1	347	Kornfeld et al. (1999)
max. 18 mos.[z]	3,959	2,138	1,821	AFDC/JOBS	4.3	338	Fein and Karweit (1997); Fein (1999); Fein and Lee (2000); Fein et al. (2001)
2 yrs.[k]	5,595	4,537	1,058	AFDC/JOBS	4.7	288	Fein et al. (1998)
27 mos.	7,568	3,784	3,784	AFDC/JOBS	4.5	354	Gordon and Agodini (1999)
4 yrs.	2,815	1,405	1,410	AFDC/JOBS	6.6	303	Bloom et al. (1999); Bloom, Kemple et al. (2000)
4 yrs.	4,803	2,396	2,407	AFDC/JOBS	5.7	636	Bloom, Melton et al. (2000); Hendra, Michalopoulos, and Bloom (2001); Bloom et al. (2002)
N.A.	N.A.	N.A.	N.A.	N.A.	N.A.	N.A.	Turturro, Benda, and Turney (1997)
thru 12/96	4,875	3,268	1,607	AFDC/JOBS	8.5	424	Camasso, Harvey, and Jagannathan (1996); Camasso et al. (1998, 1999)
thru 12/96	3,518	2,233	1,285	AFDC/JOBS	8.5	424	Camasso, Harvey, and Jagannathan (1996); Camasso et al. (1998, 1999)
1 to 2 yrs.	1,775[p]	911	864	AFDC/JOBS	6.7	377	Minkovitz et al. (1999)
4 yrs.	2,801[r]	1,076	1,725	AFDC/JOBS	7.0	280	Kerpelman, Connell, and Gunn (2000)

c. All monetary values in Canadian dollars.

d. Under Work Pays, the earnings disregard was $120 and the benefit reduction rate was 67 percent, and a higher needs standard was used for "fill-the-gap" budgeting.

e. Controls became subject to treatment conditions beginning in the fourth quarter of 1996.

Table 4.5   *(continued)*

f. A higher needs standard (equal to $424 in 1993 for a family of three) was used for "fill-the-gap" budgeting.

g. Controls assigned before January 1993 became subject to treatment conditions three years after RA.

h. Controls became subject to treatment conditions beginning in the fourth quarter of 1997.

i. Controls became subject to treatment conditions three years after RA.

j. Randomization scheduled to end in December 1999; evaluation includes participants in first eight months.

k. Those entering after June 1995 observed for up to six months after Basic and Placement track distinction was eliminated in June 1997.

l. Demonstration also implemented in four rural counties with results reported separately.

m. Sample sizes are for combined one- and two-parent families. 87% of recipient cases and 80% of applicant cases are one-parent families.

n. FDP provisions phased in between October 1992 and October 1993.

o. Implementation of the FDP provisions was delayed in two counties until January 1995. Some results only pertain to eight counties with implementation by October 1993.

p. Sample sizes refer to number of children aged three to twenty-four months with complete medical records abstraction for analysis of vaccination status at one- and two-year follow-ups; a larger sample of families were in the experiment.

q. Reforms applied to both recipients and applicants, but only former group was included in evaluation.

r. Sample sizes refer to number of children up to age six with complete medical records abstraction; 2,500 families were in the treatment and control groups.

s. Randomization continued for new applicants from November 1995 to July 1997; evaluation includes only recipients as of October 1995.

t. EMPOWER REDESIGN, implemented in August 1997 under TANF, applied to both treatment and controls.

u. VIP provisions were implemented in July 1995, but VIEW provisions were phased in at five demonstration sites between July 1995 and October 1997.

v. Evaluation also includes two counties, but staggered implementation means no exposure to new rules at time of follow-up.

w. Evaluation also includes sample of applicants between July 1995 and September 1996, but staggered implementation means little exposure to new rules at time of follow-up.

x. Evaluation also includes sample of two-parent families, but sample sizes were too small for separate analysis.

y. Randomization continued through February 1997; evaluation includes participants in first twelve months.

z. Controls became subject to treatment conditions beginning March 1997.

aa. Five-year follow-up data are available for the subsample of families with children aged one to ten at RA.

bb. Five-year follow-up data are available; however, the control group became subject to the treatment conditions after March 1997.

The studies listed in Panel C combine a financial work incentive with a work requirement. Four of these programs were administered within the conventional welfare system. These include the full WRP and MFIP programs, as well as programs in Michigan (To Strengthen Michigan Families, TSMF) and Iowa (Family Investment Program, FIP). Table 4.6 shows that MFIP and FIP provided more generous financial incentives than WRP or TSMF.

The other programs listed in Panel C also provided financial work incentives, but they were administered outside the conventional welfare system. The financial incentives took the form of earnings supplements that were available only to low-income single parents (SSP) or families who worked at least thirty hours a week (New Hope). The SSP programs were carried out in Canada; New Hope was conducted in Wisconsin.

The six evaluations in category D involve time limits in conjunction with financial work incentives and/or mandatory work or related activities. Arizona's EMPOWER (Employing and Moving People Off Welfare and Encouraging Responsibility) program combines a time limit with somewhat stricter JOBS sanctions. The other five programs—Delaware's A Better Chance (ABC) program, Indiana's IMPACT Placement Track program, the Virginia Independence Program/Virginia Initiative for Employment Not Welfare (VIP/VIEW), Florida's Family Transition Program (FTP), and Connecticut's Jobs First program—combine a time limit with financial work incentives and a work requirement. Of all the programs we consider, these incorporate the most TANF-like bundles of reforms and provide the best experimental evidence about the effects of TANF-like reforms.

Category E consists of four programs that focus on various other reforms. The Arkansas Welfare Waiver Demonstration Project (AWWDP) and New Jersey Family Development Program (FDP) each evaluate a family-cap policy. The Maryland Primary Prevention Initiative (PPI) and Georgia Preschool Immunization Project (PIP) evaluate parental responsibility requirements focused on immunizations or preventative health care for children.

Table 4.5 shows that all of the experiments were implemented in the 1990s under state waivers prior to the passage of PRWORA, with randomization periods that ranged from mid-1991 to late 1996.[15] Thus the economy was steadily improving during the period of randomization and follow-up. There is somewhat more variation across the evaluations in the state of the economy at the time the experiments began. The generosity of welfare benefits also varies across the experimental sites.

It is important to note that the reforms represented among the experiments listed in Table 4.5 are not necessarily representative of the reforms implemented across the states under PRWORA. Comparing Table 4.6 with Table 2.8 shows that, relative to states' TANF plans, the experiments involved relatively generous financial work incentives. Few involved the stringent sanction policies that many states have imposed under TANF. And few of the experiments involved the combination of low benefits, weak financial work incentives, and time limits that characterize many states' welfare programs since PRWORA was enacted.

In terms of measuring outcomes, Table 4.5 shows that about two years of follow-up data are typically available, although some programs have observed participants for up to five years postrandomization. Unless otherwise noted, the sample sizes shown are based on administrative data and represent the maximum number of study participants available for analysis. In some cases, results discussed in subsequent chapters are based on smaller samples, especially when outcomes derive from surveys that typically were administered to only a subset of the original study sample.

Table 4.6   Key reforms (treatment) of experimental studies

Name	Financial work incentives	Mandatory work-related activity	Sanctions	Time limits
A. Programs that focus on financial work incentives				
CWPDP	After 9/93: Eliminated 4-month time limit on AFDC disregard (first $30 and 33% of remaining earnings)			
WRP-IO	Enhanced disregards (first $150 and 25% of any remaining earnings)		"Vendor payment sanction" (state takes control of grant); noncompliance leads to loss of grant	
MFIP-IO	Enhanced disregards (38% of guarantee level and 38% of any remaining earnings up to 140% of FPL)			
B. Programs that focus on mandatory work or related activities				
LA Jobs-1st GAIN		• Job search first • Strong "work first" message and Job Clubs for supervised job search	Adults-only sanction for noncompliance with program activities; high enforcement	
IMPACT Basic Track		• Work first • Mandatory 20 hours a week in E&T or work-related activities		
Atlanta LFA		• Job search first • Exemption if youngest child under age 3 • Case managers indicated that E&T services were available as a second step after initial job search	Adults-only sanction for noncompliance with program activities; high enforcement	

Table 4.6 *(continued)*

| Family cap | Parental responsibility | Transitional | | Two-parent families | Other features |
		Child care	Health insur.		
				100-hour rule eliminated	• Reduction in AFDC grant (8.5% from 10/92 to 9/93) • Asset limit (including vehicle value) increased • Restricted account for education, house, or business
		Y	Y	100-hour rule and work history requirement eliminated	• Asset limit (including vehicle value) increased
				100-hour rule eliminated	• Streamlined administrative procedures • Higher disregards for step-parent earnings • Direct reimbursement of child-care providers • Food Stamp cash-out • Asset limit (including vehicle value) increased
No increase with added children born to current recipients	• Immunizations and school attendance • Pregnant/parenting minors must live with parents • Cooperate with CSE				• Personal responsibility agreement required • Assignment to tier determined by caseworker-administered assessment • Traditional case management structure (separate income maintenance and welfare-to-work program staff)

Table 4.6 *(continued)*

Name	Financial work incentives	Mandatory work-related activity	Sanctions	Time limits
Grand Rapids LFA		• Job search first • Exemption if youngest child under age 1 • Clients encouraged to enroll in E&T programs in addition to working • Caseworkers believed clients might be justified in turning down temporary or part-time jobs	Adults-only sanction for noncompliance with program activities; high enforcement	
Riverside LFA		• Job search first • Exemption if youngest child under age 3 • Clients encouraged to take low-paying or part-time jobs as a first step	Adults-only sanction for noncompliance with program activities; high enforcement	
Portland		• Job search or E&T first depending on disadvantage • Exemption if youngest child under age 1 • Job search clients encouraged to find good jobs (i.e., with benefits, higher-paying)	Adults-only sanction for noncompliance with program activities; high enforcement	
Atlanta HCD		• E&T first • Exemption if youngest child under age 3 • Clients given choice in type of education activity	Adults-only sanction for noncompliance with program activities; high enforcement	
Grand Rapids HCD		• E&T first • Exemption if youngest child under age 1 • Clients given choice in type of education activity	Adults-only sanction for noncompliance with program activities; high enforcement	
Riverside HCD		• E&T first • Exemption if youngest child under age 3 • Short stay in basic education stressed • Clients moved into active job search once literacy target achieved	Adults-only sanction for noncompliance with program activities; high enforcement	

Table 4.6 *(continued)*

| Family cap | Parental responsibility | Transitional | | Two-parent families | Other features |
		Child care	Health insur.		
					• Traditional case management structure (separate income maintenance and welfare-to-work program staff)
					• Traditional case management structure (separate income maintenance and welfare-to-work program staff)
		Y			• Integrated case management • Excluded those with serious barriers to participation
					• Traditional case management structure (separate income maintenance and welfare-to-work program staff)
					• Traditional case management structure (separate income maintenance and welfare-to-work program staff)
					• Traditional case management structure (separate income maintenance and welfare-to-work program staff) • Limited to those without diploma or GED, or low reading/math score, or limited English proficiency

Table 4.6   *(continued)*

Name	Financial work incentives	Mandatory work-related activity	Sanctions	Time limits
Columbus Integrated		• E&T first • Exemption if youngest child under age 3 • Clients given choice in type of education activity	Adults-only sanction for noncompliance with program activities; high enforcement	
Columbus Traditional		• E&T first • Exemption if youngest child under age 3 • Clients given choice in type of education activity	Adults-only sanction for noncompliance with program activities; high enforcement	
Detroit		• E&T first • Exemption if youngest child under age 1	Adults-only sanction for noncompliance with program activities; low enforcement	
Oklahoma City		• E&T first • Exemption if youngest child under age 1 • Importance of education as a way of increasing job skills stressed for all clients	Adults-only sanction for noncompliance with program activities; low enforcement	

C. Programs that tie financial work incentives to hours of work or related activities

Name	Financial work incentives	Mandatory work-related activity	Sanctions	Time limits
WRP	Enhanced disregards (first $150 and 25% of any remaining earnings)	• Half-time (single parents with youngest child under 13) or full-time (single parents with no child under 13 or 2-parent families) paid or community service job after 30 months on aid (15 months for 2-parent able-bodied primary wage earner)	"Vendor payment sanction" (state takes control of grant); noncompliance leads to loss of grant	
TSMF	Enhanced disregards (first $200 and 20% of any remaining earnings)	• Until 10/94: 20 hours/week in work, E&T, self-improvement, or community service • After 10/94: participation in Work First (applied to controls too)	After 10/94: 25% of grant, plus FSP sanction	

Table 4.6 *(continued)*

Family cap	Parental responsibility	Transitional		Two-parent families	Other features
		Child care	Health insur.		
		Y			• Integrated case management
		Y			• Traditional case management structure (separate income maintenance and welfare-to-work program staff)
		Y			• Traditional case management structure (separate income maintenance and welfare-to-work program staff)
		Y			• Integrated case management (but limited resources weakened this feature)
		Y	Y	100-hour rule and work history requirement eliminated	• Asset limit (including vehicle value) increased
	• After 10/94: Immunizations			100-hour rule and work history requirement eliminated	• Personal responsibility agreement required • All earnings and savings of dependent children disregarded • After 10/94: Vehicles excluded from asset tests; allowed deductions for investments in self-employment

Table 4.6   *(continued)*

Name	Financial work incentives	Mandatory work-related activity	Sanctions	Time limits
FIP	Enhanced disregards (first $200 and 50% of any remaining earnings)	Mandatory E&T participation at levels specified in individual agreement (including possible unpaid work experience or community service)	Assignment to Limited Benefit Plan (cash grant reduced for 3 months and then eliminated for succeeding 6 months)	
MFIP	Enhanced disregards (38% of guarantee level and 38% of any remaining earnings up to 140% of FPL)	Mandatory E&T for recipients on aid > 24 in past 36 mos. (single parents) or > 6 in past 12 mos. (two parents) and no child <1 year old (single parents only) and working < 30 hours per week	10% of grant. May be lower than sanction for controls, which was reduction of grant by adult's portion	
SSP[a]	Earnings Supplement (half difference between gross earnings and benchmark income set to $30K in NB and $37K in BC to start) for minimum of 30 hours/week		Monthly supplement withheld for third or higher episode of less-than-full-time employment	3 yrs.
SSP-Plus[a]	Earnings supplement (half difference between gross earnings and benchmark income set to $30.6K to start) for minimum of 30 hours/week		Monthly supplement withheld for third or higher episode of less-than-full-time employment	3 yrs.
SSP-A[a]	Earnings supplement (half difference between gross earnings and benchmark income set to $37K to start) for minimum of 30 hours/week		Monthly supplement withheld for third or higher episode of less-than-full-time employment	3 yrs.

Table 4.6   *(continued)*

| Family cap | Parental responsibility | Transitional | | Two-parent families | Other features |
		Child care	Health insur.		
		Y		100-hour rule and work history requirement eliminated	• Personal responsibility agreement required • Asset limit (including vehicle value) increased • Balance in Individual Investment Account and interest/dividend income disregarded
				100-hour rule and work history requirement eliminated	• Streamlined administrative procedures • Higher disregards for step-parent earnings • Direct reimbursement of child-care providers • Food Stamp cash-out • Asset limit (including vehicle value) increased
					• Must take up program w/in 1 year • Cannot simultaneously receive traditional IA • Unearned income and income from other family members disregarded
					• Must take up program w/in 1 year • Cannot simultaneously receive traditional IA • Unearned income and income from other family members disregarded • Voluntary employment-related services (résumé service, Job Club, job leads, job coaching, self-esteem workshop) • Blueprint for self-sufficiency developed
					• Had to remain on IA for 1 year and then take up program w/in 1 year • Cannot simultaneously receive traditional IA • Unearned income and income from other family members disregarded

Table 4.6   *(continued)*

Name	Financial work incentives	Mandatory work-related activity	Sanctions	Time limits
New Hope	Earnings supplement for minimum of 30 hours/week at unsubsidized or community service job			

D. Programs that focus on TANF-like bundle of reforms

EMPOWER			Automatic min. 1-, 3- and 6-month sanction of adult portion of grant for 1st, 2nd, or 3rd noncompliance with JOBS requirements	24 months in 60 months (adult only)[e]
ABC	• More generous disregards • Fill the gap budgeting	• Mandatory work activities in first 24 months • Work required in second 24 months • Pay-for-performance community service job if not able to find work	Progressive sanctions leading to case closure after 5 months of continuous noncompliance with work and parenting requirements	48 months; ineligible for 96 months [i]
IMPACT Placement Track	Fixed grant up to FPL	• Mandatory 20 hours a week in work-related activities	Noncompliance leads to loss of adult portion of grant for 2 mos. min., increasing to 36 mos. for third penalty	24 months in 60 months (adult only)[f]
VIP/VIEW[g]	Families receive full TANF grant as long as net earnings plus TANF put them below FPL[h]	• Job search required for 90 days[h] • If regular employment not found, participation in Community Work Experience Program required in exchange for benefits[h] • Exemption allowed for parents with child under 18 months, and medical exemptions tightened[h]	• Case closed if personal responsibility agreement not signed[h] • Full family sanction for noncompliance with job search or work requirements after signing agreement[h] • Other sanctions for failure to comply with CSE, parental responsibility provisions • Months in sanction count towards time limit[h]	24 months; ineligible for 36 months[h]

Table 4.6 *(continued)*

Family cap	Parental responsibility	Transitional		Two-parent families	Other features
		Child care	Health insur.		
					• Subsidized health insurance and child care
No increase with added children born to current recipients	• Pregnant/parenting minors must live with parents	Y	Y	100-hour rule eliminated	• Contributions to Individual Development Account for training and education disregarded • Teens aged 13 and over not exempted from JOBS
No increase with added children born to current recipients	• Parenting class • Immunizations and school attendance • Pregnant/parenting minors must live with parents • Substance-abuse treatment and family planning • Cooperate with CSE	Y	Y	Eligibility determination same as for one-parent families	• Personal responsibility agreement required
No increase with added children born to current recipients	• Immunizations and school attendance • Pregnant/parenting minors must live with parents • Cooperate with CSE	Y	Y	100-hour rule eliminated	• Personal responsibility agreement required • Increased asset limit if working • Assignment to tier determined by caseworker-administered assessment
No increase with added children born to current recipients (but any child support received for capped child is disregarded)	• Stronger cooperation with CSE • Immunizations and school attendance • Minors with children must live with parents	Y[h]	Y[h]	Eligibility determination same as for one-parent families	• Transportation assistance while on TANF and for one year after case closes[h] • Allowed to accumulate $5,000 in savings for use toward own business, education, or home ownership • Personal responsibility agreement required[h] • Diversion payments for forgoing welfare for 160 days

Table 4.6   *(continued)*

Name	Financial work incentives	Mandatory work-related activity	Sanctions	Time limits
FTP	Enhanced disregards (first $200 and 50% of any remaining earnings)	• Mandatory participation in job search and placement activities[j] • Intensive case management and enhanced services • Exemption if youngest child under 6 months	Sanctions for noncompliance with work and parenting requirements	24 in 60 months or 36 in 72 months depending on recipient characteristics
Jobs First	All earned income disregarded as long as earnings below FPL	• Mandatory work first employment services; E&T as last resort • Exemption if youngest child is under age 1 (and child not conceived while on welfare)	• First instance: 20% grant reduction for 3 months • Second: 35% reduction for 3 months • Third: canceled for 3 months	21 months (with possible extensions)

E. Programs that focus on other reforms

Name	Financial work incentives	Mandatory work-related activity	Sanctions	Time limits
AWWDP				
FDP[c]	Earned disregard up to 50% of grant level	• More extensive case management and supportive services • Exemption if youngest child under age 2	Strengthened	
PPI			$25 monthly penalty for failure to verify preventive care at 6-month intervals	
PIP			Loss of portion of grant for nonimmunized child	

Note: For full program names and citations, see Table 4.5. BC = British Columbia; CSE = child support enforcement; E&T = education and training; FPL = federal poverty line; FSP = Food Stamp Program; IA = Canadian Income Assistance; NB = New Brunswick.

a. All monetary values in Canadian dollars.

b. Thirty-seven percent of treatment group thought subject to family cap compared with 20 percent of controls; 52 percent and 46 percent of treatment and control groups, respectively, did not know how much more money they would get with an added child.

c. Implementation of the FDP provisions was delayed in two counties until January 1995. Some results only pertain to eight counties with implementation by October 1993.

Table 4.6 *(continued)*

Family cap	Parental responsibility	Transitional Child care	Transitional Health insur.	Two-parent families	Other features
	• School attendance and parental contact with teachers • Immunizations	Y			• Asset limit (including vehicle value) increased
$50 increase for additional child conceived while mother on aid (half the increase under AFDC)		Y	Y	Nonfinancial eligibility requirements made similar to one-parent-family requirements	• Asset limit (including vehicle value) increased • All child support passed through and first $100 disregarded
No increase with added children born to current recipients[b]	• Family planning information and services				
No increase with added children born to current recipients[d]			Y	Some financial marriage penalties eliminated	
	• Semi-annual verification of preventive health care services, including vaccinations for pre-school-age children • Verify at time of eligibility and semi-annually or annually thereafter that pre-school-age children receive vaccinations				

d. Thirty-six percent of treatment group thought no additional benefit with added child compared with 35 percent of controls.

e. Sixty-one percent of treatment group believed state had time limits compared with 56 percent of control group.

f. Sixty-nine percent of treatment group thought subject to time limits compared with 43 percent of control group.

g. VIP provisions implemented in July 1995 but VIEW provisions phased in at five demonstration sites between July 1995 and October 1997.

h. VIEW provision phased in between July 1995 and October 1997.

i. Eighty-four percent of treatment group thought subject to time limits compared with 66 percent of control group.

j. Many control group members were subject to Project Independence provisions requiring participation in mandatory work-related activity.

Most programs served both longer-term recipients and new applicants, and both single-parent and two-parent families. When results are available separately for single parents, we show sample sizes specific to that group and report single-parent results in the chapters that follow. We restrict our attention to single-parent cases because single-parent families constitute roughly 90 percent of the welfare caseload. (When results are only available for a combined sample, the single-parent families usually dominate the sample.) Likewise, we separately report sample sizes and results for ongoing recipients (those on welfare at the time of randomization) and applicants (those randomized when they applied for welfare) when available.[16]

Finally, it is worth noting how a number of the methodological issues discussed above apply to specific experiments. These methodological concerns will affect the interpretation of the results from several studies. First, in a number of the experiments, participants were confused about the program's rules. In Arizona, 56 percent of the control group, versus 61 percent of the treatment group, thought they were affected by time limits (Kornfeld et al. 1999). In Delaware a similar problem occurred, with 66 percent of the controls reporting that they thought they had a time limit, compared with 84 percent of the treatment group (Fein and Karweit 1997). Similar confusion occurred in Indiana. The impacts from these programs might have been different had the time limits been better understood.

Second, in some experiments, the treatment was not constant for the entire period between random assignment and the last available follow-up. In VIP/VIEW in Virginia and FDP in New Jersey, implementation of the treatment reforms was staggered, so that the "exposure" to the treatment varied across the study population. Another problem arises in several cases where the experimental treatment changed during the period of randomization (for example, Michigan's TSMF) or during the period of follow-up (Indiana's IMPACT). Such alteration complicates the interpretation of the treatment effects, which become a mixture of the two regimes.[17] In several other studies (for example, Arizona's EMPOWER, Delaware's ABC, Iowa's FIP), the experiment was terminated prematurely and the experimental reforms (or a modified set of reforms) were applied to all study participants.[18] This control-group cross-over limits the period during which "pure" treatment effects can be estimated. Some of the long-term results from NEWWS could also potentially be affected by control-group crossover, because at many of the sites, the control groups became eligible for program services during the fourth or fifth year of the follow-up. However, analyses by Hamilton et al. (2001)

suggest that what crossover existed had little effect on the estimated long-term impacts of the NEWWS program.

Features of Observational Studies

Several key features of the observational studies that we review are summarized in Table 4.7. The first column shows that most of the studies analyze annual state-level data from administrative sources. The CPS is the next most common source, followed by others such as vital statistics (that is, birth certificates, marriage and divorce statistics) and the SIPP. Most of the studies, including all that use aggregate state-level data, cover the entire population. Other studies focus on narrower, more welfare-prone groups, such as single mothers or women with low education levels.[19]

The sample periods of most studies begin between the late 1970s and mid-1980s; a few rely exclusively on data from the 1990s. The several years of prereform data in the studies with longer sample periods provide no information about the effects of reform, but they do help in determining the independent contribution of the economy to trends in welfare-related behavior. The sample periods end in 1996 for several studies, shortly after PRWORA was passed. Others extend to as late as 2000, providing a few years of post-PRWORA data.

Most of the observational studies focus on estimating the effects of reform as a bundle. Some estimate the effects of waiver-based reform and TANF separately. Several studies attempt to estimate the separate effects of specific reforms, such as financial work incentives, work-related activity mandates, sanctions, time limits, and family caps.

Most analyses use the unemployment rate to control for the state of the economy. Several include lagged values as well as the current value, to allow for the possibility that adjustment to economic conditions may not be instantaneous. A few studies add other measures of economic conditions, such as job growth or low-skill wages. Some studies provide no controls for the economy.

Most studies likewise include controls for demographic trends. In studies based on individual-level data, these refer to characteristics of individuals or families. In studies based on state-level data, these refer to the demographic composition of the states. Most studies also include the generosity of the states' welfare system, as measured by the size of the benefit available to a family with no other income. Some also control for other policy and political factors.

The last column of the table shows that the great majority of studies

Table 4.7   Selected features of observational studies

Study	Data source	Covered population	Sample period Begin	End
Bartik and Eberts (1999)	Annual state-level admin. data	Total pop.	1984	1996
Bitler, Gelbach, and Hoynes (2002)	CPS micro data	Women 16–54	1989	2000
Bitler et al. (2004)	State-level vital statistics	Women 15 and above	1989	2000
Blank (2001)	Annual state-level admin. data	Total pop.	1977	1996
CEA (1997)	Annual state-level admin. data	Total pop.	1976	1996
CEA (1999b)	Annual state-level admin. data	Total pop.	1976	1998
Figlio and Ziliak (1999)	Annual state-level admin. data	Total pop.	1976	1996
Grogger (2002)	SIPP micro data	Single mothers 16–54	1990	1999
Grogger (2003)	CPS micro data	Single mothers 16–54	1978	1999
Grogger (2004)	CPS micro data	Single mothers 16–54	1978	1998
Grogger and Michalopoulos (2003)	Micro-level administrative data from FTP demonstration	Families in Escambia County, FL with children < 14/15	1994	1997
Horvath-Rose and Peters (2002)	State-level vital statistics	Women 15–49	1984	1996
Huang, Garfinkel, and Waldfogel (2000)	Annual state-level admin. data	Women 15–44	1976	1996
Kaushal and Kaestner (2001)	CPS micro data	Unmarried women 18–44 with no high school diploma	1995	1999
Kearny (2002)	State-level vital statistics	Women 15–34	1989	1998

Table 4.7 *(continued)*

Policies analyzed		Controls			
Reform as a bundle	Specific reforms	Economy	Demographic	Policy environment	UCFs
AW		U, U_{-1}, U_{-2}; EG, EG_{-1}, EG_{-2}; WP, WP_{-1}, WP_{-2}; HS, HS_{-1}, HS_{-2}		B	S, Y
AW, TANF		U, U_{-1}, EG, EG_{-1}	A, E, R, MSA, CC	B, UP program, Medicaid	S, Y, state time trends
AW, TANF		U, median-wage women, median-wage men, median income	A, E, R, % urban	B, covenant marriage	S, Y, state time trends
AW		U, U_{-1}, U_{-2}, median wage, 20th% wage	A, E, R, immigration, nonmarital births	B, UP program, P, Medicaid spending	S, Y
AW	FWI, WRA-A, WRA-D, WRA-S, TL, FC	U, U_{-1}		B	S, Y, state time trends
AW, TANF	FWI, WRA-A, WRA-S, TL, FC	U, U_{-1}, U_{-2}		B, MW	S, Y, state time trends
AW		U, U_{-1}, ..., U_{-4}		B	S, Y, state time trends
Reform (AW or TANF)	TL	U	A, E, R, # kids, age youngest kid	B	S-Y fixed effects
Reform (AW or TANF)	TL	U	A, E, R, # kids, age youngest kid	B, EITC	S, Y
Reform (AW or TANF)	TL	U	A, E, R, # kids, age youngest kid	B, MW	S, Y
	TL		A, E, R, # kids, age youngest kid, past welfare use, past employment		Y, random assignment to treatment
AW	FWI, WRA-D, TL, FC, PR	U, poverty rate	E, R, wages, religion, kids in single-parent homes	Parental consent for abortion	S, Y
AW	CSE	U, U_{-1}, U_{-2}, median wage, 10th% wage	A, E, R, immigration	B, UP program, P, Medicaid spending	S, Y
AW, TANF	TL, FC	U, U_{-1}, U_{-2}	A, R, # kids <6, # kids ≥6, UI		S, Y
TANF	TL, FC, WRA-A	U	A	B	S, Y, state time trends

Table 4.7 *(continued)*

Study	Data source	Covered population	Sample period Begin	Sample period End
Levine (2002)	State-level vital statistics	Women 15–44	1985	1996
MaCurdy, Mancuso, and O'Brien-Strain (2002)	State-level admin. data (changes)	Total pop.	1996	1999
Mead (2001)	State-level admin. data (changes)	Total pop.	1994	1998
Meyer and Rosenbaum (2001)	CPS micro data	Female family heads 19–44	1984	1996
Moffitt (1999)	Annual state-level admin. data	Total pop.	1977	1995
Moffitt (1999)	CPS aggregated	Women 16–54	1977	1995
O'Neill and Hill (2001)	CPS micro data	Single mothers 18–44	1982	1999
Paxson and Waldfogel (2003)	State child protection system aggregate data	Children	1990	1998
Rector and Youssef (1999)	State-level admin. data (changes)	Total pop.	1997	1998
Schoeni and Blank (2000)	CPS aggregated	Women 16–54, educ <12	1976	1998
Wallace and Blank (1999)	Annual state-level admin. data	Total pop.	1980	1996
Wallace and Blank (1999)	Monthly state-level admin. data	Total pop.	1980	1998
Ziliak et al. (2000)	Monthly state-level admin. data	Total pop.	1987	1996

Note: A = age; AW = any waiver; B = maximum welfare benefit; CC = central city; CSE = child support enforcement; E = education; EG = employment growth; EG_{-m} = months' lag of employment growth; EITC = Earned Income Tax Credit; FC = family cap; FWI = financial work incentives; HS = fraction of employees with high school diplomas or better; HS_{-m} = months' lag of fraction of employees with high school diploma or better; MS = marital status; MSA = Metropolitan Statistical Area (urban); MW = minimum wage; P = party control; PR = parental responsibility; R = race; S = state; TL = time limit; U = unemployment rate; U_{-m} = months' lag of

Table 4.7 (continued)

Policies analyzed		Controls			
Reform as a bundle	Specific reforms	Economy	Demographic	Policy environment	UCFs
AW	FC	U	R, A, E, MS	B, parental notification, mandatory delay for abortion	S, Y, state time trends
	WRA-D, WRA-S	Change in U; change in 20th% wage	A, E, R, # kids, # young kids, % immigrants, unwed birth rate, % noncitizens	B	
	WRA-S, WRA-O		AFDC caseload in 1994	Legislative effectiveness, state individualism	
	FWI, TL	U	A, E, R, # kids, any kids < 6,3,2,1	B, MW, EITC, Medicaid, child-care spending	S, Y, month
AW	FWI, WRA-A, WRA-D, WRA-S, TL, FC	U, U_{-1}		B	S, Y, state time trends
AW		U, U_{-1}	A, E, E*Y, E*U, E*U_{-1}	B	S, Y, state time trends
AW, TANF		U, W, college wage premium	A, E, R, # kids, age youngest kid, ever married, urban-rural	B	S, trend and $trend^2$, state-year trends
AW	WRA-D, WRA-S, TL, FC	U	A, E, R, % urban, % kids	B	S, Y
	WRA-D, WRA-S	U			
AW, TANF		U, U_{-1}, EG, and each *E	A, E, A*E, R	B, B*E	S, Y, state time trends, Y*E
AW		U, U_{-1}, U_{-2}, median wage, 20th% wage	A, E, R, immigration, nonmarital births	B, UP program, P, Medicaid spending	S, Y
AW, TANF		U, U_{-1}, . . . , U_{-12}			S, state-specific month dummies
	FWI, WRA-D, TL, FC	U, U_{-1}, . . . , U_{-6}			S, month dummies

unemployment rate; UCF = unidentified confounding factors; UI = unearned family income; UP = (AFDC) Unemployed Parent program; W = wage for workers with a high school degree or less; WP = wage premium predicted from state industrial mix; WRA-A = age exemptions from work-related activities; WRA-D = deadlines for satisfying work-related activity mandates; WRA-O = work-related activities—other feature; WRA-S = sanctions for noncompliance with work-related activities; Y = year; * = interaction term in regression equation.

Table 4.8   Outcomes covered by experimental studies

Study	State	Welfare use	Employment and earnings	Income	Poverty	Marriage	Child-bearing	Child outcomes
A. Programs that focus on financial work incentives								
CWPDP	CA	X	X	X		X		
WRP-IO	VT	X	X	X				X
MFIP-IO	MN	X	X	X	X	X		X
B. Programs that focus on mandatory work or related activities								
LA Jobs-1st GAIN	CA	X	X	X	X	X	X	X
IMPACT Basic Track	IN	X	X	X	X			
Atlanta LFA	GA	X	X	X	X	X	X	X
Grand Rapids LFA	MI	X	X	X	X	X	X	X
Riverside LFA	CA	X	X	X	X	X	X	X
Portland	OR	X	X	X	X	X	X	X
Atlanta HCD	GA	X	X	X	X	X	X	X
Grand Rapids HCD	MI	X	X	X	X	X	X	X
Riverside HCD	CA	X	X	X	X	X	X	X
Columbus Integrated	OH	X	X	X	X	X	X	X
Columbus Traditional	OH	X	X	X	X	X	X	X
Detroit	MI	X	X	X	X	X	X	X
Oklahoma City	OK	X	X	X	X	X	X	X
C. Programs that tie financial work incentives to hours of work or related activities								
WRP	VT	X	X	X				X
TSMF	MI	X	X	X				X
FIP	IA	X	X	X				
MFIP	MN	X	X	X	X	X		X
SSP	Canada	X	X	X	X	X	X	X
SSP Plus	Canada	X	X	X				
SSP Applicants	Canada	X	X	X	X			
New Hope	WI	X	X	X	X			X
D. Programs that focus on TANF-like bundle of reforms								
EMPOWER	AZ	X	X	X		X	X	
ABC	DE	X	X	X		X	X	X
IMPACT Placement Track	IN	X	X	X	X			
VIP/VIEW	VA	X	X	X				
FTP	FL	X	X	X		X	X	X
Jobs First	CT	X	X	X		X	X	X
E. Programs that focus on other individual reforms								
AWWDP	AR	(X)	(X)				X	
FDP	NJ	(X)	(X)				X	
PPI	MD							X
PIP	GA							X
Total		30	30	30	19	20	19	24

Note: For full program names and citations, see Table 4.5. X = results discussed in relevant chapter; (X) = results not discussed.

Table 4.9 Outcomes covered by observational studies

Study	Welfare use	Employment	Labor supply	Earnings	Income	Poverty	Marriage	Child-bearing	Child outcomes
Bartik and Eberts (1999)	X								
Bitler, Gelbach, and Hoynes (2002)							X		
Bitler et al. (2004)							X		
Blank (2001)	X								
CEA (1997)	X								
CEA (1999b)	X								
Figlio and Ziliak (1999)	X								
Grogger (2002)	X								
Grogger (2003)	X	X	X	X	X				
Grogger (2004)	X								
Grogger and Michalopoulos (2003)	X								
Horvath-Rose and Peters (2002)								X	
Huang, Garfinkel, and Waldfogel (2000)	X								
Kaushal and Kaestner (2001)		X						X	
Kearney (2002)								X	
Levine (2002)								X	
MaCurdy, Mancuso, and O'Brien-Strain (2002)	X								
Mead (2001)	X								
Meyer and Rosenbaum (2001)		X							
Moffitt (1999)	X	X	X	X	X				
O'Neill and Hill (2001)	X	X							
Paxson and Waldfogel (2003)									X
Rector and Youssef (1999)	X								
Schoeni and Blank (2000)	X	X	X	X	X	X	X		
Wallace and Blank (1999)	X								
Ziliak et al. (2000)	X								
Total	18	6	3	3	3	1	3	4	1

employ a state fixed-effects model such as that described above, using state dummies and year dummies to control for state- and period-specific unobservables, respectively. A few go further, employing state-specific trends to control for potentially confounding factors that trend smoothly within states. A few studies do not include state dummies, but employ a specification in which the dependent variable represents the change in welfare cases. Differencing the dependent variable in this way may control for unobservables in a manner similar to state dummies.[20] A few of the studies that include state dummies do not include year dummies, but rather employ more restrictive controls for economywide period effects.

Outcomes Covered by Studies

Table 4.8 summarizes the outcomes covered by the experimental studies. The columns of the table correspond to the chapters that follow: the welfare caseload, employment and earnings, and so on. We indicate when the results include one or more measures in each category.[21] This tabulation reveals that, with the exception of the random assignment studies in category E (other reforms), all the random assignment studies cover welfare use, employment, earnings, and income. A smaller number examine poverty, family structure, and child well-being.

Table 4.9 provides similar information for the observational studies. It shows that most such studies have focused on the welfare caseload. Only six analyze employment; only three analyze labor supply, earnings, or income (and only one in the case of poverty). Marriage and fertility have been the focus of three or four studies each; and child outcomes have received the least coverage, having been the subject of only one observational study.

This chapter has covered a wealth of information needed to assess the validity of studies of welfare reform, covering issues of methodology, measurement, and important features of the specific studies we review. Of course, the need for detailed information derives from the existence of numerous studies that make use of different approaches and different data. For our purposes, this is good news; the findings in which we have the greatest confidence are those that are replicated by different studies that vary in their measurements and their approach. In the chapters that follow, we highlight where key results are robust to these differences in analytical design and where they are fragile.

CHAPTER FIVE

Welfare Use and Welfare Payments

In this chapter we focus our attention on how welfare reform has affected welfare use and welfare payments. These are two key outcomes about which the model discussed in Chapter 3 makes predictions. Welfare use is also related to welfare dependency, which has long been one of the key topics in debates over social welfare policy. In addition, welfare payments are an important component of poor families' incomes, another issue that is central to many discussions of welfare reform.

This chapter has four goals. We first determine whether the estimated effects of specific welfare reform policies on welfare use and welfare payments accord with the predictions from the model discussed in Chapter 3. We then assess the overall effects of welfare reform. Since reform as a whole comprises many separate individual reforms, some of which have contradictory effects on welfare use, the effects of reform as a bundle cannot be predicted by the model. Nevertheless, the overall effects of reform play an important role in many policy discussions, and are used by some observers to gauge the overall success of welfare reform. Next, since there is an abundance of recent research on the links between the economy and welfare use, and since the strong economy has been cast as an alternative explanation for why the welfare caseload fell in the 1990s, we summarize recent analyses on the effects of the economy on the caseload. We finish by discussing how the effects of recent reforms accord with some of the traditional goals of welfare reform.

In the sections that follow, we discuss the results from three types of studies: random assignment experiments, early observational studies, and later observational studies. The early and later generations of observational studies are separated by only a few years, but they differ in important ways that bear on the quality of the evidence that they provide. We draw on our assessment of this difference in the concluding section of the chapter, where we evaluate the overall "fit" of the estimates to the predictions from the model.

Experimental Estimates of the Effects of Specific Reforms

Figures 5.1 and 5.2 present twenty-nine impact estimates from the experimental studies reviewed in Chapter 4 that evaluate the effects of various reforms on welfare use and welfare payments. All of the studies rely on individual-level administrative data to determine average welfare recipiency status and welfare payments for treatment- and control-group members. Where possible, we report impacts for single-parent families two years after random assignment. In cases where second-year results were not available, the length of the follow-up period is noted in parentheses following the program name. We also indicate whether the results refer to new applicants, longer-term recipients, or both. In most of the experiments, applicants had higher employment rates than recipients, who were already on welfare and for whom employment rates were generally low. In some cases, this difference determines whether we compare the empirical results with predictions from Chapter 3 regarding initially working or nonworking recipients.

The estimates in Figure 5.1 represent the percentage-point treatment effect, or impact, of each program on welfare use for the given follow-up period. Figure 5.2 records the impacts on monthly welfare payments measured in U.S. dollars.[1] For comparison purposes, the average level of the outcome for the control group is provided in parentheses to the left of the chart. Asterisks denote levels of statistical significance.

The studies in Figures 5.1 and 5.2 are grouped according to the central reform or reforms they evaluate, following the categories defined in Chapter 4. We proceed by discussing the results for three categories of specific reforms—financial work incentives, mandatory requirements for work or related activities, and financial work incentives tied to work or related activities. Results for the final category of studies, which evaluate the effects of TANF-like bundles of reforms, are discussed later in the chapter.

Financial Work Incentives

Three of the experiments focus on financial work incentives: California's Work Pays Demonstration Program (CWPDP), Vermont's Welfare Restructuring Program (WRP), and Minnesota's Family Investment Program (MFIP). The CWPDP treatment group faced a lower benefit-reduction rate than the control group after the first four months of work, although the program impacts also reflect the effect of CWPDP's reduced benefit level. WRP and MFIP were dual-treatment experiments, in which

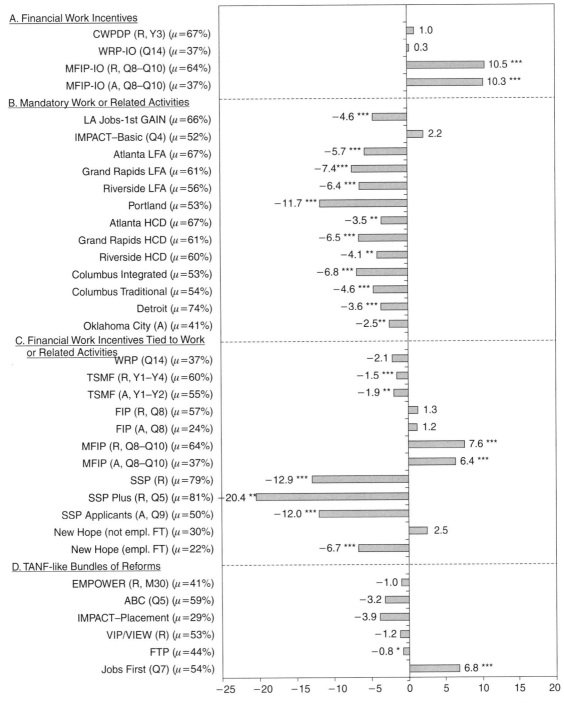

Figure 5.1

Estimated impacts of welfare reform on welfare use from experimental studies. *Source:* See Appendix Table A.1.

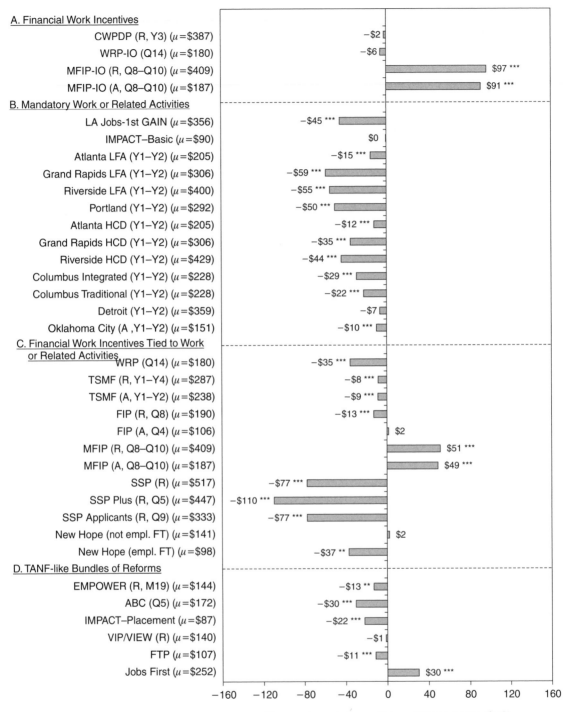

A. Financial Work Incentives

CWPDP (R, Y3) (μ=$387) — -$2

WRP-IO (Q14) (μ=$180) — -$6

MFIP-IO (R, Q8–Q10) (μ=$409) — $97 ***

MFIP-IO (A, Q8–Q10) (μ=$187) — $91 ***

B. Mandatory Work or Related Activities

LA Jobs-1st GAIN (μ=$356) — -$45 ***

IMPACT–Basic (μ=$90) — $0

Atlanta LFA (Y1–Y2) (μ=$205) — -$15 ***

Grand Rapids LFA (Y1–Y2) (μ=$306) — -$59 ***

Riverside LFA (Y1–Y2) (μ=$400) — -$55 ***

Portland (Y1–Y2) (μ=$292) — -$50 ***

Atlanta HCD (Y1–Y2) (μ=$205) — -$12 ***

Grand Rapids HCD (Y1–Y2) (μ=$306) — -$35 ***

Riverside HCD (Y1–Y2) (μ=$429) — -$44 ***

Columbus Integrated (Y1–Y2) (μ=$228) — -$29 ***

Columbus Traditional (Y1–Y2) (μ=$228) — -$22 ***

Detroit (Y1–Y2) (μ=$359) — -$7

Oklahoma City (A ,Y1–Y2) (μ=$151) — -$10 ***

C. Financial Work Incentives Tied to Work or Related Activities

WRP (Q14) (μ=$180) — -$35 ***

TSMF (R, Y1–Y4) (μ=$287) — -$8 ***

TSMF (A, Y1–Y2) (μ=$238) — -$9 ***

FIP (R, Q8) (μ=$190) — -$13 ***

FIP (A, Q4) (μ=$106) — $2

MFIP (R, Q8–Q10) (μ=$409) — $51 ***

MFIP (A, Q8–Q10) (μ=$187) — $49 ***

SSP (R) (μ=$517) — -$77 ***

SSP Plus (R, Q5) (μ=$447) — -$110 ***

SSP Applicants (R, Q9) (μ=$333) — -$77 ***

New Hope (not empl. FT) (μ=$141) — $2

New Hope (empl. FT) (μ=$98) — -$37 **

D. TANF-like Bundles of Reforms

EMPOWER (R, M19) (μ=$144) — -$13 **

ABC (Q5) (μ=$172) — -$30 ***

IMPACT–Placement (μ=$87) — -$22 ***

VIP/VIEW (R) (μ=$140) — -$1

FTP (μ=$107) — -$11 ***

Jobs First (μ=$252) — $30 ***

Program impacts for monthly welfare payments ($US)

Note: For full program names, see Table 4.5. Impacts are for two-year follow-up and for recipients (R) and applicants (A) unless otherwise noted. μ = control group mean; M = month; Q = quarter; Y = year; FT = full-time. Significant at the ***1%, **5%, *10% level.

Figure 5.2
Estimated impacts of welfare reform on monthly welfare payments from experimental studies.
Source: See Appendix Table A.2.

the "Incentives Only" treatment groups were subject only to the financial work incentives.[2]

The model in Chapter 3 predicts that expanded financial incentives should increase welfare use. As seen in panel A of Figure 5.1, results from all three experiments are consistent with that prediction. However, CWPDP and WRP-IO increased welfare use only slightly, and insignificantly, whereas MFIP increased it sizably and significantly.

Although these differences could be explained by a number of factors, differences in the generosity of the programs' financial work incentives may be particularly important. The financial incentives offered by CWPDP and WRP were what we will refer to as weak incentives. By weak, we mean that they allowed working treatment-group members to keep more of their earnings than working control-group members only under certain conditions involving the recipients' work history and hours of work.

In CWPDP, the treatment group enjoyed lower tax rates than the control group only after four months of work. However, the treatment group faced a lower maximum-benefit payment than the control group in all months. Thus the CWPDP financial incentive allowed treatment-group members to keep more of their earnings only after four months of combining work and welfare, and even then only if they worked more than a threshold number of hours. WRP-IO (and the full WRP program) provided members of the treatment group with a higher earnings disregard, but also with a tax rate that was higher than that faced by the control group for the first four months of work. As a result, only after recipients had worked for at least four months was the treatment-group tax schedule unambiguously more generous than the control-group tax schedule.

In contrast, MFIP-IO (and the full MFIP program) provided a much stronger financial incentive. Treatment-group members received at least 38 percent of the maximum benefit plus 38 percent of any additional earnings, up to 140 percent of the federal poverty line. This was unambiguously more generous than the tax structure facing the AFDC control group, independent of the recipient's work history or current hours of work.

The difference between weak and strong financial work incentives can also be stated in terms of the programs' budget sets, that is, the areas beneath their budget constraints (see Figure 3.1 for an illustration). We say that experiments involve strong financial incentives if the experimental budget set fully contains, or dominates, the control-group budget set. In other words, the experimental budget set dominates if, for a given wage, income from earnings and welfare benefits are higher for the experimental group than for the control group at all hours of work greater than zero. If not, we say the experiment involves a weak financial incentive.

In CWPDP and WRP, the budget set of the treatment group did not dominate that of the control group. Whether a working recipient enjoyed higher income under the experimental or control condition depended on her work history and current labor supply. In MFIP, the budget set of the treatment group dominated that of the control group. Treatment-group recipients always kept more of their earnings than control-group recipients. This difference may explain why CWPDP and WRP-IO had small effects on welfare use, whereas MFIP-IO had large effects.

The impacts of these programs on welfare payments, reported in panel A of Figure 5.2, are roughly similar to their impacts on welfare use. Although CWPDP and WRP-IO resulted in lower welfare payments, those impacts were insignificant and their magnitudes were negligible. At any rate, our model predicts that financial work incentives could either decrease or increase welfare payments, depending on whether the reduction in monthly payments to working recipients exceeds or falls short of the increase in the number of months that those recipients remain on welfare. MFIP, with its much stronger financial incentive, increased welfare payments much as it increased welfare use.

Mandatory Work or Related Activities

The results in panel B of Figure 5.1 show that all but one of the thirteen programs that imposed mandatory work or related activities significantly decreased welfare use. The average reduction was 5.1 percentage points. Of the programs that reduced welfare use, all but one significantly reduced welfare payments, as shown in Figure 5.2. These results are consistent with the predictions from the model.

The programs that focused on job placement reduced welfare use by a bit more than those that focused on skills development. The mean reduction in welfare use among the four placement-oriented programs—Jobs-First GAIN, Atlanta LFA, Grand Rapids LFA, and Riverside LFA—was 6 percentage points. Among the six skills-oriented programs, which included Impact Basic Track, Atlanta HCD, Grand Rapids HCD, Riverside HCD, and the programs in Columbus, Detroit, and Oklahoma City, the average reduction was 3.9 percentage points. The Portland program had the largest effects of all. This may bode well for its hybrid model, which provided a mix of placement- and skills-oriented services. Then again, Portland's larger effects may be attributable to the fact that, unlike the other sites, the Portland program excluded recipients with substantial barriers from participating in the demonstration (Freedman, Friedlander et al. 2000, ES-21).

The eleven NEWWS programs provide some evidence on the longer-run impacts of work requirements. Year-by-year impacts for five years are presented in Figure 5.3. By the fifth year of the follow-up, the average impact of these programs decreased substantially. Whereas the mean second-year impact of the NEWWS programs was −6.3 percentage points, by the fifth year, it had fallen to −3.3 percentage points. The greatest decline took place in Portland, which had the largest second-year impact.

Financial Work Incentives Tied to Work or Related Activities

A number of experiments combined bundles of reforms consisting of financial work incentives tied to work or related activities. WRP, TSMF, FIP, and MFIP were administered within the welfare system. These programs involved work-related activity mandates and provided financial work incentives in the form of higher disregards or lower benefit-reduction rates. The model in Chapter 3 predicts that financial incentives should increase welfare use, but that work-related activity mandates should decrease it. Because this combination of reforms gives rise to conflicting incentives, its net effects on welfare use cannot be predicted by the model.

Panel C of Figure 5.1 shows that two of the programs administered within the welfare system reduced welfare use, whereas the other two increased it. WRP and TSMF decreased welfare use by similar amounts, although only the TSMF impacts were significant. FIP and MFIP increased welfare use. MFIP had larger effects than FIP; only the MFIP impacts were significant.

Although the results of these programs are mixed, they follow an interesting pattern. One might expect programs that combine work requirements with weak financial work incentives to reduce welfare use, because the effect of the work requirement would outweigh the effect of the financial incentive. Likewise, one might expect programs combining work requirements with strong financial work incentives to increase welfare use. For the most part, this is the pattern observed in Figure 5.1.

As we discussed above, WRP involved a weak financial incentive. The same can be said of TSMF. Although the TSMF treatment group enjoyed a disregard of $200, which was more generous than the AFDC disregard available to the control group, the treatment group also faced a benefit-reduction rate of 80 percent, which exceeded the control-group tax rate during the first four months of work.

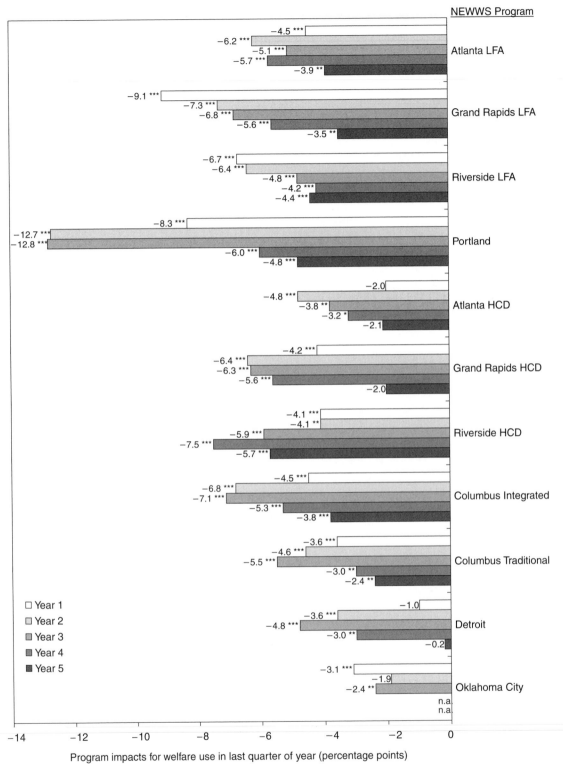

Atlanta LFA

−4.5 ***
−6.2 ***
−5.1 ***
−5.7 ***
−3.9 **

Grand Rapids LFA

−9.1 ***
−7.3 ***
−6.8 ***
−5.6 ***
−3.5 **

Riverside LFA

−6.7 ***
−6.4 ***
−4.8 ***
−4.2 ***
−4.4 ***

Portland

−8.3 ***
−12.7 ***
−12.8 ***
−6.0 ***
−4.8 ***

Atlanta HCD

−2.0
−4.8 ***
−3.8 **
−3.2 *
−2.1

Grand Rapids HCD

−4.2 ***
−6.4 ***
−6.3 ***
−5.6 ***
−2.0

Riverside HCD

−4.1 ***
−4.1 **
−5.9 ***
−7.5 ***
−5.7 ***

Columbus Integrated

−4.5 ***
−6.8 ***
−7.1 ***
−5.3 ***
−3.8 ***

Columbus Traditional

−3.6 ***
−4.6 ***
−5.5 ***
−3.0 **
−2.4 **

Detroit

−1.0
−3.6 ***
−4.8 ***
−3.0 **
−0.2

Oklahoma City

−3.1 ***
−1.9
−2.4 **
n.a.
n.a.

□ Year 1
▨ Year 2
▨ Year 3
▨ Year 4
■ Year 5

−14   −12   −10   −8   −6   −4   −2   0

Program impacts for welfare use in last quarter of year (percentage points)

Note: n.a. = not available. Significant at the ***1%, **5%, *10% level.

Figure 5.3
Estimated impacts of mandatory work or related activities on welfare use from eleven NEWWS programs, years 1 to 5. *Source:* Hamilton et al. (2001), table D.2.

In contrast, the budget set faced by the FIP treatment group, like that facing the MFIP treatment group, unambiguously dominated the budget set facing the control group. FIP involved a disregard of $200 and a tax rate of 50 percent, making it more generous than AFDC, though less generous than MFIP. Thus the results in Figure 5.1 suggest that the experiments that involved strong financial incentives increased the use of welfare on net, whereas experiments that offered weak financial incentives reduced welfare use. Results for welfare payments, presented in panel C of Figure 5.2, generally accord with the results for welfare use.

New Hope and the various SSP experiments were administered by agencies outside the usual welfare system. They involved financial work incentives in the form of earnings subsidies that were available only to individuals who worked enough to satisfy the programs' hours requirements. SSP was available only to individuals who had received welfare for at least one year. New Hope was available to families in specific low-income neighborhoods, irrespective of their welfare status.

The SSP experiments all decreased welfare use, as the model predicts for consumers who were initially receiving welfare but not working.[3] Sizable fractions of the treatment groups left welfare for the supplemental program. Although the programs reduced welfare use, they *raised* the rate of cash transfers, that is, participants' receipt of payments from either the welfare program or the supplement program (not shown). The programs also decreased welfare payments, as shown in Figure 5.2, although they increased total cash transfers (not shown).

The effects of New Hope differed between two groups of individuals. The program decreased welfare use among those who initially satisfied the hours requirement (30 hours/week), but had essentially no effect on those who did not. Since many of the individuals who initially satisfied the hours requirement were combining work and welfare, it is conceivable that New Hope reduced their welfare use by inducing them to switch from the welfare program to the supplement. Many of the individuals who did not initially satisfy the hours requirement were also combining work and welfare, but they would have had to increase their hours in order to receive the supplement.

Taken as a whole, the experimental estimates are mostly consistent with the predictions from the economic model in Chapter 3. Financial work incentives by themselves increase welfare use, and the increase is greater, the stronger the incentive. Mandates to work or participate in related activities decrease welfare use. When the two policies are combined within the welfare system, their net effect depends on the strength of the financial incentive. When the financial incentive is strong, it outweighs the effect of the work requirement, and welfare use rises. When the financial incentive is weak, the work requirement dominates, and welfare use falls. Regarding earnings supplements tied to hours requirements, three of four programs reduced welfare use among individuals who did not initially satisfy the programs' hours requirements. The one program that was available to individuals who initially satisfied the hours requirement reduced welfare use among that group.

Of course, the experiments provide only one source of evidence on the effects of welfare reform. Several observational studies have also addressed these issues. We discuss those studies in the next section.

Observational Estimates of the Effects of Specific Reforms

The observational studies are more heterogeneous than the experimental studies. Whereas the experimental studies all analyze individual-level data drawn from administrative records, the observational studies analyze several different types of data. As shown in Table 4.6, some use data from administrative records, albeit aggregated to provide monthly or annual measures of the caseload in each state. Such studies include CEA (1997), Levine and Whitmore (1998), Bartik and Eberts (1999), CEA (1999b), Figlio and Ziliak (1999), Moffitt (1999), Wallace and Blank (1999), Huang, Garfinkel, and Waldfogel (2000), Ziliak et al. (2000), and Blank (2001). Some use individual-level data from nationwide surveys such as the CPS and SIPP (Grogger 2002, 2003, 2004; O'Neill and Hill 2001). Other studies start with the CPS data, then aggregate it into cells defined by state, year, and education level (Moffitt 1999; Schoeni and Blank 2000). One involves a nonexperimental reanalysis of data from Florida's Family Transition Program (FTP) experiment (Grogger and Michalopoulos 2003). We also use reported impacts from FTP and Connecticut's Jobs First program to construct nonexperimental estimates of the mechanical effects of time limits, that is, of the extent to which welfare use falls once families start reaching the time limit.

Some studies analyze welfare use in levels, but most analyze the logarithm of the caseload, that is, the logarithm of the fraction of the state's population that is on welfare in a given year. Others analyze the percent change in the state's caseload between two points in time (Rector and Youssef 1999; Mead 2001; MaCurdy, Mancuso, and O'Brien-Strain 2002). In this case, as in the case where the dependent variable is the logarithm of the caseload, the regression coefficients that measure the effects of particular reforms can be interpreted as percent changes in the caseload resulting from the reform. Because most of the results are reported in this manner, and most that are not can be comparably transformed, we report results for the observational studies in terms of percent, rather than percentage-point, effects.

Most of the models employ some sort of generalized difference-in-difference, or state fixed-effects, strategy to control for unobservable confounding factors. Those that analyze percent changes directly do not, but by differencing the caseload over time, they may at least partially control for such factors. A few studies provide only limited controls for time effects, although they focus on the effects of reform as a bundle rather than on the effects of specific reforms (Wallace and Blank 1999; O'Neill and Hill 2001).

Most of the studies employ controls for business cycle factors in order to disentangle the effects of reform from the effects of the economy. As discussed above, the fact that welfare reform took place during the longest economic expansion in U.S. history poses a substantial collinearity problem. The collinearity problem is particularly great for studies that attempt to estimate the effects of specific reforms. Not only must they distinguish the effects of the economy from the effects of reform, they must distinguish the effects of one reform from the effects of others that were implemented at nearly the same time.

The studies exploit different dimensions of policy variation in their attempts to separate the effects of different reforms. It is useful to distinguish between two generations of studies that differ along these lines. The earlier generation exploited only the timing of reforms, characterizing them by means of dummy variables of the type discussed in Chapter 4 (CEA 1997; Moffitt 1999; Ziliak et al. 2000).[4]

The later generation of studies generally either exploits or tests for additional dimensions of variation. For example, CEA (1999b) characterizes financial work incentives in terms of the take-home earnings enjoyed by a welfare recipient with a given level of earnings. This characterization captures not only the timing of states' policy changes but also the fact that, after reform, states varied widely in the generosity of their financial incentives. Several studies categorize states' sanction policies in terms of their severity. Although this approach gives rise to the definitional issues discussed in Chapter 2, in principle it provides a more powerful test of the effect of sanctions. In a related approach, several studies not only exploit before-and-after variation in the implementation of time limits, but test whether their effect varies with the age of the youngest child in the family. Some studies involve a mix of dummy variables and fuller characterizations of reforms. CEA (1999b), for example, uses dummy variables to capture the effects of time limits, while providing fuller characterizations of both financial incentives and sanctions.

Beyond their characterizations of policy changes, the two generations of studies differ in other ways as well. Not surprisingly, the early-generation studies have less data to analyze; their sample periods end in 1996 (or 1995, in the case of Moffitt 1999). The later-generation studies generally include data through 1998 or later. Although this is a difference of only a few years, these additional years of postreform data may greatly increase the reliability of the estimated effects of reform. Finally, the early studies typically attempt to estimate the effects of multiple specific reforms, whereas most of the later studies focus on a smaller subset of reforms. Narrowing the focus to a few reforms reduces the collinearity problem, but it does so at the risk of attributing to one of the included reforms effects that are actually due to the reforms that have been omitted from the model.

Results from Early-Generation Observational Studies

Results from the three early-generation observational studies are presented in Figure 5.4. Most of the estimates are insignificant: of the sixteen estimates presented, only four are significant at the 10 percent level.[5] None is significant at higher levels of confidence.

In addition, the estimates are quite mixed. Regarding financial work incentives, shown in panel A of Figure 5.4, two estimates are positive, though negligible, whereas the third is negative. However, none is significant.

Although the estimated effects of work-requirement age exemptions shown in panel B are insignificant, they are positive, which is the opposite of what the theory would predict. Work requirements should decrease welfare use; more stringent exemption policies should decrease welfare use by increasing the number of recipients who are subject to the requirements. Since the results shown in Figure 5.4 are the coefficients on dummy variables indicating age exemptions that are more restrictive than those under JOBS, one would expect them to be negative.

Two of the studies indicate that work requirements decrease the caseload, and one of the results is significant (see panel C). It is troubling, however, that the results of CEA (1997) and Moffitt (1999) differ so much. Moffitt's (1999) analysis of specific reforms is essentially a replication of CEA (1997), although Moffitt (1999) truncated his sample period at the end of 1995, whereas CEA (1997) extended theirs through 1996. Thus the results appear to be highly sensitive to the addition of one more year of data.

Both CEA (1997) and Moffitt (1999) find that sanctions decrease welfare use (see panel D), as do Levine and Whitmore (1998; not shown),

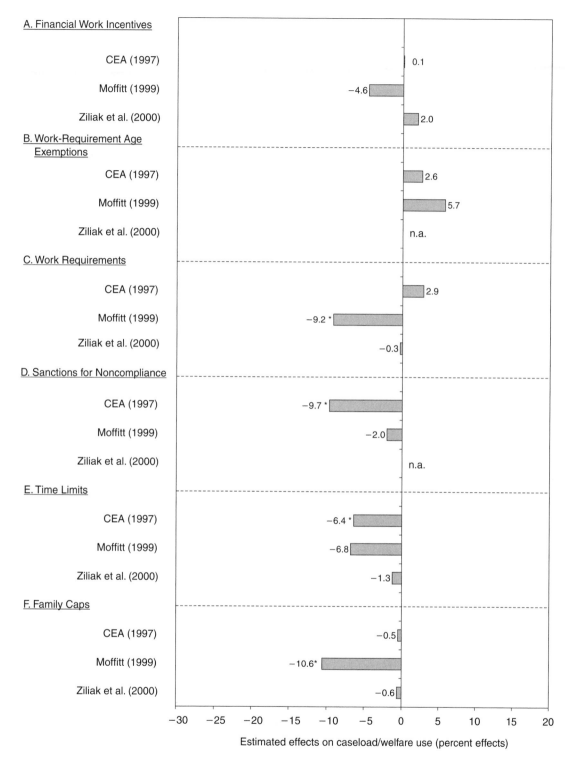

A. Financial Work Incentives
- CEA (1997): 0.1
- Moffitt (1999): −4.6
- Ziliak et al. (2000): 2.0

B. Work-Requirement Age Exemptions
- CEA (1997): 2.6
- Moffitt (1999): 5.7
- Ziliak et al. (2000): n.a.

C. Work Requirements
- CEA (1997): 2.9
- Moffitt (1999): −9.2 *
- Ziliak et al. (2000): −0.3

D. Sanctions for Noncompliance
- CEA (1997): −9.7 *
- Moffitt (1999): −2.0
- Ziliak et al. (2000): n.a.

E. Time Limits
- CEA (1997): −6.4 *
- Moffitt (1999): −6.8
- Ziliak et al. (2000): −1.3

F. Family Caps
- CEA (1997): −0.5
- Moffitt (1999): −10.6*
- Ziliak et al. (2000): −0.6

Estimated effects on caseload/welfare use (percent effects)

Note: Asterisks denote results based on coefficients that are significant at the 10 percent level or better. n.a. = not available.

Figure 5.4
Results from early observational studies of the effects of specific reforms on welfare use.

who estimated a model very similar to that of CEA (1997). CEA (1997) and Moffitt (1999) report similar negative estimates of the effects of time limits on the caseload, although only the CEA estimate is significant (see panel E). Ziliak et al. (2000) report a negative effect as well, albeit one that is quite small and insignificant.

Finally, all three authors report that family caps reduce welfare use, although Moffitt's (1999) estimate is significant and much larger than the other two (see panel F). As mentioned in Chapter 1, family caps prevent welfare benefits from increasing if the welfare recipient has an additional child. The primary intention of such policies was to reduce welfare-related childbearing. By making the welfare system less generous, they could conceivably reduce welfare use as well. However, since the few family caps that were implemented by the end of Moffitt's (1999) sample period had generally been in place for only a short time, it seems unlikely that they could have had such substantial effects on the caseload by then.

Taken as a whole, the results from these early studies are only partially consistent with the predictions from the model in Chapter 3. One might question whether this reflects more on the validity of the model or more on the limitations of the early studies. These studies were very ambitious, attempting to distinguish the effects of a large number of policies, most of which were implemented over a short period of time, both from the effects of all the other policies and from the effects of the economy. At the same time, the policies themselves are characterized sparsely, by way of dummy variables that indicate when they were in effect, but that fail to reflect any other dimension of variation that should affect behavior. The limited number of postreform data points, stemming from the short sample periods that these studies employ, exacerbates a difficult collinearity problem. The fact that some of the estimates from two of the studies differ so greatly, when the studies themselves differ primarily by one year's worth of postreform data, further suggests that collinearity causes problems for these analyses.[6]

Results from Later-Generation Observational Studies

The later generation of studies generally includes additional postreform data, which should mitigate to some extent the collinearity problem evident in the earlier studies. Some of the later studies also incorporate further dimensions of policy variation into their regression models. Figure 5.5 plots the results from these later-generation studies, again showing impacts in terms of percent effects.

Only one of the later-generation studies attempts to estimate the effects of financial work incentives (see panel A of Figure 5.5). CEA

(1999b) finds that more generous incentives, parameterized by the size of the disregard, lead to greater increases in welfare use, as the model from Chapter 3 would predict. The estimate is statistically significant.

CEA (1999b) is also the only later-generation study to estimate the effects of states' age-of-youngest-child exemptions from work requirements (see panel B). The omitted category refers to the JOBS policy. As a result, the coefficients represent the effects of imposing more restrictive exemption policies. Although the theory from Chapter 3 predicts that these policies would reduce welfare use, the estimates indicate the opposite.

Two similar studies reach differing conclusions regarding the effects of immediate work requirements, that is, of work requirements that become effective as soon as the individual starts to receive welfare (as compared with work requirements that became applicable with a delay) (see panel C). Rector and Youssef (1999) find that such requirements substantially decrease welfare use, as theory predicts. MaCurdy, Mancuso, and O'Brien-Strain (2002), however, find that such policies have no effect.

Four studies analyze the effects of sanctions (see panel D). All of these studies classify states according to the severity of their sanction policy, although the classification schemes that they employ often place states in different categories, as discussed in Chapter 2. Nevertheless, all four studies report that sanctions reduce welfare use, and the more stringent the sanction, the greater the reduction. Most of these estimates are statistically significant.

Despite the similarity of these results, some caution is warranted in interpreting the magnitude of these estimates. In other analyses not shown here, MaCurdy, Mancuso, and O'Brien-Strain (2002) regress changes in state-level caseloads between 1989 and 1992 on sanction policies implemented between 1992 and 1996. Since policy changes made after 1992 logically cannot affect behavior prior to 1992, these regressions shed some light on the policy endogeneity problem, that is, on the extent to which behavior influenced policy, rather than the other way around.

The coefficient on MaCurdy, Mancuso, and O'Brien-Strain's future full-family sanctions dummy is statistically significant and, interpreted at face value, suggests that sanctions reduced prereform caseloads by 18 percent. This finding may indicate that states with large (percentage) reductions in their caseload during the prewaiver period were more likely to seek waivers for full-family sanctions. Alternatively, the data may reflect the effects of some other policy change that typically preceded the sanctions in states that eventually received sanction waivers.

Six studies estimate the effects of time limits (see panel E). Grogger

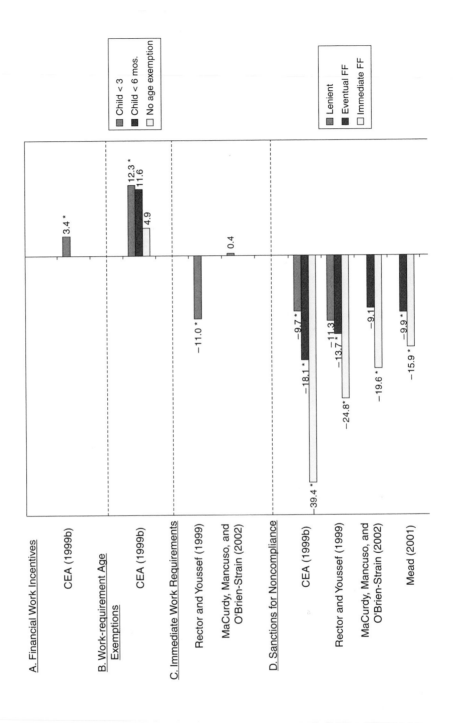

A. Financial Work Incentives

CEA (1999b)   3.4 *

B. Work-requirement Age Exemptions

CEA (1999b)   12.3 * 11.6   4.9

Child < 3
Child < 6 mos.
No age exemption

C. Immediate Work Requirements

Rector and Youssef (1999)   −11.0 *

MaCurdy, Mancuso, and O'Brien-Strain (2002)   0.4

D. Sanctions for Noncompliance

CEA (1999b)   −9.7 *   −18.1 *   −39.4 *

Rector and Youssef (1999)   −11.3   −13.7 *   −24.8 *

MaCurdy, Mancuso, and O'Brien-Strain (2002)   −9.1   −19.6 *

Mead (2001)   −9.9 *   −15.9 *

Lenient
Eventual FF
Immediate FF

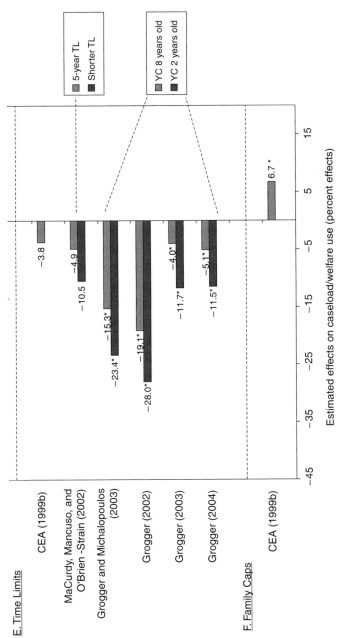

Estimated effects on caseload/welfare use (percent effects)

Note: FF = full family; TL = time limit; YC = youngest child. Asterisks denote results based on coefficients that were significant at the 10 percent level or better.

Figure 5.5
Results from later observational studies on the effects of specific reforms on welfare use.

and Michalopoulos (2003) and Grogger (2002, 2003, 2004) focus explicitly on the behavioral effects of time limits. The focus of MaCurdy, Mancuso, and O'Brien-Strain (2002) is not explicit, but since few families could have reached the time limit during their sample period, their estimates primarily reflect behavioral effects as well. The estimate from CEA (1999b) probably reflects a mix of behavioral and mechanical effects, since their time-limit variable equals one after the time limit began to bind, rather than when it was implemented.

Almost all the estimates indicate that time limits reduce welfare use. MaCurdy, Mancuso, and O'Brien-Strain (2002) find that shorter time limits have stronger effects than longer ones, although both estimates are insignificant. Grogger and Michalopoulos (2003) and Grogger (2002, 2003, 2004) find time limits to have larger effects among families with younger children.

Estimates of the mechanical effects of time limits can be constructed from Connecticut's Jobs First program and Florida's FTP.[7] Quarterly impact estimates of the effects of these programs on welfare use are presented in Figure 5.6. Since these programs involved reforms other than time limits, including relatively generous financial work incentives, the program impacts by themselves do not isolate either the behavioral or the mechanical effects of time limits. The financial work incentives do

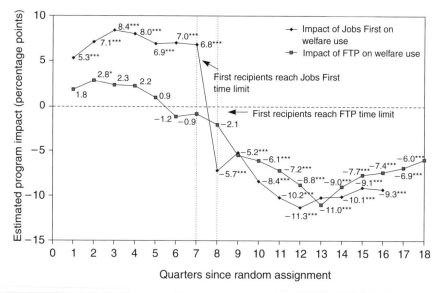

Figure 5.6
Estimated impacts of Jobs First and FTP on monthly welfare use, quarters 1 to 18. *Source:* Jobs First: Bloom et al. (2002), table B.1; FTP: Bloom et al. (2000), table B.1.

not change over time, however, whereas time limits begin to bind at a particular point in time. We construct nonexperimental difference-in-difference estimates of the mechanical effects of time limits by subtracting the pre–time limit program impact—that is, the impact from the period before recipients could have exhausted their benefits—from the post–time limit program impact.[8]

Jobs First imposed a twenty-one-month time limit, which implies that none of its recipients could have exhausted the available benefits prior to the end of quarter 7. FTP imposed a twenty-four-month time limit on most recipients, although it imposed a thirty-six-month time limit on the roughly 40 percent of recipients who were deemed to be particularly disadvantaged. None of the FTP recipients could have exhausted the available benefits prior to the end of quarter 8.

Figure 5.6 shows that both Jobs First and FTP actually increased welfare use early in the pre–time limit period, suggesting that the effects of the financial work incentives outweighed the behavioral effects of the time limits. The impact on welfare use was greater for Jobs First than for FTP. This difference is probably due to the variation in generosity of the programs' financial incentives. Whereas members of the FTP treatment group faced a $250 disregard and a 50 percent tax rate, members of the Jobs First treatment group could keep all of their earnings up to the federal poverty line (about $1,050 per month for a family of three in 1996).

Between quarter 7 and quarter 8, the Jobs First program impact fell from 6.8 percentage points to −5.7 percentage points. This decrease suggests that the mechanical effects of time limits led welfare use to fall by 12.5 percentage points, which amounts to 23 percent of the 53.9 percent rate of welfare receipt in the control group in quarter 7. The impact of FTP fell from −2.1 percentage points in quarter 8 to −5.2 percentage points in quarter 9. This reduction suggests that the mechanical effects of time limits led welfare use to fall in FTP by 3.1 percentage points, or 8.3 percent.

The mechanical effect of the Jobs First time limit appears to have been much greater than the mechanical effect of the FTP time limit. This is consistent with the difference between the pre–time limit impacts of the two programs. Owing to the greater generosity of the Jobs First financial incentive, the Jobs First treatment group accumulated months on welfare at a much faster rate than the FTP treatment group. In FTP, only 8 percent of the treatment group subject to the twenty-four-month time limit accumulated twenty-four months of welfare use within twenty-four months (D. Bloom, Kemple et al. 2000). Since the two-year limit applied to about 60 percent of the treatment group, this finding means that only about 5 percent of the treatment group as a whole accumulated enough welfare use to reach the time limit at the twenty-four-month mark. In Jobs First, in contrast, 43 percent of the treatment group accumulated twenty-one months of welfare use within twenty-one months of random assignment (D. Bloom, Melton et al., 2000). As a result, a higher fraction of the Jobs First treatment group was dropped from the rolls during the first post–time limit quarter than was true of the FTP treatment group.

These estimates consider only the very first group of recipients to reach the time limit. The mechanical effects of time limits could become larger as more recipients exhaust their benefits. If we define the post–time limit period as the first year after recipients could begin to reach the limit, rather than the first quarter, we estimate that the mechanical effects of the time limit reduced welfare use by 14.2 percentage points in Jobs First, and by 4.7 percentage points in FTP.[9]

Figure 5.7 presents quarterly impact estimates of Jobs First and FTP on monthly welfare payments. Jobs First had large positive effects on welfare payments during the pre–time limit period, and smaller, but still substantial, negative effects during the post–time limit period. Between quarters 7 and 8, when recipients first began to reach the time limit, the program impact fell by almost $50, from $30 to −$17. FTP had little effect on welfare payments during the pre–time limit period, but significant impacts throughout the post–time limit period. The mechanical

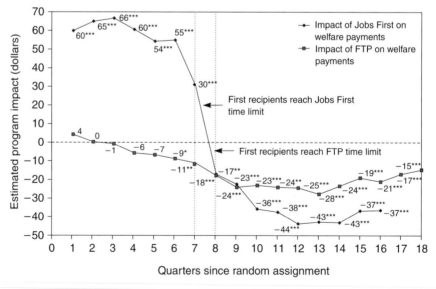

Note: Impact significant at the ***1%, **5%, *10% level.

Figure 5.7
Estimated impacts of Jobs First and FTP on monthly welfare payments, quarters 1 to 18. *Source:* Jobs First: Bloom et al. (2002), table B.1; FTP: Bloom et al. (2000), table B.1.

effects of FTP's time limit on welfare payments was smaller than that of Jobs First, as was true for welfare use. Between quarters 8 and 9, when the first FTP recipients reached the time limit, the program's average impact on monthly welfare payments fell by only $6, from −$17 to −$23.

The final policy considered by the later-generation studies is family caps. As shown in panel F of Figure 5.5, CEA (1999b) report that family caps had a significant, positive effect on welfare use. This result is hard to rationalize, considering that family caps make the welfare system less generous and, if anything, should reduce welfare use.

Otherwise, results from the later generation of observational studies are more consistent with the predictions from the model than the results from the earlier generation. The one study that analyzes the effects of financial work incentives reports that they increase welfare use, as the model predicts. One of the two studies that considers immediate work requirements finds them to reduce welfare use. All of the studies of sanctions report that they reduce welfare use, and that more punitive sanction policies have greater effects than more lenient policies. All of the studies that address the behavioral effects of time limits, either implicitly or explicitly, show that they reduce welfare use. Four studies, based on three different data sets, report that the effect of time limits is greatest among families with the youngest children.

At the same time, some results are at odds with the model. It is hard to understand how more restrictive work-requirement exemption policies could actually cause welfare use to rise. Likewise, the positive effect of family caps on the caseload is inconsistent with theoretical predictions. Evidence that the most stringent sanction policies were implemented in states with the largest prereform reductions in welfare use suggests that the estimated effects of sanctions may be exaggerated by policy endogeneity.

Estimates of the Effects of Reform as a Bundle

Since the combination of reforms implemented by states during the wavier period and subsequently under TANF may include individual reforms with conflicting effects on welfare use, estimates of the effect of reform as a bundle do not reflect on the ability of the economic model to predict behavior. Nevertheless, the overall effect of reform on welfare use is a matter of considerable policy discussion and, for many, a means of determining whether reform has been successful.

Two sets of studies provide evidence on the effect of reform as a bundle. The first includes welfare reform experiments that involve TANF-like bundles of reforms, by which we mean bundles that include time limits and either financial incentives, work requirements, or both. The second includes observational studies, which are much more numerous than experimental studies of TANF-like reform bundles. In fact, most observational studies focus on estimating the effects of reform as a bundle, rather than the effects of specific reforms. Most of the studies of specific reforms discussed above also estimate the effects of reform as a bundle. In many cases, the effect of reform as a bundle is their primary focus.

Estimates from the experimental studies appear in panel D of Figure 5.1. Since all of these estimates are based on pre–time limit data, it is not surprising that there are both positive and negative impacts. Most of the estimates, however, are insignificant. One exception is the relatively large, significant positive impact of Jobs First. As noted above, Jobs First had a very generous financial incentive with a zero percent tax rate up to the federal poverty line. These results indicate that TANF-like reform bundles can have either positive or negative impacts on welfare use, at least before their time limits begin to bind. However, one cannot infer from these estimates how reform affected welfare use in the nation as a whole, because these six experiments are not necessarily representative of the distribution of reform bundles implemented across the country.

The impact of the nationwide distribution of reforms is reflected in observational estimates, since they are based on data from all of the states. The observational estimates of the effect of reform as a bundle are reported in Figure 5.8. This figure includes results from both the early- and the later-generation studies. For the purposes of estimating the effects of reform as a bundle, the most important generational distinction concerns the sample period. All of the studies use dummy variables to capture the imposition of reform. The earlier studies estimate the effects of reform under waivers; some of the later studies distinguish the effects of waiver-based reforms from the effects of reforms under TANF. Another difference among the studies involves population coverage. Most of the studies analyze administrative data, which implicitly cover the entire population, including two-parent cases. The CPS-based studies focus on welfare-prone subsets of the population, such as single mothers or women with fewer than twelve years of education.

As seen in Figure 5.8, most of the estimates are negative, indicating that reform reduced welfare use. However, the range of estimates is rather large. Some of the variation in the results can be explained by methodological variation across the studies. The two studies that report positive estimates employ lagged dependent variables in their regression models, unlike all of the other studies. The two studies that report the largest negative estimates employ less complete controls for economy-wide trends than the other studies. We discuss these issues in turn.

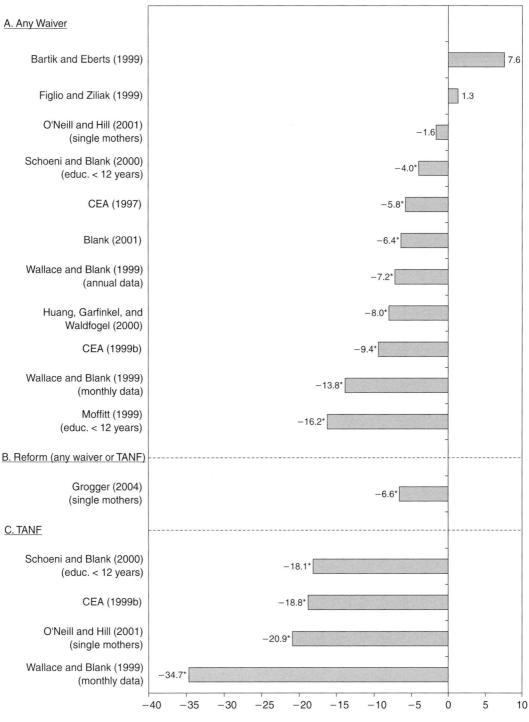

A. Any Waiver

Bartik and Eberts (1999) — 7.6

Figlio and Ziliak (1999) — 1.3

O'Neill and Hill (2001) (single mothers) — −1.6

Schoeni and Blank (2000) (educ. < 12 years) — −4.0*

CEA (1997) — −5.8*

Blank (2001) — −6.4*

Wallace and Blank (1999) (annual data) — −7.2*

Huang, Garfinkel, and Waldfogel (2000) — −8.0*

CEA (1999b) — −9.4*

Wallace and Blank (1999) (monthly data) — −13.8*

Moffitt (1999) (educ. < 12 years) — −16.2*

B. Reform (any waiver or TANF)

Grogger (2004) (single mothers) — −6.6*

C. TANF

Schoeni and Blank (2000) (educ. < 12 years) — −18.1*

CEA (1999b) — −18.8*

O'Neill and Hill (2001) (single mothers) — −20.9*

Wallace and Blank (1999) (monthly data) — −34.7*

Estimated effects on caseload/welfare use (percent effects)

Note: Asterisks denote results based on coefficients that are significant at the 10 percent level or better.

Figure 5.8
Results from observational studies of the effects of reform as a bundle on welfare use.

Figlio and Ziliak (1999) and Bartik and Eberts (1999) argue that the focus of analysts' interest should be how policy affects welfare dynamics, that is, how policy affects individuals' transitions on and off the welfare rolls. They conclude that estimating dynamic models of the welfare caseload, that is, models that include lagged dependent variables as independent variables, should provide superior estimates of the effects of welfare reform as compared with models that do not include lagged dependent variables.

This argument seems to rest on confusion over different definitions of the term "dynamics." In the welfare literature, dynamics refer to welfare transitions. In the econometrics literature, dynamics refer to regression models that include lagged dependent variables. Despite the similar terminology, these concepts are not closely related.

Intuitively, it is not obvious how adding lagged values of the caseload to a model in which the dependent variable is the current caseload could result in coefficients that could be interpreted as the effect of welfare policy changes on welfare entries, welfare exits, or even net flows. More formally, Klerman and Haider (2000) show that the conditions under which lagged-dependent-variable models identify the effects of policy changes on welfare transitions are highly restrictive. One condition requires welfare exit rates to be independent of time on welfare, which is contradicted by empirical evidence (Blank, 1989; Bane and Ellwood, 1994). Under more general conditions, it is not clear how the estimates from lagged-dependent-variable models are to be interpreted.

However, it is clear that adding lagged dependent variables to the model exacerbates an already difficult collinearity problem. As illustrated in Figure 2.1, trends in the economy are already highly correlated with the trend in welfare reform. Adding last year's welfare caseload to the model adds another variable that is highly correlated with both. One possible consequence of collinearity is that coefficients have unexpected signs, which may explain why the two studies that include lagged dependent variables estimate that reform increased, rather than decreased, the caseload. Ultimately, although we are sympathetic to the idea that welfare transitions deserve more study, we are unconvinced that adding lagged dependent variables to models of the welfare caseload is the way to proceed.

At the other end of the spectrum are the estimates based on monthly data from Wallace and Blank (1999) and the estimates from O'Neill and Hill (2001). The regressions on which these estimates are based did not include year dummies. Wallace and Blank (1999) caution that this omission may cause their estimates to overstate the effects of reform, since they might also capture the effect of other factors that could reduce welfare use, such as the expansion of the EITC or changes in Medicaid eligibility rules. O'Neill and Hill (2001) attempt to control for such factors using linear and quadratic time trends, rather than time dummies. Since the trends in welfare use over their sample period are not very quadratic, as illustrated in Figure 2.1, it is unlikely that their time trends provide adequate controls. As a result, their estimates are likely to overstate the effects of reform.

After eliminating the estimates from these four studies, the range of the estimated effects of reform as a bundle extends from −4 percent to −18.8 percent. All of those estimates are significant. The average is −10.1 percent.

That average masks some remaining heterogeneity. The estimates of the effect of waiver-based reforms tend to be lower than the estimated effects of TANF-based reforms. This seems plausible, since TANF-based reform bundles were more likely to include time limits and stricter sanctions than waiver-based reform bundles. The mean estimate of the effect of waivers is −8.1 percent, compared with −18.5 percent for reform in the TANF era.[10]

Estimates of the Effect of the Economy

As already noted, the expanding economy of the 1990s has been offered as an alternative explanation for why the welfare caseload fell. Some analysts have attempted to compare the decline in the caseload due to welfare reform with the decline attributable to the economy. Since all but one of the studies listed in Figure 5.8 also provide estimates of how the economy affects welfare use, it is instructive to summarize those estimates here.[11]

To put the estimates on a common footing, we use regression results from the various analyses to estimate how welfare use should change in response to a 2.7-percentage-point decline in the unemployment rate, like the decline that took place nationwide between 1993 and 1999. As above, we express these changes as percent effects. For some of the studies, this amounts to multiplying a regression coefficient, or a sum of regression coefficients when several lagged unemployment rates appear, by −2.7. For others, the coefficients must first be transformed by the mean level of welfare use in the regression samples. For studies that involved lagged dependent variables, we compute both a short-run and a long-run effect. The short-run effect involves only the unemployment rate coefficients, whereas the long-run effects are functions of the unemployment-rate coefficients and the coefficients of the lagged dependent variables.[12]

Figure 5.9 displays the results. All of the estimates are negative, indicating that reductions in unemployment reduce the caseloads. The magnitudes vary among the studies. In the two lagged-dependent-variable studies, the long-run effects are greater than the short-run effects. This is as one would expect, since the long-run effects allow for greater adjustment to unemployment-rate changes than the short-run effects. These are also the two largest estimates of the effects of the unemployment rate on the caseload. Bartik and Eberts's (1999) results suggest that the fall in the unemployment rate reduced the caseload by 29 percent, whereas Figlio and Ziliak's (1999) estimates associate the decline in the unemployment rate with an 18 percent decline in the caseload.

There is less heterogeneity among the remaining estimates, although some variation remains. At the low end, Grogger (2004) and CEA (1997) attribute relative declines of 5.0 percent and 8.4 percent, respectively, to the reduction in unemployment. At the other end, CEA (1999b) and Wallace and Blank (1999) credit the falling unemployment rate with reductions in the caseload of 14.6 and 16.2 percent, respectively. Averaging the results from the nine studies that do not employ lagged dependent variables yields an average estimate of 12.1 percent.

Aside from the estimates derived from lagged-dependent-variable models, there is less heterogeneity among the estimated effects of the unemployment rate than among the estimated effects of reform. This lower heterogeneity suggests that the estimated effects of the economy are somewhat less sensitive than the estimated effects of reform to some of the specification issues discussed in the last section, probably because more data are available to estimate the effects of the unemployment rate. As we noted in Chapter 2, reform took place over a short period extending from the mid- to the late 1990s. As a result, it is difficult to disentangle the effects of reform from other explanatory factors that changed at the same time. In contrast, the unemployment rate fluctuates throughout the various studies' sample periods, which in some cases extend as far back as the 1970s. There is more information with which to estimate the effects of the unemployment rate, and that information is spread out over time. As a result, the estimated effects of the unemployment rate are less sensitive to late-sample specification issues, such as the treatment of period effects, than are the estimated effects of reform.

As with the estimated effects of reform discussed in the last section, the estimated effects of the unemployment rate indicate that the strong economy of the 1990s was responsible for an important fraction of the decline in welfare use. The average estimated decline of 12.1 percent in response to a 2.7-percentage-point decline in the unemployment rate amounts to about one-fourth of the roughly 50 percent decline in the caseload that took place between 1993 and 1999. At the same time,

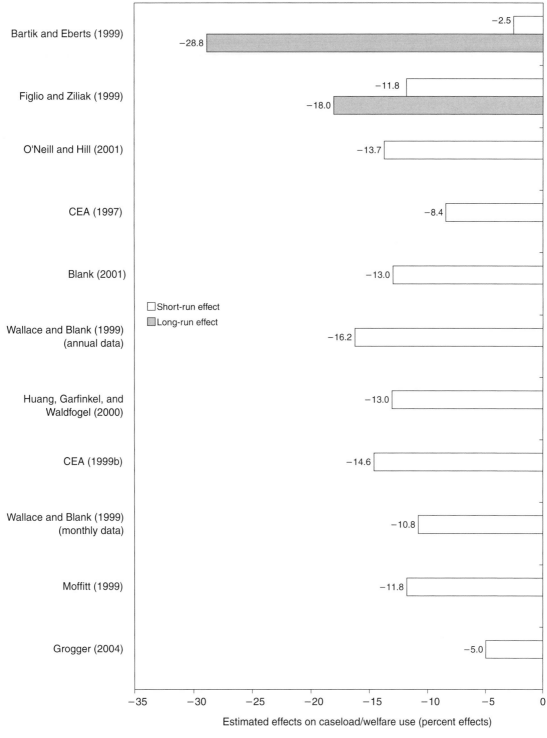

Figure 5.9
Results from observational studies of the effects of the unemployment rate on welfare use.

these estimates, in conjunction with those from the previous section, suggest that the decline in the caseload cannot be explained entirely either by the strong economy or by welfare reform.

Summary

Having discussed the various estimates in some detail, in this section we aim to distill a whole from the parts. We ask first whether the estimates accord with the predictions from Chapter 3. We then assess the results in relation to some of the traditional goals of welfare reform.

Of the three types of studies, the early-generation observational studies provide the least support for the model. At the same time, they provide the weakest basis for drawing inferences. The number of policies that these studies seek to analyze, their limited sample periods, and their limited characterizations of policy changes cause these studies to suffer from overwhelming collinearity problems. Because of these limitations, we do not rely on them for evidence to either refute or support the economic model.

The experimental and later-generation observational studies have firmer methodological legs to stand on. They also provide greater support for the model. The experimental studies of financial work incentives show that they increase welfare use and welfare payments, and that stronger incentives have larger effects. The one later-generation observational study yields similar results with respect to welfare use.

Regarding mandatory work or related activities, twelve of thirteen experiments show that they decrease welfare use and welfare payments, as predicted. None of the later-generation observational studies provides directly comparable results, but one of the two studies that analyze immediate work requirements finds that they reduce welfare use. An anomalous finding regarding work requirements involves age-of-youngest-child exemptions. The one study to address this issue, a later-generation observational study, finds that more restrictive exemptions increase welfare use, rather than decrease it.

The effects of sanctions were estimated by four later-generation observational studies. All indicated that sanctions reduced the caseload, and that stricter sanctions had greater effects. However, evidence that sanctions tended to be imposed in states with above-average prereform decreases in welfare use suggests that these estimates may overstate the true effects of sanctions.

Six later-generation observational studies indicated that time limits reduced welfare use before recipients began to exhaust their benefits. Four of those studies reported that the effects were greater among families with younger children. Observational estimates based on data from Jobs First and FTP show that in at least two states, time limits have mechanically reduced welfare use where they have begun to bind.

Family caps generated the second anomalous result. Although the model discussed in Chapter 3 made no specific predictions regarding their effects on welfare use, one might expect them to reduce it, since they make the welfare system less generous. Yet the one later-generation observational study to address family caps reported that they significantly increased the caseload.

Despite the two outstanding anomalies, however, many of the predictions from the model are consistent with the results from the studies we have reviewed. Some of those predictions are confirmed by results from several studies. Nevertheless, it would be premature to say that the model fits the data. Welfare use is only one outcome predicted by the model in Chapter 3, and the evidence in favor of the model would be far greater if its predictions held not just for welfare use, but for employment and labor supply as well.

The results presented in this chapter lead us to draw some tentative conclusions about the extent to which recent policy changes are consistent with the traditional goals of welfare reform, that is, with promoting work and reducing dependency while still alleviating need by raising living standards. Our conclusions are necessarily limited because the results discussed above have nothing to say about work. Nevertheless, policies that reduce welfare use potentially could reduce welfare dependency, to the extent that dependency is viewed as long-term reliance on welfare. Similarly, policies that increase welfare payments may potentially alleviate need, provided that increases in welfare payments are not offset by reductions in earnings or other sources of income.

Strong financial incentives, either alone or in conjunction with work requirements, are potentially consistent with the goal of alleviating need, because they increase welfare payments. At the same time, however, they increase welfare use. Conversely, work requirements reduce welfare use, and thus potentially reduce welfare dependency, but they also reduce welfare payments, which could aggravate need rather than alleviate it. Similar conclusions could be drawn regarding time limits, especially once they become binding.

Of course, policies that reduce welfare payments need not necessarily lower living standards. If they increase work effort to such an extent that increases in earnings make up for decreases in benefit payments, they can alleviate need while reducing dependency at the same time. The key is the extent to which these reforms increase employment and earnings. We address these questions in the next chapter.

❖

CHAPTER SIX

Employment, Labor Supply, and Earnings

Promoting work among welfare recipients has been a key objective of policy reform efforts since at least the early 1960s. The recent era has been no exception. Many waiver-based reforms focus primarily on requiring recipients to work or receive training, and one of PRWORA's primary goals is to promote work. Moreover, employment and labor supply are two of the central outcomes about which our economic model makes predictions. These two factors also play a key role in alleviating need.

Almost all of the major reforms discussed in Chapter 2—work requirements, time limits, and financial work incentives—should increase employment. Their effects on labor supply (that is, on hours of work) are more multifaceted. Work requirements and time limits should increase labor supply, particularly among welfare recipients who were not initially working. One exception could arise, at least in the short run, if mandatory work-related activities were satisfied via training programs that removed the participant from the labor market during the period of training.

The labor supply consequences of financial work incentives are more complicated. Although increases in employment should lead to increases in labor supply among recipients who were not working initially, conflicting income and substitution effects result in ambiguous predictions for the labor supply of working welfare recipients. In the low-income population more generally, financial work incentives may reduce labor supply by encouraging entry onto welfare. But to the extent that the states implement dual-eligibility thresholds along the lines discussed in Chapter 3, such entry effects may be mitigated.

As in Chapter 5, we examine evidence from both experimental and observational studies. Our primary goals in this chapter are, first, to test predictions of the model regarding the impact of specific reform policies on employment, labor supply, and earnings against the results from a number of studies and, second, to assess those effects in terms of the traditional goals of welfare reform. We also discuss estimates of the effect of reform as a bundle. To consider the effect of the economy on the labor market behavior of welfare-prone populations is more difficult, because few studies have addressed this issue. However, two studies have investigated a related question of considerable importance: how economic conditions affect the effects of welfare reform on earnings. Since few other studies analyze such interactions between the economy and welfare reform, we summarize the results from these studies in order to acquaint the reader with the evidence on this important topic.

Experimental Estimates of the Effects of Specific Reforms

Most of the experimental studies are based on administrative data from the states' unemployment insurance (UI) systems. In most states, every quarter, all employers covered by the UI system are required to report the earnings of each of their employees who earn $50 or more. Typically, a study participant is considered to be employed if she has any reported earnings in a given quarter, although some studies adopt an annual measure of employment instead. Likewise, some studies analyze the quarterly earnings data directly, whereas others analyze annualized earnings or even earnings over a multiyear follow-up period. Because the units of measurement vary among studies, we normalize all results in terms of monthly earnings.

One problem with administrative data is that they miss people who move between states. Each state maintains its own earnings files, so when a worker moves out of state, her earnings record in the home state shows zero earnings. But earnings records also show zero earnings when a worker becomes jobless, and it is not possible to distinguish this status from those who have moved.

Administrative data miss earnings in other ways as well. The UI system covers about 90 percent of all jobs in the United States; uncovered sectors include self-employment, federal government employment, some state and local government employment, some domestic jobs, and some agricultural jobs (U.S. Bureau of Labor Statistics, 1989). Of course the informal sector is uncovered as well, which means the UI data miss income from people who provide informal child care, take in laundry, and otherwise work for cash. A comparison of employment data from administrative and survey sources suggests that administrative data underestimate self-reported employment among welfare leavers by 10–20 percent (Isaacs and Lyon 2000, table 2C).

Another problem with these data, from the perspective of testing predictions from the model, is that they provide no direct information about hours or weeks of work. A few of the experimental studies have collected supplemental data from surveys that include such measures of labor supply, but many have not. As a result, we are often left to draw inferences about labor supply from data on earnings. Since hours are proportional to earnings, this approach may be reasonable. But since wages vary among individuals, earnings data are more variable than hours data, and the resulting estimates may be less precise. Moreover, inferences about hours based on earnings data may be misleading if reform affects wages.

Financial Work Incentives

Panel A of Figure 6.1 presents four estimates from three programs that focus on the effects of financial work incentives. According to Becerra et al. (1998), CWPDP reduced employment by 2 percentage points, which appears to contradict the prediction from the model. Results from a reanalysis of the CWPDP data, however, show that the program increased employment by a statistically significant 3.1 percentage points (Hotz, Mullin, and Scholz 2002). Since it is beyond the scope of this study to reconcile these contradictory findings, we adopt an agnostic position regarding the effects of CWPDP.

WRP-IO had positive but small and insignificant effects on employment. This finding seems consistent with the weak incentive that was offered by the program. The MFIP-IO program, with its stronger financial incentive, significantly increased employment among recipients. Among applicants, the program had no effect in the third year of the follow-up, although it did increase employment significantly during the first year (not shown).

Earnings impacts are presented in panel A of Figure 6.2. CWPDP and WRP-IO had small, insignificant impacts of the same sign as their impacts on employment. However, MFIP-IO had negative, rather than positive, effects. MFIP-IO may be a case where the income effect outweighs the substitution effect.[1] First, although the model predicts that a financial incentive should increase labor supply among initially nonworking recipients, many MFIP participants were working initially. Among recipients, 33 percent of the control group was employed in the first quarter after random assignment. Among applicants, the corresponding employment rate was 49 percent. Because many MFIP participants were employed, income effects may have played a role in the impact of the program.

Furthermore, MFIP has a relatively high benefit level, providing $9,228 per year to a family of three with no other income. Compared with other welfare programs, this level of income is relatively high. Since

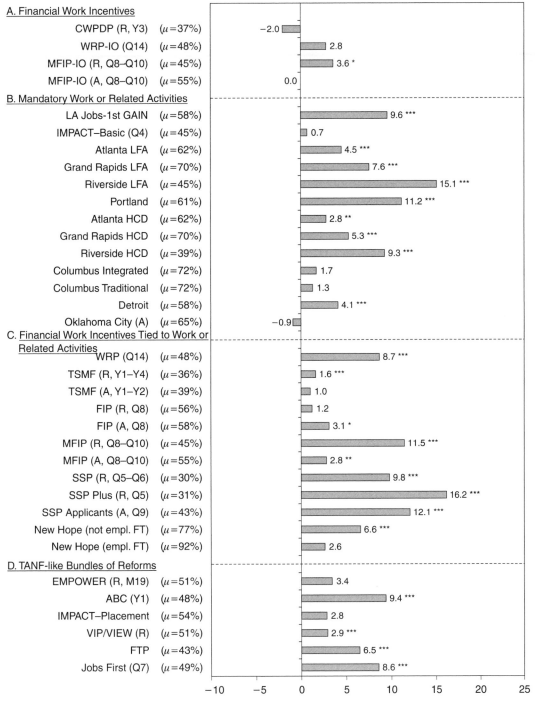

A. Financial Work Incentives

CWPDP (R, Y3)	(μ=37%)	−2.0
WRP-IO (Q14)	(μ=48%)	2.8
MFIP-IO (R, Q8–Q10)	(μ=45%)	3.6 *
MFIP-IO (A, Q8–Q10)	(μ=55%)	0.0

B. Mandatory Work or Related Activities

LA Jobs-1st GAIN	(μ=58%)	9.6 ***
IMPACT–Basic (Q4)	(μ=45%)	0.7
Atlanta LFA	(μ=62%)	4.5 ***
Grand Rapids LFA	(μ=70%)	7.6 ***
Riverside LFA	(μ=45%)	15.1 ***
Portland	(μ=61%)	11.2 ***
Atlanta HCD	(μ=62%)	2.8 **
Grand Rapids HCD	(μ=70%)	5.3 ***
Riverside HCD	(μ=39%)	9.3 ***
Columbus Integrated	(μ=72%)	1.7
Columbus Traditional	(μ=72%)	1.3
Detroit	(μ=58%)	4.1 ***
Oklahoma City (A)	(μ=65%)	−0.9

C. Financial Work Incentives Tied to Work or Related Activities

WRP (Q14)	(μ=48%)	8.7 ***
TSMF (R, Y1–Y4)	(μ=36%)	1.6 ***
TSMF (A, Y1–Y2)	(μ=39%)	1.0
FIP (R, Q8)	(μ=56%)	1.2
FIP (A, Q8)	(μ=58%)	3.1 *
MFIP (R, Q8–Q10)	(μ=45%)	11.5 ***
MFIP (A, Q8–Q10)	(μ=55%)	2.8 **
SSP (R, Q5–Q6)	(μ=30%)	9.8 ***
SSP Plus (R, Q5)	(μ=31%)	16.2 ***
SSP Applicants (A, Q9)	(μ=43%)	12.1 ***
New Hope (not empl. FT)	(μ=77%)	6.6 ***
New Hope (empl. FT)	(μ=92%)	2.6

D. TANF-like Bundles of Reforms

EMPOWER (R, M19)	(μ=51%)	3.4
ABC (Y1)	(μ=48%)	9.4 ***
IMPACT–Placement	(μ=54%)	2.8
VIP/VIEW (R)	(μ=51%)	2.9 ***
FTP	(μ=43%)	6.5 ***
Jobs First (Q7)	(μ=49%)	8.6 ***

−10   −5   0   5   10   15   20   25

Program impacts for employment (percentage points)

Note: For full program names, see Table 4.5. Impacts are for two-year follow-up and for recipients (R) and applicants (A) unless otherwise noted. μ = control group mean; M = month; Q = quarter; Y = year; FT = full-time. Significant at the ***1%, **5%, *10% level.

Figure 6.1
Estimated impacts of welfare reform on employment from experimental studies. *Source:* See Appendix Table A.3.

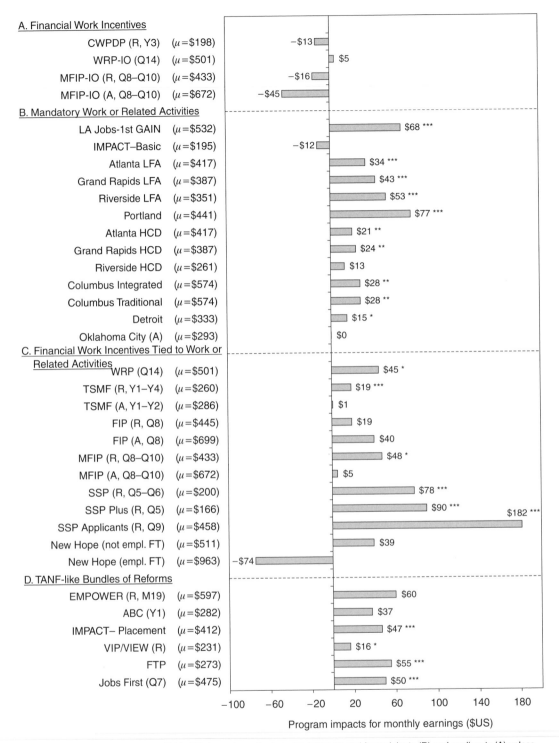

A. Financial Work Incentives

CWPDP (R, Y3)	($\mu=\$198$)	−$13
WRP-IO (Q14)	($\mu=\$501$)	$5
MFIP-IO (R, Q8–Q10)	($\mu=\$433$)	−$16
MFIP-IO (A, Q8–Q10)	($\mu=\$672$)	−$45

B. Mandatory Work or Related Activities

LA Jobs-1st GAIN	($\mu=\$532$)	$68 ***
IMPACT–Basic	($\mu=\$195$)	−$12
Atlanta LFA	($\mu=\$417$)	$34 ***
Grand Rapids LFA	($\mu=\$387$)	$43 ***
Riverside LFA	($\mu=\$351$)	$53 ***
Portland	($\mu=\$441$)	$77 ***
Atlanta HCD	($\mu=\$417$)	$21 **
Grand Rapids HCD	($\mu=\$387$)	$24 **
Riverside HCD	($\mu=\$261$)	$13
Columbus Integrated	($\mu=\$574$)	$28 **
Columbus Traditional	($\mu=\$574$)	$28 **
Detroit	($\mu=\$333$)	$15 *
Oklahoma City (A)	($\mu=\$293$)	$0

C. Financial Work Incentives Tied to Work or Related Activities

WRP (Q14)	($\mu=\$501$)	$45 *
TSMF (R, Y1–Y4)	($\mu=\$260$)	$19 ***
TSMF (A, Y1–Y2)	($\mu=\$286$)	$1
FIP (R, Q8)	($\mu=\$445$)	$19
FIP (A, Q8)	($\mu=\$699$)	$40
MFIP (R, Q8–Q10)	($\mu=\$433$)	$48 *
MFIP (A, Q8–Q10)	($\mu=\$672$)	$5
SSP (R, Q5–Q6)	($\mu=\$200$)	$78 ***
SSP Plus (R, Q5)	($\mu=\$166$)	$90 ***
SSP Applicants (R, Q9)	($\mu=\$458$)	$182 ***
New Hope (not empl. FT)	($\mu=\$511$)	$39
New Hope (empl. FT)	($\mu=\$963$)	−$74

D. TANF-like Bundles of Reforms

EMPOWER (R, M19)	($\mu=\$597$)	$60
ABC (Y1)	($\mu=\$282$)	$37
IMPACT– Placement	($\mu=\$412$)	$47 ***
VIP/VIEW (R)	($\mu=\$231$)	$16 *
FTP	($\mu=\$273$)	$55 ***
Jobs First (Q7)	($\mu=\$475$)	$50 ***

Program impacts for monthly earnings ($US)

Note: For full program names, see Table 4.5. Impacts are for two-year follow-up and for recipients (R) and applicants (A) unless otherwise noted. μ = control group mean; M = month; Q = quarter; Y = year; FT = full-time. Significant at the ***1%, **5%, *10% level.

Figure 6.2
Estimated impacts of welfare reform on monthly earnings from experimental studies. *Source:* See Appendix Table A.3.

our theory would lead us to expect larger income effects at higher levels of income, a dominant income effect is a possible explanation for MFIP-IO's negative, though insignificant, impacts on earnings.

Mandatory Work or Related Activities

Panel B of Figure 6.1 presents impact estimates from thirteen programs that involved mandatory work or related activities. The results are generally consistent with the prediction from the model. Twelve of the programs had positive effects on employment, nine of which were significant. The one negative impact was small and insignificant.

On average, these programs increased employment by 5.6 percentage points, which amounts to an average 10 percent gain over the control groups. The placement-oriented programs resulted in larger average employment gains than the skills-oriented programs, which generally required the participant to take part in classroom activities. The average employment increase among the placement-oriented programs was 9.2 percentage points, compared with 3 percentage points among the skills-oriented programs.

The earnings impacts from these programs, presented in panel B of Figure 6.2, are similarly consistent with the prediction from the model. Eleven of thirteen programs produced positive effects on earnings, nine of which were significant at least at the 5 percent level. The one negative effect was insignificant.

The average earnings gain over the first two years of the follow-up exceeded $58 per month, or $700 per year. Only four of the programs failed to increase earnings by at least $400 annually. Again the gains were greater for the placement-oriented programs than for the skills-oriented programs. Among the four placement-oriented programs, annual earnings gains averaged $594. Among the skills-focused programs, they averaged $186.

Five-year employment impacts from NEWWS are presented in Figure 6.3; five-year earnings impacts are shown in Figure 6.4. These findings provide some evidence on the longer-run effects of work requirements. As in Chapter 5, there is evidence of program fade-out. Annual employment impacts in years 4 and 5 averaged 2.0 percentage points, compared with 4.8 percentage points in years 1 and 2. Long-term annual earnings impacts averaged $324, compared with short-term impacts of $378. For the most part, the program impacts fell over time, not because treatment-group employment and earnings fell, but because the labor market outcomes of the control group caught up with those of the treatment group.

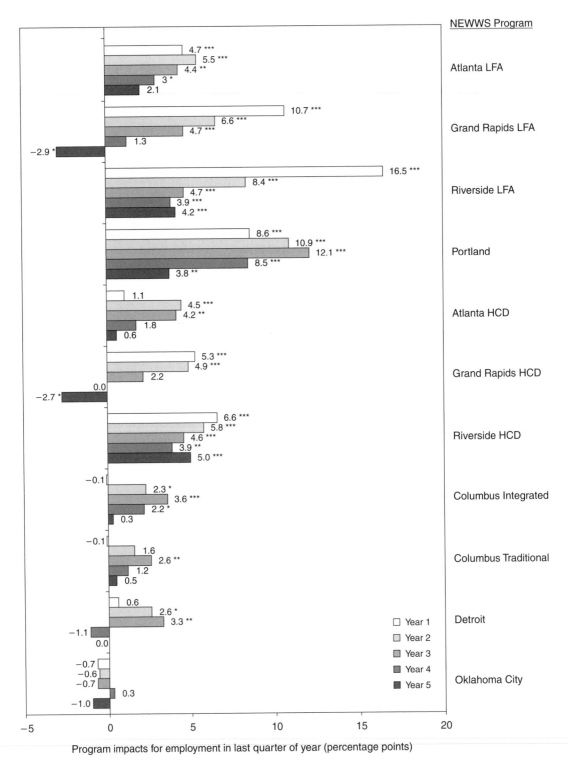

Atlanta LFA
4.7 ***
5.5 ***
4.4 **
3 *
2.1

Grand Rapids LFA
10.7 ***
6.6 ***
4.7 ***
1.3
−2.9 *

Riverside LFA
16.5 ***
8.4 ***
4.7 ***
3.9 ***
4.2 ***

Portland
8.6 ***
10.9 ***
12.1 ***
8.5 ***
3.8 **

Atlanta HCD
1.1
4.5 ***
4.2 **
1.8
0.6

Grand Rapids HCD
5.3 ***
4.9 ***
2.2
0.0
−2.7 *

Riverside HCD
6.6 ***
5.8 ***
4.6 ***
3.9 **
5.0 ***

Columbus Integrated
−0.1
2.3 *
3.6 ***
2.2 *
0.3

Columbus Traditional
−0.1
1.6
2.6 **
1.2
0.5

Detroit
0.6
2.6 *
3.3 **
−1.1
0.0

Oklahoma City
−0.7
−0.6
−0.7
0.3
−1.0

☐ Year 1
☐ Year 2
▨ Year 3
▨ Year 4
■ Year 5

Program impacts for employment in last quarter of year (percentage points)

−5   0   5   10   15   20

Note: Significant at the ***1%, **5%, *10% level.

Figure 6.3
Estimated impacts of mandatory work or related activities on employment from eleven NEWWS programs, years 1 to 5. *Source:* Hamilton et al. (2001), table C.1.

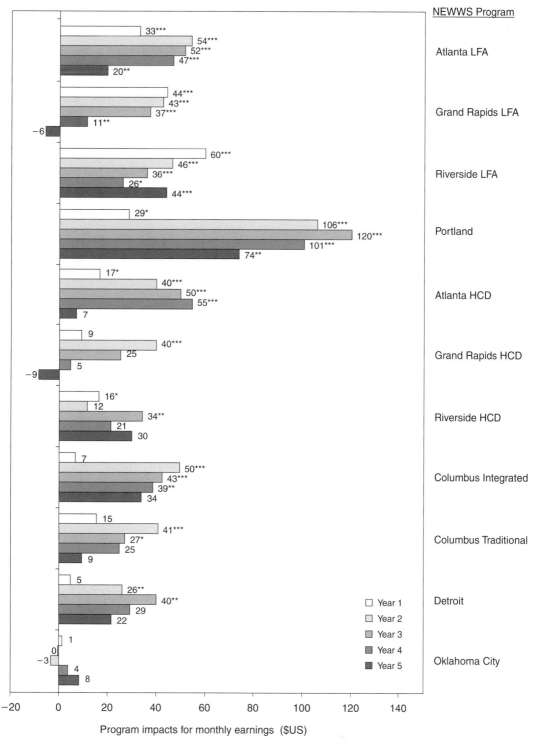

Atlanta LFA — 33***, 54***, 52***, 47***, 20**

Grand Rapids LFA — 44***, 43***, 37***, 11**, −6

Riverside LFA — 60***, 46***, 36***, 26*, 44***

Portland — 29*, 106***, 120***, 101***, 74**

Atlanta HCD — 17*, 40***, 50***, 55***, 7

Grand Rapids HCD — 9, 40***, 25, 5, −9

Riverside HCD — 16*, 12, 34**, 21, 30

Columbus Integrated — 7, 50***, 43***, 39**, 34

Columbus Traditional — 15, 41***, 27*, 25, 9

Detroit — 5, 26**, 40**, 29, 22

Oklahoma City — 1, 0, −3, 4, 8

☐ Year 1
☐ Year 2
☐ Year 3
▨ Year 4
▩ Year 5

Program impacts for monthly earnings ($US)

Note: Significant at the ***1%, **5%, *10% level.

Figure 6.4
Estimated impacts of mandatory work or related activities on monthly earnings from eleven NEWWS programs, years 1 to 5. *Source:* Hamilton et al. (2001), table C.2.

In the three sites that ran placement- and skills-oriented programs simultaneously, the gap between the impacts of the two types of programs faded over time. For the first two years of the program, the average impacts of the placement-oriented programs on annual employment and earnings were 8.7 percentage points and $561, respectively. The average impacts among the skills-focused programs were 4.7 percentage points and $267. For years 3 through 5, the average impacts of the placement-oriented programs on annual employment and earnings were 2.8 percentage points and $355. For skills-focused programs the average impacts in years 3 through 5 were 2.2 percentage points and $291. The longer-term differentials between the placement- and skills-oriented programs are much smaller than the differentials that appeared during the first two years of the program. This smaller difference suggests that some of the early differential may have been due to the fact that participants in the placement-oriented programs were looking for work during the initial period of the program, rather than taking part in the classroom activities to which participants in the skills-focused programs devoted some of their time.[2]

Financial Work Incentives Tied to Work or Related Activities

Panel C of Figures 6.1 and 6.2 presents twelve estimates from eight programs that link financial incentives to work. Among the four programs that were administered within the welfare system, all increased employment. However, the effects are quite heterogeneous. The impacts of these programs on earnings are similarly heterogeneous, generally following their impacts on employment.

WRP had stronger effects on employment and earnings than WRP-IO. This greater impact suggests that a requirement to work in exchange for welfare may be effective in increasing employment and earnings, even when it has little effect on welfare use, as was seen in Figure 5.1.

Michigan's TSMF program had small positive effects on employment, mirroring its small negative effects on welfare use. TSMF had a weak financial incentive and its welfare-to-work program was not particularly placement-oriented during its first two years. When the program did adopt a work-first approach, the work-related activity mandate was applied to *both* the treatment and the control group (although the control group was subject to lesser sanctions for violating the work mandate). With little effective difference in the conditions applying to the treatment and control groups, one might expect to find small effects.

The FIP program combined a fairly strong financial incentive with an education-focused welfare-to-work program. The combined policies increased the fraction of participants who combined work and welfare in a manner that was similar for both recipients and applicants (not shown). However, the program decreased the fraction of ongoing recipients who abandoned welfare for work, although it had no such effect on new applicants. It may be that applicants were more likely to satisfy the work-related activity mandate by working, whereas ongoing recipients were more likely to satisfy it by taking part in the skills-focused welfare-to-work program. Such a difference could explain why the program increased employment and earnings more among applicants than among ongoing recipients. Unfortunately, the evaluation provides no information on welfare-to-work participation rates that could be used to verify this explanation.

Like WRP, MFIP had stronger effects on employment and earnings than did its incentives-only counterpart. The earnings impact from MFIP is positive, whereas the impact from MFIP-IO was negative. Work requirements may thus provide a means of overcoming the negative income effects that may arise from a strong financial incentive in the presence of a relatively high benefit level.

With one exception, the four programs that operated outside the traditional welfare system had substantial impacts on labor market behavior. The SSP programs generated sizable gains in both employment and earnings. New Hope led to significant increases in employment among families who were not initially satisfying the program's hours requirement. Its employment effect on those who initially satisfied the hours requirement was small, but this may be due to "ceiling effects." These families were working at least 30 hours per week when the experiment began, and the control group maintained employment rates of 92 percent. With near-universal employment among the control group, it would be difficult for the program to generate sizable employment gains.

New Hope had a negative, albeit insignificant, effect on the earnings of families who initially satisfied the program's hours requirement. Like the participants in MFIP, this group of New Hope participants had annual incomes averaging about $11,000, which is high by the standards of welfare programs. Of course, they were working nearly full-time as well. As a result, the income effect may have dominated the substitution effect for this group.

Entry effects could also have reduced earnings. Unlike the other programs, which were available only to welfare recipients, New Hope was also available to low-income families who were not receiving welfare. For those families, the New Hope earnings supplement raised income at any level of labor supply (at or above 30 hours/week) while reducing the effective wage. Thus the income and substitution effects reinforced each other, which should have decreased the labor supply and earnings of this group.

Two recent studies provide evidence on longer-term effects of SSP (Michalopoulos et al. 2002; Zabel, Schwartz, and Donald 2004). The positive impact that this program had on employment and earnings was smaller in the long run than in the short run.[3] As with NEWWS, this reduction was mostly due to control-group catch-up by the end of the fifty-four-month follow-up period. Notably, the rate of full-time employment for the SSP treatment group remained roughly stable over time, falling only slightly even after the earnings supplement ended at the thirty-six-month mark. In contrast, the rate of full-time employment for the control group steadily increased over time.

Taken as a whole, the evidence from these experiments is fairly consistent with the predictions from the model. Most of the policies increase employment, and most of the positive impact estimates are significant. The few negative estimates are statistically insignificant. Some of the positive estimates may be smaller than expected due to specific program features.

Most of the earnings impacts are positive. All of the exceptions are insignificant. Two of the negative earnings impacts involve groups of participants with initial employment rates and incomes that are high by the standards of welfare populations. Thus the negative, albeit insignificant, impacts may be due to income effects. New Hope had the largest negative impact. It was also the one program available to working nonwelfare recipients and, therefore, the one program where entry effects may also have played a role.

Observational Estimates of the Effects of Specific Reforms

Compared with the case of welfare use, there are fewer observational studies of the effects of welfare reform on employment, labor supply, and earnings. Four observational studies analyze the effects of reform as a bundle. Only three study the effects of specific policy reforms. The results for these three analyses appear in Figure 6.5.

All the observational studies are based on data from the March CPS. They therefore use fairly similar measures of employment and earnings. Employment is typically measured as a dummy variable that equals one if the survey respondent worked for pay in the year preceding the survey and equals zero otherwise. Respondents also indicate the number of weeks they worked for pay in the previous year, which provides a useful measure of labor supply. In addition, respondents report their income

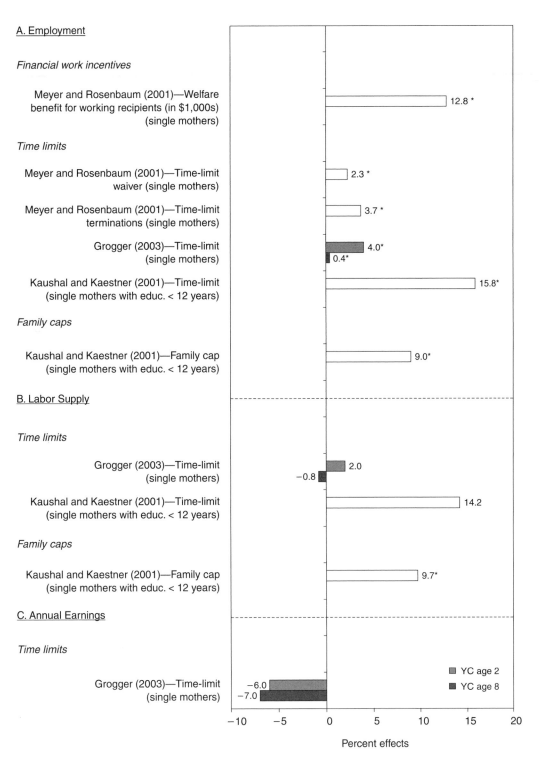

A. Employment

Financial work incentives

Meyer and Rosenbaum (2001)—Welfare benefit for working recipients (in $1,000s) (single mothers) — 12.8 *

Time limits

Meyer and Rosenbaum (2001)—Time-limit waiver (single mothers) — 2.3 *

Meyer and Rosenbaum (2001)—Time-limit terminations (single mothers) — 3.7 *

Grogger (2003)—Time-limit (single mothers) — 4.0* / 0.4*

Kaushal and Kaestner (2001)—Time-limit (single mothers with educ. < 12 years) — 15.8*

Family caps

Kaushal and Kaestner (2001)—Family cap (single mothers with educ. < 12 years) — 9.0*

B. Labor Supply

Time limits

Grogger (2003)—Time-limit (single mothers) — 2.0 / −0.8

Kaushal and Kaestner (2001)—Time-limit (single mothers with educ. < 12 years) — 14.2

Family caps

Kaushal and Kaestner (2001)—Family cap (single mothers with educ. < 12 years) — 9.7*

C. Annual Earnings

Time limits

Grogger (2003)—Time-limit (single mothers) — −6.0 / −7.0

YC age 2
YC age 8

−10   −5   0   5   10   15   20

Percent effects

Note: Asterisks denote results based on coefficients that were significant at the 10 percent level or better. YC = youngest child. The white bars denote studies where no differentiation was made regarding children's age.

Figure 6.5
Results from observational studies of the effects of specific reforms on employment, labor supply, and earnings.

from earnings in the previous year. As in the econometric literature on welfare use, some researchers analyze the individual-level data directly, whereas others first aggregate the data into cells defined by the respondent's education, age, state, and year.

Many of the analytical issues that arise in observational studies of the caseload also arise in studies of employment and earnings. Welfare reform is only one of several factors that contributed to recent changes in the labor market behavior of single mothers. The strong economy played an important role, as did the EITC (Hotz, Mullin, and Scholz 2001; Meyer and Rosenbaum 2001; Grogger 2003). Other, largely unobservable factors may have played a role as well. As in the caseload literature, researchers have attempted to account for such confounding influences by including controls in their regression models for the economy, characteristics of survey respondents, other policy variables, and state-specific fixed effects. With one exception, all include year dummies to control for other economywide trends which could have affected labor market behavior.

The generational distinction that appeared in the observational studies of the effects of specific reforms on welfare use is less pronounced in the studies of labor market outcomes. Meyer and Rosenbaum (2001) estimate an approximation to a structural model in which they characterize financial work incentives in a manner that accounts for the generosity of states' financial work incentives (a later-generation approach). However, they use dummy variables to capture both the behavioral and the mechanical effects of time limits (an early-generation approach). Grogger (2003) allows the behavioral effects of time limits to depend on the age of the youngest child in the family, although he uses a single dummy variable to control for the effects of other reforms. Only Kaushal and Kaestner (2001) rely exclusively on dummy variables to characterize specific welfare reforms (in their case, time limits and family caps).

Meyer and Rosenbaum estimate that increasing financial work incentives so as to raise the monthly benefit payment to working recipients by about $85 increases employment by 12.8 percent. They report that implementing time limits increases employment by 2.3 percent; actual terminations due to time limits raise employment another 3.7 percent. Grogger (2003) finds that time limits generally increase employment in a manner that is greatest for families with the youngest children. This is consistent with the model of Grogger and Michalopoulos (1999, 2003), but the effect on employment is smaller than it was for welfare use and only marginally significant ($p < 0.10$). Grogger finds no significant evidence that time limits affect labor supply or earnings. Kaushal and Kaestner report much larger effects for time limits. They estimate that time limits increase employment and labor supply among single mothers with fewer than twelve years of education by 15.8 and 14.2 percent, respectively, although only the former estimate is significant. They also find family caps to have sizable and significant effects on both of these measures of labor market activity. This is surprising because, as we will see in Chapter 8, they do not find a statistically significant effect of family caps on fertility.

As in Chapter 5, Figures 6.6 and 6.7 present quarterly impact estimates from Jobs First and FTP that can be used to estimate the mechanical effects of time limits on employment and earnings, respectively. A key question is whether time limits should have any mechanical effects on employment or earnings. The language of PRWORA and state policies clearly lead one to expect time limits to mechanically affect welfare use: subject to exemption and extension policies, most welfare families are legally barred from receiving benefits once they have reached the limit. In contrast, there is no legal link between the time limit and employment. Being dropped from the rolls may enhance former recipients' desire to work, but such work may not be readily forthcoming. Alternatively, recipients who anticipate the advent of their time limit may seek work well beforehand, with the result that their employment does not change at the time they are dropped from the rolls.

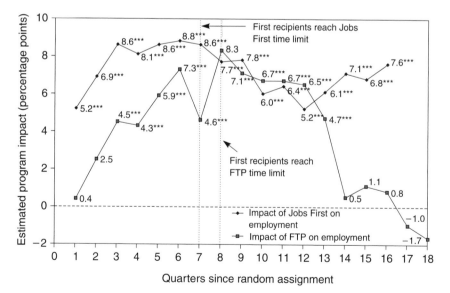

Note: Impact significant at the ***1%, **5%, *10% level.

Figure 6.6
Estimated impacts of Jobs First and FTP on employment, quarters 1 to 18. *Source:* Jobs First: Bloom et al. (2002), table B.1; FTP: Bloom et al. (2000), table B.1.

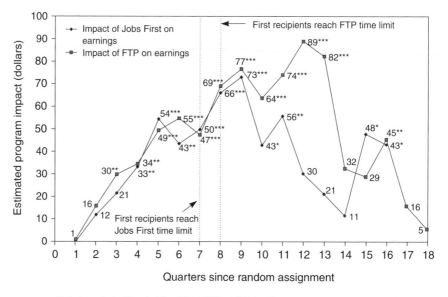

Note: Impact significant at the ***1%, **5%, *10% level.

Figure 6.7
Estimated impacts of Jobs First and FTP on monthly earnings, quarters 1 to 18. *Source:* Jobs First: Bloom et al. (2002), table B.1; FTP: Bloom et al. (2000), table B.1.

During the pre–time limit period, both programs increased employ-ment (Figure 6.6). The Jobs First increase was greater, which is consis-tent with its stronger financial incentive. However, in neither program is there strong evidence that the time limit had a mechanical effect on em-ployment. In Jobs First, the decline in the program's employment impact between quarters 7 and 8 is 0.9 percentage points. This contrasts sharply with the 12.5-percentage-point decline in the program's impact on wel-fare use between the same two quarters. The employment impact contin-ues to fall gradually through quarter 12, after which it rises again.

The pre–time limit impact of FTP was somewhat more variable than that of Jobs First. The post–time limit change was similar, however; it fell from 8.3 percentage points to 7.1 percentage points between quarters 8 and 9. It continued to decline a bit for the next three quarters. The im-pact of the program fell more sharply between quarters 12 and 13 and particularly between quarters 13 and 14. Although this pattern differs from that of Jobs First, it cannot clearly be linked to the mechanical ef-fects of the time limit.[4]

The time trends in the earnings impacts of the programs are somewhat different, but still provide little to suggest that the time limit has much of a mechanical effect (Figure 6.7). In Jobs First, the program's earnings im-pact continues to rise for two quarters after recipients begin reaching the limit. It falls fairly sharply between quarters 9 and 14, after which it rises almost as sharply. The earnings impact of FTP falls between quarters 9 and 10, but otherwise rises fairly steadily from quarter 7 to quarter 12. It falls sharply in quarter 14, after which it follows roughly the same trend as the program's employment impact.

Estimates of the Effects of Reform as a Bundle

Two sources provide evidence on the effects of reform as a bundle: experiments that involved TANF-like reform bundles and observational studies. The evidence from the experimental studies is presented in panel D of Figures 6.1 and 6.2. All of these programs yielded positive impacts on both employment and earnings, most of which were significant. These findings contrast with the mixed effects that these programs had on welfare use, but then the contrast is not so surprising. Whereas the reforms bundled together in these programs have potentially conflicting effects on welfare use, they have reinforcing effects on employment.

Results from observational studies are presented in Figure 6.8. All of the estimated effects of reform on employment are positive. Four of the five of them fall between 2.9 and 3.9 percent. The outlier is O'Neill and Hill's (2001) estimate of the effect of TANF, which may have to do with the limited controls that they employ for period effects.

Three of the four estimates of the effects of reform on labor supply are positive and significant, ranging from 4 to 8 percent. The one negative estimate, from Schoeni and Blank (2000), is insignificant. Only two of the four estimates of the effects of reform on earnings are significant, although all are positive.

Although none of the estimates of the effects of reform as a bundle can be used to test the theory from Chapter 3, almost all of them are consistent with it. The model indicated that nearly all the central reforms implemented under PRWORA should raise employment, and nearly all the estimates suggest that collectively, they did. These data suggest that reform played an important role in increasing the employment of the welfare-eligible population.

Estimates of the Effect of the Economy

Only two of the authors listed in Figure 6.8 estimate the effect of the economy on labor market behavior. Grogger's (2003) estimates imply that a 2.7-percentage-point decrease in the unemployment rate, such as that which took place between 1993 and 1999, should have increased employment among single mothers by 4.2 percent. O'Neill and Hill's

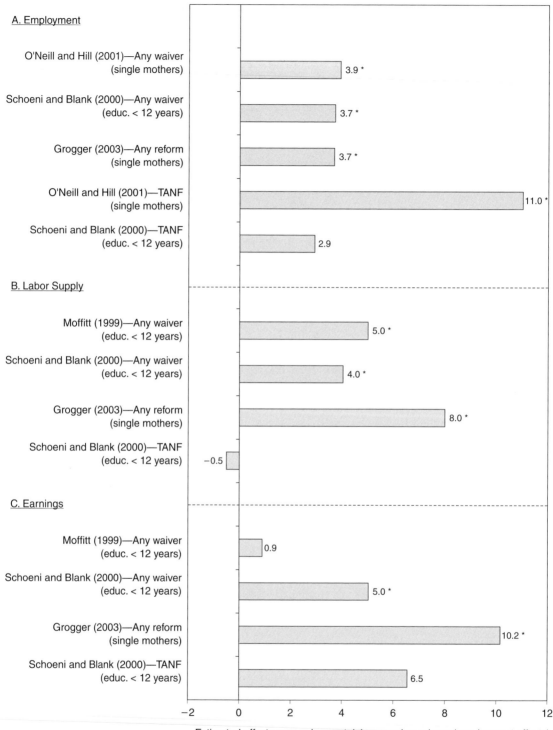

A. Employment

O'Neill and Hill (2001)—Any waiver (single mothers) 3.9 *

Schoeni and Blank (2000)—Any waiver (educ. < 12 years) 3.7 *

Grogger (2003)—Any reform (single mothers) 3.7 *

O'Neill and Hill (2001)—TANF (single mothers) 11.0 *

Schoeni and Blank (2000)—TANF (educ. < 12 years) 2.9

B. Labor Supply

Moffitt (1999)—Any waiver (educ. < 12 years) 5.0 *

Schoeni and Blank (2000)—Any waiver (educ. < 12 years) 4.0 *

Grogger (2003)—Any reform (single mothers) 8.0 *

Schoeni and Blank (2000)—TANF (educ. < 12 years) −0.5

C. Earnings

Moffitt (1999)—Any waiver (educ. < 12 years) 0.9

Schoeni and Blank (2000)—Any waiver (educ. < 12 years) 5.0 *

Grogger (2003)—Any reform (single mothers) 10.2 *

Schoeni and Blank (2000)—TANF (educ. < 12 years) 6.5

Estimated effects on employment, labor supply, and earnings (percent effects)

Note: Asterisks denote results based on coefficients that are significant at the 10 percent level or better.

Figure 6.8
Results from observational studies of the effects of reform as a bundle on employment, labor supply, and earnings.

(2001) estimates imply that single mothers' employment would have risen by 6.9 percent. Both effects are substantial in relation to the observed 20 percent increase in employment among single mothers between 1993 and 1999. O'Neill and Hill's estimate is probably larger than Grogger's because of their use of limited controls for period effects, as discussed above. Grogger is the only analyst to report the effects of unemployment on labor supply; his estimate implies that the 1993–1999 fall in unemployment should have increased labor supply by 4 percent, explaining roughly one-sixth of the observed 24.5 percent increase among single mothers.

Two recent studies have taken up a different but important question regarding the effect of the economy. Rather than ask how the economy affects labor market behavior, they ask how the economy affects the impacts of welfare-to-work (and similar) programs on earnings. That is, they seek to estimate interactions between the state of the economy and the earnings impacts of welfare-to-work and job-training programs.

This issue has taken on increased importance in light of the recent performance of the economy. Nevertheless, it is unclear on a priori grounds how weakness in the economy should affect the earnings impact of job training programs. Some have argued that employment programs only work when there are jobs, so the effects would be larger in a better economy and smaller in a worse economy. Others have argued that in a good economy, the programs are unnecessary because people would find jobs anyway. This line of argument suggests that effects would be smaller in a better economy and larger in a worse economy.

H. Bloom, Hill, and Riccio (2001) analyze individual-level data from fifty sites in twenty-five counties in eight states of MDRC's random assignment studies of welfare-to-work programs. They find that a one-percentage-point increase in the unemployment rate reduces the program impact by $94 (significant at $p = 0.004$). Relative to the average earnings impact of $879, this amounts to an 11 percent reduction in the impact of such programs. This is a sizable interaction effect.

However, Greenberg, Michalopoulos, and Robins (2001) reach different conclusions. They analyze the effect of government training programs on earnings using study-level data, combining experimental evaluations and nonexperimental evaluations while controlling for study characteristics. Their analysis includes both welfare programs and other government training programs. They separately consider men, women, and youth. For women—the primary group in welfare-to-work programs and the group most comparable to that studied by Bloom, Hill, and Riccio (2001)—they find no interaction between the state of the economy and the impact of job-training programs.

Why do the results differ between these two studies? On the one hand, the contrasting findings may have to do with differences in the design of the studies, such as the use of individual-level versus study-level data. On the other, they may have to do with limited variation in the state of the economy across studies, in which case no design would have much power to detect an interaction between economic conditions and the effects of welfare-to-work programs. Despite keen interest in the relationship between welfare reform and the state of the job market, there is no conclusive evidence to suggest how recent weakness in labor markets should influence the effects of reform.

Summary

The model from Chapter 3 predicted that all of the major welfare reforms should increase employment. Most of the evidence is consistent with those predictions. Of thirty-five experimental estimates of the effects of various (combinations of) reforms on employment, thirty-two were positive and twenty-three of those were significant. The negative estimates were small and insignificant. The one observational estimate of the effect of financial work incentives indicated that they increased employment, as predicted. The two observational estimates of the behavioral effects of time limits on employment were both positive. Kaushal and Kaestner (2001) find them to have sizable effects. Grogger (2003) finds some evidence that time limits have greater behavioral effects among families with younger children, although the effects that he reports are fairly small and only marginally significant. There is also a discrepancy in the data regarding the mechanical effects, if any, of time limits on employment. Meyer and Rosenbaum (2001) find that employment rises once states began to drop families from the rolls. However, trends in the employment impacts of Jobs First and FTP show no clear changes around the time when participants began to reach their limits.

The predictions of the model regarding labor supply (and, indirectly, earnings) are more complicated due to the conflicting income and substitution effects that arise from financial work incentives. None of the pure financial incentive experiments significantly increased earnings. The programs involving mandatory work-related activities did increase earnings, although the magnitude of the increase declined by the end of the fifth year, mostly due to catch-up on the part of the controls. Most of the programs that tied financial work incentives to work or related activities increased earnings, although the one exception may be instructive. New Hope, the only program that was open to nonwelfare recipients, decreased earnings among families who were satisfying the program's hours requirement at the time that the program began, albeit insignificantly. This decrease may arise from the fact that for participants who were working initially, the program generated income and substitution effects that should have reinforced each other to reduce hours (though not below the program's thirty-hour requirement). The effects of both New Hope and SSP faded in the long run, again mostly because the control group caught up with the treatment group.

The results from studies of the effects of reform as a bundle similarly indicate that reform increased the employment and earnings of welfare-eligible populations. Nevertheless, none of the estimates suggests that reform raised earnings by very much. Among the experimental studies, the most successful program increased annual earnings by less than $2,200; after that, the next-most successful program raised annual earnings by $1,080. Reform generally raised earnings, although not by amounts that are likely to raise many poor families out of poverty.

As in the previous chapter, we can draw several conclusions from this evidence regarding the extent to which recent policy reforms achieve some of the traditional goals of welfare reform. Also as in Chapter 5, the conclusions we can draw are somewhat limited because the results discussed above focus on a single set of outcomes. Nevertheless, they speak to the goal of promoting work, and in conjunction with the results from the last chapter, we can make some preliminary statements about the extent to which they alleviate need. Taken in combination, the results we have described point to trade-offs among the goals of reducing dependency, promoting work, and alleviating need.

The results here suggest that almost all the recent policy reforms promote work. The vast majority of the estimates discussed above are consistent with increased employment, as are the estimated effects of reform as a bundle. The trade-offs have to do with the extent to which the different policies, or combinations of policies, reduce dependency and alleviate need. Strong financial incentives increase employment and earnings, and as seen earlier, they increase welfare payments as well. Because they increase both earnings and welfare payments, they presumably reduce need by raising incomes. However, they do so at the cost of additional welfare use.

Work requirements increase earnings as well as employment. In Chapter 5 we concluded that they also reduce welfare use and welfare payments. Work requirements seem to meet the goals of reducing dependency and promoting work, but whether they alleviate need depends on whether they increase earnings by more than they reduce welfare payments. There is some evidence that time limits increase employment, but little evidence that they increase earnings. Time limits may reduce dependency and promote work, but it seems even less likely that they alleviate need. In the next chapter we analyze the effects of reform on income and poverty, which allows us to address questions of alleviating need more directly.

❖

CHAPTER SEVEN

Income and Poverty

Raising living standards has been another key objective of welfare policy, and many reform efforts have been designed with this goal in mind. One way to capture the effect of reform on living standards is to examine its effect on income, a measure widely used to gauge a family's command over resources. Poverty is another metric commonly defined on the basis of whether a family's income exceeds a specified needs standard. For some observers, these outcomes are among the most important to consider when evaluating the consequences of welfare reform.

For the most part, the model in Chapter 3 makes ambiguous predictions about the effects of reform on income, the main components of which are earnings and welfare payments. Reforms such as work requirements and time limits may cause earnings to rise while causing welfare payments to fall. Thus the net change in income will depend on the magnitudes of these opposing effects. Financial work incentives have ambiguous effects on earnings, leading to ambiguous effects on income. Consequently, despite the importance of the effects of reform on income for policy purposes, they cannot be used to test the adequacy of the economic model.

Whereas the effect of reform on income depends on how reform affects different components of income, the effect of reform on poverty also depends on where in the income distribution any change in income takes place. For example, if income changes are small and occur only among those already well below the poverty line, then the poverty rate would remain unchanged. Alternatively, if income changes are small on average but occur among those close to the poverty line, then there may be a change in the proportion of families classified as poor.

In Chapter 2 we noted that recent income trends have been positive. The mean incomes of female-headed families have risen and poverty rates have fallen. There is keen interest in determining whether these changes are the direct result of welfare reform, or whether they stem

155

mostly from other factors, such as the economy or policy changes like the minimum wage or the EITC. Thus our primary goal in this chapter is to assess what we know about the effects of welfare reform on income and poverty.

As is true for other aspects of welfare-related behavior, the causal impact of welfare reform on income has been evaluated using both experimental and observational methods. Although administrative data provide the primary source of information on outcomes in Chapters 5 and 6, only a narrow measure of income and poverty can be constructed by relying solely on administrative data. Both experimental and observational studies also employ survey data to construct broader measures of income and to calculate poverty rates.

Conceptually, the ideal income measure would capture all sources of income available to the recipient in her own name, as well as sources available through income pooled at the family or household level. Those income sources would include earnings, cash and noncash government means-tested transfers (for example, welfare, food stamps, Supplemental Security Income, general assistance, Medicaid), other government transfers (for example, unemployment insurance, disability insurance, Social Security), private transfers (for example, child support or alimony), and income from assets (for example, interest, dividends). Income would also be measured net of taxes paid and tax credits received (for example, EITC). Some would also argue that income should be measured net of work-related expenses such as out-of-pocket child care and transportation costs, but this is rarely done in practice.[1] If these costs are deducted from income, a single mother moving from welfare to work may experience a decline in net income if the increase in her earnings is not large enough to offset the loss of welfare benefits and the increased out-of-pocket work-related expenses.

Family income is typically defined as all income sources for the unit of individuals who are related by blood, marriage, or adoption. A non-married partner of the recipient might be considered part of the family group as well, especially if income is pooled. To the extent that income pooling occurs within the household, between related or unrelated individuals, the income for the entire household would be measured.

The complexities of income measurement, both conceptually and in practice, mean that such an ideal measure is rarely available. In the studies we review in this chapter, the measures of income and poverty vary. All the observational studies analyze data from the CPS. Thus they use a fairly comprehensive measure of family income, although they typically do not account for taxes, tax credits, or noncash transfers (including food stamps).

Experimental studies often employ a measure based on administrative data that we refer to as "combined income." It includes the recipient's earnings, cash assistance (for example, welfare payments and any financial work incentives such as earnings supplements), and food stamps. In some cases, taxes and tax credits such as the EITC are imputed as well. Combined income is a relatively narrow construct because it involves only the recipient's income from a few sources (although for many female-headed families, these are the main sources of income). Some experimental studies also collect information on a broader array of income sources directly from participants. These survey data, either alone or in combination with administrative data, are used to measure a broader concept of income that may include other public and private transfers, and earnings and unearned income of other family members.

In comparing studies, one must therefore keep in mind that the measurement of income (and hence poverty) may be incomplete (that is, not all sources are measured or imputed) or may suffer from underreporting of certain income sources. Measures of family income in some studies may include cash sources only, while income measures in other studies may include the value of in-kind benefits such as food stamps. Income may be measured before taxes, so that taxes paid or tax credits received are not accounted for. Income data collected through survey methods may be measured using a recall period as short as one month or as long as a year. The unit of observation may vary from the narrowest perspective of the recipient's income to the broadest perspective of family or household income. Even when income measures are the same over time or across studies, income data collected in surveys are often plagued by underreporting; efforts to relate changes in policies to changes in income measures may be biased by such measurement error.

In those studies that calculate a poverty rate, the standard approach is to compare the measure of income with a needs standard that is usually specific to the family type (size and number of adults versus children). Almost all studies use the poverty cutoffs defined by the Census Bureau to calculate the official poverty rate, even though the income concept these investigations use generally differs from the official measure used by the Census Bureau (family pretax cash income). In some cases, the measure of income is more comprehensive than the official measure (for example, the EITC and value of food stamps are included). In other cases, it is less comprehensive (for example, income from assets, private transfers, and non-welfare-related public transfers are excluded). The income measure may also be based on only individual income, whereas the Census Bureau poverty cutoffs are intended to apply to family income. Thus the concept of poverty as applied in these studies does not necessarily capture the same concept as the official measure, and poverty rates are not necessarily comparable across studies.[2]

Some researchers would argue that income, especially the way it is usually measured in surveys, may not be the best indicator of material well-being (Edin and Lein 1997; Haskins 2001; Meyer and Sullivan 2003, 2004). For example, income may not fully capture a family's command over resources if it has savings available to draw on during periods of low income, if it is able to borrow money from family or friends, or if it can incur debt to pay for unexpected costs. For this reason, consumption or expenditures are often considered a better gauge of a family's well-being, because this measure reflects the value of what a family actually consumes.

Despite the potential advantage of consumption as a measure of well-being, we are not aware of any studies that use the difference-in-difference methodology to measure the effect of state welfare waiver policies or TANF on consumption. Meyer and Sullivan (2004) examine consumption data for the Consumer Expenditure Survey and Panel Study of Income Dynamics. However, they do not explicitly estimate the impact of welfare waivers or TANF as a bundle, or of specific welfare reform policies. Rather, they test for differences across four time intervals: 1984–1990, 1991–1993, 1994–1995, and 1996–1998.[3] Their difference-in-difference methodology compares consumption trends for single mothers with single women and married mothers. Their findings indicate that consumption for single mothers did not decline in the 1990s, either in absolute terms or relative to the comparison groups of women. In fact, consumption may have improved somewhat, even for women with the least education. Meyer and Sullivan interpret their results to suggest that recent changes in tax and welfare policy have not had detrimental effects on the material conditions of single mothers and their children. Two related studies examine changes in food insecurity after 1994; they also do not estimate the effect of state waivers or TANF per se, but do effectively consider changes over time (Borjas 2001a; Winship and Jencks 2002).[4]

With this background, the remainder of this chapter focuses on the relationship between welfare reform and income and poverty measures. The next section considers the results from random assignment studies. A discussion of the observational studies follows. Although the primary focus is on the effect of various welfare reform policies on income and poverty, one study allows us to compare the effect of the economy on income trends to the effect of welfare reform. In the final section we conclude by summarizing the relationship between reform policies, the economic model, and the traditional objectives of reform.

Experimental Estimates of the Effects of Specific Reforms

All the experimental studies reviewed in previous chapters analyze at least one measure of income. Some consider only the more narrow measure of combined income, others examine a broader measure of family or household income, and a few analyze both. Some also include a measure of poverty. Figures 7.1 and 7.2 summarize the results.

Some studies report impact estimates not only for total income but for a number of different sources of income as well. Specific income sources reported include welfare payments and earnings, which we have discussed in the last two chapters, as well as food stamp payments, child support payments, private transfers, and so on. Although we do not present impact estimates for these other sources of income, we discuss them in the text when doing so is useful in interpreting the total income impacts. Since incomes are measured over varying time intervals, we normalize all estimated impacts to the monthly equivalent.

Financial Work Incentives

Three studies assess the impact of financial work incentives: WRP-IO, CWPDP, and MFIP-IO (see panel A of Figures 7.1 and 7.2). CWPDP does not report a combined income measure, so the estimated impact reported in Figure 7.1 was constructed from the separate impacts of the program on the recipient's earnings and welfare and food stamp payments. The impact estimate so constructed is close to 0, a negative $3 per month in the third year of follow-up. Food stamp payments were the only income component on which CWPDP has a significant positive impact (not shown). The program's impacts on earnings and welfare payments were negative but insignificant (see Figures 5.2 and 6.2).

Administrative data from WRP-IO show a $2 gain in recipient combined monthly income. However, data from the forty-two-month follow-up survey show a $139 gain in monthly household income (including the EITC). The difference between these estimates is difficult to reconcile. WRP-IO had no significant impact on welfare or food stamp payments, and no significant impact on earnings at the forty-two-month follow-up. The program had a large but insignificant positive impact on the reported earnings of other family members (not shown).

MFIP-IO had some favorable impacts on both income and poverty. The strongest results are for recipients. As measured by administrative data, recipient combined income rose by $81 a month and poverty fell by 8.3 percentage points in quarters 8 to 10. However, as measured by the thirty-six-month follow-up survey, there was an $11 decrease in

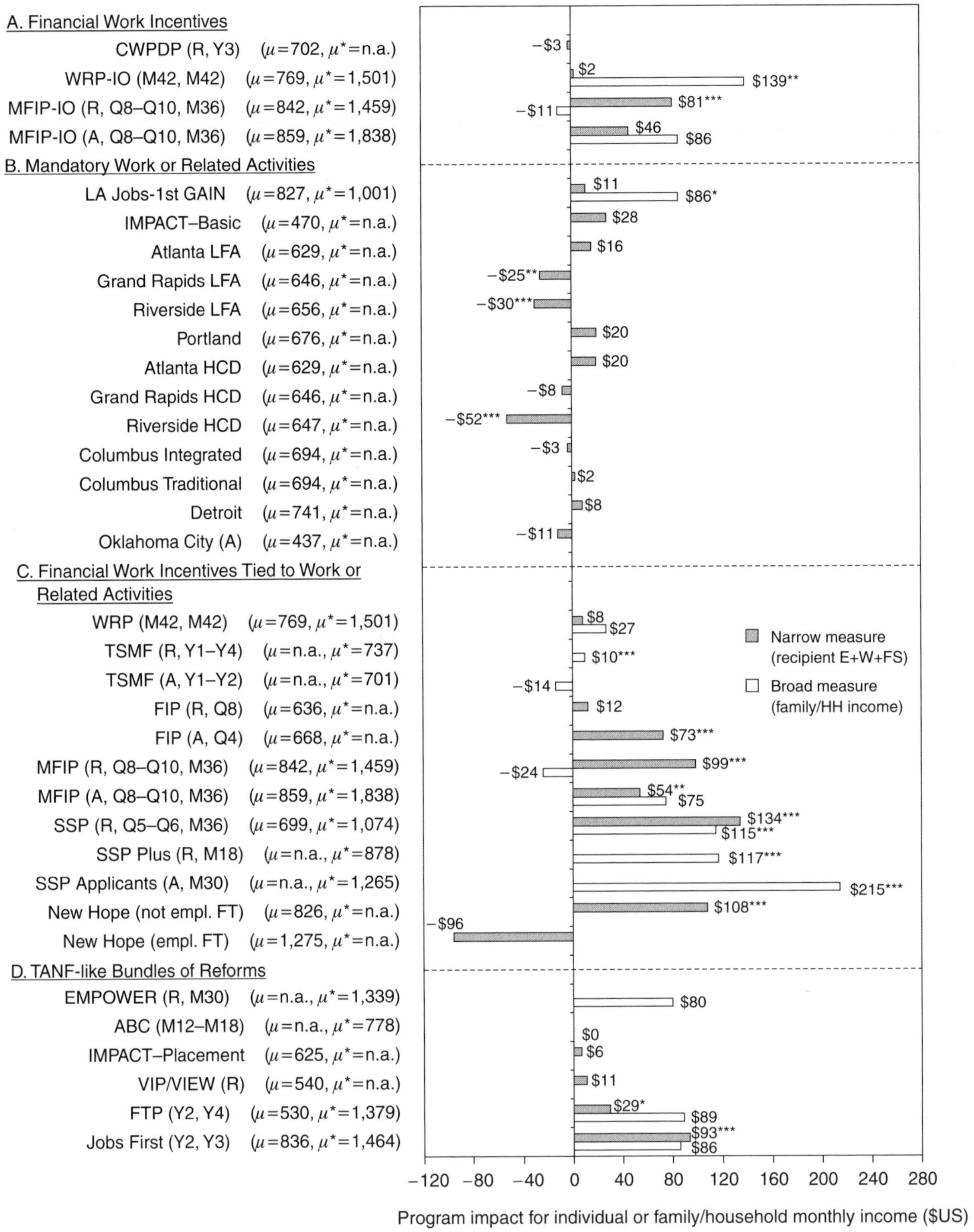

A. Financial Work Incentives

CWPDP (R, Y3) (μ=702, μ*=n.a.) −$3

WRP-IO (M42, M42) (μ=769, μ*=1,501) $2 $139**

MFIP-IO (R, Q8–Q10, M36) (μ=842, μ*=1,459) −$11 $81***

MFIP-IO (A, Q8–Q10, M36) (μ=859, μ*=1,838) $46 $86

B. Mandatory Work or Related Activities

LA Jobs-1st GAIN (μ=827, μ*=1,001) $11 $86*

IMPACT–Basic (μ=470, μ*=n.a.) $28

Atlanta LFA (μ=629, μ*=n.a.) $16

Grand Rapids LFA (μ=646, μ*=n.a.) −$25**

Riverside LFA (μ=656, μ*=n.a.) −$30***

Portland (μ=676, μ*=n.a.) $20

Atlanta HCD (μ=629, μ*=n.a.) $20

Grand Rapids HCD (μ=646, μ*=n.a.) −$8

Riverside HCD (μ=647, μ*=n.a.) −$52***

Columbus Integrated (μ=694, μ*=n.a.) −$3

Columbus Traditional (μ=694, μ*=n.a.) $2

Detroit (μ=741, μ*=n.a.) $8

Oklahoma City (A) (μ=437, μ*=n.a.) −$11

C. Financial Work Incentives Tied to Work or Related Activities

WRP (M42, M42) (μ=769, μ*=1,501) $8 $27

TSMF (R, Y1–Y4) (μ=n.a., μ*=737) $10***

TSMF (A, Y1–Y2) (μ=n.a., μ*=701) −$14

FIP (R, Q8) (μ=636, μ*=n.a.) $12

FIP (A, Q4) (μ=668, μ*=n.a.) $73***

MFIP (R, Q8–Q10, M36) (μ=842, μ*=1,459) −$24 $99***

MFIP (A, Q8–Q10, M36) (μ=859, μ*=1,838) $54** $75

SSP (R, Q5–Q6, M36) (μ=699, μ*=1,074) $134*** $115***

SSP Plus (R, M18) (μ=n.a., μ*=878) $117***

SSP Applicants (A, M30) (μ=n.a., μ*=1,265) $215***

New Hope (not empl. FT) (μ=826, μ*=n.a.) $108***

New Hope (empl. FT) (μ=1,275, μ*=n.a.) −$96

Narrow measure (recipient E+W+FS)
Broad measure (family/HH income)

D. TANF-like Bundles of Reforms

EMPOWER (R, M30) (μ=n.a., μ*=1,339) $80

ABC (M12–M18) (μ=n.a., μ*=778) $0

IMPACT–Placement (μ=625, μ*=n.a.) $6

VIP/VIEW (R) (μ=540, μ*=n.a.) $11

FTP (Y2, Y4) (μ=530, μ*=1,379) $29* $89

Jobs First (Y2, Y3) (μ=836, μ*=1,464) $93*** $86

−120 −80 −40 0 40 80 120 160 200 240 280

Program impact for individual or family/household monthly income ($US)

Note: For full program names, see Table 4.5. Impacts are for two-year follow-up and for recipients (R) and applicants (A) unless otherwise noted. μ = control group mean for narrow income measure; μ* = control group mean for broad income measure; M = month, Q = quarter; Y = year; E = earnings; W = welfare payments; FS = food stamp payments; HH = household; FT = full-time; n.a.=not applicable or not available. Significant at the ***1%, **5%, *10% level.

Figure 7.1
Estimated impacts of welfare reform on monthly income from experimental studies. *Source:* See Appendix Table A.4.

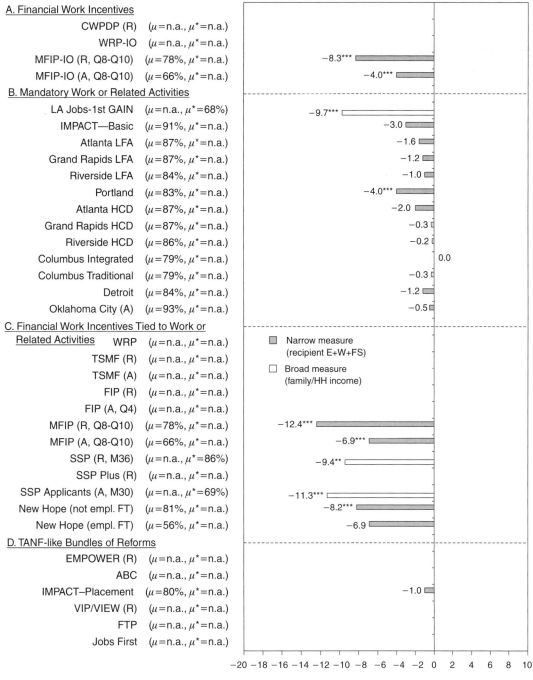

A. Financial Work Incentives
CWPDP (R) (μ=n.a., μ^*=n.a.)
WRP-IO (μ=n.a., μ^*=n.a.)
MFIP-IO (R, Q8-Q10) (μ=78%, μ^*=n.a.) −8.3***
MFIP-IO (A, Q8-Q10) (μ=66%, μ^*=n.a.) −4.0***
B. Mandatory Work or Related Activities
LA Jobs-1st GAIN (μ=n.a., μ^*=68%) −9.7***
IMPACT—Basic (μ=91%, μ^*=n.a.) −3.0
Atlanta LFA (μ=87%, μ^*=n.a.) −1.6
Grand Rapids LFA (μ=87%, μ^*=n.a.) −1.2
Riverside LFA (μ=84%, μ^*=n.a.) −1.0
Portland (μ=83%, μ^*=n.a.) −4.0***
Atlanta HCD (μ=87%, μ^*=n.a.) −2.0
Grand Rapids HCD (μ=87%, μ^*=n.a.) −0.3
Riverside HCD (μ=86%, μ^*=n.a.) −0.2
Columbus Integrated (μ=79%, μ^*=n.a.) 0.0
Columbus Traditional (μ=79%, μ^*=n.a.) −0.3
Detroit (μ=84%, μ^*=n.a.) −1.2
Oklahoma City (A) (μ=93%, μ^*=n.a.) −0.5
C. Financial Work Incentives Tied to Work or Related Activities
WRP (μ=n.a., μ^*=n.a.)
TSMF (R) (μ=n.a., μ^*=n.a.)
TSMF (A) (μ=n.a., μ^*=n.a.)
FIP (R) (μ=n.a., μ^*=n.a.)
FIP (A, Q4) (μ=n.a., μ^*=n.a.)
MFIP (R, Q8-Q10) (μ=78%, μ^*=n.a.) −12.4***
MFIP (A, Q8-Q10) (μ=66%, μ^*=n.a.) −6.9***
SSP (R, M36) (μ=n.a., μ^*=86%) −9.4**
SSP Plus (R) (μ=n.a., μ^*=n.a.)
SSP Applicants (A, M30) (μ=n.a., μ^*=69%) −11.3***
New Hope (not empl. FT) (μ=81%, μ^*=n.a.) −8.2***
New Hope (empl. FT) (μ=56%, μ^*=n.a.) −6.9
D. TANF-like Bundles of Reforms
EMPOWER (R) (μ=n.a., μ^*=n.a.)
ABC (μ=n.a., μ^*=n.a.)
IMPACT–Placement (μ=80%, μ^*=n.a.) −1.0
VIP/VIEW (R) (μ=n.a., μ^*=n.a.)
FTP (μ=n.a., μ^*=n.a.)
Jobs First (μ=n.a., μ^*=n.a.)

Narrow measure (recipient E+W+FS)
Broad measure (family/HH income)

−20 −18 −16 −14 −12 −10 −8 −6 −4 −2 0 2 4 6 8 10

Program impact for poverty rate based on individual or family/household monthly income (percentage points)

Note: For full program names, see Table 4.5. Impacts are for two-year follow-up and for recipients (R) and applicants (A) unless otherwise noted. μ = control group mean for narrow income measure; μ^* = control group mean for broad income measure; M = month, Q = quarter; Y = year; E = earnings; W = welfare payments; FS = food stamp payments; HH = household; FT = full-time; n.a.=not available. Significant at the ***1%, **5%, *10% level.

Figure 7.2
Estimated impacts of welfare reform on poverty from experimental studies. *Source:* See Appendix Table A.4.

monthly family income. This discrepancy may be due to differential re-porting bias between the treatment and the control groups, which im-plies that the results based on administrative data are more reliable.[5] To the extent that MFIP-IO generated income gains, they were the result of higher welfare and (cashed-out) food stamp payments generated by the financial work incentives: MFIP-IO raised combined welfare and food stamp payments for both applicants and recipients, by about the same dollar amount ($91–$97 dollars per month; not shown). Other-wise, MFIP-IO generally had smaller effects on the applicant group.

Mandatory Work or Related Activities

All the programs that focus on mandatory work-related activities report measures of income and poverty at the end of two years (see panel B of Figures 7.1 and 7.2). Three of the NEWWS programs had sig-nificant negative impacts on recipient combined income based on admin-istrative data, ranging from −$25 to −$52 per month. Results from the other programs all show smaller insignificant impacts, either negative (three NEWWS programs) or positive (five NEWWS programs, Los An-geles, and IMPACT).[6] The only statistically significant impact for the broader measure of household income comes from combined adminis-trative and survey data from Los Angeles Jobs-First GAIN.[7] It shows an $86 impact on monthly household income inclusive of the EITC and payroll taxes, which amounts to a 9 percent increase. The larger positive impact for this measure compared with the measure of recipient income is due to a larger impact in respondent-reported earnings (versus admin-istrative data) and to the EITC (Freedman, Knab et al. 2000).

With two exceptions, most of the poverty impacts are insignificant and small in magnitude. All are negative (or zero), even in those cases where incomes fell on average. The two significant impacts for Los An-geles Jobs-First GAIN and Portland were associated with larger income gains on average. At the same time, Los Angeles Jobs-First GAIN and several of the NEWWS programs resulted in a slight increase in families with recipient combined income below 50 percent of the poverty line. This result suggests that, although these programs are neutral or positive for recipients near the poverty line, they may make those near the bot-tom of the income distribution worse off (Freedman, Friedlander et al. 2000; Freedman, Knab et al. 2000; not shown).

Five-year data for the eleven NEWWS programs provide longer-run information on recipient combined income (plus the EITC, net of payroll taxes). The impacts on monthly income for each follow-up year are shown in Figure 7.3. By year 5, there is only one significant income im-pact in any of the sites (a negative impact in Riverside HCD; data are not

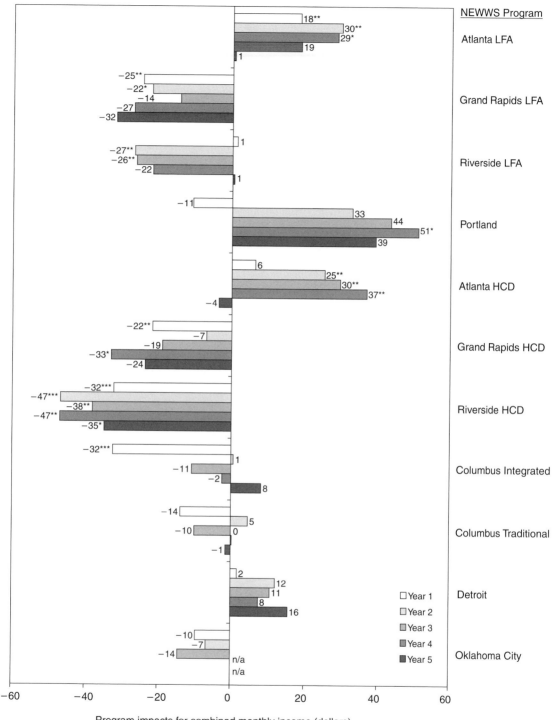

Figure 7.3

Estimated impacts of mandatory work or related activities on combined monthly income from eleven NEWWS programs, years 1 to 5. *Source:* Hamilton et al. (2001), table E.1.

available for Oklahoma). The year-5 impact estimates are almost equally divided among negative impacts, impacts close to zero, and positive impacts.

There is no clear difference between the placement- and skills-oriented programs. Portland's mixed approach has the largest five-year income and two-year poverty impacts. That program, however, excluded some recipients with substantial barriers to work, so it is not clear if similar impacts would be found for a more disadvantaged population. Furthermore, the timing pattern in the impact estimates is not consistent across sites, although the program impact fades in a majority of them. For example, Portland has increasing positive impacts in years 2 and 3 followed by the largest positive impact of all the sites in year 4 ($51 dollars per month or just over $600 in annual combined income; $p < .10$). But the impact shrinks in year 5. At the other extreme, Riverside HCD has negative and significant impacts of $35 or more per month (over $400 per year) in all but the first year, although the year 5 impact is somewhat less negative than year 4.

The modest impacts of these programs on income and poverty are consistent with the combination of negative impacts on welfare payments (see Figure 5.2) and positive earnings impacts (see Figure 6.2). The decline in welfare payments, in turn, was due to the high benefit-reduction rates under the old AFDC rules (which applied to both the treatment and the control groups in NEWWS) that caused welfare payments to fall as earnings rose. Declines in food stamp payments among these programs were also almost always significant as well (not shown).

Financial Work Incentives Tied to Work or Related Activities

WRP and TSMF, which combined weak financial work incentives and mandatory work-related activities, had small and generally insignificant effects on income (see panel C of Figure 7.1). FIP and MFIP, which combined strong financial work incentives with mandatory work-related activities, generally had positive and significant effects on income. In the case of MFIP recipients, a survey-based measure of family income yielded a negative impact, in contrast to the sizable positive impact from the measure based on administrative data. As discussed above, this discrepancy is likely to be the result of differential reporting biases for treatment versus control group members, again implying that the estimates based on administrative data are more reliable (Miller et al. 2000). MFIP also produced substantial reductions in poverty rates (see panel C of Figure 7.2).

The difference in the impacts that these four programs had on income is consistent with their different impacts on welfare payments (see Figure 5.2) and earnings (see Figure 6.2). WRP and TSMF, with their weak financial incentives, generated relatively small declines in welfare payments and relatively small gains in earnings. These two effects roughly offset each other, resulting in small changes in income. FIP decreased welfare payments among recipients but left them roughly unchanged among applicants. It raised the earnings of both groups, but the increase was greater among applicants. As a result, income rose slightly among recipients, but substantially among applicants. As discussed in Chapter 6, the differences between groups in the impacts of the program may have to do with differences in the way the two groups satisfied the program's work-related activity mandate. MFIP, with its generous financial incentive, increased both welfare payments and earnings. As a result, income rose substantially (at least as measured by administrative data).

Of the four programs that tie financial incentives to work outside the welfare system, three—the SSP programs—substantially increased income (and reduced poverty when reported).[8] New Hope increased income (and reduced poverty) by a similar amount among families who did not initially satisfy its hours requirement. Among families initially working full-time, however, New Hope decreased income and reduced poverty by substantial, but insignificant, amounts.

SSP decreased welfare payments by essentially the same amount by which it increased earnings (see Figures 5.2 and 6.2). It increased incomes because of the earnings supplements paid to working participants. Among families not initially employed full-time, New Hope increased earnings, albeit insignificantly, and had essentially no effect on welfare payments. Like SSP, its earnings supplements played an important role in raising incomes. Among families working full-time initially, New Hope decreased earnings and welfare payments. Although this group also received earnings supplements, they were insufficient to generate any income gains for this group.

Observational Estimates of the Effects of Specific Reforms

Only a handful of observational studies have analyzed family income, and even fewer have examined poverty (see Figure 7.4). Three observational studies estimate the effect of reform as a bundle. Only one estimates the effect of a specific reform policy. As in the last two chapters, we add to what is known about the effects of specific reforms by using data from Jobs First and FTP to construct difference-in-difference estimates of the mechanical effects of time limits.

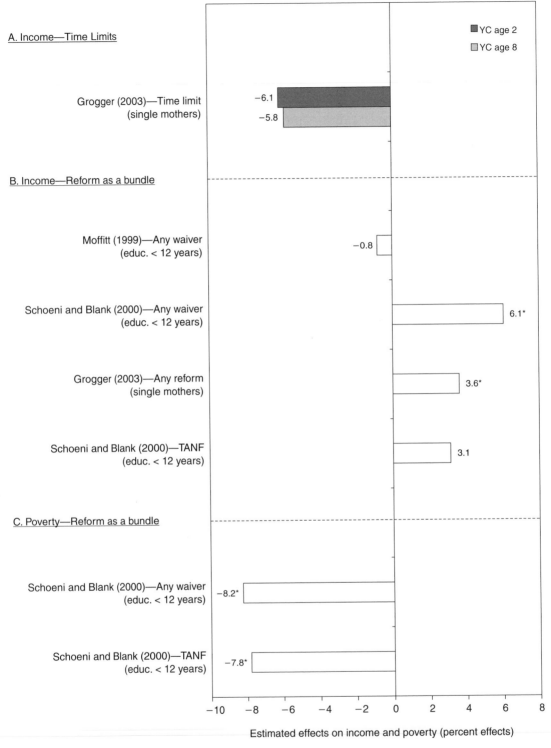

A. Income—Time Limits

Grogger (2003)—Time limit
(single mothers)
−6.1
−5.8

B. Income—Reform as a bundle

Moffitt (1999)—Any waiver
(educ. < 12 years)
−0.8

Schoeni and Blank (2000)—Any waiver
(educ. < 12 years)
6.1*

Grogger (2003)—Any reform
(single mothers)
3.6*

Schoeni and Blank (2000)—TANF
(educ. < 12 years)
3.1

C. Poverty—Reform as a bundle

Schoeni and Blank (2000)—Any waiver
(educ. < 12 years)
−8.2*

Schoeni and Blank (2000)—TANF
(educ. < 12 years)
−7.8*

YC age 2
YC age 8

−10   −8   −6   −4   −2   0   2   4   6   8

Estimated effects on income and poverty (percent effects)

Note: Asterisks denote results based on coefficients that are significant at the 10 percent level or better. YC = youngest child. The white bars denote studies where no differentiation was made regarding children's age.

Figure 7.4
Results from observational studies of the effects of reform on income and poverty.

All the existing studies in this literature analyze the CPS, which is the primary nationally representative data source with information on annual family income. The Annual Demographic Supplement to the March CPS is the source used by the Census Bureau to calculate poverty rates on an annual basis; hence these studies can implement a measure of income (annual family pretax cash income) and poverty that follows the concepts employed by the Census Bureau in their calculations.

Like the studies of welfare use and earnings that are based on survey data, some of these analyses use aggregated micro data, whereas others analyze the individual-level micro data directly. Some analyze the level of income; others analyze the logarithm of income. The study populations include either all women or female-headed families in a given age range (typically sixteen to fifty-four). Like other observational studies, the income models typically include controls for the business cycle (for example, current and lagged unemployment rate), demographic characteristics of the recipient (for example, age, education, and race/ethnicity), and other policy variables (for example, maximum welfare-benefit level, minimum wage, and EITC). All include state and year dummies to control for state and period effects. Some models also include state-specific time trends.

Time Limits

Grogger's (2003) study is the only observational analysis of income to consider the effect of a specific TANF reform, in this case, the behavioral effects of time limits. In addition to estimating the impact of reform as a bundle (discussed below), Grogger's linear and log models of income, like the models of welfare use, employment, labor supply, and earnings discussed in Chapters 5 and 6, allow the effect of time limits to vary with the age of the youngest child. In this case, the effect is not statistically significant. However, the estimated impact is limited to the period before most recipients began reaching the time limit.

To estimate the mechanical effects of time limits, we construct difference-in-difference estimates based on results from Jobs First and FTP, as in Chapters 5 and 6. Figure 7.5 plots quarterly impact estimates of the effects of the two programs on monthly combined recipient income. Both programs increased income in the pre–time limit period, the result of their financial work incentives. The increase was greater in Jobs First, which had the more generous incentive.

Jobs First's impact on income began to fall after quarter 5. Between quarters 7 and 8, when the program's time limit first began to bind, its impact fell from $89 to $50. Relative to the control group's mean

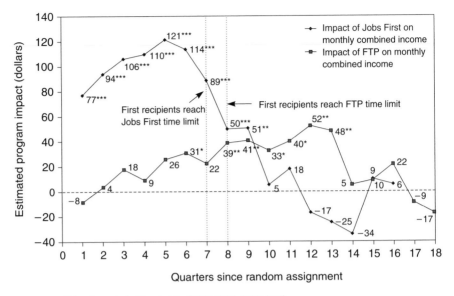

Figure 7.5
Estimated impacts of Jobs First and FTP on monthly income, quarters 1 to 18. *Source:* Jobs First: Bloom et al. (2002), table B.1; FTP: Bloom et al. (2000), table B.1.

monthly earnings in quarter 7 of $842, this decrease represents a 4.6 percent decline. The program's impact continued to decline thereafter, the result of decreases in welfare use (see Figure 5.6) and earnings (see Figure 6.7). By quarter 10, the program's impact on income was insignificantly different from zero and it remained so through quarter 16.

The pattern in FTP is different. Because recipients accumulated months on welfare at a slower rate in FTP, the mechanical effect of its time limit was smaller. In conjunction with its positive effect on earnings, this caused the impact of FTP on income to remain roughly constant, or to even rise slightly, for five quarters after its time limit first began to bind in quarter 8. After quarter 13, the program's impact on income fell, the result of its falling impact on earnings (see Figure 6.7). The decline in the program's impact on income was much smaller than the corresponding decline in its impact on earnings. The reason is that its negative impact on welfare use began to abate (see Figure 5.6).

In comparing Jobs First and FTP, it appears that FTP participants could more readily cushion the decline in earnings impacts with increases in welfare use. Presumably, they were able to do so because fewer of them actually reached the time limit. For the Jobs First participants who exhausted their benefits, using welfare to cushion the decline in earnings that followed quarter 9 was not an option.

Estimates of the Effects of Reform as a Bundle

As shown in panel D of Figures 7.1 and 7.2, four of the six experimental programs that include TANF-like bundles of reforms—EMPOWER, IMPACT, VIP/VIEW, and ABC—yielded no significant impacts on income or, when measured, poverty. Of these four programs, IMPACT had the largest positive (and significant) impact on earnings (see Figure 6.2), but it also resulted in a significant reduction in welfare payments (see Figure 5.2). As noted in Chapter 4, a sizable fraction of the control group in three of these four studies believed that the time limits applied to them, which would bias the estimated impacts of these programs toward zero. FTP and Jobs First yielded positive income impacts during the pre–time limit period for measures of recipient combined income. However, as discussed above, those impacts faded once recipients began to exhaust their benefits. The impact estimates for broader measures of household income, also measured after time limits begin to take effect, are likewise insignificant, albeit positive.

Bitler, Gelbach, and Hoynes (2003) reanalyze the Jobs First data to determine the distributional impacts of the reforms. They estimate treatment effects at different percentiles of the distribution of combined quarterly income (earnings plus TANF and food stamps) and find that mean effects conceal considerable variation across the distribution. In the pre–time limit period (the first seven quarters), the treatment effect for combined quarterly income is $0 for the bottom tenth of the distribution, positive but less than $200 until about the 50th percentile, and then peaks at $800 at about the 80th percentile. This compares with their estimated mean treatment effect of $296 for the pre–time limit period. In the post–time limit period, the mean treatment effect is $10. When the entire distribution is considered, the treatment effect is zero until the 18th percentile; negative between the 18th and 43rd percentile and above the 90th percentile; and positive elsewhere. At the extremes, the effects range from −$300 to $300, considerably different from the mean effect near zero.

All three observational studies summarized in panel B of Figure 7.4 estimate the determinants of annual pretax family income. Moffitt (1999) covers the shortest interval of time and finds no statistically significant effects of waivers on income for women aged sixteen to fifty-four (not shown), or for the subset with less than twelve years of schooling. Schoeni and Blank (2000), with four additional years in their time series, find that waiver-based reform raises family income by 6.1 percent for women with fewer than twelve years of schooling (a statistically significant effect). The effect of TANF is 3.1 percent for the same group, but statistically insignificant. These researchers found no effect of waivers or TANF on the incomes of women with higher levels of education (not shown), which would be expected given that this group is less likely to be affected by welfare reform.

Grogger (2003) combines waivers and TANF into one measure of any reform and finds that family income among female family heads rises by 3.6 percent for women whose youngest child is under age 1 (9.8 percent for a model estimated in logs, not shown).[9] The interaction between the reform dummy and age of the youngest child (not shown) suggests that the impact on family income declines with the youngest child's age, an effect that is significant only in the log model. The larger effect Grogger finds may result from the fact that he limits his sample to female-headed families. This population is likely to be most affected by welfare reform: hence the larger estimated impact.

Schoeni and Blank (2000) also consider the distributional effects of waivers and TANF by estimating equations of the log of the 20th and 50th percentiles of family income for women aged sixteen to fifty-four, and the 20th/50th ratio (not shown). Waivers are estimated to raise family incomes for high school dropout women at the 20th and 50th percentiles by about 8–10 percent (a statistically significant effect). TANF, however, only has a statistically significant and positive effect on the 50th percentile of family income for women in the lowest education category. The lack of an effect at the 20th percentile leads to an estimated widening of the 20th–50th gap because of the implementation of TANF.

Only Schoeni and Blank (2000) model the poverty rate. Their results are shown in panel C of Figure 7.4. Consistent with their findings for income, Schoeni and Blank report a statistically significant decline in the poverty rate for women with fewer than twelve years of schooling, equal to about 8 percent for both the implementation of waivers and the implementation of TANF. There is no evidence to suggest that waivers or TANF affected the poverty rate for women with twelve or more years of schooling (not shown).

Estimates of the Effect of the Economy

Of the studies listed in Figure 7.4, the effect of the economy on income or poverty can be ascertained only for Grogger's (2003) study.[10] The estimate from that analysis indicates that a 2.7-percentage-point decline in the unemployment rate—the magnitude of the decline that occurred between 1993 and 1999—would have increased the average income of single mothers by 2.8 percent. Given that single mothers' incomes increased 23 percent between 1993 and 1999, the economic expansion, as captured by the fall in the unemployment rate, can explain about 12 percent of the increase in income. On the one hand, this impact is smaller than the corresponding estimates of the effect of the economy on the welfare caseload (see Chapter 5) and single mothers' employment and labor supply (see Chapter 6). On the other hand, the estimated effect of the economy on the incomes of single mothers, at 2.8 percent, is only just below the estimated effects of reform for the same group (see Grogger's (2003) result plotted in Figure 7.4).

Summary

The studies reviewed in this chapter provide a varied picture of the effect of reform on both income and poverty. Above we noted that the estimated effects of income are not directly useful for testing the predictions of the model in Chapter 3. Nevertheless, it is crucial to understand how reform has affected these important measures of families' economic well-being, particularly since one of the traditional goals of welfare policy is to alleviate need.

The evidence from experimental and observational studies indicates that some reform policies can raise incomes and reduce poverty and thereby alleviate need, although this is not the case for all reforms. Generous financial work incentives generate the strongest income gains and antipoverty effects, especially when they are tied to work. As noted in Chapter 5, however, the trade-off for alleviating need is that financial work incentives increase welfare use, running counter to the objective of reducing dependency. Work requirements alone have relatively weak effects on family income and poverty, but they do raise self-sufficiency by increasing the proportion of income from earnings. Finally, time limits appear to have little anticipatory effect on income, although this conclusion is based on a single study.

Although the antipoverty effectiveness of financial work incentives appears to be quite robust, recipients' income levels remain relatively low. Consequently their rates of poverty remain relatively high. For example, in the experimental studies that include financial work incentives (see panels A, C, and D of Figure 7.2), the poverty rate for the treatment group falls below 50 percent in just one case. The proportion with very low incomes may not move much at all, and many of those raised above the poverty line still remain "near poor."

In terms of welfare reform as a bundle, the evidence suggests that incomes for disadvantaged women have risen and their poverty rate has fallen, at least in the period before time limits become binding. This result may be surprising in light of the fact that, with the exception of gen-

erous financial work incentives, none of the individual reforms appears
to raise income or reduce poverty by amounts that are large enough to
explain the overall favorable impacts. Most states have not implemented
financial work incentives as generous as those that generated the strongest income gains in the experimental studies, so it is unlikely that this
policy reform can explain the favorable income and poverty trends. One
explanation for this apparent contradiction is that welfare reform raised
the incomes of those who were deterred by the reforms from entering
welfare in the first place. Such "nonentrants" would not be captured in
the experimental studies, because the experiments are limited to families
receiving (or applying for) welfare. Alternatively, the estimates of reform
as a bundle based on observational studies may overstate the true effect
of reform because of inadequate controls for confounding factors.

Moreover, the observational estimates are based on data reported
prior to the beginning of time limits' mechanical effects. As time limits
begin to affect a larger share of the recipient population, the overall income gains may not be sustained, but a lot will depend on the rate at
which recipients exhaust their benefits. Jobs First and FTP both increased income during the pre–time limit period. In Jobs First, where recipients accumulated months on welfare and exhausted their benefits relatively quickly, those gains disappeared shortly after the time limit began
to bind. In FTP, where accumulation rates were lower and fewer recipients exhausted their benefits, income gains persisted a bit longer.

It is important to keep in mind that much of this chapter has focused
on income measures that are rarely as comprehensive as would be desired to fully evaluate changes in well-being. Most observational studies
consider only family income before taxes and exclusive of in-kind benefits, and underreporting of income may bias results. Many of the experimental evaluations use a concept of income limited to earnings and social welfare benefits (for example, welfare and food stamp benefits in the
U.S. experiments) for the recipient. Even if a comprehensive income
measure were available, it might not fully reflect the individual or family's command over resources. Other studies of consumption patterns,
mentioned at the outset of this chapter, suggest that the income patterns
discussed here are reflected in consumption patterns as well. Nevertheless, further research on broader measures of well-being would usefully
complement efforts that have focused on traditional, if limited, measures
of income.

CHAPTER EIGHT

Family Structure

Jacob Alex Klerman

As noted in Chapter 1, in addition to promoting work and reducing dependency, PRWORA's goals specifically included family structure considerations: to see that children are cared for in their own homes, to promote marriage, to encourage the formation and maintenance of two-parent families, and to reduce the incidence of out-of-wedlock childbearing. A number of reforms implemented by the states were designed to directly affect marriage and childbearing. For example, states aimed to diminish any disincentive toward marriage associated with welfare eligibility rules by eliminating differences in eligibility for two-parent versus one-parent families (for example, the "100-hour rule" and work history requirement).[1] In order to reduce childbearing among mothers already on welfare, a number of states instituted family caps, which eliminated (or reduced) the increase in the welfare benefit for any child born while the mother was on welfare. Minor residency requirements, which require teen parents to live with their own parents in order to receive welfare benefits, are designed to make unwed teen childbearing less attractive. Other provisions of welfare reform not specifically intended to affect marriage or childbearing (or fertility, as it is sometimes referred to in the literature) could have indirect effects on these outcomes, as well.

The economic model in Chapter 3 provides predictions regarding the impact of welfare policies on welfare use and labor market behavior. Decisions regarding marriage and childbearing are arguably more complex, although the economic approach can be used to model these decisions as well. Hence, as we shift our attention to consider the impacts of welfare reform on family structure, we begin in the next section by extending our theoretical model to incorporate decisions regarding marriage and childbearing. We then consider the evidence from experimental and observational studies on the effects of welfare reform on these two outcomes, respectively.

Theoretical Framework and Methodological Issues

In order to make predictions about the effects of welfare reform on family structure, we need to extend the theoretical model presented in Chapter 3. The available data sources to analyze marriage and childbearing outcomes also differ to some extent from those that are available to study welfare use, labor market behavior, and income. In this section, we first extend the theory that is relevant for analyzing the effects of welfare reform on family structure. We then consider the special methodological issues raised by the nature of the available data.

Expanding the Theoretical Framework

To analyze the implications for welfare reform on marriage and childbearing and expand the theoretical framework discussed in Chapter 3, we consider a consumer who has preferences regarding marriage and children as well as regarding leisure and income. She maximizes her utility by choosing whether to marry and whether to have a child, in addition to whether to receive welfare and how much to work.

These choices will be affected by a myriad of factors that determine preferences and the opportunity set. As with the simple case developed in Chapter 3, welfare benefits and labor market opportunities may affect consumers' choices. When the model is expanded to include marriage and childbearing, consumers' opportunity sets will be affected by the pool of potential spouses and the jobs available to them, as well as by the direct utility of marriage and children.

Our interest, however, is in the effect of welfare reform policies on marriage and childbearing, holding these other factors constant. Assume for the moment that welfare is available to single mothers, but not to childless or married women.[2] Consider a woman jointly making life choices regarding marriage, childbearing, work, and welfare receipt. Like her decisions about work and welfare, her decisions about how many children to have and whether to marry will depend upon the utility associated with those choices. In this simplified environment, a welfare program will lower the costs of unwed childbearing relative to the other alternatives. Since only unmarried motherhood makes the woman eligible for welfare, the existence of a welfare program reduces the relative benefits of marriage and increases the benefits of having at least one child and having that child while unmarried.

Similarly, policy changes that make welfare relatively more attractive (for example, higher benefit levels or financial work incentives) can be expected to reduce marriage and raise both the share of women having at least one child and the share of women having at least one nonmarital birth. Conversely, policy changes that make welfare relatively less attractive (for example, a family cap, mandatory work-related activities, or time limits) can be expected to increase marriage and reduce both the share of women having at least one birth and the share with at least one nonmarital birth.

This simple model assumes that welfare is not available to married couples. However, welfare was available to married couples under the AFDC Unemployed Parent (AFDC-UP) program and continues to be available under TANF. Compared with a welfare program that is only available to unmarried women, making welfare payments available to married couples reduces the disincentives for marriage and marital childbearing. Thus policies that make welfare available to or more attractive for two-parent families would be expected to increase marriage and marital births.

Even allowing for welfare payments to married parents, this simplified model of marriage and childbearing abstracts from a number of potentially important factors that influence behavior. First, marriage and childbearing choices are inherently durable, that is, they affect utility in the future as well as today. For that reason, choices regarding marriage and childbearing are best viewed within a dynamic framework where expected future costs and benefits enter into current decision making. Second, marriage and particularly childbearing are time-intensive activities that may involve trade-offs with time devoted to market and nonmarket activities. For example, increased work may limit the time available to search for a suitable marriage partner. Then again, interactions at the workplace may ease marital search and provide a better set of potential spouses.

The notion of a marriage market suggests other mechanisms by which welfare reform might affect marriage. For example, if welfare-to-work programs succeed in raising earnings and income, they might make women more attractive as spouses and thus raise the propensity to marry. Higher income, however, would also make women more self-sufficient and perhaps less likely to marry. As yet another example, low income may increase the emotional and financial strain on a marriage, so that welfare reforms that raise total income might be expected to increase marriage and, in particular, to help those currently married to stay married.

Accounting for these other considerations, the predicted effects of welfare reform on marriage and childbearing are more ambiguous than what would follow from the simple stylized model. While the simple model would predict, for example, that financial work incentives would decrease marriage because they make welfare more attractive, the increased employment associated with such incentives may enhance the prospects for marriage through workplace interactions. The higher income that results from financial work incentives may also increase the likelihood that married couples remain married. As another example, if increased work effort limits opportunities for marital search, then work requirements may decrease marriage, even though they make welfare less attractive.

Predictions for two types of policy reforms may be less ambiguous. To encourage marriage, many states have reduced or eliminated the differential treatment of two-parent families under their TANF programs, either through equalized eligibility rules (for example, elimination of the 100-hour rule or work history requirement) or through more liberal treatment of the spouse's earnings (for example, disregards). But these eligibility and disregard changes were never adopted in isolation. In the experimental evaluations, for example, such reforms often accompanied financial work incentives, which as argued above may have mixed impacts on marriage.

The one policy reform whose effect on childbearing seems fairly clear is the family cap. By reducing the increase in benefits to women who have children while on welfare, family caps should reduce births to welfare recipients.[3] Nevertheless, because the dollar amounts involved tend to be small, the family cap may have little effect on behavior.

Methodological Issues

Although welfare reform was motivated in part by trends in marriage and childbearing, these outcomes are less well studied in both the experimental and the observational literatures. Of the random assignment studies we have analyzed in previous chapters, WRP, IMPACT, TSMF, FIP, New Hope, SSP Plus, SSP Applicants, and VIP/VIEW do not analyze either marriage or childbearing. CWPDP, MFIP, and SSP examine only marriage, while AWWDP and FDP consider only childbearing. The remaining programs—L.A. Jobs-First GAIN, the eleven NEWWS programs, EMPOWER, ABC, FTP, and Jobs First—analyze both outcomes. One observational study considers marriage, while four observational studies consider childbearing.

Compared with the research on outcomes examined in Chapters 5, 6, and 7, the more limited research on marriage and childbearing can be attributed to several factors. First, although PRWORA was motivated in part by goals related to marriage and childbearing, most of the state programs evaluated under waivers were designed primarily to influence work and welfare use. Even so, a few of the random assignment evaluations that included family caps, minor residency requirements, and changes in two-parent eligibility requirements do not evaluate either marriage or childbearing (for example, IMPACT and VIP/VIEW).

Second, unlike welfare use, employment, and earnings, marriage and childbearing behavior are harder to measure using administrative data on welfare recipients (although this is the source of information on childbearing for FDP and AWWDP), especially for those off of welfare. Thus those experimental studies that do not have participant surveys cannot easily analyze these outcomes.

Third, even when resources are devoted to measuring these outcomes in experimental studies, changes in marital status and additional childbearing while on welfare are relatively rare events. Moreover, changes in marriage and childbearing behavior may not take place immediately. As a result, studies with small samples or short follow-up periods may be less likely to detect changes in these outcomes. In addition, survey data in experimental studies often have smaller samples and are subject to measurement error (for example, recall bias and differential non-response), leading these analyses to have lower power.[4] Consequently, when these outcomes are included in impact analyses, there may be limited statistical power to detect changes in behavior.

Fourth, welfare reform may have its most important effects on the marriage and childbearing behavior of women who are not on welfare. Although welfare reform may affect the likelihood that a woman on welfare has additional children, gets married, or stays married, it should also affect marriage- and childbearing-related decisions for women who are at risk of welfare participation. Indeed, many first-time welfare entries historically were precipitated by a first birth to an unmarried woman. Such entries were particularly important from a policy perspective, because they disproportionately resulted in long-term welfare spells (Bane and Ellwood 1994).

However, as noted in Chapter 4, conventional experimental studies are not designed to capture welfare entry effects. Thus, to the extent that welfare reform reduces first births to unmarried women, this effect will not be detected by experiments. This significant limitation of the existing experiments underlines the need for high-quality observational studies.

Several sources of data are available to study marriage and childbearing using econometric methods. Two studies we discuss below use the CPS to analyze current marital status and household composition; a third study relies on aggregate state-level vital statistics data on marriage and divorce rates.[5] In the case of childbearing, several studies employ information on individual births available from birth certificate records compiled by the National Center for Health Statistics. These vital statistics data include information on essentially all births, whether or not the mother is on welfare. Studies based on these data thus have very large samples and can account for entry effects.

The large samples also permit subgroup analyses, which allow for some consistency checks. For example, we would expect the effects of reform on childbearing to be larger for the subgroups with a larger proportion of women on welfare (or with a higher probability of entering welfare). Failure to find such effects can be interpreted as evidence against a claim of causality. Unfortunately, these vital statistics data do not include information on current, past, or future welfare receipt, and, in general, they have not been linked to administrative data from the welfare or UI systems.

Experimental Estimates of the Effects of Specific Reforms on Marriage

Figure 8.1 presents percentage-point impact estimates for the effects of various reforms on marriage. All of these results are based on survey data. In most cases, the outcome analyzed is whether the participant is married and living with a spouse at the time of the interview. As in previous chapters, we report initial follow-up results (usually about two years postrandomization) and, where available, longer-term results (usually about five years postrandomization). As in other chapters, the row labels indicate the length of the follow-up interval and whether the result refers to applicants or recipients. The average rate of marriage among the control group is provided in parentheses. Asterisks denote significance levels.

Financial Work Incentives

We begin by considering financial work incentives. Panel A of Figure 8.1 presents results for two programs that provided financial work incentives for single recipients (and two-parent recipients). CWPDP had no significant effect on marriage for single-parent cases (a 0.1-percentage-point increase), but significantly increased marriage for two-parent cases (a 6.2-percentage-point increase). The effect appears to be the result of less divorce (Hu 2003). The interpretation of these results is, however, complicated by policy bundling. While the CWPDP waiver included a financial work incentive, it also included a cut in the AFDC benefit level (at zero earnings) and removed some of the restrictions on the eligibility of two-parent families (specifically the 100-hour rule). It is

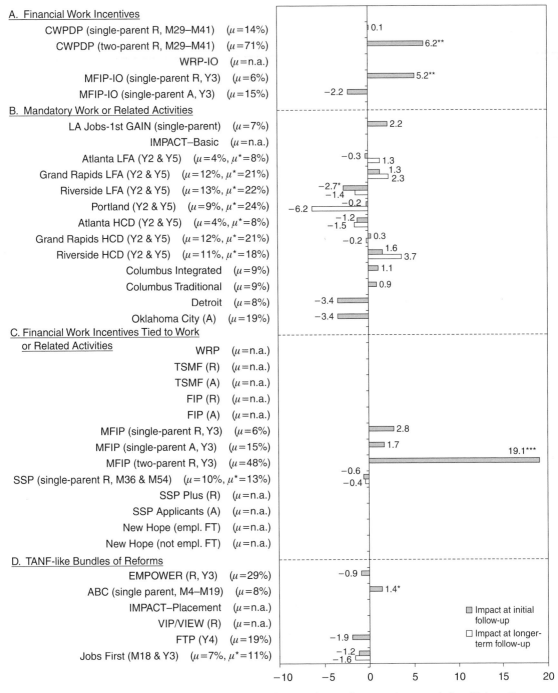

A. Financial Work Incentives

- CWPDP (single-parent R, M29–M41) (μ=14%) — 0.1
- CWPDP (two-parent R, M29–M41) (μ=71%) — 6.2**
- WRP-IO (μ=n.a.)
- MFIP-IO (single-parent R, Y3) (μ=6%) — 5.2**
- MFIP-IO (single-parent A, Y3) (μ=15%) — −2.2

B. Mandatory Work or Related Activities

- LA Jobs-1st GAIN (single-parent) (μ=7%) — 2.2
- IMPACT–Basic (μ=n.a.)
- Atlanta LFA (Y2 & Y5) (μ=4%, μ^*=8%) — −0.3, 1.3
- Grand Rapids LFA (Y2 & Y5) (μ=12%, μ^*=21%) — 1.3, 2.3
- Riverside LFA (Y2 & Y5) (μ=13%, μ^*=22%) — −2.7*, −1.4
- Portland (Y2 & Y5) (μ=9%, μ^*=24%) — −0.2, −6.2
- Atlanta HCD (Y2 & Y5) (μ=4%, μ^*=8%) — −1.2, −1.5
- Grand Rapids HCD (Y2 & Y5) (μ=12%, μ^*=21%) — 0.3, −0.2
- Riverside HCD (Y2 & Y5) (μ=11%, μ^*=18%) — 1.6, 3.7
- Columbus Integrated (μ=9%) — 1.1
- Columbus Traditional (μ=9%) — 0.9
- Detroit (μ=8%) — −3.4
- Oklahoma City (A) (μ=19%) — −3.4

C. Financial Work Incentives Tied to Work or Related Activities

- WRP (μ=n.a.)
- TSMF (R) (μ=n.a.)
- TSMF (A) (μ=n.a.)
- FIP (R) (μ=n.a.)
- FIP (A) (μ=n.a.)
- MFIP (single-parent R, Y3) (μ=6%) — 2.8
- MFIP (single-parent A, Y3) (μ=15%) — 1.7
- MFIP (two-parent R, Y3) (μ=48%) — 19.1***
- SSP (single-parent R, M36 & M54) (μ=10%, μ^*=13%) — −0.6, −0.4
- SSP Plus (R) (μ=n.a.)
- SSP Applicants (A) (μ=n.a.)
- New Hope (empl. FT) (μ=n.a.)
- New Hope (not empl. FT) (μ=n.a.)

D. TANF-like Bundles of Reforms

- EMPOWER (R, Y3) (μ=29%) — −0.9
- ABC (single parent, M4–M19) (μ=8%) — 1.4*
- IMPACT–Placement (μ=n.a.)
- VIP/VIEW (R) (μ=n.a.)
- FTP (Y4) (μ=19%) — −1.9
- Jobs First (M18 & Y3) (μ=7%, μ^*=11%) — −1.2, −1.6

☐ Impact at initial follow-up
☐ Impact at longer-term follow-up

Program impact for percentage married and living with spouse at time of follow-up interview

Note: For full program names, see Table 4.5. Impacts are for two-year follow-up and for single-parent and two-parent recipients (R) and applicants (A) unless otherwise noted. μ = control group mean at initial follow-up; μ^* = control group mean at longer-term follow-up; M = month, Q = quarter; Y = year; FT = full-time; n.a. = not available. Significant at the ***1%, **5%, *10% level.

Figure 8.1
Estimated impacts of welfare reform on marriage from experimental studies. *Source:* See Appendix Table A.5.

not clear which of the components of the bundle caused the marital status effect.

MFIP-IO provided financial work incentives and several other reforms designed to encourage marriage. In particular, some restrictions on eligibility for two-parent families were eliminated (specifically the 100-hour rule and the work history requirement), and the treatment of stepparent earnings was liberalized. Consistent with this intention, the experimental evaluation of the financial work incentives alone (that is, MFIP-IO) suggests that marriage increased. For single-parent recipients, the proportion married at the time of the thirty-six-month follow-up interview is 11.0 percent in the treatment group versus 5.8 percent in the control group, a statistically significant difference of 5.2 percentage points. For single-parent applicants, treatment-group members are slightly less likely to be married (2.2 percentage points), but the difference is not significant.

Mandatory Work or Related Activities

The results of panel B of Figure 8.1 show mixed results of the effect of mandatory work or related activities on the fraction married and living with their spouse as of the two-year follow-up survey. Six are positive, and six are negative. Most involve only a small change. Of the twelve studies, only Riverside LFA has a marginally statistically significant ($p < 0.10$) negative impact on the likelihood of being married. For seven of the NEWWS sites, there are also five-year follow-up results. In none of them (including Riverside LFA) can we reject the hypothesis of no effect. Again, the sites are divided in sign and the point estimates are small. We conclude that there is no evidence for any effect of mandatory work programs on marriage.

Financial Work Incentives Tied to Work or Related Activities

Among the experiments that evaluated financial work incentives tied to work or related activities, three consider effects on marriage.[6] Beyond combining financial incentives and work requirements, all three programs also decreased marriage penalties (see Table 4.5). Panel C of Figure 8.1 shows mixed results, but the figures hide some important details. For MFIP urban single-parent recipients, the impact estimate of 2.8 percentage points recorded in Figure 8.1 just misses statistical significance at the 10 percent level. For rural single parent-recipients, the impact (not shown) is 7.9 percentage points, which also just misses significance at the 10 percent level. Pooling the two samples yields an impact of 3.6 percentage points, which is significant at the 5 percent level (not shown). Given that just 7.0 percent of the control group is married at the time of follow-up, this impact represents a 51.4 percent increase. A test of the difference in marriage rates for urban recipients in MFIP-IO versus MFIP indicates that the addition of mandatory work requirements to a financial work incentives program had no effect, consistent with the findings for the evaluations that examine work requirements alone.

Results for MFIP applicants are quite different. In the urban counties, as seen in Figure 8.1, MFIP increased marriage by an insignificant 1.7 percentage points. In the rural counties (not shown), MFIP decreased marriage by an insignificant −0.6 percentage points. The pooled estimate (not shown) yields a decrease of 0.2 percent, which is not significant.

In addition, the MFIP evaluation considered the impact of the full program on marriage for the sample of two-parent families. For two-parent families, the MFIP intervention increased the proportion remaining married by 19.1 percentage points. The effect is statistically significant at the 1 percent level and represents an increase of 40 percent.

In considering this effect, it is important to note that at randomization most of these women were married with their spouse present. In the control group, however, rates of separation are high. Three years later, slightly less than half (48.3 percent) of these women were married and living with their spouse. Analyses of other aspects of couples' living arrangements suggest that the positive impact on whether two-parent families stay together is concentrated among those who were married (rather than cohabiting) at random assignment. The effect works partially through a drop in the divorce rate (about 6.5 percentage points). The balance of the effect is due to higher rates of married couples continuing to live together, rather than separating. Furthermore, these results are confirmed and strengthened by an analysis of official divorce records. Five years postrandomization, the control group had a 20 percent divorce rate, while the experimental families had an 11 percent divorce rate (Miller et al. 2000; not shown).

The SSP evaluation also considered effects on marriage at both the thirty-six-month and the fifty-four-month follow-up. Canada's Income Assistance program counts a husband's income when calculating the welfare benefit. If the husband works, this will usually result in a lower benefit and would be expected to discourage marriage. To lower this disincentive and encourage marriage, SSP disregards income contributed by a husband or common-law spouse when calculating the earnings supplement.

SSP analyzes program impacts on marital status, as well as a broader measure that includes both formal marriage and Canadian common-law relationships.[7] Using this combined marriage and common-law relationship concept, SSP had insignificant impacts for the participants' marital status as of the thirty-six-month interview. The impact on marriage is small and negative (the impact recorded in Figure 8.1); the impact on common-law relationships is small and positive (not shown); neither effect is statistically different from zero. During the thirty-six-month follow-up period, there is no significant difference in the fraction ever married or in a common-law relationship or in the duration of such a union.

The interpretation of the SSP results is, however, complicated by considering the two provinces—British Columbia and New Brunswick—separately. For most outcomes considered in the SSP evaluation, impacts do not differ significantly across the two provinces. Marriage is one of the few exceptions. The proportion ever married or in a common-law relationship over the thirty-six-month follow-up period fell significantly in British Columbia (by 3.1 percentage points, or 18 percent of the value for the control group) and rose significantly in New Brunswick (by 4.1 percentage points, or 20 percent). If marriage is measured as marital status at the time of the thirty-six-month follow-up interview, the contrast between the two provinces is not as sharp and the impact for New Brunswick is not statistically different from zero. There is no significant impact in either province on the proportion in a common-law relationship as of the follow-up interview, suggesting that these effects worked primarily through marriage.

Michalopoulos et al. (2000) discuss the possible reasons for the difference in results across provinces. They note that the results within each province are robust across subgroups, so that the small differences in baseline characteristics between the two provinces do not explain the differences in the impact on marriage. They also note that the impacts on income and full-time employment were similar across the two provinces, and the policy changes removing the marriage penalty were identical.

They suggest two possible explanations for the divergence across provinces. The first relates to the marriage market. During the period of the experiment, the unemployment rate for men was considerably higher in New Brunswick than in British Columbia. They speculate that these poor job prospects for men made the additional employment, earnings, and income provided by SSP more attractive. It should be noted, however, that this argument—that poor economic prospects for men encourage them to marry—is the opposite of the standard argument that marriage among African-American women is low because there are few marriageable men (Wilson and Neckerman 1986). A second possible explanation concerns cultural differences. New Brunswick is more rural, and majority Catholic; British Columbia is more urban, and has fewer Catholics. Michalopoulos and his colleagues conclude: "The opposite direction of impacts by province underscores the importance of the geographic and cultural context in translating employment and earnings impacts into effects on family structure" (Michalopoulos et al. 2000, 67). With the same intended treatment and only two sites, more definite conclusions are not possible.

Figure 8.1 also shows the results for SSP as of the fifty-four-month follow-up. Since the earnings supplement was only available for up to thirty-six months, this longer-term follow-up takes place about eighteen months after the supplement ended. For the full SSP sample, there is no effect on the proportion ever married in the eighteen months prior to the survey. This also holds for those ever in a common-law relationship or those in either a common-law relationship or a marriage. More important, as of this follow-up, there are no longer any differences in outcomes by province. Thus the differences in marriage outcomes by province that were evident during the period when the earnings supplement was available did not persist once the supplement ended.

There are no observational studies of the effects of specific reforms on marriage. This lack of studies is particularly unfortunate because, as noted earlier, welfare reform's effect on family structure might be expected to operate primarily through entry effects that are not captured by random assignment studies.

In summary, the literature indicates that mandatory work requirements have no impact on marriage. None of the random assignment studies allows a pure test of the effect of financial work incentives, since all such programs also include provisions to encourage marriage through changes in eligibility rules or the treatment of the second parent's earnings. For these bundled policies, there is some evidence of increases in marriage for one-parent cases (MFIP-IO recipients, MFIP pooled urban and rural recipients, and SSP in New Brunswick while the earnings supplement was in effect), but there is also evidence to the contrary (CWPDP, MFIP applicants, and SSP in British Columbia). There are two pieces of evidence to suggest that financial work incentives combined with reforms to reduce penalties for marriage help maintain two-parent families (CWPDP and MFIP). In both of those cases, the impact is substantively large and statistically significant.

Estimates of the Effects of Reform as a Bundle on Marriage

Since the combination of reforms implemented by states may have conflicting effects on marriage, estimates of the effect of reform as a bundle do not reflect on the ability of our model to predict behavior. Nevertheless, the overall effect of reform on marriage is a matter of considerable policy interest.

As in the previous chapters, two sets of studies provide evidence on the effect of reform as a bundle. The first is welfare reform experiments that involved TANF-like bundles of reforms, by which we mean bundles that included time limits and either financial work incentives, work requirements, or both. The second consists of three observational studies that examine either current marital status, or marriage and divorce rates.[8]

We begin with the experimental evaluations of TANF-like bundles. Panel D of Figure 8.1 presents results for four programs. The follow-up periods range from as little as four months (ABC, for those entering latest) to four years (FTP). EMPOWER, FTP, and Jobs First have negative but insignificant impacts on the likelihood of being married (or married and living with one's spouse). EMPOWER and Jobs First also consider changes in marital status. Those effects are also insignificant.

ABC is the only study to show a statistically significant ($p < 0.10$) increase in marriage, and this occurs even though the follow-up period is short, averaging twelve months (with a range from four to nineteen months). Analyses for subgroups show a significant positive impact on marriage for women under age twenty-five, those who are capable of having additional children, those never married, and those with less than twelve years of schooling. The differences between age and education groups are also statistically significant.

For the observational studies, panels A, B, and C of Figure 8.2 display the results for current marital status, the marriage rate (reflecting entry into marriage), and the divorce rate (reflecting exit from marriage), respectively. Bitler, Gelbach, and Hoynes (2002) use data from the March CPS to estimate difference-in-difference models for marital status and household composition for both a sample of children under sixteen years of age and a sample of women ages sixteen to fifty-four. Figure 8.2 (panel A) shows that the implementation of any waiver or of TANF in states that had a waiver had no significant effect on current marital status for the sample of women, while there is an estimated 3.1 percent decline in the propensity to be married in states that implemented TANF but had no prior waiver. A separate analysis shows that this latter effect is primarily due to a statistically significant increase in being divorced or separated (rather than in being never married). In other results (not shown), the only significant effect of reform on household composition among women is a 3 percent decline in the number of men over age sixteen in the household as a result of TANF implementation in states that ever had a waiver. For the child sample (results not shown), there is no discernible relationship between these reform variables and either household composition or the marital status of the co-resident parent(s).[9]

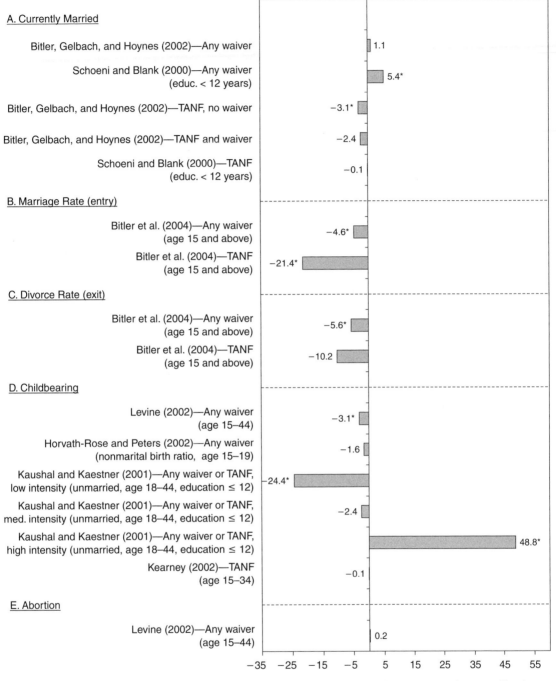

A. Currently Married

Bitler, Gelbach, and Hoynes (2002)—Any waiver — 1.1

Schoeni and Blank (2000)—Any waiver
(educ. < 12 years) — 5.4*

Bitler, Gelbach, and Hoynes (2002)—TANF, no waiver — −3.1*

Bitler, Gelbach, and Hoynes (2002)—TANF and waiver — −2.4

Schoeni and Blank (2000)—TANF
(educ. < 12 years) — −0.1

B. Marriage Rate (entry)

Bitler et al. (2004)—Any waiver
(age 15 and above) — −4.6*

Bitler et al. (2004)—TANF
(age 15 and above) — −21.4*

C. Divorce Rate (exit)

Bitler et al. (2004)—Any waiver
(age 15 and above) — −5.6*

Bitler et al. (2004)—TANF
(age 15 and above) — −10.2

D. Childbearing

Levine (2002)—Any waiver
(age 15–44) — −3.1*

Horvath-Rose and Peters (2002)—Any waiver
(nonmarital birth ratio, age 15–19) — −1.6

Kaushal and Kaestner (2001)—Any waiver or TANF,
low intensity (unmarried, age 18–44, education ≤ 12) — −24.4*

Kaushal and Kaestner (2001)—Any waiver or TANF,
med. intensity (unmarried, age 18–44, education ≤ 12) — −2.4

Kaushal and Kaestner (2001)—Any waiver or TANF,
high intensity (unmarried, age 18–44, education ≤ 12) — 48.8*

Kearney (2002)—TANF
(age 15–34) — −0.1

E. Abortion

Levine (2002)—Any waiver
(age 15–44) — 0.2

−35 −25 −15 −5 5 15 25 35 45 55

Estimated effects on family structure (percent effects)

Note: Results are for women 16–54 unless otherwise noted. Asterisks denote results based on coefficients that are statistically significant at the 10 percent level or better.

Figure 8.2
Results from observational studies of the effects of reform as a bundle on marriage, divorce, and childbearing.

Schoeni and Blank (2000) use the March CPS to consider the propensity to be married and also the propensity to be a female head of household. As seen in panel A of Figure 8.2, their difference-in-difference specification suggests that for high school dropouts, any waiver increases marriage (by about 5 percent) and depresses female headship (by about 8 percent, result not shown). For those with exactly twelve years of schooling (results not shown), waivers have a significant negative effect on marriage (the opposite of the effect for high school dropouts) and a positive (but not statistically significant) effect on female headship. For those with more than twelve years of schooling (results not shown), waivers again have a significant positive effect on marriage, but not on female headship.

Schoeni and Blank (2000) also estimate the effect of TANF using interstate variation in the date of implementation of each state's TANF program. These models show almost no significant effect of TANF on marriage or female headship. The only exception is a 2-percentage-point increase in female headship for those with more than a high school diploma (not shown).

Bitler et al. (2004) use aggregate state-level vital statistics data to model transitions into marriage (the marriage rate) and out of marriage (the divorce rate). Compared with the CPS data, the vital statistics records provide a nearly complete sample of all marriages and divorces, capturing the flow in and out of marriage rather than the current stock of married women analyzed in the studies discussed above. The main drawback is that the data are aggregated at the state level, which precludes the use of individual controls. As seen in panels B and C of Figure 8.2, Bitler et al. (2004) find a negative relationship between welfare reform and flows into and out of marriage, with a statistically significant 4.6 percent and 21.4 percent decline in the marriage rate attributable to waivers and TANF, respectively; and a 5.6 percent decline in the divorce rate due to waivers.[10] In general the negative impact of TANF exceeds that for waivers, although there is less cross-state variation for identifying the TANF effect. While the effect of reform on marriage is sensitive to alternative specifications and data sources, the coefficient is always either negative or statistically insignificant. There is no evidence from Bitler and her colleagues' study that marriage rates increase due to welfare reform.

In summary, the evidence from the experimental studies on the effect of TANF as a bundle is mixed. The observational studies are equally inconclusive, with one study suggesting that waivers increased the propensity to be married, and another finding the opposite for TANF. A third study suggests a decline in new marriages but also a drop in divorces due to waivers and TANF. More study of this issue is needed to reconcile these divergent findings.

Experimental Estimates of the Effects of Specific Reforms on Childbearing

We now turn to childbearing, considering first experimental estimates and then observational estimates. Figure 8.3 presents experimental impact estimates of the effects of various reforms on childbearing. These experimental studies usually measure childbearing as the proportion of the sample having one or more children since randomization or since the last follow-up as reported by treatment- and control-group respondents. Again note that entry effects—in particular, the decision to have the initial child that could make a woman eligible for welfare—are not captured by the standard random assignment study design. In addition, none of the childbearing measures distinguishes between marital and nonmarital childbearing.

There are no experimental estimates of the effect of financial work incentives on childbearing. Our discussion therefore begins with the effect on childbearing of mandatory work or related activities. We then consider financial work incentives tied to work or related activities, followed by a childbearing-specific policy, family caps.

Mandatory Work or Related Activities

As seen in panel B of Figure 8.3, of the twelve studies that focus on mandatory work or related activities, only Columbus Traditional has even a borderline statistically significant ($p < 0.10$) negative impact on the portion having a birth in the two years following random assignment. The signs of the impacts in the other sites are more often positive than negative. For seven of the sites (but not Columbus), there are also five-year follow-up results.[11] For none of these sites can we reject the hypothesis of no effect. Again the signs are mixed, with more positive impact estimates than negative impact estimates. The evidence suggests that work mandates have no impact on childbearing.

Financial Work Incentives Tied to Work or Related Activities

At the thirty-six-month and fifty-four-month follow-ups, SSP collected information on whether treatment- and control-group members had any new children in the family in the eighteen months prior to the survey. At both follow-ups, there was no significant difference in child-

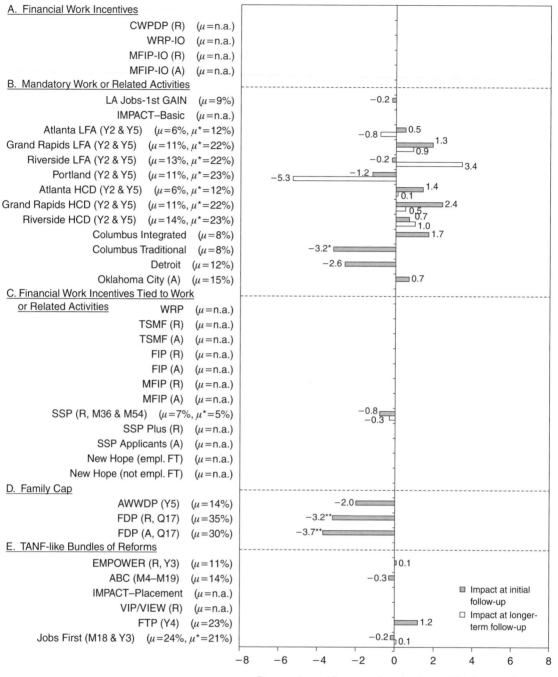

A. Financial Work Incentives

CWPDP (R) (μ=n.a.)
WRP-IO (μ=n.a.)
MFIP-IO (R) (μ=n.a.)
MFIP-IO (A) (μ=n.a.)

B. Mandatory Work or Related Activities

LA Jobs-1st GAIN (μ=9%) — −0.2
IMPACT–Basic (μ=n.a.)
Atlanta LFA (Y2 & Y5) (μ=6%, μ^*=12%) — −0.8, 0.5
Grand Rapids LFA (Y2 & Y5) (μ=11%, μ^*=22%) — 1.3, 0.9
Riverside LFA (Y2 & Y5) (μ=13%, μ^*=22%) — −0.2, 3.4
Portland (Y2 & Y5) (μ=11%, μ^*=23%) — −5.3, −1.2
Atlanta HCD (Y2 & Y5) (μ=6%, μ^*=12%) — 1.4, 0.1
Grand Rapids HCD (Y2 & Y5) (μ=11%, μ^*=22%) — 2.4, 0.5
Riverside HCD (Y2 & Y5) (μ=14%, μ^*=23%) — 0.7, 1.0
Columbus Integrated (μ=8%) — 1.7
Columbus Traditional (μ=8%) — −3.2*
Detroit (μ=12%) — −2.6
Oklahoma City (A) (μ=15%) — 0.7

C. Financial Work Incentives Tied to Work or Related Activities

WRP (μ=n.a.)
TSMF (R) (μ=n.a.)
TSMF (A) (μ=n.a.)
FIP (R) (μ=n.a.)
FIP (A) (μ=n.a.)
MFIP (R) (μ=n.a.)
MFIP (A) (μ=n.a.)
SSP (R, M36 & M54) (μ=7%, μ^*=5%) — −0.8, −0.3
SSP Plus (R) (μ=n.a.)
SSP Applicants (A) (μ=n.a.)
New Hope (empl. FT) (μ=n.a.)
New Hope (not empl. FT) (μ=n.a.)

D. Family Cap

AWWDP (Y5) (μ=14%) — −2.0
FDP (R, Q17) (μ=35%) — −3.2**
FDP (A, Q17) (μ=30%) — −3.7**

E. TANF-like Bundles of Reforms

EMPOWER (R, Y3) (μ=11%) — 0.1
ABC (M4–M19) (μ=14%) — −0.3
IMPACT–Placement (μ=n.a.)
VIP/VIEW (R) (μ=n.a.)
FTP (Y4) (μ=23%) — 1.2
Jobs First (M18 & Y3) (μ=24%, μ^*=21%) — −0.2, 0.1

■ Impact at initial follow-up
□ Impact at longer-term follow-up

Program impact for percentage having a child since random assignment as of follow-up interview

Note: For full program names, see Table 4.5. Impacts are for two-year follow-up and for recipients (R) and applicants (A) unless otherwise noted. Outcome for AWWDP is average number of births since RA times 100, which is approximately the same as the percentage having a child since RA. μ = control group mean at initial follow-up; μ^* = control group mean at longer-term follow-up; M = month, Q = quarter; Y = year; RA = random assignment; FT = full-time; n.a.= not available. Significant at the ***1%, **5%, *10% level.

Figure 8.3
Estimated impacts of welfare reform on childbearing from experimental studies. *Source:* See Appendix Table A.6.

bearing between the treatment group and the controls. Thus there appear to be no effects of financial work incentives tied to work or related activities on childbearing, both while the earnings supplement is in effect and up to eighteen months after the supplement ends.

Family Cap

Two experiments, AWWDP and FDP, evaluated a family cap. Unlike the studies of work mandates that use survey data, these two studies rely on administrative data from the welfare system to identify births after random assignment. Such administrative data only record births while on welfare. Thus the concept of childbearing analyzed by these two studies differs from the other experimental studies of childbearing that also capture births to women who have left welfare.

The evaluation of the AWWDP in Arkansas finds no effect on childbearing measured by the average number of births after random assignment (0.14 for the control group versus 0.16 for the experimental group).[12] In addition, there was no statistically significant effect on receipt of family planning services or use of birth control. However, several methodological issues suggest caution in interpreting these findings. First, the sample used for the analysis of childbearing is very small: the researchers use a 5 percent random subsample of the population available for study. Thus, for their analysis of births, the sample sizes in the treatment and control groups are 86 and 88, respectively. Such small samples make it unlikely that even substantial effects could be detected.

Second, the AWWDP evaluators report that "a substantial portion of workers explained the cap on benefits to clients in both the experimental and control groups" (Turturro, Benda, and Turney 1997, 2). As a result, many recipients were confused as to which rules applied to them. In a small survey of study participants ($N = 102$), about half did not know how their benefits would change with an additional child (45.7 in the experimental group versus 51.8 percent in the control group). Inasmuch as members of the control group believed that they were subject to the family cap, the experiment will underestimate the effect of a universally applied family cap.

Results for New Jersey are quite different. In New Jersey, the family cap was instituted as part of FDP, a wide-ranging waiver package including enhanced welfare-to-work services, financial work incentives, transitional Medicaid, and elimination of some marriage penalties. For recipients, comparisons of the experimental and control groups imply that the entire package of reforms led to a statistically significant 3.2-percentage-point decline in the proportion having an additional birth (see panel D of

Figure 8.3). This represents a 9.2 percent decline relative to the control group mean of 34.9 percent. There was no effect on whether participants had an abortion, however (not shown).

For applicants, FDP resulted in a decline in childbearing of 3.7 percentage points or 12.3 percent of the control group mean, similar to the impact on recipients. In addition, unlike the result for recipients, abortions among applicants increased 14 percent. This effect appears to be concentrated in the early months of the experiment.

FDP also affected family planning. Survey responses indicate that, compared with those in the control group, those in the treatment group were 4 percentage points more likely to use family planning in the last year (30.9 percent versus 26.6 percent). Regression analyses of sterilization and family planning visits from Medicaid files are also consistent with a moderate to large effect on childbearing practices, and the timing of these effects is also plausible.

Like AWWDP, however, methodological issues suggest caution in interpreting the FDP findings. First, there is some evidence of problems with randomization. More than one-quarter of case workers admitted to evaluators that they used discretion when making assignments to the treatment and control groups (Camasso, Harvey, and Jagannathan 1996; Kearney 2002), which would invalidate the randomization and thus the statistical inference. Second, like the Arkansas demonstration, the FDP client survey suggests that understanding of the program was very poor.[13] Combining the groups that reported either that their cash benefits would not increase or that none of their benefits (including food stamps and Medicaid) would increase, survey results suggest that only 3.5 percent more of the experimental group believed that the cash benefit would not increase with the birth of a new child.

If understanding of the program was truly this weak, then the childbearing and abortion effects that were found are surprising. Confusion about the family cap would be expected to bias the effects of the program downward. These results would then imply even larger effects when the program was understood. Another interpretation, however, is possible. FDP was broader than the family cap. It also involved an enhanced earnings disregard, enhanced case management, and relaxation of the marriage penalty. Thus even if recipients did not understand the family cap, childbearing effects might have resulted from these other program components.

Nevertheless, confusion by the treatment and control groups regarding the policies that applied to them would still lead to a downward bias in the estimated program impact. Partially to address this concern, the New Jersey evaluation also conducted a before-and-after econometric

analysis. Using the same administrative data, Camasso et al. (1999) estimated a regression model for childbearing with controls for demographic characteristics (for example, age, marital status, education, and
number of children), earnings, history of AFDC use, the unemployment
rate, the FDP participation rate, county dummies, and a linear time
trend. The effect of FDP was estimated as the deviation from the time
trend implied by this regression model. Again large negative effects of
FDP on childbearing were detected, as were moderate positive effects on
abortions. Note, however, that by our standards for judging observational studies, this study's design is weak. If childbearing began to decline (or the decline accelerated) nationally for welfare recipients (as Figure 2.4 suggests), this approach would have attributed that decline to
FDP. A stronger design would have included some form of control for
trends in states that did not implement a family cap.[14]

Observational Estimates of the Effects of Specific Reforms on Childbearing

Figure 8.4 presents the percent effect of specific reforms on childbearing
outcomes for observational studies. For most of these studies, the outcome analyzed is a birth rate (births per woman in an age range). We begin by considering time limits and family caps, for which we have multiple estimates. We then review Horvath-Rose and Peters's (2002) results
for the effect of several other policies on the nonmarital childbearing
ratio.

Time Limits

Panel A of Figure 8.4 presents results for the three observational
studies that consider the effect of time limits on childbearing. Kearney
(2002) estimates the effect of time limits on the total number of births
to fifteen- to thirty-four-year-old women using difference-in-difference
methods (with state-specific time trends) and birth certificate data from
vital statistics. She finds no significant effect.

Kaushal and Kaestner (2001) use CPS data to estimate the effect of
time limits on the birth rate (births per woman in the last year). Their estimates can be interpreted as a restricted difference-in-difference-in-difference specification. They include year and state fixed effects and they
interact the reform dummy with a dummy variable identifying the population assumed to be most affected by welfare reform.[15] Their first affected group is unmarried women with twelve or fewer years of education. They compare this affected group with two unaffected or control

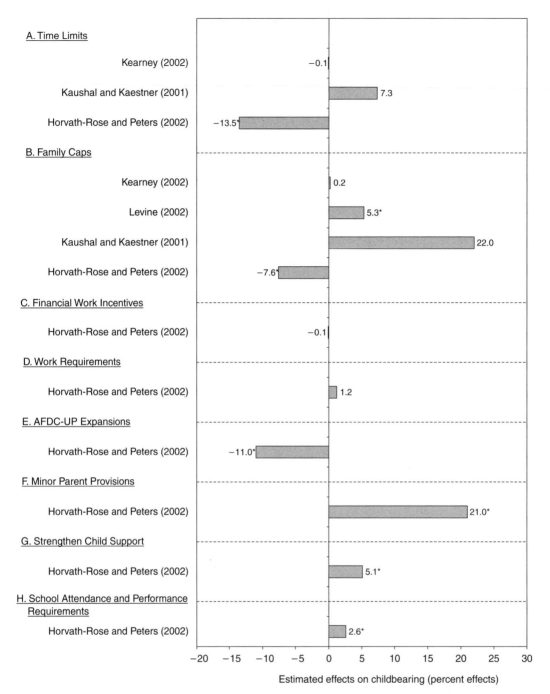

A. Time Limits

Kearney (2002) −0.1

Kaushal and Kaestner (2001) 7.3

Horvath-Rose and Peters (2002) −13.5*

B. Family Caps

Kearney (2002) 0.2

Levine (2002) 5.3*

Kaushal and Kaestner (2001) 22.0

Horvath-Rose and Peters (2002) −7.6*

C. Financial Work Incentives

Horvath-Rose and Peters (2002) −0.1

D. Work Requirements

Horvath-Rose and Peters (2002) 1.2

E. AFDC-UP Expansions

Horvath-Rose and Peters (2002) −11.0*

F. Minor Parent Provisions

Horvath-Rose and Peters (2002) 21.0*

G. Strengthen Child Support

Horvath-Rose and Peters (2002) 5.1*

H. School Attendance and Performance Requirements

Horvath-Rose and Peters (2002) 2.6*

Estimated effects on childbearing (percent effects)

Note: Outcomes are: Kearney (2002): births to women 15–34; Levine (2002): births to women 15–44; Kaushal and Kaestner (2001): births to women 18–44 with ≤ 12 years of education; and Horvath-Rose and Peters (2002): nonmarital birth ratio for women 15–19. Asterisks denote results based on coefficients that are significant at the 10 percent level or better.

Figure 8.4
Results from observational studies of the effects of specific reforms on childbearing.

groups: married women with twelve or fewer years of education (results shown in Figure 8.4) and unmarried women with an associate degree. Their second affected group, unmarried women with at least one child and twelve or fewer years of schooling, is appropriate for considering the effects of a family cap on subsequent childbearing. Again two control groups are employed: married women with children and twelve or fewer years of schooling; and unmarried women with children and an associate's degree. For each of the four affected-comparison group combinations Kaushal and Kaestner (2001) consider, they find an insignificant positive effect of time limits.

Horvath-Rose and Peters (2002) analyze a different outcome, the nonmarital birth ratio, defined as the fraction of births that are to unmarried women. Like Kearney (2002), they use birth certificate data, in this case to compute the nonmarital birth ratio. Their models also include state and year fixed effects. As seen in Figure 8.4, unlike the other two observational studies of births or birth rates, Horvath-Rose and Peters find a significant and negative effect of time limits on the nonmarital birth ratio for teens aged fifteen to nineteen.

Family Cap

Panel B of Figure 8.4 presents the results for analyses of the impact of family caps. Kearney (2002), using the methodology discussed above, finds no effect. Her estimate is very small, but so is the standard error, so that the basic analysis can reject an effect of 1 percent or more. This conclusion is robust to the inclusion of state-specific time trends, alternative coding of the family cap, alternative timing of the effect on childbearing, and using the birth rate rather than the number of births. Analyses by parity, race-ethnicity, and age (not shown) show no consistent effect. In sum, Kearney finds no evidence for the theoretically predicted negative effect of a family cap on childbearing.

Levine (2002) estimates difference-in-difference models (including state-specific time trends) of births and birth rates using vital statistics data. He also finds, contrary to the theory, that the family cap raises childbearing, and the effect is statistically significant. The effect is consistent across the age, education, and parity subgroups he examines.

Kaushal and Kaestner (2001), using the methodology discussed above with the CPS, also estimate the effect of a family cap on the birth rate. The estimate recorded in Figure 8.4 is for unmarried women with less than twelve years of schooling (compared with married women with less than twelve years of schooling). This impact is positive but insignificant, as are the impacts for the three other affected-comparison group combinations that they consider. Some of the point estimates are large in percentage terms (including the one shown in Figure 8.4), but their standard errors are even larger. Moreover, the largest estimate represents an increase of only 1.1 percentage points.

Finally, Horvath-Rose and Peters (2002) explore the effect of a family cap on the nonmarital birth ratio as discussed above. They find, as shown in Figure 8.4, that family caps lower the nonmarital birth ratio among teenagers by a statistically significant 7.6 percent overall. The negative impact for whites is 10.0 percent compared with 2.8 percent for blacks (results not shown). For adults aged twenty and above, the corresponding effects for whites and blacks are reductions of 17 and 8 percent, respectively (results not shown). With the exception of the black teenager effect (significant at the 10 percent level), these effects are statistically significant at the 5 percent level.

These results for the effects of the family cap diverge from those found in the other observational studies. Furthermore, Horvath-Rose and Peters's model produces curious estimates for a number of other policy changes in addition to family caps. We discuss these next.

Other Reforms

Panels C to H of Figure 8.4 display Horvath-Rose and Peters's estimates for the effects for other specific reform waivers. The magnitudes are sometimes even larger than the effects for the family cap, but their signs are mixed. In the case of financial work incentives (see panel C) and work requirements (see panel D), there appears to be no effect. AFDC-UP expansion waivers significantly decrease the nonmarital birth ratio (see panel E), especially for teenagers (an 11 percent decline; not shown) and white teens (a 13 percent decline; not shown). Contrary to expectation, however, minor parent provisions are estimated to raise the nonmarital birth ratio by 21 percent for teens, with effects that are statistically significant at the 5 percent level (see panel F). Strengthening child support and school attendance and performance requirements also appear to raise childbearing (see panels G and H).

Estimates of the Effects of Reform as a Bundle on Childbearing

Finally, we consider the effects of welfare reform as a bundle on childbearing. We consider both evidence from experimental studies of TANF-like bundles and from observational studies. As seen in panel E of Figure 8.3, the four programs that focus on TANF-like bundles of reforms all find small and insignificant impacts on births over a follow-up interval ranging from four months (ABC) to four years (FTP). The estimates are divided in sign, none is statistically significant, and in the one case for which we have results at two follow-up intervals (Jobs First), the sign changes.

Notably, EMPOWER also measures the impact on births to unwed minors who were part of the assistance unit at the time of random assignment. Births to such unwed minors decrease significantly: as of the three-year follow-up, 4 percent of the control group cases had a birth to an unwed minor since random assignment compared with 1.6 percent of cases in the experimental group. Conceptions to unwed minors since random assignment also showed a statistically significant 1.8-percentage-point decline.

As seen in Table 4.5, EMPOWER's reforms included a family cap, as well as a minor residency requirement and a provision removing the exemption from JOBS participation for teens under age sixteen (those age thirteen and above must now participate). Because these three reforms are bundled with the program's other reforms, it is not possible to ascribe the reduction in unwed teen childbearing to these specific policies. It is also worth noting that the control group in EMPOWER became subject to the treatment-group provisions two years into the three-year follow-up period. Thus some of the measured impact of the EMPOWER reforms on adult and teen childbearing may have been diluted by the control-group crossover.

Panel C of Figure 8.2 displays estimates of the percent effects of reform as a bundle on childbearing from the observational studies. The results are mixed. Kearney (2002) estimates a negative, tiny, and statistically insignificant effect of TANF. Levine's (2002) estimate shows a 3 percent decrease in the birth rate, an effect that is highly significant. However, if this result were causal, we would expect it to be larger for less-educated women, who are more likely to receive welfare. This pattern across education groups is not observed in the data, which suggests caution in interpreting the estimated negative effect as causal.

Kaushal and Kaestner (2001) also find effects of reform as a bundle, but the sign patterns are difficult to interpret. The only statistically significant negative effect is for low-intensity reforms and then only for their first treatment-comparison group combination. If there were truly an effect of reform, we would expect to find larger (in absolute value) effects with more-intensive reforms. However, Kaushal and Kaestner find no statistically significant effect of medium-intensity reforms (in any model). Furthermore, they find that high-intensity reforms significantly increase childbearing for the first two treatment-comparison group combinations.

Horvath-Rose and Peters (2002) also find that waivers decreased the nonmarital birth ratio by about 1.6 percent for teens (results shown but insignificant), but also for older women (results not shown), as well as for whites and blacks in these two age groups.

Levine (2002) applies the same methods used to study childbearing to data on abortions from the Alan Guttmacher Institute (see panel E of Figure 8.2). For that outcome, he finds no evidence of an effect of any waiver on the abortion rate. Furthermore, these results are consistent with disaggregation by age, although the data do not allow disaggregation by education or parity. We conclude that there is little evidence that welfare reform as a whole lowers childbearing.

Summary

Given the complexity of marriage and childbearing behavior, it may come as little surprise that economic models generally yield ambiguous predictions regarding the effects of welfare reform. As a result, empirical evidence cannot be construed as either refuting or supporting the economic model. Nevertheless, the evidence is crucial for informing policy discussions, many of which were once motivated by concerns that AFDC had adverse effects on family structure.

For marriage, the experimental evidence strongly suggests that programs that mandate work have no effect. There is a small amount of evidence that financial work incentives, when combined with liberalized two-parent eligibility rules or more generous treatment of a spouse's earnings, may increase marriage. The evidence suggests that this combination of policies may be more effective in reducing separation or divorce among already married couples than in increasing marriage among single mothers. There are no observational studies of marriage that consider the impact of specific reform policies.

The experimental evidence strongly suggests that programs that mandate work have no effect on childbearing. The one observational study that examines this policy also finds no effect (although there are reasons to discount this study as discussed below).

The impact of family caps is the only other policy reform that has been evaluated using both random assignment and experimental methodologies. Although there are some differences across studies, they can be partially reconciled. Of the two random assignment studies, one (New Jersey) finds large negative effects. One of the four observational studies (Horvath-Rose and Peters 2002) estimates an impact in the same direction. However, there appear to be methodological problems with both of the random assignment studies, and Horvath-Rose and Peters's results provide anomalous estimates across the several policies they consider. Of the three remaining observational studies, Kaushal and Kaestner (2001) rely on the CPS, which has low power. Hence the effect is insignificant. This leaves two observational studies, Kearney (2002) and Levine (2002), both of which exploit the larger sample sizes available through vital statistics data. Whereas Kearney (2002) finds a precisely estimated effect close to zero, Levine (2002) reports a positive and significant effect, which is contrary to expectation. This difference cannot be readily resolved. The lack of evidence in support of the expected behavioral response to family caps may stem from the fact that the dollar magnitudes associated with the family caps are generally small.

Fewer studies have examined the impact of other specific reform policies on childbearing, so all the available evidence comes from three observational studies. Excluding the problematic studies discussed above, the evidence regarding the impact of time limits shows no effect. The only study to examine any other specific policies (including financial work incentives) is Horvath-Rose and Peters (2002), who often report anomalous results. Thus the sum of the evidence suggests that family caps, and perhaps time limits as well, have had no effect on childbearing. The effect of other specific reform policies on childbearing remains unexplored.

When welfare reform is considered as a bundle, there is one observational study that suggests that waivers increased marriage rates, and another that indicates the opposite for TANF. One study suggests that TANF and waivers reduce flows both into and out of marriage. In contrast, with the exception of one study, none of the random assignment experiments suggests that TANF-like reforms affect marriage. Likewise, there is little evidence from either experimental or observational studies to indicate that reform as a bundle affected childbearing. The one observational study to find significant impacts of reform provides counterintuitive results, with more intensive reforms raising childbearing. One intriguing result from EMPOWER is a significant decrease in unwed childbearing among the daughters who were part of the assistance unit at the time of random assignment. This result provides some insight into possible entry effects for reform as a whole.

These weak results for both marriage and childbearing are not entirely surprising. With the exception of family caps and policies to liberalize the treatment of two-parent families, the reforms studied here were not primarily designed to affect family structure. Given the nature of decisions regarding marriage and childbearing, the policy changes may have been too small to effect significant change. Furthermore, any changes in behavior may take longer to materialize. With the available evidence to date, however, there are no notable trade-offs between welfare reform policies that have been studied and marriage and childbearing outcomes, in contrast to outcomes discussed in prior chapters.

It is important to recognize, however, that the experimental methodology is arguably less informative for family structure outcomes than for most other outcomes. The primary effect of welfare reform on family structure may involve childbearing- or marriage-related decisions that historically have influenced welfare entry: the decision to have a first child, the decision to marry the father, and among couples, the decision to stay married. Because experimental studies consider only women already receiving or applying for welfare, they miss changes in entry behavior among those at risk of going on welfare. At the same time, the available observational studies have weaknesses that limit the ability to draw solid inferences about potential entry effects.

CHAPTER NINE

Child Outcomes

The model introduced in Chapter 3 focuses on the relationship between welfare policies and decisions regarding welfare use, work effort, and income. The previous chapter extends that model to consider the impact of reform on marriage and childbearing. In this chapter, we further extend the model to examine the impact of reform policies on children and consider the evidence from experimental and observational studies.[1]

Throughout the process of reform, there has been considerable attention paid to the potential for both negative and positive impacts of various welfare policies on the well-being of children. There are a number of reasons to expect welfare reform to affect child outcomes. First, the primary objective of some welfare reform policies, such as parental responsibility requirements regarding school attendance, immunizations, well-child care, or parenting classes, is to directly change parental behavior or investments in their children. Second, welfare reform policies may change other aspects of behavior that in turn affect child well-being. For example, as we saw in Chapter 6, work effort by mothers with children may change as a result of welfare reform policies. Research suggests that maternal employment may affect child health and development, although the evidence indicates that the effect depends on the nature of the mother's job, the change in family resources, the quality of child care and activities for older children, and the mother's psychological well-being (Morris et al. 2001).

Family income may also be affected by welfare reform through changes in welfare payments, earnings, and other transfers. A body of research similarly indicates that family income can affect child development, showing a link between childhood poverty and detrimental outcomes for children. (See, for example, the studies in Duncan and Brooks-Gunn 1997, and the reviews provided by Haveman and Wolfe 1995; and Mayer 1997.) Other factors relevant for children's development that might be affected by welfare reform include maternal schooling, child care utilization and quality, access to health insurance, marriage and childbearing, and living arrangements. Indeed, we have seen evidence in prior chapters that welfare reform as a whole, and specific reforms in particular, have affected welfare receipt, work effort, and family income.

To interpret the evidence on the effect of welfare policies on child well-being, we begin in the next section by presenting a theoretical framework of the relationship between child well-being and reform policies. We also discuss a number of methodological issues that arise in the literature that aims to determine the causal impact of reform on children. We then present the findings from the experimental studies that measure the impact of specific reforms on child outcomes, followed by a parallel discussion for observational studies. A discussion of the impact of reform as a bundle follows.

Theoretical Framework and Methodological Issues

As investigations of the links between child outcomes and welfare reform have multiplied, researchers have suggested multiple hypotheses about the ways in which changes in welfare policy might affect child well-being (see, for example, Duncan and Chase-Lansdale 2001). In this section, we first outline a theoretical framework that extends the economic model of Chapter 3 and then discuss some of the methodological issues that arise in the empirical research that are unique to the analysis of child outcomes.

Expanding the Theoretical Framework

The choice-theoretic framework presented in Chapter 3 can be adapted to consider the determinants of child outcomes in the context of family decision making.[2] The approach draws upon the standard economic model of household production (Becker 1965, 1981). That model posits that parents maximize their own well-being (or utility), including the well-being of their children, subject to an overall budget constraint (which equates the inputs purchased and their prices with the income available from work and other sources) and production functions that govern how inputs such as parental time and other purchased goods and services are translated into the child outcomes valued by parents (for example, schooling attainment, health status). Assuming that decisions regarding the number of children to have are already made (that decision was the subject of the prior chapter), at each point in time, parents make choices about the allocation of their own time between work, time spent with children or in other home production activities, and leisure.[3] Parents also influence how their children's time is allocated (for example, in schooling or nonschooling activities) and the other resources that are devoted to their children, such as books and toys, health care, the neighborhood in which they live, the schools they attend, and so on. These choices are affected by underlying parental tastes, preferences, and endowments (such as prior investments in their own schooling) and are constrained by wages available in their labor market, nonlabor income sources, and the prices they face for purchased goods and services.

Like the model presented in Chapter 3, this decision-making framework necessitates that parents make trade-offs, such as between time spent working to earn more income and time available to spend with their children, between the purchase of goods and services that benefit adults in the family and those that enhance the home environment or directly benefit children (for example, school tuition, tutors, after-school activities). As children age, they begin to make their own choices about how they spend their time (for example, time spent in school, on homework, or in delinquent activities) and the inputs that go into their own human capital production (for example, attitudes toward school, teenage childbearing, and other aspects of positive and negative social behavior).

Within this framework, welfare reform may affect parental investments in their children (or children's own choices), and hence child well-being, in several ways. Some welfare reform policies, such as parental responsibility requirements, can be thought of as policies that are aimed to directly enhance parental investments in their children. In the same way that work mandates modeled in Chapter 3 are expected to increase work effort, parental responsibility mandates that require parents to attend parenting classes, to obtain preventive health care, or to ensure school attendance are expected to increase the proportion of children who receive better parenting, obtain the required care, or attend school. However, to the extent that some parents do not meet these expectations in the absence of mandates, whether they will do so under mandates is a function of the costs associated with compliance (for example, travel, time, and out-of-pocket costs to attend parenting classes or visit health care providers, or the time and other costs of monitoring school attendance) versus the costs of not complying (a function of the certainty and severity of the sanctions levied on those who do not comply). Furthermore, whether an increase in compliance translates into improvements in children's well-being depends upon the extent to which changes in these inputs "produce" better outputs (for example, improved child behavior or health, or better schooling outcomes).

Beyond these direct effects, welfare reform may indirectly influence child outcomes through their effects on other family decisions. As discussed in Chapter 3, the three key welfare reform policies—financial work incentives, work-related activity requirements, and time limits— are expected to affect parental choices about welfare use and work and, ultimately, the level of family income. Changes in work effort may affect the time available for parents to spend with and invest in their children, substituting market time for time spent at home. The substitution to- ward more market time may increase income, which then affects the re- sources available to purchase other goods and services that are inputs into the production of child quality. Thus these policies may be expected to affect child well-being indirectly through their impact on work (and therefore time spent at home), income (and therefore other purchased in- puts), and other aspects of family decision making.

In terms of time use, the impact of welfare reform policies on children is expected to be a function of how both the quantity and the quality of time available for children change, as well as the quality of the care that is substituted for parental care. Prior research indicates that maternal work may affect child health and development, although the relation- ship depends on a number of factors. The quantity and quality of time working parents provide their children is associated with the nature of their work (for example, work hours, stress), their parenting style, and parental physical and mental health, although these relationships are not necessarily causal (see the summaries of this literature provided by Mor- ris et al. 2001 and Brooks-Gunn et al. 2001). Welfare programs that sup- port parents' investments in their own schooling may have spillover benefits; higher parental education has been causally linked with better child outcomes (Magnuson and McGroder 2002)

For a single-mother family, welfare reform's emphasis on work or par- ticipation in activities leading to work is likely to lead to the substitution of nonmaternal care for maternal care. This substitution is likely to be largest for pre–school-age children, in contrast with older children who would be in school even if their mother were not working. Subsidized child care, even once families leave welfare, is a component of most state TANF programs. High-quality center-based care has been demonstrated in random assignment evaluations to improve behavioral and cognitive functioning in disadvantaged preschool-age children (see the review by Karoly et al. 1998), and high-quality child care more generally has been linked to better child outcomes (for recent reviews, see Vandell and Shumow 1999; Vandell and Wolfe 2000; and Vandell and Pierce 2003). Poor-quality care, on the other hand, may leave children no better off, or even worse off. Thus the impact of welfare reform will depend upon par- ents' child-care decisions, which in turn depend on the price and quality of the care options available to them. These impacts may well differ for younger versus older children and youth.

Family decisions about welfare use and work, along with other sources of income (for example, other social safety net programs, child support, income from savings), determine the financial resources available to families to purchase goods and services that support the raising of children, including those resources that affect the quality of the home, neighborhood, and school environments. There is an increasing body of evidence that finds a positive relationship between family income and child health and development, with evidence that this relationship is particularly strong at younger ages (Duncan and Brooks-Gunn 1997). Welfare policies that raise incomes may therefore improve child well-being. In contrast, policies that reduce income may be more harmful. Given the findings in Chapter 7 that generous financial work incentives can raise family incomes, particularly when combined with work mandates, we would expect these policies to have more favorable impacts on children than work mandates alone, which were generally associated with little or no change in family income.

As discussed in Chapter 8, welfare reform policies may also affect other areas of family decision making such as childbearing and family formation. To the extent that welfare reform policies reduce childbearing, or out-of-wedlock childbearing, there may be benefits for existing children; available resources can be devoted to a smaller number of children in the family (the "quality-quantity" trade-off). Policies that promote or maintain two-parent families may also have beneficial effects for children to the extent that the time and financial resources available for child rearing increase. However, as we have seen, it appears that the welfare reforms implemented to date have small or inconsistent impacts on childbearing and marriage. Thus it is likely that any associated impacts on child well-being are small as well.

Finally, welfare reform policies may also affect the decisions that older children and youth make about their own behavior. For example, the model presented in Chapter 8 regarding childbearing also applies to adolescents. Policies such as minor residence requirements, work requirements, and time limits may generally make welfare less attractive and therefore may be expected to reduce teen childbearing and early entry onto welfare. If welfare is a less attractive alternative, young people may choose instead to devote more time to investing in their schooling and future labor market prospects. How they do so may depend upon the ways in which welfare reform has affected other aspects of decision making. For example, some youth may increase the time they spend in the labor market in order to contribute to family income, or they may spend time caring for younger siblings. These uses of time may detract from investments in their own schooling.

In sum, the model we have outlined posits that welfare reform policies will have direct and indirect impacts on child well-being by altering parental decisions about the quality and quantity of their own time devoted to raising their children, and the inputs of goods and services that are purchased to care for and nurture their children. Direct impacts arise through mandates to ensure certain behaviors or to obtain particular goods and services. Indirect impacts occur through reform policies' effects on parental work effort, welfare receipt, and family income. Other intervening or intermediate behaviors include those affecting child care, residential location, family composition, parental schooling, parent psychological well-being (for example, self-esteem, sense of self-efficacy, stress, depression, substance abuse), child socialization (for example, for older children, messages about work, responsibility, and self-sufficiency), and access to services (for example, health care).

These direct and intermediate impacts are then expected to affect child outcomes in a number of domains, including cognitive development, behavioral and emotional adjustment, school achievement and attainment, antisocial and delinquent behavior, child safety, and physical and mental health. Welfare reform might be expected to have both negative and positive effects on children's outcomes, and some outcomes might remain unchanged because of opposing forces. We would also expect child impacts to vary with the age of the child. Finally, various aspects of child development may respond to welfare reform more quickly or more slowly. For example, child behavior problems at both younger and older ages may manifest themselves within a short time frame, while it may take longer for effects on child health to become apparent.

Methodological Issues

The same methodological approaches—random assignment experiments and observational studies using the difference-in-difference methodology—could, in principle, be used to evaluate the empirical relationship between welfare reform policies and child outcomes. In terms of the observational methodology, however, many of the child outcomes of interest are not measured routinely as part of large nationally representative surveys, such as the CPS. In addition, specialized smaller-scale surveys may not have sufficient sample sizes to support the difference-in-difference methodology. Likewise, there are few administrative databases that track relevant outcomes in a consistent manner over both geographic space and time. Consequently, in contrast to outcomes such as welfare use, employment and earnings, and income, there are considerably fewer observational studies that analyze child outcomes; in fact, we are aware of only one difference-in-difference study that analyzes direct measures of child well-being.[4] Instead, the research on child outcomes and welfare reform has been conducted in the context of experimental evaluations.

Since our assessment of the impact of welfare reform on child well-being will, of necessity, draw almost exclusively on random assignment studies—and then only on a subset of the studies discussed in prior chapters—a number of caveats must be kept in mind. First, child-outcome data in experimental studies are usually collected through surveys of parents, though in some cases children and teachers may be the respondents. Such survey samples are often by design smaller than the overall study population, and thus are often smaller than those shown in Table 4.5. Smaller samples reduce statistical power.

Second, unlike some of the earlier chapters, where there is considerable uniformity in the outcome measure across studies, child well-being can be conceptualized in many ways, with a myriad of indicators within any given domain such as child behavioral problems, academic success, physical and mental health, or some other area of functioning. Cross-study comparisons are made more difficult when studies do not focus on the same domains, or when they do not use a similar set of indicators within a domain or the same metric or scale for a given indicator.

In some cases, the measures are straightforward indicators of child outcomes. Clear examples include whether a grade has been repeated or whether a child has made an emergency room visit since random assignment. In other cases, the indicators are standard scales or test batteries with well-understood psychometric properties (for example, reliability and validity).[5] For example, the Behavioral Problems Index (BPI) is a frequently used measure of child problem behavior, and it appears in the child-outcome impact analyses for several of the demonstration studies. But the BPI is not the only measure of problem behavior used in these studies, so differences across studies in child behavior measures may arise from the scales themselves and from the dimensions of behavior they measure rather than from true differences in behavior.

Finally, the limitations of experimental studies discussed in Chapter 4—the inability to capture program entry effects, questions about generalizing from a local demonstration to national reform, and problems with maintaining ideal experimental conditions—will also affect the ability to generalize from the experimental studies to the national experience, particularly with respect to the impact of welfare reform as a whole.

Experimental Estimates of the Effects of Specific Reforms

A child-outcome component has been included in a number of the welfare experiments, with most studies, as already noted, relying primarily on data collected from parents (and sometimes teachers or the children themselves). A few experimental studies also use administrative data for outcomes such as child maltreatment and foster care. However, across the experimental studies, data on child outcomes are not universally available. Of the studies listed in Table 4.5, the programs in Arizona (EMPOWER), Arkansas (AWWDP), Indiana (IMPACT), Iowa (FIP), New Jersey (FDP), and Virginia (VIP/VIEW) do not report results for child outcomes in the domains we list above.[6] The other evaluations report results for at least one child outcome for at least one treatment-control contrast.[7]

In light of the measurement issues discussed in the previous section, we have organized the presentation of the results from the experimental literature in a format different from the one we used in earlier chapters. First, we have grouped the measures of child outcomes into four broad domains: behavior, school performance, health, and other.[8] The first domain captures both positive and negative aspects of behavior, ranging from such measures as the BPI or an index of positive social behaviors for younger children, to being suspended or expelled from school, to being involved in criminal or delinquent activity (for older children). The second domain includes various measures of school performance and achievement, including subject-specific test scores (for example, reading and math), parental reports of school performance, the extent of grade repetition, and use of special education. General measures of health status are included in the third domain, along with other indicators of health and safety, such as reports of child abuse and neglect. A fourth residual domain captures other outcomes such as foster care placements and participation in clubs or organizations.

Given the multiple measures that are often not comparable across studies, we first provide an overall qualitative perspective of the results across studies in Figure 9.1.[9] In this figure, we record the number of measures in a given domain where the impact estimate was in a favorable direction (whether numerically positive or negative)—plotted with circle symbols—and the number of measures where the impact estimate was in an unfavorable direction—plotted with square symbols. Each symbol represents one impact estimate for a given study. In each case, we plot the impact estimates that are statistically significant ($p \leq .10$) using solid symbols, and plot those that are statistically insignificant using open symbols. Impact estimates that are zero are recorded with a clover symbol.

As noted in the discussion of our theoretical framework, the impact of welfare reform may vary with the age of the child. Drawing on the age stratifications used in each study, we first tabulate outcomes for all children, if available, followed by those for various age strata, as available. Although the studies use somewhat different age cutoffs to define their age strata, we separately record results for three age groups, based on the age at the time of follow-up: preschool-age children (up through age 5), primary-school-age children (typically ages 5 to 12), and secondary-school-age children and above (typically ages 12 and above).[10] We indicate for each study what age cutoffs are used. In some studies, two age groups are available for the two older-age strata (that is, primary and secondary grades) and we record the results for each. Because of the outcome domains considered and the metrics available, infants and toddlers at follow-up are often excluded from the experimental studies.

To bring an additional quantitative perspective to the results for primary-school-age children, Figures 9.2, 9.3, and 9.4 display the effect sizes for selected measures of child behavior (Figure 9.2), school achievement (Figure 9.3), and health status (Figure 9.4) when they are available.[11] In each figure, a positive effect size indicates a result in the favorable direction (whether numerically positive or negative); a negative effect size indicates an unfavorable result. Typically, results are available for children ages 5 to 12 at the time of follow-up, but the age range in the NEWWS sites is limited to ages 8 to 10. Figure 9.2 reports results for a measure of behavior problems (in most cases, the BPI) and a measure of positive social behavior (in most cases, the Positive Behavior Scale). Figure 9.3 plots results for a measure of school achievement (in some cases based on a test score; in others, based on parent or teacher reports), as well as a measure of grade repetition. Finally, Figure 9.4 records results for a measure of general health status, typically as reported by the child's parent. In each case, Appendix Table A.7 provides more detail on the specific measures for each study.

We now turn to a summary of the results for experimental evaluations of programs that involved specific policy reforms.

Financial Work Incentives

Both MFIP-IO and WRP-IO evaluated the impact of financial work incentives on child outcomes (see panel A of Figure 9.1). Compared with MFIP, WRP examined a more limited set of child indicators. In general, WRP-IO shows no consistent effect for the limited set of child indicators studied for the sample of nearly 1,200 children (D. Bloom, Hendra, and Michalopoulos 2000). Although children in the treatment group had a significantly higher likelihood of missing a day or more of school in the last month (shown as a solid square in the "schooling" row for all children), they also had a significantly higher rate of participation

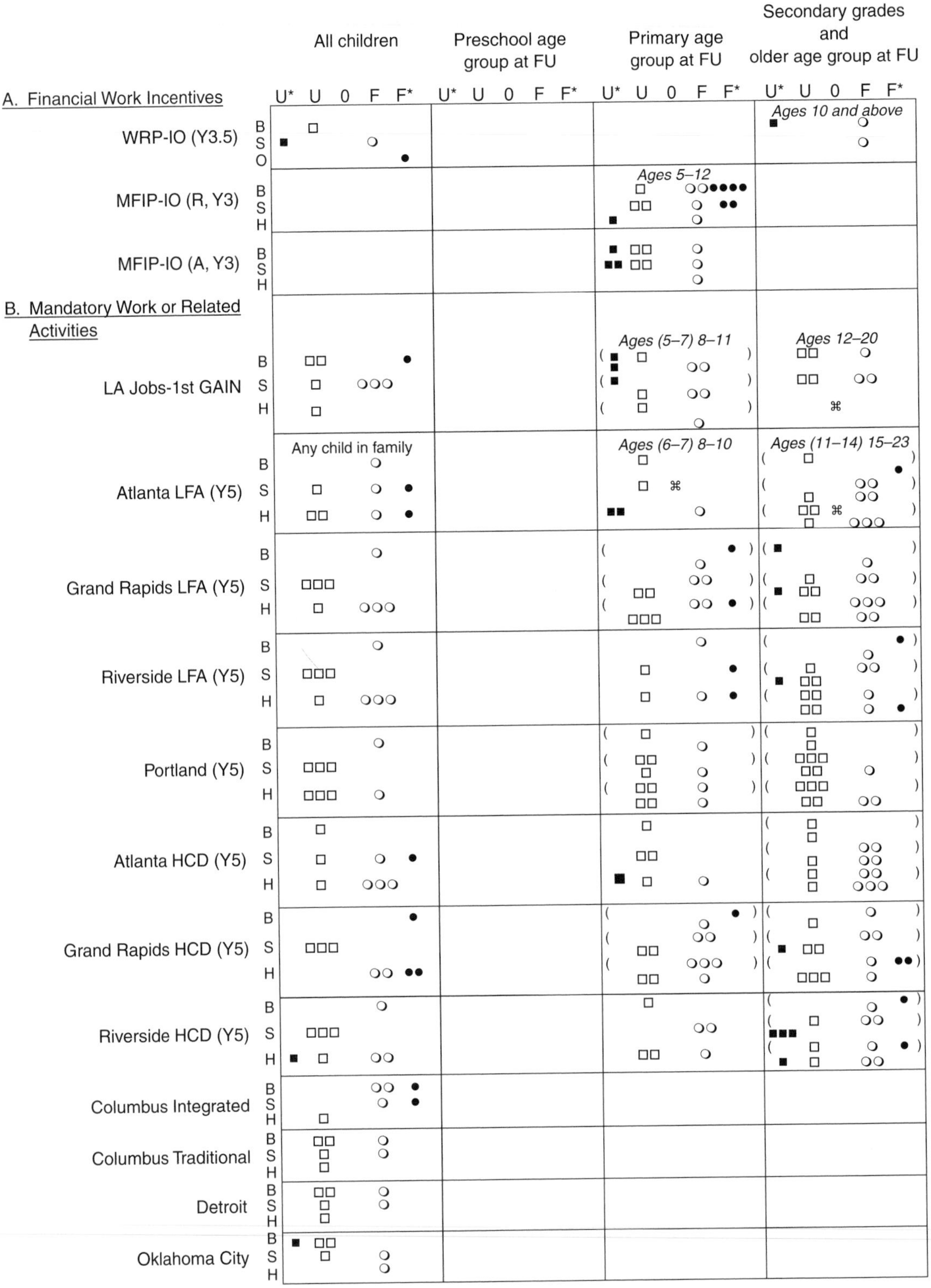

All children   Preschool age group at FU   Primary age group at FU   Secondary grades and older age group at FU

A. Financial Work Incentives

U* U 0 F F*   U* U 0 F F*   U* U 0 F F*   U* U 0 F F*

WRP-IO (Y3.5) — B S O — Ages 10 and above

MFIP-IO (R, Y3) — B S H — Ages 5–12

MFIP-IO (A, Y3) — B S H

B. Mandatory Work or Related Activities

LA Jobs-1st GAIN — B S H — Ages (5–7) 8–11 — Ages 12–20

Atlanta LFA (Y5) — B S H — Any child in family — Ages (6–7) 8–10 — Ages (11–14) 15–23

Grand Rapids LFA (Y5) — B S H

Riverside LFA (Y5) — B S H

Portland (Y5) — B S H

Atlanta HCD (Y5) — B S H

Grand Rapids HCD (Y5) — B S H

Riverside HCD (Y5) — B S H

Columbus Integrated — B S H

Columbus Traditional — B S H

Detroit — B S H

Oklahoma City — B S H

Figure 9.1
Estimated impacts of welfare reform on child outcomes from experimental studies. *Source:* See Appendix Table A.7.

		All children					Preschool age group at FU					Primary age group at FU					Secondary grades and older age group at FU				
		U*	U	0	F	F*	U*	U	0	F	F*	U*	U	0	F	F*	U*	U	0	F	F*
C. Financial Work Incentives Tied to Work or Related Activities																					
WRP (Y3.5)	B				○												*Ages 10 and above* □			○	
	S		□□																	○	
	O					●															
TSMF (Y1–Y4)	H		□														*Ages 12 and above*			○	
	O		□																	○	
MFIP (R, Y3)	B											*Ages 5–12*			○○○○	●●●	*Ages 13 and above* □				
	S														○○	●●●			⌘	○○	
	H											■	□								
MFIP (A, Y3)	B											■	□□		○		■				
	S												□□□		○○		■■	□			
	H												□								
SSP (R, Y3)	B						*Ages 3–5* □□					*Ages 6–11* □		○○			*Ages 12–18* ■■■■■			○	
	S									○			⌘	○	●●		■	□□□			
	H							□		○○		□			●●			□		○○	
New Hope	B			○	●		*Ages 3–5*			○○○		*Ages 6–12* □		○○○○		*Ages 12–18* ■	□				
	S			○○										○	●		■■■				●●
D. Parental Responsibility Requirements																					
PPI	H						*Ages 2–4* □□		○												
PIP	H											*Ages 4–10*			●						
E. TANF-like Bundles of Reforms																					
ABC (Y1–Y3)	H	■		○○																	
	O			○																	
FTP (Y4)	B											*Ages 5–12* ■	□□		○		*Ages 13–17* ■	□□□			
	S												□□	⌘	○		■	□			
	H												□			●				○	
Jobs First (Y3)	B													○	●●●●			□		○○	●
	S												□□	⌘	○		■	□□			
	H														○			□			

Column Symbol

Column	Symbol	Description
U*	■	Statistically significant impact in unfavorable direction at $p \le .10$.
U	□	Impact in unfavorable direction at $p > .10$.
0	⌘	Impact equal to 0.
F	○	Impact in favorable direction at $p > .10$.
F*	●	Statistically significant impact in favorable direction at $p \le .10$.

Note: Impacts are for two-year follow-up and for recipients (R) and applicants (A) unless otherwise noted. B = outcomes in behavioral domain; S = outcomes in school performance and achievement domain; H = outcomes in health domain; O = other outcomes; Y = year; FU = follow-up.

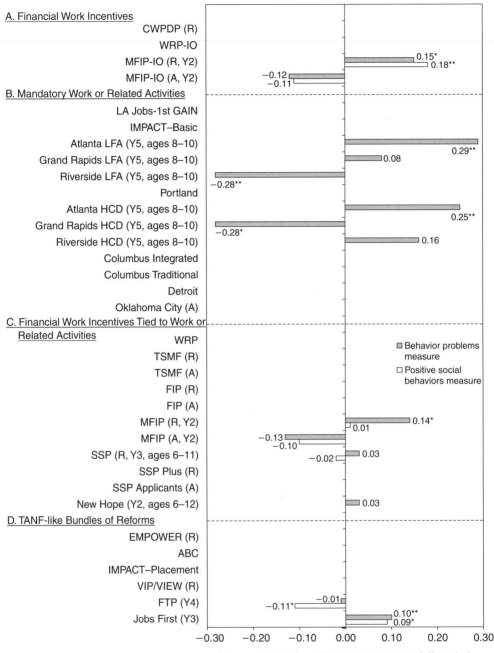

Figure 9.2

Estimated impacts of welfare reform on primary-school-aged children's behavior from experimental studies. *Source:* See Appendix Table A.7.

Note: For full program names, see Table 4.5. Positive effect sizes indicate favorable impact; negative effect sizes indicate unfavorable impact. Impacts are for follow-up period indicated and for children aged 5–12 of recipients (R) and applicants (A) unless otherwise noted. Y = year. Significant at the ***1%, **5%, *10% level.

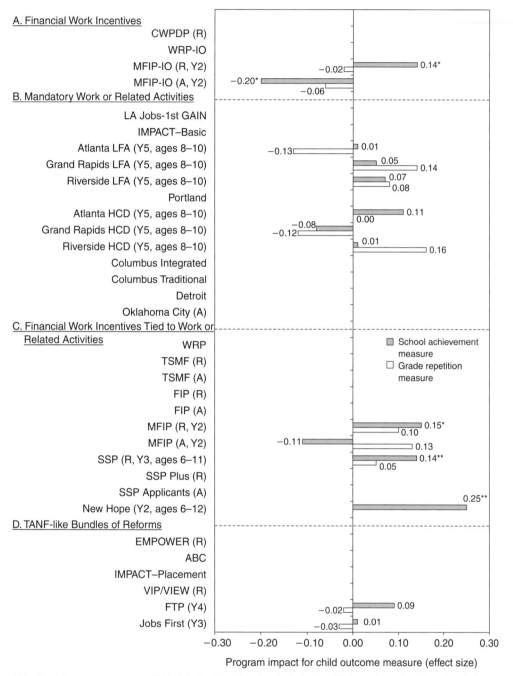

Figure 9.3

Estimated impacts of welfare reform on primary-school-aged children's school achievement from experimental studies. *Source:* See Appendix Table A.7.

Note: For full program names, see Table 4.5. Positive effect sizes indicate favorable impact; negative effect sizes indicate unfavorable impact. Impacts are for follow-up period indicated and for children aged 5–12 of recipients (R) and applicants (A) unless otherwise noted. Y = year. Significant at the ***1%, **5%, *10% level.

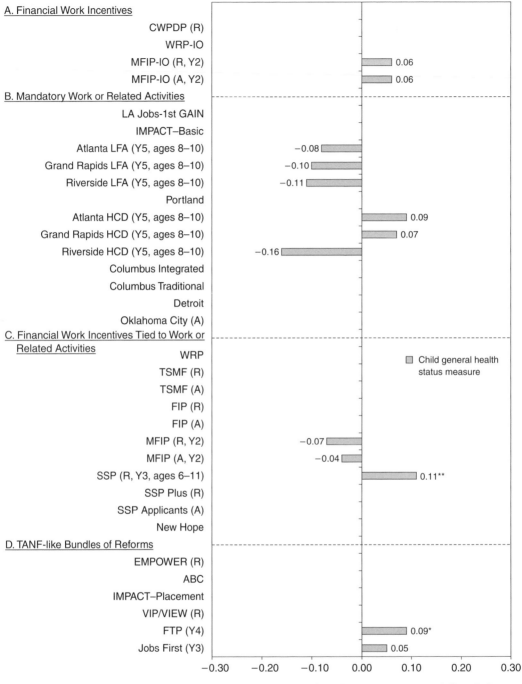

A. Financial Work Incentives
- CWPDP (R)
- WRP-IO
- MFIP-IO (R, Y2) — 0.06
- MFIP-IO (A, Y2) — 0.06

B. Mandatory Work or Related Activities
- LA Jobs-1st GAIN
- IMPACT–Basic
- Atlanta LFA (Y5, ages 8–10) — −0.08
- Grand Rapids LFA (Y5, ages 8–10) — −0.10
- Riverside LFA (Y5, ages 8–10) — −0.11
- Portland
- Atlanta HCD (Y5, ages 8–10) — 0.09
- Grand Rapids HCD (Y5, ages 8–10) — 0.07
- Riverside HCD (Y5, ages 8–10) — −0.16
- Columbus Integrated
- Columbus Traditional
- Detroit
- Oklahoma City (A)

C. Financial Work Incentives Tied to Work or Related Activities
- WRP
- TSMF (R)
- TSMF (A)
- FIP (R)
- FIP (A)
- MFIP (R, Y2) — −0.07
- MFIP (A, Y2) — −0.04
- SSP (R, Y3, ages 6–11) — 0.11**
- SSP Plus (R)
- SSP Applicants (A)
- New Hope

D. TANF-like Bundles of Reforms
- EMPOWER (R)
- ABC
- IMPACT–Placement
- VIP/VIEW (R)
- FTP (Y4) — 0.09*
- Jobs First (Y3) — 0.05

Legend: ▨ Child general health status measure

Program impact for child outcome measure (effect size)

Note:: For full program names, see Table 4.5. Positive effect sizes indicate favorable impact; negative effect sizes indicate unfavorable impact. Impacts are for follow-up period indicated and for children aged 5–12 of recipients (R) and applicants (A) unless otherwise noted. Y = year. Significant at the ***1%, **5%, *10% level.

Figure 9.4

Estimated impacts of welfare reform on primary-school-aged children's health status from experimental studies. *Source:* See Appendix Table A.7.

in clubs and organizations (shown as a solid circle in the "other" row for all children). For those age 10 and above, shown in the last panel of columns, the treatment group reported a statistically significant higher rate of ever being in trouble with the police (26.8 percent versus 17.2 percent for controls), but there were favorable insignificant differences in behavior problems and school dropout behavior.

The MFIP child analysis (both the Incentives Only and full program) focuses on a random subset of families in the evaluation sample who entered the study in the first six months (April to October 1994) and who had at least one child aged 5 to 12 at the time of the survey, three years after random assignment (Gennetian and Miller 2000). This age cohort combines children who were both preschool age and school age at the time of random assignment, groups that are analyzed separately in some of the other experiments. Much of the data collected refers to a single "focal" child rather than to all children in the family.[12] As with other MFIP analyses, results are available separately for long-term recipients and applicants, with about 600 and 400 children in the combined treatment and control groups, respectively.

In general, MFIP-IO produced largely favorable effects for children of long-term recipients. Statistically significant beneficial impacts were concentrated in the behavioral and schooling domains. For example, Figures 9.2 and 9.3 show statistically significant favorable impacts—with effect sizes in the range of 0.14 to 0.18—for measures of behavior problems, positive social behaviors, and school achievement for recipient children. The impact for one health indicator, emergency room visits for any child in the family, was unfavorable and statistically significant for recipients (see Figure 9.1). For applicants, most effects were not significant, but some in the behavior and school performance domains were unfavorable and statistically significant. Other results (not shown) indicate that MFIP-IO improved the physical home environment and reduced harsh parenting for recipient children, while the reverse was true for applicants (Gennetian and Miller 2000). Recall that in Chapter 7, MFIP-IO had stronger effects on income for long-term recipients than for recent applicants. Also, applicant children in the control group performed better than recipient children in the control group, indicating there was less room for the program to improve child outcomes among the more advantaged applicant children.

Mandatory Work or Related Activities

Panel B of Figure 9.1 records the child outcomes measured as part of L.A. Jobs-First GAIN (Freedman, Knab, et al. 2000), as well as the eleven NEWWS programs (Hamilton, Freedman, and McGroder 2000; Hamilton et al. 2001). These programs, which focus on mandatory work-related activities, collected information at the two-year or five-year follow-up on the children of recipients and applicants, either single parents (Los Angeles) or all parents (NEWWS).

L.A. Jobs-First GAIN collected child-level information at the two-year follow-up for close to 1,600 children (Freedman, Knab et al. 2000). Information collected covered areas such as academic achievement and school performance, behavioral and emotional adjustment, and safety. Results are recorded for all children, as well as for children classified by age at the time of follow-up: 5 to 7, 8 to 11, and 12 to 20. There are over 400 children in each age group. Since the two youngest age groups fall into our second age stratum (that is, primary grades), the results for these two groups are recorded in the third panel of columns. In this case, for each domain, results for the youngest age group (that is, 5 to 7) are bracketed by parentheses, followed by the results for the oldest age group.

As seen in Figure 9.1, for the pooled sample of children, there was only one statistically significant effect (and that only at the 10 percent level): a more favorable outcome on school expulsions/suspensions (9.3 percent treatment versus 12.9 percent for controls). Younger children in the primary-school age group (those ages 5 to 7) were significantly more likely to have a special physical, emotional, or mental condition that made their parents' work difficult. They were also more likely to repeat a grade (6.2 percent versus 0.4 percent for controls). For the older primary-school-age children (those ages 8 to 11), the treatment group attended special classes for physical, emotional, or mental conditions at a significantly higher rate (15.5 percent versus 9.8 percent for the control group). The other impact estimates were mixed and insignificant. For the oldest age stratum, those ages 12 to 20 at the follow-up, there were no statistically significant differences on any of the indicators. In some cases, the impact estimates were favorable and in others not favorable.

Outcomes in the NEWWS evaluation—collected at the two-year follow-up for four programs and at the five-year follow-up for the other seven programs—focused on maternal reports of behavioral adjustments, school progress, and health and safety for all children aged 18 or under at random assignment. Sample sizes range from 500 to 1,200 as of the final follow-up. For three programs—Grand Rapids LFA, Portland, and Grand Rapids HCD—results are available for children ages 6 to 7 and 8 to 10 as of the five-year follow-up. For these three programs, the results for these two age groups are shown in the third panel of columns for primary-school-age children, with parentheses around the first row of symbols for the youngest age group, followed by results for the older age group. For the two Atlanta and two Riverside programs, results for children at the youngest ages are only available for those aged 8 to 10 at the five-year follow-up. All seven programs also report results for those aged 11 to 14 and aged 15 to 23 as of the five-year follow-up. Results for these two age groups are shown in the final panel of columns for secondary-school-age children and above, again with parentheses bracketing the results for the younger age range. For the four remaining NEWWS sites, the results recorded in the first column for all children are for children aged 6 and above as of the two-year follow-up.

Overall, the NEWWS child-outcome results show no clear pattern of beneficial or harmful effects for children up to age 14 at follow-up (those who were pre-school age to primary-school age at the time of random assignment). Both favorable and unfavorable effects are found across all the domains, sometimes for the same program. Typically, only a small subset of the measured outcomes have statistically significant impacts. As noted above, results are available for three sites for children aged 6 to 7 at follow-up, a group that was aged 1 to 2 at the time of random assignment. There are mostly favorable effects for this age group in the two Grand Rapids programs and more unfavorable, but insignificant, effects for the Portland program.

In six NEWWS programs (LFA and HCD programs in Atlanta, Grand Rapids, and Riverside), the Child Outcomes Study (COS) collected additional measures for a focal child aged 3 to 5 at randomization (ages 8 to 10 as of the five-year follow-up), focusing in more detail on academic functioning, social skills and behavior, and health and safety based on reports from mothers, teachers, and the children. Sample sizes range between 250 and 550, depending on the measure and the site. Figures 9.2 to 9.4 plot results for this subsample of the NEWWS study, because this is the only sample with data on measures of child behavior, school achievement, and health status comparable to other studies. As seen in the three figures, the COS results also show no clear pattern of favorable or unfavorable effects across the six NEWWS sites. In the behavior domain, large statistically significant favorable impacts were found for Atlanta LFA and Atlanta HCD, while the reverse was true for Riverside LFA and Grand Rapids HCD. None of the impacts for school achievement or health status was statistically significant. In a more thorough analysis, Hamilton et al. (2001) conclude that there is no strong relationship between child outcomes and the placement- or skills-oriented approach.

Turning back to Figure 9.1, for the older adolescents and young adults (those aged 15 to 23 as of the five-year follow-up, who were preadolescents to adolescents at random assignment), there is a higher prevalence of statistically significant unfavorable effects, especially for schooling outcomes in the Riverside HCD program, the program with the largest employment increase and the largest income decline by year 5 (see Figures 6.3 and 7.3). Significant unfavorable schooling outcomes are also found for Grand Rapids LFA, Riverside LFA, and Grand Rapids HCD, three other programs with employment increases and income declines through at least the second or third year of follow-up.

It appears from these results that reductions in welfare dependency without significant gains in income result in ambiguous effects on child outcomes, with examples of both favorable and unfavorable effects. For pre–school-age and primary-school-age children at random assignment, most results for outcomes measured five years later were insignificant. Among the significant impacts, which number slightly greater than what would be expected by chance, favorable effects were somewhat more prevalent than unfavorable ones. There is more consistent evidence of unfavorable impacts for adolescents and young adults, especially in the school achievement domain. Across these studies, there is no clear relationship between program impacts on income and impacts on children, although there is some evidence discussed above that associates worse adolescent outcomes with higher employment and lower income. On the basis of the theoretical framework discussed above, these results are not unexpected, given that these programs had little if any effect on income. At the same time, the greater work effort on the part of mothers does not appear to have been very harmful to younger children, but the same cannot be said for adolescents.

Financial Work Incentives Tied to Work or Related Activities

Child impacts are available for WRP and TSMF, programs that combined weak financial work incentives within the welfare system with mandatory work-related activities (see panel C of Figure 9.1). The results for the full WRP evaluation show even fewer significant impacts than the Incentives Only component of the program (D. Bloom, Hendra, and Michalopoulos 2000). The only significant impact is a higher rate of participation for all children in clubs and organizations (34.2 versus 26.5 percent). There is no clear pattern with respect to the relative contribution of work requirements on top of the incentive program.

The evaluation of the Michigan TSMF program is one of the few to rely exclusively on administrative data to assess child outcomes (Werner and Kornfeld 1997). The evaluation shows no significant impacts for any of the measures considered: substantiated reports of abuse and ne-glect, placement in foster care, and employment and earnings (for chil-dren aged 12 and above at follow-up). The labor market outcomes for youth were examined because Michigan's program allowed a 100 per-cent disregard of earnings from dependent children. Despite this pro-gram feature, TSMF does not appear to have significantly affected work effort on the part of teens.

The results for the full MFIP, which combined strong financial work incentives with work mandates, are similar to those seen earlier for MFIP-IO (compare panels A and C of Figure 9.1). In particular, chil-dren aged 5–12 of long-term recipients experienced several favorable im-pacts concentrated in the behavior and school domains. Many of the same indicators that are significant in panel A are likewise significant in panel C. Moreover, the effect sizes for the behavior problems and school achievement measures plotted in Figures 9.2 and 9.3 for MFIP recipients are comparable to those found for MFIP-IO recipients. When selected indicators were considered for recipient pre–school-age children (those younger than age 6 at random assignment) versus school-age children, the latter group had stronger impacts (not shown). Two school perfor-mance measures and the BPI showed favorable effects for the older sub-group. There were no significant effects for the youngest children, those who were pre–school-age at the start of the experiment. Compared with the older cohort, adult MFIP participants with pre–school-age children experienced a larger increase in employment and income.

A comparison of the two MFIP interventions (full MFIP versus MFIP-IO) for recipients indicates that the favorable effects on children's behav-ior and school performance can be attributed to the financial work in-centives component of the program. With the exception of one indica-tor of positive social behavior where MFIP had a worse outcome than MFIP-IO, the behavior and school performance indicators were little changed between MFIP-IO and MFIP. Thus while the financial work incentives improved several measures of behavior and school perfor-mance, the services and work requirements were generally neutral. This finding suggests that adding mandatory work-related activities to a pro-gram with generous financial work incentives is neutral for children, de-spite the fact that adding the work requirements further increased full-time employment and lowered welfare benefits.

For recent applicants, the full MFIP generally had no effect on the child indicators measured for those aged 5 to 12 at follow-up. The one exception was a measure of whether the focal child had been suspended or expelled since random assignment. Small sample sizes make it more problematic to separate the effects of work requirements versus financial work incentives for the applicants in the study. Compared with the long-term recipients, children in the recent applicant group began with fewer disadvantages and were more heterogeneous, which may explain some of the differential impact.

MFIP also provides a more limited number of measures, mostly in the schooling domain, for children aged 13 and above at the time of follow-up (aged 10 and above at random assignment). The impacts for these adolescents are mixed in sign and insignificant for long-term recipients, but they are all unfavorable and, with one exception, statistically significant for the adolescent children of recent applicants. It is unclear whether these unfavorable impacts might be associated with the work requirement or financial work incentive components of the program, although recent applicants were not subject to the MFIP work requirements for much of the follow-up period.

Child impacts are available for two of the programs—SSP and New Hope—that tie financial incentives outside the welfare system to work (see panel C of Figure 9.1). The SSP evaluation assessed child outcomes three years postrandomization (Morris and Michalopoulos 2000).[13] Outcome measures covered the child's social and antisocial behavior, school progress and achievement, and health and safety. In addition, it is among the few studies to administer achievement tests to children—the Peabody Picture Vocabulary Test-Revised (a standard measure of receptive vocabulary) for children aged 4 to 7 and a math skills test for children aged 7 to 15—to directly assess academic performance. SSP reports results stratified into three age groups (3 to 5, 6 to 11, and 12 to 18 at follow-up), with about 1,000 children each in the youngest and oldest age strata, and about 450 in the middle stratum.

The impacts for SSP are strikingly consistent within age strata. For the youngest children, who were infants and toddlers at the time of random assignment, none of the outcomes was significantly affected by the program. Of the significant impacts for children aged 6–11, all were favorable and centered on measures of school achievement (math score and maternal report of achievement in specific subjects) and health (general health and presence of long-term health problems).[14] The effect sizes, shown in Figures 9.2 to 9.4, are 0.14 for the significant math achievement measure and 0.11 for the significant health status measure. Indeed, the health impact for SSP children aged 6–11 reported in Figure 9.4 is one of only two significant effects.

In contrast, for the oldest age group in the SSP study, all the statistically significant effects were in the unfavorable direction, with detrimental effects concentrated in the behavior domain. For instance, children aged 12–18 at follow-up had higher rates of school behavior problems, minor delinquent activity (15- to 18-year-olds only), and use of tobacco, alcohol, and drugs, with effect sizes that range from about 0.10 to 0.20 standard deviations. At the same time, there were no significant impacts for many of the other indicators measured for this age group, including math and reading test scores. It is worth noting that adult outcomes for SSP families with children aged 12–18 at follow-up were as favorable as they were for families with children in the youngest and middle cohorts.

The New Hope Child and Family Study collected parental assessments of child behavior and school progress for a focal child aged 3–12 at the two-year follow-up (Bos et al. 1999). Teachers also provided ratings on indicators in these domains for children in kindergarten and above. In addition, information was collected directly from children starting at age 6. Results are presented for all children and for three age groups at follow-up: 3–5, 6–8, and 9–12, although results for the last two groups are often pooled. The sample sizes for many of the impact results shown in Figure 9.1 are among the smallest of the studies we consider, ranging from under 250 combined treatment and control children aged 3–5 and 6–8 to over 600 children of all ages with parental reports of school behavior. In addition to these results, Bos and Vargas (2001), in a separate analysis, report results for adolescents aged 12 to 18 based on data collected from all children in the New Hope sample.

Even though the New Hope parental outcomes, such as employment, earnings, and income, shown in previous chapters, differed by employment status at the time of random assignment, there were few differences in child outcomes across the two groups. Pooled results are summarized in Figure 9.1. With the exception of the adolescent results, only two of the outcomes recorded in the table show a significant favorable effect, while none shows a significant unfavorable effect.[15] The significant favorable effects for the pooled sample are for the teacher report of positive social behavior (children ages 3 to 12) and for school performance (children ages 5 to 12), with an effect size that equals about 0.25 of a standard deviation in each case (the latter result is shown in Figure 9.3). With one exception, the other measures for both children aged 3 to 5 and those aged 6 to 12 are in the favorable direction, but small sample sizes mean that small differences are unlikely to be detected.

The impacts for New Hope adolescents are mixed, with both favorable and unfavorable statistically significant impacts across the behavior and school achievement domains. On the positive side, New Hope adolescents are less likely to be in special education and more likely to be in a gifted or talented program. On the negative side, they are more likely to have a higher number of contacts by the school for behavior or academic problems, to have repeated a grade, and to be performing more poorly in school.

Although the SSP and New Hope earnings supplements were available for at most three years, both studies also included a longer-term follow-up of child outcomes (results not shown). SSP collected additional data on children fifty-four-months postrandomization, with results stratified by children aged 1 to 2, 3 to 4, 13 to 15, and 16 to 17 as of random assignment (Michalopoulos et al. 2002). Although fewer measures were collected at this later follow-up, the treatment–control group comparisons suggest that some of the favorable effects of SSP persisted even after the earnings supplements ended, while other unfavorable effects disappeared. For example, for those 7.5 to 9.5 years of age at follow-up (aged 3 to 4 at random assignment), children in SSP were more likely to have above-average school achievement (as reported by their parents), less likely to have ever used special education, and to have somewhat better health on average. For the youngest children studied, those aged 1 to 2 at random assignment, the measures of academic functioning, behavior, and health showed no significant differences.

Those aged 17 and above at the final follow-up (ages 13 and above at random assignment) showed few differences, in contrast to some of the unfavorable effects as of the thirty-six-month follow-up found for adolescents. As of the fifty-four-month follow-up, these children who were now transitioning to adulthood were no more or less likely to have dropped out of school, to have completed the twelfth grade, to be attending college, to be working, or to have ever been arrested. The one unfavorable impact was a higher incidence of ever having a baby among children of SSP participants who were aged 20.5 to 22.5 years as of the fifty-four-month follow-up (ages 16 to 17 at random assignment). However, the higher level of childbearing did not translate into differential outcomes with respect to schooling or work.

The New Hope analysis focused on children aged 6 to 16 as of the five-year follow-up, three years after the initial two-year follow-up reported in Figure 9.1 (Huston et al. 2003). Most notably, the favorable effects of New Hope on children's achievement persisted past the three-year period of New Hope program benefits. Among all children aged 6 to 16, there were significant favorable effects for the Woodcock-Johnson (a standardized achievement test) broad reading and letter-word scores, and on parent-rated reading achievement and the positive behavior scale. There were no significant differences in teachers' reports of school achievement or of positive or problem behaviors; in children's self-reports of delinquent or risky behavior; or in parent's reports of child health outcomes. Most of these effects were similar for children stratified by age, although some differences emerge. Comparisons across time are limited to some extent, because some of the measures with unfavorable outcomes for adolescents at the two-year follow-up are not reported for the same age group three years later. Nevertheless, it appears that favorable effects for the youngest children may persist even beyond the period when families are eligible for the earnings supplement.

Together these results, combined with those for programs that included financial work incentives alone, suggest that more work and more income generally have neutral or favorable effects for younger children (preschool- and primary-school age), with the possibility that effects may persist over time. However, they may have detrimental effects on adolescents, at least for some areas of development and perhaps only in the short run. The favorable effects are concentrated in the behavior and school performance domains for the younger children; the negative impacts for the older youth fall primarily in the behavior domain. These results are consistent with the broader literature that evaluates the relationship between family income and child outcomes across the life course. Duncan and Brooks-Gunn (1997), in their synthesis of recent studies on this topic, conclude that "family economic conditions in early and middle childhood appear to be far more important for shaping ability and achievement than they do during adolescence" (597). Another recent analysis of pooled data from many of the experiments we include here also concludes that school achievement gains, in particular, are concentrated among younger children and only in those programs that provide earnings supplements, that is, those programs that raise family incomes (Clark-Kauffman, Duncan, and Morris 2003).

The MFIP applicants, a more advantaged group, provide the one exception, where even younger children experienced some unfavorable impacts in a program involving financial work incentives. Since the income gains for these families were still positive, albeit smaller than those for recipients, it is not clear what other factors can explain these less favorable outcomes.

Parental Responsibility Requirements

Two studies that evaluated parental responsibility requirements, PPI and PIP, assessed child outcomes. Since these two demonstrations focused on requirements regarding preventative health care (PPI) or immunizations (PIP), the main outcomes of interest pertain to the domain of child health for younger children.

The PPI program in Maryland required families with children aged 3–

24 months to verify that their children received preventative health care, including immunizations. Data collected from the medical records of nearly 1,800 treatment and control children, one and two years after randomization, provided information on preventative visits per year and on whether children were up to date for three specific vaccinations (Minkovitz et al. 1999). The results show no significant treatment-control differences at either the first or the second year follow-up in measures of vaccination status or receipt of well-child care.

Georgia's PIP, which required families to demonstrate proof of up-to-date immunization status semiannually (up to 1996) or annually (after 1996), served families with children aged 6 or younger. Medical records were examined for about 2,800 treatment and control children in the demonstration four years after randomization (Kerpelman, Connell, and Gunn 2000). In each of the four years postrandomization, children in the treatment group were significantly more likely to be current on at least four, and most often all five, of their vaccinations. For example, four years after randomization, 87.5 percent of treatment children were up to date on their polio vaccination compared with 80.1 percent of the control group. The impacts for this vaccination and two other vaccinations with relatively high rates of immunization even in the control group (specifically DTP, Diphtheria–Tetanus Toxoids–Pertussis, and MMR, Measles-Mumps-Rubella) are considered large given the potential for a "ceiling effect" (that is, efforts to increase immunization rates often reach a "ceiling" beyond which further increases to 100 percent coverage are difficult to achieve).

One possible explanation for the favorable impacts of PIP, compared with the lack of results for PPI, is that PIP had larger sanctions than PPI. In the case of PIP, the sanction equaled a portion of the nonimmunized child's grant. PPI effectively levied a $10 per month sanction against a family that was out of compliance.[16] Another explanation may be that recipients responded more to the PIP initiative because the intervention was focused only on changing immunization outcomes—with expectations that were easier to understand and comply with—compared with the broader set of requirements under PPI regarding health care (for example, preventative care more generally and prenatal care) and school attendance (Kerpelman, Connell, and Gunn 2000).

Observational Estimates of the Effects of Specific Reforms

Given the measurement issues discussed earlier, it is not surprising that there are so few observational studies of the impact of welfare reform on child outcomes. Most of the outcomes of interest—such as impacts on cognitive, emotional, and social development; behavior problems; school performance; and child health—are simply not collected for large nationally representative samples over time. Without such data, it is difficult to implement the difference-in-difference methodology required to control for unobserved confounding factors.

We are aware of just one relevant observational study, which uses administrative data on child maltreatment and the difference-in-difference methodology to investigate the impact of specific reform policies under TANF (and waivers as a whole). Paxson and Waldfogel (2003) use annual state-level administrative data on child maltreatment and foster care to model the relationship between these outcomes and welfare policies, measured by the existence of a pre-TANF waiver, the existence of a family cap under AFDC or TANF, and then specific policies post-TANF (work requirements, sanctions, and time limits). The outcomes they model by state and year from 1990 to 1998 include the log of reports of child abuse and neglect (in total and disaggregated), substantiated cases of abuse and neglect and the substantiation rate (substantiated cases as a fraction of all reported cases), and the number of children in out-of-home (primarily foster) care. Controls are included for the size, age, and race composition of the child population; the fraction of children in urban areas; the proportion of children whose mother has less than a high school degree; the unemployment rate; state welfare benefit levels; and state and year fixed effects. Controls are not included, however, for other state-level child welfare policy variables that were changing over this period.

Paxson and Waldfogel produce some evidence suggesting that welfare policy may affect child maltreatment outcomes, but many of the estimated effects are not statistically significant. The statistically significant coefficients indicate that immediate work requirements under TANF are associated with an increase in out-of-home care, while a first full-family sanction under TANF is estimated to raise reports of physical abuse, reports of neglect, and substantiated cases of abuse. Among the other effects, a family cap lowers substantiated cases and the substantiation rate but raises out-of-home care. Paxson and Waldfogel hypothesize that a family cap reduces abuse by limiting family size, but the other studies reviewed in Chapter 8 suggest that family caps do not have a major impact on childbearing. None of the coefficients on the TANF time limit measure is statistically significant.

Taken together, the welfare policy variables are only jointly significant in the models of substantiated cases, reported cases of neglect, and out-of-home care. As with the observational studies reviewed in other chapters, there may be too little variation in the time period—with data extending only to 1998—to separately sort out the effects of the different welfare policy variables on child outcomes. In addition, the absence of controls for other potentially relevant policy variables may bias the estimated welfare policy impacts.

Estimates of the Effects of Reform as a Bundle

Of the experimental studies that evaluate TANF-like bundles of reforms, ABC, FTP, and Jobs First report analyses of child outcomes (see panel E of Figure 9.1 and panel D of Figures 9.2 to 9.4). Delaware's ABC evaluation examined child protective services administrative data for nearly 4,000 children in the treatment and control groups to assess the impact of the program on substantiated reports of child abuse and neglect (in aggregate and for subcomponents of maltreatment) and placements in foster care (Fein and Lee 2000). The results show a statistically significant increase in the incidence of child neglect in years 1 and 3, but not in year 2.[17] For example, in year 1, 2.6 percent of the control group had a substantiated report of child neglect compared with 4.1 percent for the treatment group. No significant differences were found for other types of maltreatment (for example, physical and emotional abuse or sexual abuse) and foster care placements.

The combination of benefit decreases and increased work effort in years 1 and 3 is suggested by Fein and Lee (2000) as an explanation for the pattern of significance on the measure of child neglect. In contrast, while benefits fell in the second year, earnings did not increase. This interpretation is consistent with Paxson and Waldfogel (1999), who estimate that increased maternal employment in single-parent families increases child maltreatment. Since income—which is sometimes negatively associated with the incidence of abuse and neglect in Paxson and Waldfogel's (1999) study—did not increase, the negative employment effect in years 1 and 3 would be expected to dominate.

The evaluation of FTP covered behavior problems, school outcomes, health status, and, for older children, delinquency and childbearing measured four years postrandomization (D. Bloom et al. 2000). There are few statistically significant impact estimates on a range of child outcome measures, evaluated separately for about 1,100 children aged 5–12, and nearly 750 children aged 13–17. For the younger age group, which includes both preschool-age and school-age children at random assignment, FTP led to a statistically significant unfavorable outcome on the positive social behavior scale (see Figure 9.2), but the mother's report of the child's general health was significant and favorable (see Figure 9.4). There were no statistically significant impacts for the youngest children in terms of current school achievement as reported by the mother, use of special education, or school suspensions, with impact estimates in both the favorable and the unfavorable direction.

For the older children, FTP resulted in an increase in the rate of school suspensions (41 percent for the treatment group versus 33 percent for the control group), equal to 0.17 of a standard deviation. The maternal report of educational success was also unfavorable and marginally significant. No significant differences in other outcomes for the older children, such as grade repetition, ever being arrested, or having a baby were found in the four-year follow-up; however, all but one of these insignificant impact estimates was in the unfavorable direction. The contrast between the younger and older children in FTP is not as sharp as it was for the age differences observed in SSP.

The Jobs First three-year follow-up survey collected information on school achievement for all children under age 18. In addition, Jobs First collected more detailed information on behavior and functioning for about 1,500 focal children aged 5 to 12 at follow-up and collected information on childbearing and contact with the police for a sample of about 1,000 adolescents aged 13 to 17 (D. Bloom et al. 2002).[18] For the focal children, the impacts are largely favorable and, in the case of behavioral outcomes, also statistically significant (although the effect sizes never exceed 0.1; see Figure 9.2). For adolescents, however, the results are more mixed. Impacts in the schooling and health domains are all unfavorable, although only one impact (current school achievement) reaches statistical significance, perhaps because of smaller sample sizes. At the same time, adolescents of Jobs First participants were less likely to be convicted of a crime.

These results, though far from conclusive, suggest that welfare reform as a whole may affect several domains of child well-being, including antisocial and problem behavior, school achievement, and health, but the specific impacts and their differences by child age are less well understood. The ABC results suggest a possible unfavorable impact on child maltreatment (specifically neglect). For the school-age children at follow-up, FTP and Jobs First show both favorable and unfavorable impacts in the behavior domain, no effects on the school performance measures, and one favorable effect for health. Likewise, for adolescents, there is mixed evidence in the behavior domain, more consistent evidence of unfavorable impacts on school performance, and no significant impact in the health domain. Since the programs implemented in Connecticut, Delaware, and Florida are not representative of the range and mix of programs implemented across all fifty states, it is impossible to ascertain the overall nationwide impact of reform from these studies.

As noted in prior chapters, the observational studies provide an alternative methodology for estimating the overall impact of waivers or TANF as a bundle. Paxson and Waldfogel's (2003) observational study of child maltreatment outcomes and out-of-home care included a state waiver dummy, but it was never statistically significant for any of the outcomes considered. In the absence of similar observational analyses of other child outcomes in domains such as behavior and cognition, school progress, other aspects of child health, and so on, it is not possible to draw solid inferences about the direction and magnitude of the impacts of waivers or of TANF as a whole on the multidimensional concept of child well-being.

Summary

The studies reviewed in this chapter paint a complex portrait of the effects of welfare reform on the multiple domains and varied indicators of child well-being.[19] Consistent with the theoretical framework presented at the outset, the literature reveals that there is scope for both positive and negative effects on child well-being of various components of reform. Positive and negative effects were observed for indicators that capture socioemotional behavior, academic performance, and health. The most favorable effects, and ones that may persist over time, are associated with financial work incentives, most likely because of the increase in family income that is accompanied by combining work and welfare. But even for these programs, there is some evidence of unfavorable impacts for some subgroups of participants, especially for adolescent children of participants and for younger children of participants who do not experience large income gains. Work requirements do not appear to have either strong favorable or unfavorable impacts on children, although again there is evidence of unfavorable impacts for adolescents, especially in the school performance domain. There is too little evidence regarding the specific impacts of time limits to draw firm conclusions.

The relationship between specific reform policies and child outcomes suggests that there may be policy trade-offs like those discussed in the chapters on welfare use, employment and earnings, and income and poverty. Notably, policies that raise incomes (for example, financial work incentives) are associated with more favorable effects for children, particularly younger children, but these policies do not necessarily reduce dependency. At the same time, policies that lower welfare use (for example, work incentives) have the potential to affect younger children negatively, especially if incomes decline. Adolescents, however, appear to do less well under each of the reforms that have been studied, perhaps indicating a trade-off between welfare reform and adolescent well-being. The inclusion of services targeted toward adolescents could potentially improve their outcomes relative to what has been observed to date.

Considering the impact of welfare reform as a bundle, we find relatively little evidence on which to draw solid inferences based on either observational or experimental data. There is just one observational study, and it fails to find an impact of welfare waivers on child maltreatment. In the case of the three experimental studies that evaluated the impact on child well-being of TANF-like bundles of reform, it is difficult to extrapolate, because the policy combinations evaluated are not representative of the full range and mix of policies implemented by the states under PRWORA. To the extent that there are favorable effects from these studies, they are concentrated in outcomes for children who are school aged at the time of follow-up. The unfavorable impacts, in contrast, are concentrated in outcomes for adolescents, particularly in the area of school performance.

Thus the impacts of welfare reform appear to differ with the stage of the child's development, regardless of the policy component or bundle of reforms considered, and for a given age, impacts may be favorable or unfavorable depending on the outcome domain considered. On the basis of the experimental evaluations that assess child well-being, it appears that there are countervailing forces that both promote and diminish healthy child behavioral, social, cognitive, and physical development. The resulting impacts of welfare reform policies on child outcomes are likely to depend on the strength of the opposing forces and the child's stage of development and other circumstances. Moreover, it is possible that some consequences for children will not materialize until more time has passed under the new policy regime, with the potential for cumulative favorable and unfavorable impacts. Effects that are small now, whether positive or negative, may become more pronounced as more time passes.

❖

CHAPTER TEN

Theory, Evidence, and Policy Trade-offs

We have presented a substantial amount of detail concerning the effects of various welfare reform policies on several measures of welfare-related behavior. In this concluding chapter, we pull these parts together into a more coherent whole, providing an accessible summary of the evidence on the effects of welfare reform. Where possible, we assess whether the results are consistent with the predictions from the model discussed in Chapter 3. We discuss which policy reforms achieve which policy objectives and point out where important trade-offs arise.

Our summary is organized around a more elaborate version of the matrix presented in Table 3.1. We begin by describing our approach for summarizing the empirical evidence presented in previous chapters. We then focus on the effects of reform on welfare use, labor market behavior, and income. These are the aspects of welfare-related behavior about which the model in Chapter 3 makes the clearest predictions. They are also related to the traditional policy goals of alleviating need, promoting work, and reducing dependency. We examine whether the empirical evidence is consistent with the predictions from the model and what trade-offs among policy goals arise from different reform policies.

We next summarize the effects of different reform policies on marriage, childbearing, and the well-being of children. In each of these cases, an extended model was required to understand how welfare reform policies may affect behavior, and the predictions from the model were generally ambiguous. Nevertheless, these aspects of behavior have provided much of the impetus for recent reform efforts, and many observers consider them key for assessing the success of welfare reform. A final section identifies the gaps in our knowledge base and lays out a research agenda for the future.

Summarizing the Empirical Evidence

The policy-outcome matrix introduced in Chapter 3 provides a useful organizing principle for our summary. The matrices presented below have many more columns than the illustrative matrix in Table 3.1, reflecting the numerous aspects of welfare-related behavior that we have covered in the intervening chapters.

We add a number of rows to the matrix as well. We add one row for family caps and, in the case of child outcomes, a row for parental responsibility requirements. We have divided the row for time limits into two: one for their behavioral effects and one for their mechanical effects. Finally, we add three rows for the experiments that combine financial work incentives with work requirements. One row pertains to programs that combine mandatory work-related activities with weak financial work incentives, both of which were administered within the welfare system (specifically WRP and TSMF). Two rows pertain to programs that tie strong financial work incentives to work, with one row each for programs administered within and outside of the traditional welfare system (FIP and MFIP, and SSP and New Hope, respectively). The model yields ambiguous predictions about programs that combine financial work incentives with work requirements, because the two reforms can have opposing effects on behavior. But by dividing such programs into these three categories, we are able to identify evidence that can be explained in terms of the model.

Each cell in the policy-outcome matrix summarizes a tally of results from both experimental and observational studies and conveys graphically three pieces of information: the number of results that bear on that particular policy-outcome combination, the signs of those results, and the results' statistical significance.[1] Because the magnitudes of the results from the experimental and observational studies are difficult to compare, we provide no information in the summary figures on the quantitative magnitudes of the results. In principle, they could all be stated in relative terms, as we did in summarizing the observational studies in earlier chapters. However, even relative comparisons are not entirely meaningful, because the preform levels of welfare-related behavior were often so different between the experimental and observational populations. This difference stems, in part, from the differences in the populations being studied. Although the impacts for the random assignment studies capture changes in behavior for welfare recipients and applicants, the observational studies also reflect changes in behavior for the population at risk of receiving welfare. Thus the magnitudes from the two types of studies may differ because of entry effects.

The definition of a "result," the unit that is tallied to produce the entries in each policy-outcome cell, differs between the experimental and observational studies. For the experimental studies, a result is the same as an impact estimate, so each impact estimate presented in Figures 5.1, 5.2, 6.1, and so on is tallied as one result.[2] This approach means that

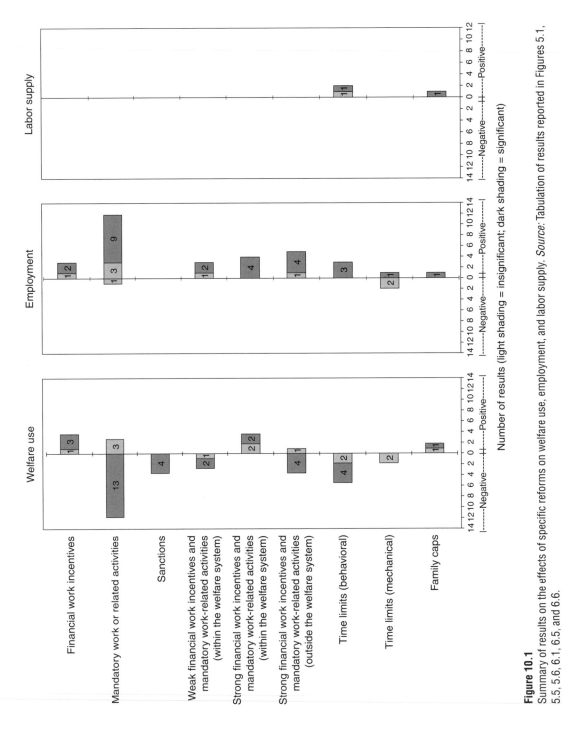

Figure 10.1
Summary of results on the effects of specific reforms on welfare use, employment, and labor supply. *Source:* Tabulation of results reported in Figures 5.1, 5.5, 5.6, 6.1, 6.5, and 6.6.

studies that provide separate estimates for recipients and applicants contribute two results, whereas those that provide only aggregated estimates provide one result. Nevertheless, since applicants and recipients are distinct groups, each result corresponds roughly to a statistically independent estimate. A similar rationale is used in the case of the marriage impacts to separately count results for single-parent and two-parent samples. Throughout the matrix, a result is counted as significant if the estimate was statistically significant at the 10 percent level or higher.

For the observational studies, a result may pertain either to a single estimate or to a set of estimates. This determination is best explained with reference to Figure 5.5. CEA's (1999b) single estimate of the effects of financial work incentives counts as one result. However, the three estimates that CEA (1999b) provides for the effects of sanctions also count as a single result. We proceed in this way because the three coefficient estimates are clearly dependent, but, more important, because the logic behind allowing sanctions of differing levels of severity to have different effects on the caseload was to test not only whether sanctions reduced welfare use but whether stricter sanctions had greater effects. Thus the three statistical estimates stand together as a single result reflecting on the effects of sanctions. In such cases where several statistical estimates underlie a single result, the result is counted as significant if a weak majority of the estimates is significant at the 10 percent level or better.

Welfare, Labor Market Behavior, and Income

Figure 10.1 summarizes the effects of various welfare reform policies on welfare use, employment, and labor supply. Figure 10.2 summarizes their effects on welfare payments, earnings, income, and poverty. The number of negative results for each policy-outcome combination is represented by the bars extending to the left from the y-axis. The number of positive results is represented by the bars extending to the right. The number of insignificant results is represented by the lighter segment of the bar, whereas the number of significant estimates is represented by the darker segment of the bar.

Two points are evident from just a cursory inspection of the figures. First, some policies' effects have been much more thoroughly studied than others'. Largely because of the NEWWS evaluation, the number of studies of the effects of work requirements ranges from twelve (in the case of welfare payments, earnings, and poverty) to sixteen (in the case of welfare use).[3] At the other end of the spectrum, only a handful of studies are available on the effects of time limits, most of which focus on welfare use. The third panel of Figure 10.1 illustrates that few studies of any

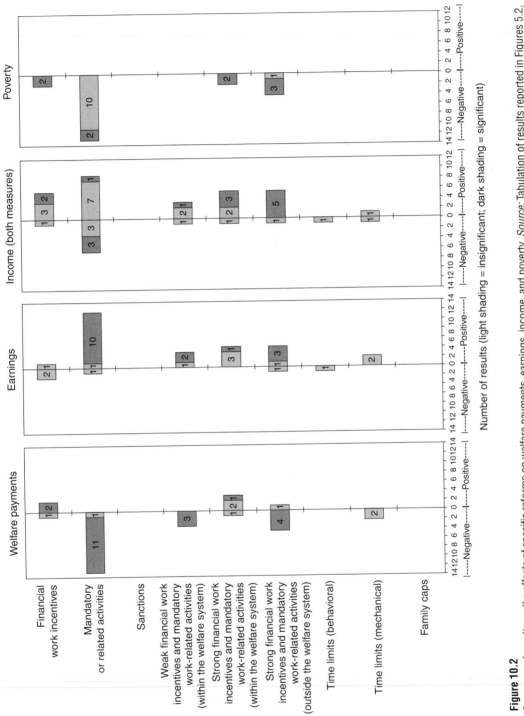

Figure 10.2

Summary of results on the effects of specific reforms on welfare payments, earnings, income, and poverty. *Source:* Tabulation of results reported in Figures 5.2, 6.2, 6.5, 6.7, 7.1, 7.2, 7.4, and 7.5.

policy reforms have focused directly on labor supply. The impact of reform on poverty has also been relatively understudied, as seen in the fourth panel of Figure 10.2.

Second, as seen in Figure 10.1, it appears that almost all of the reforms have increased employment. Different policies, however, have had quite different effects on welfare use and welfare payments and, as a result, on recipients' income. We discuss the effects of each of the three major policy reforms in turn.

Financial Work Incentives

Theory predicts that financial work incentives should increase welfare use and employment. Although only a small number of studies focus exclusively on financial work incentives, most of the results are consistent with these predictions. Of the results regarding welfare use, all four are positive and three are significant (see the first row of Figure 10.1). All three results regarding employment are positive, and two of those are significant.

Results are similar for welfare programs that combine strong financial work incentives with mandatory work-related activities (see the fifth row of Figure 10.1). Although these programs have theoretically ambiguous effects on welfare use, all four yield results showing that welfare use rises (two of which are significant). This finding suggests that the effects of strong financial work incentives outweigh the effects of the work requirements. Programs administered outside the welfare system that tie strong financial incentives to work reduce welfare use (see the sixth row of Figure 10.1). But they also increase the use of transfer payments as participants receive the earnings supplement through which the financial incentive is provided (not shown). Both types of programs increase employment, which is consistent with the model, since both financial incentives and work requirements are predicted to increase employment independently.

The conclusions differ for programs that combine weak financial work incentives with work mandates (see the fourth row in Figure 10.1). All three programs are estimated to have reduced welfare use, and two of the estimates are significant. This result suggests that the effects of the work requirements outweigh the effects of the weak financial work incentives. Indeed, the impacts for these programs resemble those of programs that involve work mandates alone.

Most programs have effects on welfare payments that are similar to their effects on welfare use (see the first panel of Figure 10.2). Their effects on earnings are more ambiguous than their effects on employment.

Of the three results regarding the effects of financial work incentives on earnings, two are negative, one is positive, and none is significant (see the second panel of Figure 10.2). This finding is consistent with the prediction in Table 3.1. Financial work incentives give rise to both substitution effects, which should increase labor supply and earnings, and income effects, which should decrease them. Linking strong financial incentives to work, whether within or outside the welfare system, seems to mitigate any negative effects of the financial incentive on earnings, but there are still more insignificant results for the earnings effects of such policies than for their corresponding effects on employment.

The effects of financial work incentives on income—both the narrow and broad income measures discussed in Chapter 7—are theoretically ambiguous. Such incentives have ambiguous effects on both earnings and welfare payments, which are the primary sources of income for low-income families. Although few studies have focused exclusively on financial work incentives, it appears that their generally positive effect on welfare payments offsets their ambiguous effects on earnings (see the third panel of Figure 10.2). Of six results, five show that financial work incentives increase income, although only two are significant. Results for strong financial incentives tied to work, either within or outside the welfare system, are less ambiguous. Of the twelve results for income, ten are positive, and eight of those are significant (see rows 5 and 6 of Figure 10.2). Programs with weak financial work incentives combined with work mandates have somewhat more ambiguous effects on income, since only one of four estimates is significant.

There are fewer results for poverty. Of the eight results that involve either financial work incentives alone or strong financial incentives tied to work, all are negative and seven are significant. We have no evidence that reform programs of these types increase poverty.

As a whole, the majority of the evidence regarding the effects of financial work incentives, particularly those that are substantially more generous than AFDC, is consistent with the predictions from the model in Chapter 3. The available evidence indicates that financial work incentives raise both welfare use and employment. Their predicted effects on labor supply are ambiguous, and that ambiguity appears in the results regarding their effects on earnings. Although the theory makes no predictions regarding their effects on income, the income and poverty results are generally favorable.

Mandatory Work or Related Activities

Work requirements have been studied more than any other reform, as indicated by the length of the bars in the second row of Figures

10.1 and 10.2. Although a few of the results suggest that work requirements increase welfare use, all of those results are insignificant. A much larger set of results shows that they decrease welfare use and welfare payments, which accords with the predictions in Table 3.1.

Mandatory work-related activities were also predicted to increase employment. Twelve of thirteen employment results are positive, and nine of those are significant. The only negative result is insignificant. Although no studies analyze the effects of work requirements on labor supply directly, eleven of the twelve results pertaining to earnings are positive, of which ten are significant. This pattern is generally consistent with the prediction that work requirements should increase labor supply.

Because mandatory work-related activities decrease welfare payments while increasing earnings, their effects on income are theoretically ambiguous. The empirical evidence reflects this ambiguity. Of fourteen results pertaining to income, six are negative and eight are positive. Three of the negative results are significant, compared with one of the positive results. Many of the underlying estimates, reported in Figure 7.1, are small in magnitude. Furthermore, there is little evidence that the results vary in systematic ways, such as according to the focus of the welfare-to-work program. It appears that, on average, the gain in earnings just offsets the loss in welfare payments, leaving income roughly unchanged.

The poverty results are a bit more favorable. All twelve results indicate that mandatory work programs decrease poverty, suggesting that incomes tend to rise among participants who are toward the top of the recipient income distribution. Of course, the fact that ten of the twelve results are insignificant tempers the notion that these programs effectively alleviate poverty. But there is no evidence that they cause poverty to rise.

Sanctions

Whereas financial work incentives and work mandates have been relatively well studied, other policy reforms have been analyzed less thoroughly. As a result, their effects are less well understood. Sanctions are an important case in point, as the third row of Figures 10.1 and 10.2 shows. Many states have enacted sanctions that are substantially more stringent than those under JOBS. Moreover, many families have lost their welfare benefit, or at least part of their benefit, because of sanctions. No experiments, however, have been conducted to isolate sanctions' effects. Some observational studies of the caseload indicate that stricter sanctions have greater effects on welfare use, which is consistent with the predictions from Chapter 3. At the same time, evidence showing that substantial declines in welfare use preceded the imposition of such sanctions by several years clouds the interpretation of those findings. There are no studies of the effects of sanctions on any other outcome.

Time Limits

Time limits have been better studied than sanctions, but less well studied than mandatory work-related activities. No experiments have been designed to isolate the effects of time limits. Several observational studies have analyzed time limits' behavioral effects, that is, how limits affect behavior before recipients exhaust their benefits. These studies form the basis for the cell entries in the third-to-last row of Figures 10.1 and 10.2. The mechanical effects of time limits are summarized in the cell entries in the next-to-last row of the figure. They are based on non-experimental estimates from two random assignment studies, along with one observational study of employment, and provide some insights into what happens once recipients begin reaching the time limit.

All six of the results regarding the behavioral effects of time limits suggest that they reduce welfare use during the pre–time limit period. Four of those results are significant. Four studies find greater effects among families with younger children, which is consistent with the prediction from the model in Chapter 3. Three significant results indicate that time limits increase employment during the pre–time limit period. Two indicate that time limits have positive behavioral effects on labor supply, although only one of those is significant. The behavioral effects of time limits on earnings and income have been the topic of a single study, which yielded insignificant results.

There are even fewer results regarding the mechanical effects of time limits, and with one exception, all the results are insignificant.[4] Two results show that welfare use and welfare payments fall once recipients begin to exhaust their benefits. Results regarding employment and earnings are mixed, only one result is significant, and none of the evidence suggests that either employment or earnings change much once recipients start reaching the limit. The two results regarding income are mixed. Once a higher proportion of the caseload reaches its time limit, the consequences of those limits could increase substantially.

Family Caps

Finally, two studies examine the effect of family caps on welfare use, employment, and labor supply. But curiously, both of the existing results show that family caps increase welfare use, although only one estimate is significant. This seems odd, since family caps make the welfare system less generous, which should decrease welfare use to the extent that they have any effect at all. A single significant result suggests that family caps raise employment and labor supply.

Relating the Results to the Economic Model

As we have discussed in earlier chapters, most of the determinate predictions of the economic model involve welfare use and labor market behavior. To what extent do the results accord with the predictions?

A number of individual estimates appear to contradict the theory, despite the fact that we eliminated from consideration studies where such contradictions might have been expected due to severe collinearity problems. One that stands out is the estimate from CEA (1999b), which suggests that more restrictive exemptions from work requirements increase, rather than decrease, the welfare caseload. Another is the finding, again from CEA (1999b), that family caps increase welfare use. Although the theory from Chapter 3 makes no explicit predictions regarding family caps, one might generally expect policies that decrease the generosity of the welfare system to decrease welfare use, rather than increase it. The finding, by MaCurdy, Mancuso, and O'Brien-Strain (2002), that immediate work requirements have no effect on welfare use is curious in light of the numerous experimental studies showing that mandatory work-related activities reduce welfare use significantly.

Some variation in statistical estimates is inevitable, of course, and in assessing the fit of the model, we should be at least as concerned with the majority of the results as with the exceptions. Most of the studies that we have reviewed provide support for the predictions of the model. Eleven experimental studies and a smattering of observational analyses have focused on the effects of work requirements. With only a few exceptions, the results show that work requirements decrease welfare use and increase employment, as predicted. The same patterns appear in the studies that link work requirements to weak financial incentives, where one might expect the effects of the work requirement to dominate those of the financial incentive.

A handful of observational studies and two experiments have focused directly on financial work incentives. Their results show that financial incentives generally increase welfare use and employment, again as predicted. These results are bolstered by those from experiments that tied strong financial incentives to work, where one might expect the financial incentive to dominate the work requirement. Those programs increased transfer receipt (either welfare receipt, in the case of programs administered by the welfare system, or subsidy payments, in the case of those administered outside the welfare system) while increasing employment.

The behavioral effects of time limits have been less extensively studied. Six (of six) observational studies indicate that time limits decrease welfare use, and four find that such effects are greatest among the families with the youngest children, consistent with the prediction from the model. Three studies find that they increase employment. Four studies show that sanctions have reduced welfare caseloads, and that stronger sanctions have greater effects.

The support for the economic model found in both experimental and observational studies implies that economic theory can help in making predictions about the potential effects of future welfare reforms, particularly those that have yet to be implemented and evaluated. For example, Congress must periodically reauthorize the TANF program. This process provides opportunities at the federal level to consider further reforms to the program, such as proposals to change the hours of work needed to satisfy work requirements. On the basis of the support we find for the economic model, we would predict that stiffer requirements, all else equal, would further reduce welfare use and increase employment. Although the model does not make an unambiguous prediction about the effect of such work requirements on income, the empirical results suggest that incomes would remain relatively unchanged, unless the work requirements are combined with strong financial work incentives.

Policy Trade-offs

Different policy objectives involve different trade-offs. Figure 10.1 shows that nearly all the policy reforms we have considered succeed in promoting work. They differ, however, in the extent to which they reduce welfare use and increase income. As a general rule, the policy reforms either increase employment and reduce welfare use or they increase employment and raise incomes. No mix of policies achieves all three objectives.

Financial incentives raise incomes as they increase employment, because they allow recipients to keep more of their benefits as their earnings rise. The trade-off for higher incomes is higher levels of welfare use.

Mandates for work or related activities, in contrast, reduce welfare use as they raise employment. They have little effect on income, either positive or negative. It appears that increases in earnings that stem from work requirements just offset the loss in welfare benefits that they entail. In a system where benefits are cut nearly dollar-for-dollar as earnings rise, this result is not surprising.

However, it is possible to mandate work and raise incomes at the same time, provided that mandatory work-related activities are combined with a strong financial incentive. This is seen in the fifth row of Figures 10.1 and 10.2. The lower tax rates arising from the financial incentive allow recipients to keep more of their benefits as their earnings increase, resulting in higher incomes. The cost, as in the case of financial incentives by themselves, is higher levels of welfare use.

It is important to stress that even those combinations of policies that raise incomes do so by modest amounts. One of the most effective experimental programs was MFIP, which combined a strong financial incentive with mandatory work activities. MFIP increased incomes by 12 to 15 percent for long-term recipients throughout the three-year follow-up period. Even in MFIP, however, participants' incomes remained low, averaging $12,000 a year, including the EITC. More than half the participants had incomes from work and transfer programs that still fell below the federal poverty line. MFIP was a relatively generous program; less generous programs have generally had smaller effects on income. These programs may alleviate need somewhat, but they do not eliminate poverty.

The terms of the policy trade-off are less clear for time limits. Figure 10.1 suggests that their behavioral effects generally reduce welfare use and increase employment. With only a single, insignificant estimate to go on, it is not possible to draw conclusions about time limits' effect on income. Few estimates of the mechanical effects of time limits are available, and it is impossible to determine the significance of most of the estimates that we considered. Although a benefit cutoff could have potentially important effects on a family's behavior and income, there is little evidence to date on the magnitude of such effects.

Marriage, Childbearing, and Child Outcomes

Figure 10.3 draws on both experimental and observational studies to summarize the research findings on marriage and childbearing, while Figure 10.4 provides a summary of the results for child outcomes based exclusively on experimental studies. In the case of child outcomes, the matrix differs to some extent from earlier figures. Since there are no studies of the impact of sanctions, time limits, or family caps on child outcomes, those rows have been eliminated. Instead, a row for parental responsibility requirements has been added. In addition, given that child well-being is multidimensional, we present results for three domains: behavior, school achievement, and health (shown in the rows). Because impacts may vary with the age of the child, we summarize results separately for children on the basis of their age at the time of follow-up (shown in the panels): preschool, primary grades, and above. When multiple im-

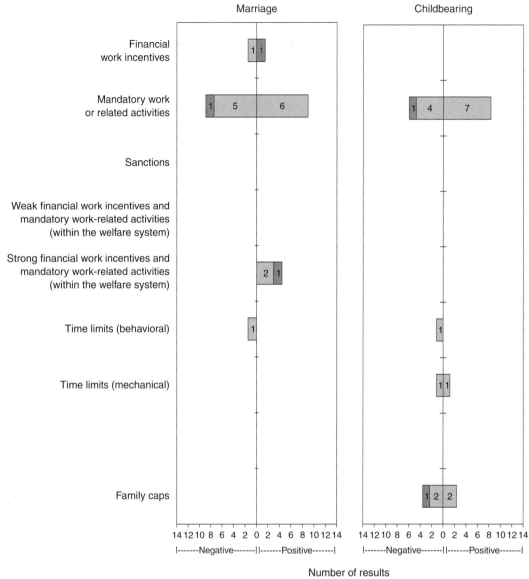

Figure 10.3
Summary of results on the effects of specific reforms on marriage and childbearing. *Source:* Tabulation of results reported in Figures 8.1, 8.2, 8.3, and 8.4.

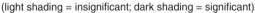

pact estimates are available for a given domain in a given experimental study, we tally the results in such a way that each study contributes just one result to the figure. This generates fractional "results" in increments of 0.5, or one-half of a result, when the multiple measures are of conflicting sign.[5]

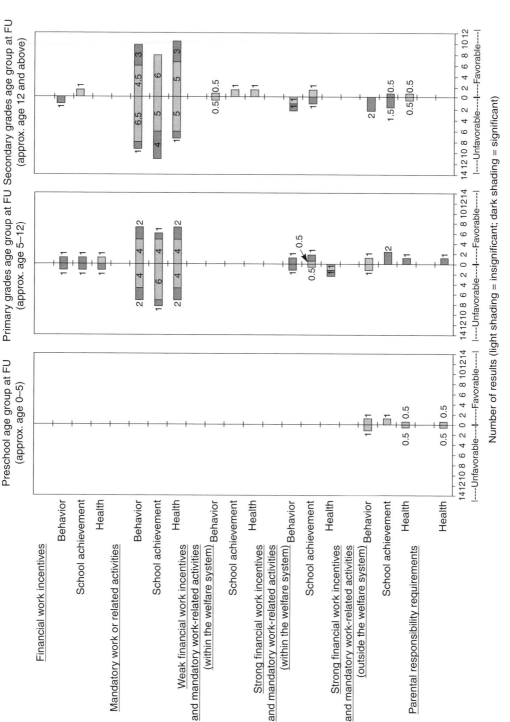

Figure 10.4
Summary of results on the effects of specific reforms on child outcomes. *Source:* Tabulation of results reported in Figure 9.1.

One apparent feature of both figures is that there have been fewer studies of these aspects of welfare-related behavior than of welfare receipt and labor market activity. Another pronounced feature is that many more of the results are insignificant.

Financial Work Incentives

There is no evidence on the relationship between financial work incentives and childbearing per se. The experimental studies that evaluate the impact of financial work incentives on marriage also include reforms to two-parent eligibility rules. As seen in Figure 10.3, there is one significant result to suggest that this combination of policies may increase marriage. There is also one significant result to indicate that these reforms plus work mandates can encourage marriage. These findings are all based on the MFIP evaluation, and the impacts are largest for two-parent families. This suggests that such programs may be more effective at keeping two-parent families intact than in leading single parents to marry. However, the insignificant overall result for the Canadian SSP, and the mixed results for the two provinces, suggests caution in interpreting the MFIP results.

The impact on child well-being is even more uncertain and based on limited evidence. The evidence base available to assess the impact of financial work incentives on outcomes for pre–school-aged children at the time of follow-up is almost nonexistent (see the first panel of Figure 10.4). For primary-school-aged children, strong financial work incentives (alone or combined with work mandates) have mixed effects on behavior and school achievement (see the second panel of Figure 10.4). The significant favorable results derive from the MFIP-IO and MFIP recipient groups, while the unfavorable results derive from applicant groups.[6] As noted in Chapter 9, the applicants in MFIP were a more advantaged group, so the children were relatively better off and there may have been less room for the program to have an impact. In addition, income gains were not as favorable for applicants as for recipients, which may also explain the less favorable impact on applicant child outcomes. Favorable effects for primary-school-aged children were also observed in programs that provided financial incentives tied to work outside the welfare system. There is even some evidence from longer-term follow-ups in SSP and New Hope that the favorable effects may persist after the earnings supplements have ended. Thus it appears that for primary-school-aged children, the increased income from reforms that incorporate strong financial work incentives may lead to some improvements in children's outcomes in certain domains.

In contrast, for adolescents (those aged 12 and above at follow-up), programs that include financial work incentives consistently appear to increase behavior problems and school achievement problems, although again the evidence base is very shallow, with just one or two significant results in the unfavorable direction (see the third panel of Figure 10.4). These unfavorable results are associated both with programs that had smaller impacts on income (for example, WRP-IO and MFIP applicants) and with studies that had larger income impacts (for example, SSP and New Hope). There is only one favorable result associated with a financial work incentive for adolescents, in this case in the school achievement domain.[7]

Mandatory Work or Related Activities

Mandated work-related activities represent the only policy reform whose effects on marriage and childbearing have been analyzed by more than a handful of studies. These policies have essentially no impact on marriage or childbearing as of the two-year follow-up data used to tally the results in Figure 10.3. In each case, only one result of twelve is statistically significant (a negative result in each case), and the remaining insignificant results are roughly evenly divided in sign. If the tallies had been based on the five-year follow-up estimates that are available for seven of the NEWWS programs, they would be almost identical. Thus even from a somewhat longer-run perspective, these programs have virtually no impact on marriage or childbearing.

The evidence provides a mixed picture of the impact of these programs on child well-being. There are no results available for preschool-aged children. For children in the primary grades, the evidence is mixed in all domains. The results are almost evenly divided in sign, with one or two statistically significant results in both favorable and unfavorable directions. The significant favorable results tend to be associated with younger children in the age range (those aged 6 to 7), while the significant unfavorable results are associated with the older children in the age range (those aged 8 to 10). Likewise, the results are equally mixed for adolescents in each domain, and the unfavorable effects are concentrated in the school achievement domain and among the oldest children in the age range (those aged 15 to 23 at follow-up).

Time Limits

There is almost no evidence on the effect of time limits on childbearing, and none at all for marriage and child well-being. In the case of childbearing, two observational studies provided insignificant results of opposite sign. Thus the literature is largely silent on the effect of time limits on these important outcomes.

Family Caps and Parental Responsibility

Figures 10.3 and 10.4 also document that we know relatively little about how family caps and parental responsibility requirements affect even those outcomes where their effects should be most visible. The limited available evidence points to a mixed impact of family caps on childbearing, with four out of five results being insignificant and of mixed sign. Parental responsibility requirements, specifically those related to well-baby and well-child services (for example, vaccinations), have been assessed in terms of their direct impact on the behaviors they seek to change, with some limited evidence of favorable effects on young children's health. Some evidence also indicates that the one program with stronger sanctions for noncompliance produced larger effects, which is consistent with the theory.

Relating the Results to the Model and Resulting Policy Trade-offs

In the case of marriage and childbearing, as discussed in Chapter 8, predictions from the model are largely ambiguous. In some cases, policy bundling makes it difficult to disentangle the separate effects of policies that might be expected to have more definitive impacts. In other cases, policy reforms have complex effects on different aspects of behavior such that the resulting predictions regarding marriage and childbearing are ambiguous.

Furthermore, we would expect policy reforms to change the behavior not just of those on welfare, but also of those at risk of becoming welfare recipients. Such effects cannot be identified in random assignment studies, a problem that highlights the need for well-executed observational studies on these outcomes. Such studies are relatively rare to date, which leaves unresolved the broader impacts of reform.

In general, the empirical evidence provides very little evidence to suggest that reform policies have had significant impacts on marriage or childbearing. The main exception to this rule is MFIP, which despite the attention it has received remains an outlier. The lack of sizable effects may result from opposing forces that cancel each other out (for example, work requirements that make welfare less attractive may promote marriage, whereas greater work effort due to work mandates may reduce the time available for marital search). Alternatively, the changes in policy may be too small to affect childbearing and marriage. Family caps are a case in point. Although there are methodological reasons to discount the findings to date, the effects of family caps on benefit payments may be too small to change childbearing decisions.

Finally, marriage and childbearing involve long-term choices, so policy changes may have little effect on such behavior among current cohorts of recipients. The impacts of recent policy changes may not materialize until more time has passed and they begin to affect decisions about marriage and childbearing among future cohorts at risk of entering welfare. Nevertheless, the lack of evidence of any consistent impact of welfare reform policies on marriage and childbearing suggests that there are no notable policy trade-offs to consider between these outcomes and reform.

The expected impact of welfare reform policies on child well-being was largely ambiguous according to the theoretical framework presented in Chapter 9. The theoretical model suggests that impacts on children should depend upon changes in the quality and quantity of time parents spend with their children, the quality of the care that is substituted for parental care as work effort increases, and the change in financial resources available to the family for investing in their children's well-being. Given the complex nature of such behavioral changes, we might expect that the impacts would vary depending on the domain of child well-being considered and on the child's stage of development. Indeed, the empirical results bear out this expectation, with evidence for favorable, unfavorable, and neutral impacts of individual reform policies on various domains of child well-being and for impacts that appear to differ for younger versus older children.

In the case of parental responsibility requirements, it appears that efforts to directly change parental decisions about the inputs of goods and services that are purchased in support of their child's health and development can have the desired effect, provided the requirements can be readily understood, the barriers to carrying out the mandates are not significant, and there are meaningful sanctions to encourage compliance.

Changes in welfare use, employment, income, marriage, and childbearing can have indirect impacts on child well-being in complex ways that are not easy to disentangle. Nevertheless, the empirical evidence suggests that programs that raise incomes can improve well-being for school-aged children in some domains. At the same time, outcomes appear to be uniformly more unfavorable for adolescents, regardless of the policy reform and whether incomes increase. This result indicates that adolescents may be more negatively affected by the increase in maternal work effort, possibly through reduced supervision or an increased propensity to take on adultlike roles within the family, such as providing child care for younger siblings.

These findings regarding the relationship between child outcomes and welfare reform imply that there may be policy trade-offs that parallel those discussed above regarding welfare use, employment and earnings, and income and poverty. Financial work incentives, which tend to raise incomes, tend to have favorable effects on younger children. Such policies, however, will not lower welfare use. In contrast, those policies that reduce dependency may have more negative effects on younger children to the extent that incomes remain unchanged or decline. The effects of reform on adolescents appear to be more uniformly negative, at least given the types of reforms studied in the available experimental studies. Whether this indicates a fundamental policy trade-off between improving adolescent well-being and welfare reform is unclear. It may be possible, with additional resources devoted to services targeted toward adolescents (for example, after-school programs or mentoring programs), to improve their outcomes as well.[8]

Welfare Reform as a Bundle

A number of observational studies and the six random assignment studies that involved TANF-like bundles of reforms provide estimates of the effects of reform as a bundle, allowing us to look beyond specific policy reforms. Results from those studies are presented in Figure 10.5.[9]

The results shown in Figure 10.5 generally indicate that reform as a bundle has resulted in a decline in welfare use and welfare payments and in an increase in employment, earnings, and income. These effects are similar to those of mandatory work-related activities combined with weak financial work incentives. This pattern seems plausible, since many states implemented modest financial work incentives combined with work requirements.

Beyond welfare use, work, and income, the evidence is thin.[10] All the results for poverty suggest a decrease, with three of four results significant. In the case of marriage, two significant results suggest an increase in marriage, while three insignificant results and two significant results have the opposite sign. The impacts of reform as a bundle on childbearing are mixed with no significant results. This finding is consistent with the experimental results, which showed that none of the individual reform policies appears to strongly affect childbearing.

Figure 10.5
Summary of results on the effects of reform as a bundle. *Source:* Tabulation of results reported in Figures 5.1, 5.2, 5.7, 6.1, 6.2, 6.8, 7.1, 7.2, 7.4, 8.1, 8.2, 8.3, and 8.4.

Number of results
(light shading = insignificant; dark shading = significant)

It is important to note that, regardless of the number of results, the entries in Figure 10.5 represent the effects of reform as a bundle during the pre–time limit period. Post–time limit evidence is very limited, and most studies summarized in this figure cover time periods prior to when recipients could have exhausted their benefits. Once recipients reach the limit in substantial numbers, these effects could change.

What We Don't Know about Welfare Reform

The results shown in Figures 10.1 and 10.2 indicate that the existing evidence is generally consistent with the outcomes about which our model makes the clearest predictions. The figures also point to a number of trade-offs that policymakers must face in structuring the welfare system. At the same time, those figures, along with Figures 10.3 and 10.4, help us to see what is not known about the effects of welfare reform. Although a solid base of research exists on the impacts of mandatory work-related activities, and nearly as much research has focused on financial work incentives (either alone or when tied to work), other reform policies, such as time limits, sanctions, family caps, and parental responsibility requirements, have received less attention. Likewise, some outcomes are relatively understudied, such as poverty, marriage, childbearing, and child well-being.

To summarize the state of knowledge about welfare reform in quantitative terms, we note that the matrix composed of Figures 10.1 through 10.4 consists of 132 cells. Of those cells, 61 are empty, and another 12 contain only insignificant results. Many of the 59 remaining cells contain a single significant result.

Furthermore, even where a substantial research base exists, most results pertain to the short run. The majority of the studies present evidence from follow-up periods of roughly two years, although the NEWWS programs and a few others provide results based on four or five years of follow-up data. The limited available evidence suggests that the effects of reform tend to fade over time, largely because the control group eventually catches up to the treatment group.

The short-run nature of the evidence especially limits our understanding of how reform affects marriage and childbearing. Marriage and childbearing change more slowly than other aspects of behavior. As a result, we would expect the effects of welfare reform on such outcomes to become apparent only over a longer horizon. With mostly short-run results to draw on, it is not surprising that most of the evidence is mixed and statistically insignificant.

The short-run nature of the data also poses a problem for assessing the ways in which welfare reform affects the well-being of children. Although some aspects of a child's well-being, such as behavior, may alter quickly in reaction to changes in her parent's behavior, other aspects, such as cognitive skills, are likely to take much longer to respond. Furthermore, even effects apparent in the short term may change as children are exposed to cumulatively lower levels of welfare use and higher levels of employment on the part of their parents. In the short term, some evidence points to favorable impacts on primary-school-aged children in the behavior and school achievement domains associated with programs that include more generous financial work incentives, either alone or tied to work requirements. But the available evidence shows both favorable and unfavorable impacts associated with work requirements in these same domains. In the case of adolescents, there is more consistent evidence of unfavorable behavioral and school-achievement impacts up to five years after reform. Whether these same patterns will continue in the longer run—or whether they will be attenuated or exacerbated—remains to be determined.

A more general problem is the shortfall of research that would enable us to understand how reform has affected families' decisions to go on welfare to begin with. Random assignment experiments are a powerful research design for revealing how policy reforms affect families' decisions to leave the welfare rolls, but they provide no information at all on how families decide to join the rolls. Observational studies of welfare use reflect the effects of entry decisions, but they do not distinguish them specifically. To date, there have been few observational studies that focus specifically on welfare entry.

This omission is important for several reasons. Theoretical considerations lead us to expect that most policy reforms should affect both entry and exit. Recent empirical work indicates that as much as half of the recent decline in the caseload is attributable to declining rates of entry. Furthermore, as we argued in Chapter 8, understanding the full effects of reform on marriage and childbearing will require that we understand how reform affects the link between childbearing and first-time welfare entry. The notion that young unmarried women might have children in order to qualify for welfare was among the most contentious issues in the welfare reform debate of the 1990s (Weaver 2000), but it has received no direct research attention.

Marriage and childbearing may also be the routes by which welfare reform ultimately has its most long-lasting effects, even though reform has appeared to have little if any effect on family formation to date. These long-term effects derive from the nature of marriage and childbearing decisions, which are likely to represent the end of a long process of information gathering and decision making. Decisions about whether to have sex, with whom to have sex, and whether to use contraception precede pregnancy and childbearing. Economic theory suggests that those choices should be influenced by the generosity of the welfare system, as should related choices about education and expectations about work. At the time that reform is imposed, many of those choices will already have been made, both by cohorts currently at risk of going on welfare and particularly by cohorts already receiving welfare. To the extent that many of the antecedent choices were made before welfare reform, one might expect that welfare reforms would have little effect on the childbearing of cohorts currently at risk of welfare use.

The situation for future cohorts could be quite different. Confronted with a less generous welfare system, future cohorts of young women could make different decisions about sexual behavior, schooling, and work. If so, then welfare reform could have long-term effects on out-of-wedlock childbearing, even if it has had no short-term effect. These effects in turn could have an important impact on welfare entry. By extension, reform could have lasting effects on the level of the welfare caseload, as cohorts that come of age in the postreform environment replace cohorts that came of age prior to reform.

Another gap in our understanding concerns the relationship between the state of the economy and welfare-related outcomes. As we noted at the outset, the welfare reform era of the 1990s coincided with an extremely robust economy. The empirical evidence we have reviewed in preceding chapters confirms that the economic expansion contributed substantially to favorable outcomes such as falling welfare rolls and rising employment, earnings, and incomes among single mothers. These studies do not, however, reveal whether the effects of reform were affected by the state of the economy. In other words, they do not show whether the economy and reform interacted to produce even more favorable outcomes than would have obtained had the economy not been so strong. This issue is a crucial one, given the downturn in the economy that started in 2000 and the slow recovery that has followed to date. The interaction between welfare programs and markets for low-wage workers is an area that requires further study.

The body of research we have assembled in this book underscores the need for further experimentation and further observational studies to address these remaining questions. Experimental evaluations played an important role in assessing the effect of reforms carried out on a state or local level prior to the implementation of nationwide reforms. In the same way, as states continue to experiment with new policies and approaches, randomized trials may be appropriate for evaluating the effects of various alternatives to current policy. Indeed, experimental evaluations are under way to evaluate the effectiveness of programs serving particularly disadvantaged segments of the welfare population, and to evaluate alternative approaches to promoting job retention and advancement among TANF recipients. Meta-analysis of prior experimental studies may also shed light on the relationships between policies and outcomes.

Observational studies can continue to complement experimental evidence and address other questions that cannot be readily addressed with randomized trials. Time limits represent an important example. Although the time has probably passed for conducting experiments to understand their behavioral effects, their mechanical effects will soon become increasingly important: as of early 2002, the latest year for which data are available, roughly 231,000 families had hit their time limits, most of whom lived in states with time limits that were shorter than the federal five-year maximum (D. Bloom, Farrell, and Fink 2002). The number of families exhausting their benefits may grow sharply in the near future as recipients in other states reach the federal five-year time limit. Studies to assess how families respond are critical.

Sanction policies, the reform that is perhaps the least well understood, provide another example. Econometric analyses that incorporate information on the likelihood of sanctioning and the monetary value of sanctions would provide a more complete understanding of this policy than the studies that are currently available. It would be useful to know how sanctions have affected outcomes other than welfare use, such as employment, income, and child well-being.

Likewise, as already noted, entry effects need to be better understood, both to fully grasp how reform has affected welfare use and labor market behavior and to understand how it affects entry-related childbearing. In this area, experimentation has less to offer. What is needed are high-quality econometric studies that focus directly on entry, particularly childbearing-related entry.

Evidence from future observational studies would be more useful if researchers more fully characterized the variation in specific policy reforms across the states. Sanctions can be characterized by their monetary penalties; financial work incentives can be characterized by the benefit payment available to working recipients, as some researchers have done. More fully characterizing the policy environment is essential if observational studies are to move beyond estimating the effects of reform as a bundle. Although existing national databases pose limitations on such efforts, approaches that utilize richer representations of states' policies are more likely to yield success in estimating the effects of specific reforms than approaches that rely on policy-specific dummy variables (Adams and Hotz 2001; Moffitt and Ver Ploeg 2001).

Focusing on the gaps in our understanding of the effects of welfare reform should not obscure the progress that has been made. To some extent such gaps are inevitable. Policy evaluations take time to conduct, and few of the reforms being evaluated have been in place for more than a decade. The methods available to researchers studying the reforms of the 1990s and beyond will continue to add to our knowledge base in the years ahead. The gaps in our current understanding represent an extensive agenda for future research.

APPENDIXES

NOTES

REFERENCES

INDEX

Sources for Experimental Study Results

This appendix provides source information for the results from experimental studies presented in Figure 5.1 (see Table A.1), Figure 5.2 (see Table A.2), Figures 6.1 and 6.2 (see Table A.3), Figures 7.1 and 7.2 (see Table A.4), Figure 8.1 (see Table A.5), Figure 8.3 (see Table A.6), and Figure 9.1 (see Table A.7). With the exception of Table A.7, each table records the outcome measure for the experimental study, the citation, and the source table.

In Table A.7, the detailed results for the child outcome impacts summarized in Figure 9.1 are recorded. For each study, Table A.7 records the outcome measures in each domain and whether the impact was in a favorable or unfavorable direction.[1] The statistical significance of each impact is indicated, along with the effect size for the impact estimate when it is available. The directional indicator and the effect size are in bold type for those impact estimates that are statistically significant.

Table A.1   Sources for results on welfare use from experimental studies

Program	Data source	Measure	Citation	Citation table
A. Financial work incentives				
CWPDP	A	Received welfare, year 3	Becerra et al. (1998)	B4.17
WRP-IO	A	Received welfare, quarter 14	Hendra and Michalopoulos (1999)	2
MFIP-IO (Recipients)	A	Average quarterly welfare receipt, year 3	Miller et al. (2000)	4.2
MFIP-IO (Applicants)	A	Average quarterly welfare receipt, year 3	Miller et al. (2000)	5.2
B. Mandatory work or related activities				
LA Jobs-1st GAIN	A	Received welfare, quarter 8	Freedman, Knab et al. (2000)	2
IMPACT–Basic	A	Received welfare, quarter 4	Fein et al. (1998)	4.3
11 NEWWS programs	A	Received welfare, quarter 8	Freedman, Friedlander et al. (2000)	ES-5
C. Financial work incentives tied to work or related activities				
WRP	A	Received welfare, quarter 14	Hendra and Michalopoulos (1999)	2
TSMF (Recipients)	A	Average monthly welfare receipt, years 1–4	Werner and Kornfeld (1997)	3-3
TSMF (Applicants)	A	Average monthly welfare receipt, years 1–2	Werner and Kornfeld (1997)	3-3
FIP	A	Received welfare, quarter 8	Fraker and Jacobson (2000)	A.3
MFIP (Recipients)	A	Average quarterly welfare receipt, year 3	Miller et al. (2000)	4.2
MFIP (Applicants)	A	Average quarterly welfare receipt, year 3	Miller et al. (2000)	5.2
SSP	A	Average monthly receipt of Income Assistance, year 2	Michalopoulos et al. (2000)	2.1
SSP Plus	A	Received Income Assistance, quarter 5	Quets et al. (1999)	4.3
SSP Applicants	A	Received Income Assistance, quarter 9	Michalopoulos, Robins, and Card (1999)	3
New Hope	A	Average monthly welfare receipt, year 2	Bos et al. (1999)	4
D. TANF-like bundles of reforms				
EMPOWER	A	Average monthly welfare receipt, months 1–36	Kornfeld et al. (1999)	4-1
ABC	A	Received welfare, quarter 5	Fein and Karweit (1997)	10
IMPACT–Placement	A	Received welfare, quarter 8	Fein et al. (1998)	4.2
VIP/VIEW	A	Received welfare, quarter 8	Gordon and Agodini (1999)	D.1
FTP	A	Received welfare, year 2	Bloom, Kemple et al. (2000)	3.1
Jobs First	A	Received welfare, quarter 7	Bloom, Melton et al. (2000)	B.1

Note: A = administrative data.

Table A.2 Sources for results on welfare payments from experimental studies

Program	Data source	Measure	Citation	Table
A. Financial work incentives				
CWPDP	A	AFDC payment, year 3	Becerra et al. (1998)	B4.33
WRP-IO	A	ANFC payment, quarter 14	Bloom, Hendra, and Michalopoulos (2000)	2
MFIP-IO (Recipients)	A	Average quarterly AFDC+FS+GA payment, quarter 8–10	Miller et al. (2000)	4.2
MFIP-IO (Applicants)	A	Average quarterly AFDC+FS+GA payment, quarter 8–10	Miller et al. (2000)	5.2
B. Mandatory work or related activities				
LA Jobs-1st GAIN	A	AFDC/TANF payment, year 2	Freedman, Knab et al. (2000)	4.1
IMPACT–Basic	A	AFDC/TANF payment, year 2	Fein et al. (1998)	4.3
11 NEWWS programs	A	AFDC payment, years 1 to 2	Freedman, Friedlander et al. (2000)	6-1
C. Financial work incentives tied to work or related activities				
WRP	A	ANFC payment, quarter 14	Hendra and Michalopoulos (1999)	3
TSMF (Recipients)	A	Average annual AFDC/SFA payment, years 1 to 4	Werner and Kornfeld (1997)	4-2
TSMF (Applicants)	A	Average annual AFDC/SFA payment, years 1 to 2	Werner and Kornfeld (1997)	4-2
FIP (Recipients)	A	FIP payment, quarter 8	Fraker and Jacobson (2000)	V.1
FIP (Applicants)	A	FIP payment, quarter 4	Fraker and Jacobson (2000)	V.3
MFIP (Recipients)	A	Average quarterly AFDC+FS+GA payment, quarter 8–10	Miller et al. (2000)	4.2
MFIP (Applicants)	A	Average quarterly AFDC+FS+GA payment, quarter 8–10	Miller et al. (2000)	5.2
SSP	A	Income Assistance payment, year 2	Michalopoulos et al. (2000)	2.1
SSP Plus	A	Average monthly Income Assistance payment, quarter 5	Quets et al. (1999)	4.3
SSP Applicants	A	Average monthly Income Assistance payment, quarter 9	Michalopoulos, Robins, and Card (1999)	3
New Hope	A	Welfare payment, year 2	Bos et al. (1999)	4
D. TANF-like bundles of reforms				
EMPOWER	A	Average monthly cash assistance payment, year 2	Kornfeld et al. (1999)	4-7
ABC	A	Cash welfare payment, quarter 5	Fein and Karweit (1997)	10
IMPACT–Placement	A	AFDC/TANF payment, year 2	Fein et al. (1998)	4.3
VIP/VIEW	A	AFDC/TANF payment, year 2	Gordon and Agodini (1999)	D.2
FTP	A	AFDC/TANF payment, year 2	Bloom, Kemple et al. (2000)	3.1
Jobs First	A	AFDC/TANF payment, year 2	Hendra, Michalopoulos, and Bloom (2001)	1

Note: A = administrative data; FS = food stamps; GA = general assistance; SFA = State Family Assistance program (Michigan).

Table A.3   Sources for results on employment and earnings from experimental studies

Program	Data source	Measure	Citation	Citation table
A. Financial work incentives				
CWPDP	A	Average employment, earnings, year 3	Becerra et al. (1998)	B4.1, B4.9
WRP-IO	A	Ever employed, average quarterly earnings, quarter 14	Bloom, Hendra, and Michalopoulos (2000)	2
MFIP-IO (Recipients)	A	Average quarterly employment, earnings, quarters 8–10	Miller et al. (2000)	4.2
MFIP-IO (Applicants)	A	Average quarterly employment, earnings, quarters 8–10	Miller et al. (2000)	5.3
B. Mandatory work or related activities				
LA Jobs-1st GAIN	A	Ever employed, average quarterly earnings, year 2	Freedman, Knab et al. (2000)	2
IMPACT–Basic	A	Employed in quarter 4; earnings in year 1	Fein et al. (1998)	4.3
11 NEWWS programs	A	Ever employed, earnings, years 1 to 2	Freedman, Friedlander et al. (2000)	ES-5
C. Financial work incentives tied to work or related activities				
WRP	A	Ever employed, average quarterly earnings, quarter 14	Bloom, Hendra, and Michalopoulos (2000)	2
TSMF (Recipients)	A	Average annual employment, earnings, years 1 to 2	Werner and Kornfeld (1997)	2-4
TSMF (Applicants)	A	Average annual employment, earnings, years 1 to 5	Werner and Kornfeld (1997)	2-6
FIP	A	Average employment, earnings, quarter 8	Fraker and Jacobson (2000)	A.1
MFIP (Recipients)	A	Average quarterly employment, earnings, quarters 8–10	Miller et al. (2000)	4.2
MFIP (Applicants)	A	Average quarterly employment, earnings, quarters 8–10	Miller et al. (2000)	5.2
SSP	A	Average monthly employment, annual earnings, year 2	Michalopoulos et al. (2000)	2.1
SSP Plus	A	Employment, earnings, quarter 5	Quets et al. (1999)	4.1
SSP Applicants	A	Employment, earnings, quarter 9	Michalopoulos, Robins, and Card (1999)	4
New Hope	A	Ever employed, total earnings, year 2	Bos et al. (1999)	2
D. TANF-like bundles of reforms				
EMPOWER	A	Employed, month 19	Kornfeld et al. (1999)	5-6
ABC	A	Ever employed, total earnings, year 1	Fein and Karweit (1997)	9
IMPACT–Placement	A	Employed in quarter 8; earnings in year 2	Fein et al. (1998)	4.2
VIP/VIEW	A	Average employment, earnings, year 2	Gordon and Agodini (1999)	C.1, C.2
FTP	A	Employment, earnings, year 2	Bloom, Kemple et al. (2000)	3.1
Jobs First	A	Ever employed, earnings, quarter 7	Bloom, Melton et al. (2000)	B.1

Note: A = administrative data.

Table A.4   Sources for results on income and poverty from experimental studies

Program	Data source	Narrow measure	Data source	Broad measure	Citation	Citation table
A. Financial work incentives						
CWPDP	A	E+W+FS, year 3			Becerra et al. (1998)	B4.9, B4.33, B4.41
WRP-IO	A	E+W+FS, quarter 14	S	HH income + EITC, month 42	Bloom, Hendra, and Michalopoulos (2000)	2, 4
MFIP-IO (Recipients)	A	Average quarterly E+W+FS, quarters 8–10	S	Family income, month 36	Miller et al. (2000)	4.5, 4.6
MFIP-IO (Applicants)	A	Average quarterly E+W+FS, quarters 8–10	S	Family income, month 36	Miller et al. (2000)	5.4, 5.5
B. Mandatory work or related activities						
LA Jobs-1st GAIN	A	E+W+FS, year 2	A, S	HH income + EITC − payroll taxes, month 24	Freedman, Knab et al. (2000)	p. 112 (in text)
IMPACT–Basic	A	E+W+FS, year 2			Fein et al. (1998)	4.12
11 NEWWS programs	A	E+W+FS, year 2			Freedman, Friedlander et al. (2000)	7.4
C. Financial work incentives tied to work or related activities						
WRP	A	E+W+FS, quarter 14	S	HH income + EITC, month 42	Bloom, Hendra, and Michalopoulos (2000)	2, 4
TSMF (Recipients)			A	Average annual family income, years 1–4	Werner and Kornfeld (1997)	4-7
TSMF (Applicants)			A	Average annual family income, years 1–2	Werner and Kornfeld (1997)	4-7
FIP (Recipients)	A	E+W, quarter 8			Fraker and Jacobson (2000)	VI.1
FIP (Applicants)	A	E+W, quarter 4			Fraker and Jacobson (2000)	VI.4
MFIP (Recipients)	A	Average quarterly E+W+FS, quarters 8–10	S	Family income, month 36	Miller et al. (2000)	4.5, 4.6
MFIP (Applicants)	A	Average quarterly E+W+FS, quarters 8–10	S	Family income, month 36	Miller et al. (2000)	5.4, 5.5
SSP	A	Average monthly E+W, quarters 5–6	A, S	Average monthly family income, quarters 11–12	Michalopoulos et al. (2000)	3, 2.3

Table A.4 *(continued)*

Program	Data source	Narrow measure	Data source	Broad measure	Citation	Citation table
SSP Plus			A, S	Average monthly family income, quarters 5–6	Quets et al. (1999)	4.4
SSP Applicants			A, S	Average monthly family income, quarters 9–10	Michalopoulos, Robins, and Card (1999)	6
New Hope	A	E+W+FS+EITC, year 2			Bos et al. (1999)	S5
D. TANF-like bundles of reforms						
EMPOWER			A, S	HH income, month 30	Kornfeld et al. (1999)	6-1
ABC			S	Average monthly HH income, months 12–18	Fein and Karweit (1997)	14
IMPACT–Placement	A	E+W+FS, year 2			Fein et al. (1998)	4.12
VIP/VIEW	A	E+W+FS, year 2			Gordon and Agodini (1999)	E.3
FTP	A	E+W+FS, year 2	S	HH income, month 48	Bloom, Kemple et al. (2000)	3.1,5
Jobs First	A	E+W+FS, year 2	S	HH income, month 36	Bloom et al. (2002)	1.4

Note: A = administrative data; E = earnings; EITC = Earned Income Tax Credit payments; FS = food stamp payments; HH = household; S = survey data; W = welfare payments.

Table A.5   Sources for results on marriage from experimental studies

Program	Data source	Measure	Citation	Citation table
A. Financial work incentives				
CWPDP	S	Married at 29–41 month FU	Hu (2003)	4
MFIP-IO (Recipients)	S	Married at 36-month FU	Miller et al. (2000)	4.7
MFIP-IO (Applicants)	S	Married at 36-month FU	Miller et al. (2000)	5.6
B. Mandatory work or related activities				
LA Jobs-1st GAIN	S	Married and living with spouse at 2-year FU	Freedman, Knab et al. (2000)	6.3
11 NEWWS programs	S	Married and living with spouse at 2-year FU	Hamilton, Freedman, and McGroder (2000)	3
11 NEWWS programs	S	Married and living with spouse at 5-year FU	Hamilton et al. (2001)	9.2
C. Financial work incentives tied to work or related activities				
MFIP (Single parent recipients)	S	Married at 36-month FU	Miller et al. (2000)	4.7
MFIP (Single parent applicants)	S	Married at 36-month FU	Miller et al. (2000)	5.6
MFIP (Two parent)	S	Married at 36-month FU	Miller et al. (2000)	6.1
SSP	S	Married at 36-month FU	Michalopoulos et al. (2000)	3.5
SSP	S	Ever married in last 18 months at 54-month FU	Michalopoulos et al. (2002)	5.8
D. TANF-like bundles of reforms				
EMPOWER	S	Married at 3-year FU	Kornfeld et al. (1999)	7-3
ABC	S	Married and living with spouse at 4–19 month FU	Fein (1999)	2
FTP	S	Married and living with spouse at 4-year FU	Bloom, Kemple et al. (2000)	5
Jobs First	S	Married and living with spouse at 18-month FU	Bloom, Melton et al. (2000)	4.7
Jobs First	S	Married and living with spouse at 3-year FU	Bloom et al. (2002)	6

Note: FU = follow-up; S = survey data.

Table A.6   Sources for results on childbearing from experimental studies

Program	Data source	Measure	Citation	Citation table
B. Mandatory work or related activities				
LA Jobs-1st GAIN	S	Had a child since RA as of 2-year FU	Freedman, Knab et al. (2000)	6.3
11 NEWWS programs	S	Had a child since RA as of 2-year FU	Hamilton, Freedman, and McGroder (2000)	3
11 NEWWS programs	S	Had new baby present in household as of 5-year FU	Hamilton et al. (2001)	9.3
C. Financial work incentives tied to work or related activities				
SSP	S	Any new children in family in last 18 months at 36-month FU	Michalopoulos et al. (2002)	5.8
SSP	S	Any new children in family in last 18 months at 54-month FU	Michalopoulos et al. (2002)	5.8
D. Family caps				
AAWDP	A	Number of births since RA as of 5-year FU	Kornfeld et al. (1999)	5-1
FDP (Recipients)	A	Number of births since RA as of 17-quarter FU	Camasso et al. (1999)	13
FDP (Applicants)	A	Number of births since RA as of 17-quarter FU	Camasso et al. (1999)	16
E. TANF-like bundles of reforms				
EMPOWER	S	Conceived a child since RA as of 3-year FU	Kornfeld et al. (1999)	7-2
ABC	S	Conceived a child since RA as of 4–19 month FU	Fein (1999)	6
FTP	S	Had a child since RA as of 4-year FU	Bloom, Kemple et al. (2000)	5
Jobs First	S	Had a child since RA as of 18-month FU	Bloom, Melton et al. (2000)	4.7
Jobs First	S	Had a child since RA as of 3-year FU	Bloom et al. (2002)	6

Note: A = administrative data; FU = follow-up; RA = random assignment; S = survey data.

Table A.7 Sources for results on child outcomes from experimental studies

Name (Population) [Follow-up length]	Outcome domain	Measure	Impact/ Signif.	Effect size	Measure	Impact/ Signif.	Effect size
		All children			**Youngest age group (ages at FU)**		
A. Financial work incentives							
WRP-IO (Single parents R&A) [3.5 years]	Behavior	• Suspended/expelled since last RA	U	—			
	School	• Absences last mo.	**U***	—			
		• Repeated grade since RA	F	—			
	Other	• CU participates clubs/orgs.	**F***	—			
MFIP-IO (Urban single-parent recipients) [3 years]	Behavior						
	School						
	Health						
(Urban single- parent applicants) [3 years]	Behavior						
	School						
	Health						
B. Mandatory work or related activities							
LA Jobs-1st GAIN (Single-parent R&A) [2 years]					*Age 5–7*		
	Behavior	• Ever suspended/ expelled	**F***	—			
		• Ever in class for behav. prob.	U	—	• Ever in class for behav. prob.	U	—

Table A.7   *(continued)*

Middle age group (ages at FU)			Oldest age group (ages at FU)		
Measure	Impact/ Signif.	Effect size	Measure	Impact/ Signif.	Effect size
			Age 10 and above		
			• Behavior prob. since RA	F	—
			• Ever in trouble w/police	**U****	—
			• Ever dropped out	F	—
Age 5–12					
• CU total BPI	**F***	**0.15**			
• CU externalizing BPI	**F***	—			
• CU internalizing BPI	**F***	—			
• CU high level of behav./emot. prob.	F	—			
• CU pos. social behav. (PBS)	**F****	**0.18**			
• CU behav. prob. at school	F	—			
• Suspended/expelled since RA	U	—			
• CU avg. perf. in school	**F***	**0.14**			
• CU perf. in school below avg.	F	—			
• CU engagement in school	**F****	**0.20**			
• Repeated grade since RA	U	0.02			
• In spec. educ. since RA	U	—			
• ERV for accident/injury since RA	**U****	—			
• CU overall health	F	0.06			
• CU total BPI	U	0.12			
• CU pos. social behav. (PBS)	U	0.11			
• CU behav. prob. at school	F	—			
• Suspended/expelled since RA	**U***	—			
• CU avg. perf. in school	**U***	**0.20**			
• CU perf. in school below avg.	U	—			
• CU engagement in school	**U****	**0.28**			
• Repeated grade since RA	U	0.06			
• In spec. educ. since RA	F	—			
• CU overall health	F	0.06			
Age 8–11			*Age 12–20*		
• Ever suspended/expelled	F	—	• Ever suspended/expelled	F	—
• Ever in class for behav. prob.	**U***	—	• Ever in class for behav. prob.	U	—

Table A.7 *(continued)*

Name (Population) [Follow-up length]	All children				Youngest age group (ages at FU)		
	Outcome domain	Measure	Impact/ Signif.	Effect size	Measure	Impact/ Signif.	Effect size
LA Jobs-1st GAIN *(continued)*		• Ever behav. prob. affect P work	U	—	• Ever behav. prob. affect P work	U*	—
	School	• CU school perf.	F	—			
		• Ever honor roll/ award	U	—			
		• Ever repeated grade	F	—	• Ever repeated grade	U***	—
		• Ever dropped out	F	—			
	Health	• Ever ERV for accident/injury	U	—	• Ever ERV for accident/injury	U	—
Atlanta LFA (R&A w/child <18 at RA) [5 years]		*Any child in family*			*Age (6–7) 8–10*		
	Behavior	• Suspended/expelled in yrs 3–5	F	0.07	• Suspended/expelled in yrs 3–5	U	0.01
	School	• Repeated grade in yrs 3–5	F*	**0.10**	• Repeated grade in yrs 3–5	0	0.00
		• CU use of spec. educ.	U	0.02	• CU use of spec. educ.	U	0.04
		• Ever dropped out	F	0.03			
	Health	• ERV for accident/ injury in yrs 3–5	F	0.07	• ERV for accident/ injury in yrs 3–5	F	0.02
		• CU condition requires med. care	U	0.04	• CU condition requires med. care	U**	**0.20**
		• CU condition affects M wk/school	U	0.05	• CU condition affects M wk/school	U***	**0.26**
		• Had baby as teen (<18) since RA	F**	**0.12**			
Grand Rapids LFA (R&A w/child <18 at RA) [5 years]	Behavior	• Suspended/expelled in yrs 3–5	F	0.04	• Suspended/expelled in yrs 3–5	(F***) F	**(0.27)** 0.06
	School	• Repeated grade in yrs 3–5	U	0.10	• Repeated grade in yrs 3–5	(F) U	(0.05) 0.10
		• CU use of spec. educ.	U	0.01	• CU use of spec. educ.	(F) U	(0.10) 0.07
		• Ever dropped out	U	0.04			
	Health	• ERV for accident/ injury in yrs 3–5	F	0.02	• ERV for accident/ injury in yrs 3–5	(F) U	(0.03) 0.02
		• CU condition requires med. care	U	0.03	• CU condition requires med. care	(F**) U	**(0.20)** 0.08
		• CU condition affects M wk/school	F	0.05	• CU condition affects M wk/school	(F) U	(0.05) 0.01
		• Had baby as teen (<18) since RA	F	0.07			
Riverside LFA (R&A w/child <18 at RA) [5 years]	Behavior	• Suspended/expelled in yrs 3–5	F	0.06	• Suspended/expelled in yrs 3–5	F	0.08

Table A.7 *(continued)*

Middle age group (ages at FU)			Oldest age group (ages at FU)		
Measure	Impact/ Signif.	Effect size	Measure	Impact/ Signif.	Effect size
• Ever behav. prob. affect P work	F	—	• Ever behav. prob. affect P work	U	—
• CU school perf.			• CU school perf.	U	—
• Ever honor roll/award	F	—	• Ever honor roll/award	U	—
• Ever repeated grade	U	—	• Ever repeated grade	F	—
	F	—	• Ever dropped out	F	—
• Ever ERV for accident/injury	F	—	• Ever ERV for accident/injury	0	—
Age 11–14			*Age 15–23*		
• Suspended/expelled in yrs 3–5	U	0.00	• Suspended/expelled in yrs 3–5	F**	**0.16**
• Repeated grade in yrs 3–5	F	0.06	• Repeated grade in yrs 3–5	F	0.05
• CU use of spec. educ.	F	0.04	• CU use of spec. educ.	U	0.04
• Ever dropped out	n/a	—	• Ever dropped out	F	0.03
• ERV for accident/injury in yrs 3–5	0	0.00	• ERV for accident/injury in yrs 3–5	F	0.04
• CU condition requires med. care	U	0.02	• CU condition requires med. care	U	0.03
• CU condition affects M wk/school	U	0.06	• CU condition affects M wk/school	F	0.04
			• Had baby as teen (<18) since RA	F	0.11
• Suspended/expelled in yrs 3–5	U*	**0.18**	• Suspended/expelled in yrs 3–5	F	0.03
• Repeated grade in yrs 3–5	U	0.14	• Repeated grade in yrs 3–5	U**	**0.16**
• CU use of spec. educ.	F	0.06	• CU use of spec. educ.	U	0.10
• Ever dropped out	F	0.08	• Ever dropped out	U	0.08
• ERV for accident/injury in yrs 3–5	F	0.09	• ERV for accident/injury in yrs 3–5	F	0.09
• CU condition requires med. care	F	0.04	• CU condition requires med. care	U	0.11
• CU condition affects M wk/school	F	0.06	• CU condition affects M wk/school	U	0.09
			• Had baby as teen (<18) RA	F	0.00
• Suspended/expelled in yrs 3–5	F**	**0.14**	• Suspended/expelled in yrs 3–5	F	0.01

Table A.7 *(continued)*

Name (Population) [Follow-up length]	All children				Youngest age group (ages at FU)		
	Outcome domain	Measure	Impact/ Signif.	Effect size	Measure	Impact/ Signif.	Effect size
Riverside LFA *(continued)*	School	• Repeated grade in yrs 3–5	U	0.01	• Repeated grade in yrs 3–5	F***	**0.18**
		• CU use of spec. educ.	U	0.06	• CU use of spec. educ.	U	0.03
		• Ever dropped out	U	0.05			
	Health	• ERV for accident/ injury in yrs 3–5	F	0.03	• ERV for accident/ injury in yrs 3–5	U	0.01
		• CU condition requires med. care	F	0.09	• CU condition requires med. care	F	0.10
		• CU condition affects M wk/school	F	0.06	• CU condition affects M wk/school	F**	**0.13**
		• Had baby as teen (<18) since RA	U	0.07			
Portland (R&A w/child <18 at RA) [5 years]	Behavior	• Suspended/ expelled in yrs 3–5	F	0.01	• Suspended/expelled in yrs 3–5	(U) F	(0.03) 0.16
	School	• Repeated grade in yrs 3–5	U	0.14	• Repeated grade in yrs 3–5	(U) F	(0.19) 0.03
		• CU use of spec. educ.	U	0.10	• CU use of spec. educ.	(U) U	(0.08) 0.02
		• Ever dropped out	U	0.04			
	Health	• ERV for accident/ injury in yrs 3–5	U	0.01	• ERV for accident/ injury in yrs 3–5	(F) U	(0.15) 0.20
		• CU condition requires med. care	U	0.07	• CU condition requires med. care	(U) U	(0.09) 0.16
		• CU condition affects M wk/school	U	0.04	• CU condition affects M wk/school	(U) F	(0.01) 0.06
		• Had baby as teen (<18) since RA	F	0.12			
Atlanta HCD (R&A w/child <18 at RA) [5 years]	Behavior	• Expelled/suspended in yrs 3–5	U	0.01	• Expelled/suspended in yrs 3–5	U	0.00
	School	• Repeated grade in yrs 3–5	F*	**0.11**	• Repeated grade in yrs 3–5	U	0.05
		• CU use of spec. educ.	F	0.05	• CU use of spec. educ.	U	0.04
		• Ever dropped out	U	0.03			
	Health	• ERV for accident/ injury in yrs 3–5	F	0.09	• ERV for accident/ injury in yrs 3–5	F	0.05
		• CU condition requires med. care	F	0.06	• CU condition requires med. care	U**	**0.18**
		• CU condition affects M wk/school	U	0.05	• CU condition affects M wk/school	U	0.10
		• Had baby as teen (<18) since RA	F	0.03			

Table A.7   *(continued)*

Middle age group (ages at FU)			Oldest age group (ages at FU)		
Measure	Impact/ Signif.	Effect size	Measure	Impact/ Signif.	Effect size
• Repeated grade in yrs 3–5	U	0.06	• Repeated grade in yrs 3–5	**U****	**0.14**
• CU use of spec. educ.	F	0.01	• CU use of spec. educ.	U	0.10
• Ever dropped out	F	0.06	• Ever dropped out	U	0.01
• ERV for accident/injury in yrs 3–5	U	0.03	• ERV for accident/injury in yrs 3–5	F	0.05
• CU condition requires med. care	U	0.03	• CU condition requires med. care	**F****	**0.12**
• CU condition affects M wk/school	F	0.01	• CU condition affects M wk/school	U	0.01
			• Had baby as teen (<18) since RA	U	0.07
• Suspended/expelled in yrs 3–5	U	0.20	• Suspended/expelled in yrs 3–5	U	0.04
• Repeated grade in yrs 3–5	U	0.03	• Repeated grade in yrs 3–5	F	0.06
• CU use of spec. educ.	U	0.27	• CU use of spec. educ.	U	0.06
• Ever dropped out	U	0.00	• Ever dropped out	U	0.11
• ERV for accident/injury in yrs 3–5	U	0.00	• ERV for accident/injury in yrs 3–5	U	0.09
• CU condition requires med. care	U	0.04	• CU condition requires med. care	F	0.02
• CU condition affects M wk/school	U	0.03	• CU condition affects M wk/school	U	0.10
			• Had baby as teen (<18) since RA	F	0.10
• Expelled/suspended in yrs 3–5	U	0.02	• Expelled/suspended in yrs 3–5	U	0.05
• Repeated grade in yrs 3–5	F	0.10	• Repeated grade in yrs 3–5	F	0.04
• CU use of spec. educ.	F	0.09	• CU use of spec. educ.	F	0.02
			• Ever dropped out	U	0.05
• ERV for accident/injury in yrs 3–5	F	0.08	• ERV for accident/injury in yrs 3–5	F	0.01
• CU condition requires med. care	F	0.09	• CU condition requires med. care	F	0.04
• CU condition affects M wk/school	U	0.06	• CU condition affects M wk/school	F	0.00
			• Had baby as teen (<18) since RA	U	0.02

Table A.7   *(continued)*

Name (Population) [Follow-up length]	Outcome domain	All children Measure	Impact/ Signif.	Effect size	Youngest age group (ages at FU) Measure	Impact/ Signif.	Effect size
Grand Rapids HCD (R&A w/child <18 at RA) [5 years]	Behavior	• Suspended/expelled in yrs 3–5	F*	**0.10**	• Suspended/expelled in yrs 3–5	**(F**)** F	**(0.19)** 0.02
	School	• Repeated grade in yrs 3–5	U	0.13	• Repeated grade in yrs 3–5	(F) **U***	(0.07) **0.17**
		• CU use of spec. educ.	U	0.00	• CU use of spec. educ.	(F) U	(0.01) 0.09
		• Ever dropped out	U	0.02			
	Health	• ERV for accident/ injury in yrs 3–5	F*	**0.11**	• ERV for accident/ injury in yrs 3–5	(F) F	(0.11) 0.08
		• CU condition requires med. care	F	0.10	• CU condition requires med. care	(F) U	(0.12) 0.06
		• CU condition affects M wk/school	F**	**0.12**	• CU condition affects M wk/school	(F) U	(0.10) 0.00
		• Had baby as teen (<18) since RA	F	0.00			
Riverside HCD (R&A w/child <18 at RA) [5 years]	Behavior	• Suspended/expelled in yrs 3–5	F	0.05	• Suspended/expelled in yrs 3–5	U	0.04
	School	• Repeated grade in yrs 3–5	U	0.06	• Repeated grade in yrs 3–5	F	0.08
		• CU use of spec. educ.	U	0.04	• CU use of spec. educ.	F	0.07
		• Ever dropped out	U	0.11			
	Health	• ERV for accident/ injury in yrs 3–5	F	0.03	• ERV for accident/ injury in yrs 3–5	U	0.02
		• CU condition requires med. care	F	0.00	• CU condition requires med. care	F	0.05
		• CU condition affects M wk/school	U*	**0.13**	• CU condition affects M wk/school	U	0.01
		• Had baby as teen (<18) since RA	U	0.09			
Columbus Integrated (R&A with all children 6+) [2 years]	Behavior	• CU help for behav./ emot. prob.	F	—			
		• CU class for behav./ emot. prob.	F*	—			
		• Suspended/expelled since RA	F	—			
	School	• Repeated grade since RA	F	—			
		• CU use of spec. educ.	F**	—			
	Health	• ERV for accident/ injury since RA	U	—			

Table A.7   *(continued)*

Middle age group (ages at FU)			Oldest age group (ages at FU)		
Measure	Impact/ Signif.	Effect size	Measure	Impact/ Signif.	Effect size
• Suspended/expelled in yrs 3–5	F	0.05	• Suspended/expelled in yrs 3–5	U	0.05
• Repeated grade in yrs 3–5	U	0.09	• Repeated grade in yrs 3–5	**U****	**0.16**
• CU use of spec. educ.	F	0.14	• CU use of spec. educ.	U	0.09
• Ever dropped out	F	0.14	• Ever dropped out	U	0.07
• ERV for accident/injury in yrs 3–5	F	0.10	• ERV for accident/injury in yrs 3–5	F	0.00
• CU condition requires med. care	**F***	**0.16**	• CU condition requires med. care	U	0.02
• CU condition affects M wk/school	**F****	**0.19**	• CU condition affects M wk/school	U	0.02
			• Had baby as teen (<18) since RA	U	0.02
• Suspended/expelled in yrs 3–5	**F*****	**0.21**	• Suspended/expelled in yrs 3–5	F	0.02
• Repeated grade in yrs 3–5	U	0.11	• Repeated grade in yrs 3–5	**U****	**0.18**
• CU use of spec. educ.	F	0.01	• CU use of spec. educ.	**U***	**0.15**
• Ever dropped out	F	0.05	• Ever dropped out	**U***	**0.14**
• ERV for accident/injury in yrs 3–5	**F***	**0.15**	• ERV for accident/injury in yrs 3–5	F	0.08
• CU condition requires med. care	U	0.06	• CU condition requires med. care	F	0.07
• CU condition affects M wk/school	F	0.03	• CU condition affects M wk/school	**U***	**0.17**
			• Had baby as teen (<18) since RA	U	0.11

Table A.7   *(continued)*

Name (Population) [Follow-up length]	All children				Youngest age group (ages at FU)		
	Outcome domain	Measure	Impact/ Signif.	Effect size	Measure	Impact/ Signif.	Effect size
Columbus Traditional (R&A with all children 6+) [2 years]	Behavior	• CU help for behav./ emot. prob.	U	—			
		• CU class for behav./ emot. prob.	F	—			
		• Suspended/expelled since RA	U	—			
	School	• Repeated grade since RA	F	—			
		• CU use of spec. educ.	U	—			
	Health	• ERV for accident/ injury since RA	U	—			
Detroit (R&A with all children 6+) [2 years]	Behavior	• CU help for behav./ emot. prob.	U	—			
		• CU class for behav./ emot. prob.	U	—			
		• Suspended/expelled since RA	F	—			
	School	• Repeated grade since RA	F	—			
		• CU use of spec. educ.	U	—			
	Health	• ERV for accident/ injury since RA	U	—			
Oklahoma City (R&A with all children 6+) [2 years]	Behavior	• CU help for behav./ emot. prob.	**U****	—			
		• CU class for behav./ emot. prob.	U	—			
		• Suspended/expelled since RA	U	—			
	School	• Repeated grade since RA	U	—			
		• CU use of spec. educ.	F	—			
	Health	• ERV for accident/ injury since RA	F	—			

C. Financial work incentives tied to work or related activities

WRP (Single-parents R&A) [3.5 years]	Behavior	• Suspended/expelled since RA	F	—			

Table A.7   *(continued)*

Measure	Middle age group (ages at FU)		Measure	Oldest age group (ages at FU)	
	Impact/ Signif.	Effect size		Impact/ Signif.	Effect size
			Age 10 and above		
			• Behav. prob. since RA	F	—
			• Ever in trouble w/police	U	—

Table A.7   *(continued)*

Name (Population) [Follow-up length]	Outcome domain	All children			Youngest age group (ages at FU)		
		Measure	Impact/ Signif.	Effect size	Measure	Impact/ Signif.	Effect size
WPR *(continued)*	School	• Absences last mo.	U	—			
		• Repeated grade since RA	U	—			
	Other	• CU participates clubs/orgs.	F***	—			
TSMF (Single-parent R&A) [1 to 4 years]	Health	• Substantiated reports A/N	U	—			
	Other	• Foster care placements	U	—			
MFIP (Urban single-parent recipients) [3 years]	Behavior						
	School						
	Health						
(Urban single-parent applicants) [3 years]	Behavior						
	School						
	Health						

Table A.7 *(continued)*

Middle age group (ages at FU)			Oldest age group (ages at FU)		
Measure	Impact/ Signif.	Effect size	Measure	Impact/ Signif.	Effect size
			• Ever dropped out	F	—
			Age 12 and above		
			• Employment	F	—
			• Earnings	F	—
Age 5–12			*Age 13 and above*		
• CU total BPI	**F***	**0.14**			
• CU externalizing BPI	**F****	—			
• CU internalizing BPI	F	—			
• CU high level of behav./emot. prob.	**F*****	—			
• CU pos. social behav. (PBS)	F	0.01			
• CU behav. prob. at school	F	—	• CU behav. prob. at school	U	
• Suspended/expelled since RA	F	—			
• CU avg. perf. in school	**F***	**0.15**	• CU avg. perf. in school	0	
• CU perf. in school below avg.	**F****	—	• CU perf. in school below avg.	F	
• CU engagement in school	**F****	**0.17**			
• Repeated grade since RA	F	0.10	• Repeated grade since RA	F	
• In spec. educ. since RA	F	—			
• ERV for accident/injury since RA	**U***	—			
• CU overall health	U	0.07			
• CU total BPI	U	0.13			—
• CU pos. social behav. (PBS)	U	0.10			
• CU behav. prob. at school	F	—	• CU behav. prob. at school	**U*****	
• Suspended/expelled since RA	**U***	—			
• CU avg. perf. in school	U	0.11	• CU avg. perf. in school	**U****	—
• CU perf. in school below avg.	U	—	• CU perf. in school below avg.	**U***	—
• CU engagement in school	U	0.13			
• Repeated grade since RA	F	0.13	• Repeated grade since RA	U	
• In spec. educ. since RA	F	—			
• CU overall health	U	0.04			

Table A.7 *(continued)*

Name (Population) [Follow-up length]	Outcome domain	All children Measure	Impact/ Signif.	Effect size	Youngest age group (ages at FU) Measure	Impact/ Signif.	Effect size
SSP (Single-parent recipients) [3 years]	Behavior				*Age 3–5* • CU behav. prob. • CU pos. social behav.	U U	0.01 0.06
	School				• CU reading score (PPVT-R)	F	0.05
	Health				• CU avg. health • CU any long-term health prob. • Injuries in last 6 mos.	U F F	0.05 0.04 0.04
New Hope (Poor families with one or more children aged 1–11) [2 years]	Behavior	• CU total pos. behav. (P) • CU total pos. behav. (T)	F **F****	0.03 **0.25**	*Age 3–5* • CU total behav. prob. (P) • CU externalizing prob. (P) • CU internalizing prob. (P)	F F F	0.12 0.11 0.09
	School	• CU normal school progress (P) • CU school achievement (P)	F F	0.09 0.09			

D. Parental responsibility requirements

| PPI (R&A) [2 years] | Health | | | | *Age 2–4* • Number of well-child visits • At least 1 well-child visit/yr. • Up-to-date vaccinations | U F U | — — — |

Table A.7   *(continued)*

Middle age group (ages at FU)			Oldest age group (ages at FU)		
Measure	Impact/ Signif.	Effect size	Measure	Impact/ Signif.	Effect size
Age 6–11			*Age 12–18*		
• CU behav. prob.	F	0.03	• CU school behav. prob.	**U***	**0.09**
• CU pos. social behav.	U	0.02	• CU delinquent activity (12–14) (C)	F	0.06
• CU school behav. prob.	F	0.01	• CU delinquent activity (15–18) (C)	**U****	**0.21**
			• CU any smoking (C)	**U***	**0.11**
			• CU drinks once/week or more (C)	**U*****	**0.20**
			• CU any drug use (C)	**U***	**0.12**
• CU reading score (6–7) (PPVT-R)	F	0.13			
• CU math score (7–11)	**F****	**0.14**	• CU math score	U	0.03
• CU avg. school subject achievement (P)	**F****	**0.11**	• CU avg. school subject achievement	**U***	**0.11**
• Ever repeated grade (P)	0	0.05	• Ever repeated grade	U	0.03
			• Ever dropped out (15–18)	U	0.09
• CU avg. health	**F****	**0.11**	• CU avg. health	F	0.05
• CU any long-term health prob.	**F****	**0.09**	• CU any long-term health prob.	U	0.02
• Injuries in last 6 mos.	U	0.01	• Injuries in last 6 mos.	F	0.03
Age 6–12			*Age 12–18*		
• CU total behav. prob. (P)	F	0.03	• Contacts for behav. prob. since RA	**U*****	**0.3**
• CU externalizing prob. (P)	F	0.02	• Suspended/expelled since RA	U	0.0
• CU internalizing problems (P)	F	0.02			
• CU total social competency (C)	U	0.06			
• CU total aggression score (C)	F	0.07			
• CU SSRC acad. scale (5–12) (T)	**F****	**0.25**	• CU avg. perf. in school	**U***	**0.2**
• CU not making normal progress (5–12) (T)	F	0.09	• CU perf. in school below avg.	**U***	**0.2**
			• CU use of spec. educ.	**F****	**0.2**
			• CU in gifted/talented program	**F***	**0.2**
			• Repeated a grade since RA	**U*****	**0.3**

Table A.7   *(continued)*

Name (Population) [Follow-up length]	Outcome domain	All children			Youngest age group (ages at FU)		
		Measure	Impact/ Signif.	Effect size	Measure	Impact/ Signif.	Effect size
PIP (Recipients) [4 years]	Health						
E. TANF-like bundles of reforms							
ABC (Single-parent R&A) [1 to 3 years]	Health	• Substantiated reports of neglect— yrs 1, 3	**U****	—			
		• Substantiated reports of neglect —yr 2	F	—			
		• Substantiated reports of other abuse—yrs 1, 2, 3	F	—			
	Other	• Foster care placements—yr 3	F	—			
FTP (R&A) [4 years]	Behavior						
	School						
	Health						
Jobs First (R&A) [3 years]	Behavior						
	School						
	Health						

Note: For full program names and citations, see Table 4.5.

0 = impact estimate is zero; F = impact estimate is in favorable direction; U = impact estimate is in unfavorable direction.

* = statistically significant at the 10 percent level; ** = statistically significant at the 5 percent level; *** = statistically significant at the 1 percent level. Boldface cells indicate any statistically significant impact.

Effect size = absolute value of difference between program and control group outcome expressed as a proportion of the standard deviation of the outcome for the control group or for both groups combined.

Table A.7 *(continued)*

Middle age group (ages at FU)			Oldest age group (ages at FU)		
Measure	Impact/ Signif.	Effect size	Measure	Impact/ Signif.	Effect size
Age 4–10					
• Up-to-date vaccinations	**F***	—			
Age 5–12			*Age 13–17*		
• Suspended since RA	F	0.02	• Suspended since RA	**U****	**0.17**
• Expelled since RA	U	0.13	• Expelled since RA	U	0.02
• CU total BPI	U	0.01	• Arrested since RA	U	0.01
• CU pos. social behav. (PBS)	**U***	**0.11**	• Found guilty since RA	U	—
• CU achievement	F	0.09	• CU achievement	**U***	**0.14**
• CU engagement in school	0	0.00			
• In spec. educ. since RA	U	0.07	• In spec. educ. since RA	U	0.09
• Repeated a grade since RA	U	0.02			
• CU general health	**F***	**0.09**	• Had a baby since RA	F	0.03
• ERV for accident/injury since RA	U	0.01			
Age 5–12			*Age 13–17*		
• Suspended since RA	F	0.04	• Suspended since RA	F	0.00
• CU total BPI	**F****	**0.10**	• Expelled since RA	U	0.11
• CU externalizing BPI	**F***	**0.09**	• Arrested since RA	F	0.09
• CU internalizing BPI	**F****	**0.10**	• Found guilty since RA	**F****	**0.14**
• CU pos. social behav. (PBS)	**F***	**0.09**			
• CU achievement	0	0.01	• CU achievement	**U*****	**0.24**
• CU engagement in school	F	0.07			
• In spec. educ. since RA	U	0.04	• In spec. educ. since RA	U	0.12
• Repeated a grade since RA	U	0.03	• Repeated a grade since RA	U	0.07
• CU general health	F	0.05	• Had a baby since RA	U	0.05

A/N = abuse or neglect; BCS/SRC = Braken Basic Concept Scale/School Readiness Composite; BPI = Behavior Problems Index; C = child report; CU = current; ERV = emergency room visit; FU = follow-up; M = maternal report; P = parent/parent report; PBS/SCS = Positive Behavior Scale/Social Competence Subscale; PPVT-R = Peabody Picture Vocabulary Test–Revised; RA = random assignment; R&A = recipients and applicants; SSRC = Social Skills Rating System; T = teacher report; — = not available.

———— ❖ ————

Methodology for Summary
Figures in Chapter 10

This appendix provides additional detail regarding the summaries of the random assignment and observational studies presented in Chapter 10. In that chapter, we tally the results of the studies we reviewed in Chapters 5 to 9 according to the major policy or groups of policies they evaluate, as well as for reform as a bundle.

The assignment of random assignment studies and observational studies to the eleven policy rows in the matrixes in Figures 10.1 to 10.5 is recorded in Table B.1. With a few exceptions, each of the studies we reviewed in Chapters 5 to 9 contributed the tallies in the Chapter 10 figures. Several studies were omitted from the tallies because of methodological concerns identified in the relevant chapters. These omitted investigations include the early generation observational studies of the caseload discussed in Chapter 5 (see Figure 5.4). In the case of the fertility tallies, methodological concerns discussed in Chapter 8 led us to omit Levine (2002) and Horvath-Rose and Peters (2002). Methodological issues also led us to exclude from the child outcome tallies the study by Paxson and Waldfogel (2003) discussed in Chapter 9. Finally, we omitted the results from CWPDP because of conflicts between early and later analyses of the experimental data.

As noted in Chapter 10, the tallies in Figures 10.1 to 10.5 illustrate graphically the number of results that pertain to that policy-outcome pair, the signs of the results, and the statistical significance of the results. For the included random assignment studies, with one exception discussed below, each row in the relevant figures in the previous chapters (for example, Figures 5.1, 5.2, 6.1, and so on) contributed one "result" to be included in the tallies. Thus studies that provide results separately for recipients and applicants contributed two results. In the case of the marriage impacts, studies that provide results for single-parent and two-parent samples also contributed two results. Although this procedure gives more weight to studies that disaggregated results for these groups,

Table B.1   Assignment of studies for summary matrixes

Policy or policy bundle	Random assignment studies	Observational studies
1. Financial work incentives	WRP-IO MFIP-IO	CEA (1999b) Meyer and Rosenbaum (2001)

2. Mandatory work or related activities	L.A. Jobs-1st GAIN
	IMPACT–Basic Track
	NEWWS Programs:
	   Atlanta LFA
	   Grand Rapids LFA
	   Riverside LFA
	   Portland
	   Atlanta HCD
	   Grand Rapids HCD
	   Riverside HCD
	   Columbus Integrated
	   Columbus Traditional
	   Detroit
	   Oklahoma City
		CEA (1999b)
		MaCurdy, Mancuso, and O'Brien-Strain (2002)
		Rector and Youssef (1999)

3. Sanctions		CEA (1999b) MaCurdy, Mancuso, and O'Brien-Strain (2002) Mead (2001) Rector and Youssef (1999)
4. Weak financial work incentives and mandatory work-related activities (within the welfare system)	WRP TSMF	
5. Strong financial work incentives and mandatory work-related activities (within the welfare system)	FIP MFIP	
6. Strong financial work incentives and mandatory work-related activities (outside the welfare system)	SSP SSP-Plus SSP-A New Hope	
7. Time limits (behavioral)		CEA (1999b) Grogger (2002) Grogger (2003) Grogger (2004) Grogger and Michalopoulos (2003) Kaushal and Kaestner (2001) Kearney (2002) MaCurdy, Mancuso, and O'Brien-Strain (2002) Meyer and Rosenbaum (2001)
8. Time limits (mechanical)	FTP Jobs First	Meyer and Rosenbaum (2001)

Table B.1 *(continued)*

Policy or policy bundle	Random assignment studies	Observational studies
9. Family cap	AAWDP FDP	CEA (1999b) Kaushal and Kaestner (2001) Kearney (2002)
10. Parental responsibility	PPI PIP	
11. Reform as a bundle	EMPOWER IMPACT VIP/VIEW ABC FTP Jobs First	Bartik and Eberts (1999) Bitler, Gelbach, and Hoynes (2002) Bitler et al. (2004) Blank (2001) CEA (1997) CEA (1999b) Figlio and Ziliak (1999) Grogger (2003) Grogger (2004) Huang, Garfinkel, and Waldfogel (2000) Kearney (2002) Moffitt (1999) O'Neill and Hill (2001) Schoeni and Blank (2000) Wallace and Blank (1999)

Note: The first ten rows for individual reform policies or groups of policies correspond to the rows in Figures 10.1 to 10.4. The eleventh row for reform as a bundle corresponds to Figure 10.5. For full names of and citations for the random assignment programs, see Table 4.5.

we view them as contributing approximately statistically independent estimates.

The one exception is our tally of the results from the random assignment studies for income and poverty, where in Figures 7.1 and 7.2 results were reported for both a narrow measure (based on administrative data) and a broad measure (based on survey data) for the same study population when they were available. In these cases, we counted each estimate as a separate result. Since a few studies provided only one measure or the other, this approach allowed us to include a greater number of studies in Figure 10.2 than would have been possible if we had restricted our attention to the estimates based on one measure only. Although this procedure may appear to give more weight to studies that reported both measures, it did not greatly change the results in the figure. Survey-based estimates were not systematically smaller or larger than the measures based on administrative data, and in some cases the impact estimates were of opposite sign.

For some of the outcomes discussed in Chapters 7 to 9, we reported results for multiple measures for a particular experiment, either capturing different concepts of the outcome (for example, narrow and broad measures of income in Figures 7.1 and 7.2, and different measures of child health and development in Figure 10.1), or corresponding to measurements at early and later follow-up intervals (as in Figures 8.1 and 8.3 for marriage and fertility, respectively). In the case of marriage and fertility, we tallied only the result from the initial follow-up period, typically the two-year follow-up, since that interval is closest to what is available in other studies. This restriction made little difference, however, since the pattern of short-term and long-term results from the NEWWS programs and Jobs First is almost identical in terms of sign and significance. In the case of the child outcomes, within the three major domains of child outcomes covered in Figure 10.1 (behavior, school achievement, and health), we used a weighting procedure (discussed below) so that each study contributed one result.

The definition of a "result" differed somewhat for the included observational studies. For example, in Figure 5.5, a number of studies employed a specification where a given policy is captured by multiple coefficient estimates. In those cases, we tallied a single result based on the pattern of the estimates. This approach reflects the fact that the estimates reported in the figure are not independent, and were designed to capture whether a policy had an effect overall and whether the effect differed for stronger or weaker versions of the policy.

For each result that an experimental or observational study contributed, the sign and significance were used to classify the result into one of four categories: negative and significant, negative and insignificant, positive and insignificant, and positive and significant. In all cases, a 10 percent cutoff was used to determine statistical significance. If the result was based on a single impact estimate or coefficient estimate, this determination was straightforward. In the case of observational studies with multiple coefficients characterizing a specific policy reform (for example, strength of sanctions and other examples in Figure 5.5), the signs were generally in the same direction and the result was tallied as significant if a weak majority of the coefficients was significant. For example, Rector and Youssef's (1999) estimates contribute a single significant result to the tally, whereas CEA's (1999b) estimates of the effects of age exemptions contribute a single insignificant result.[1]

In the case of reform as a bundle, when the same observational study produced estimates for both waivers and TANF that were of the same sign, a single result was recorded. The result was counted as significant if either estimate was significant. In a few cases, the signs differed between the waiver and TANF estimates. These studies contributed two results, with the sign and significance determined by the respective impacts for the waiver and TANF variables.

As noted above, among the experimental studies, the results for child outcomes reported in Figure 10.1 often provide multiple impact estimates within the same domain (for example, behavior, school achievement, and health). In order not to give more weight to studies that collected more measures within a domain, each study still contributed one result for each domain with available impact estimates. When multiple measures were available in the same domain, if all the signs agreed (as was often the case), the result was recorded with that sign. If any of the results was significant, the result was recorded as significant. When the signs differed, if any of the outcomes was significant, the sign associated with that result was assigned and the result was recorded as significant. If there were significant results of opposite sign, the result was split: a weight of 0.5 was given in each direction (that is, unfavorable and favorable) in the "significant" category. If none of the results of varying signs was significant, then a weight of 0.5 was given in each direction in the "insignificant" category.

❖ Notes

1. Introduction

1. The available research also addresses the impact on other welfare-related outcomes including the use of other government programs (for example, Medicaid and food stamps), material hardship and food insecurity, and health insurance coverage. For a synthesis of the research related to these outcomes, see Grogger, Karoly, and Klerman (2002).
2. Of course, this would be true of any model, not just economic models. For analyses that incorporate extra-economic perspectives, see Ellwood (1988) or Bane and Ellwood (1994).

2. Background

1. For a more in-depth treatment of this history, see Berkowitz (1991), Weaver (2000), and Heclo (2001).
2. The National Center for Heath Statistics stopped collecting detailed divorce data in 1996. See *http://www.cdc.gov/nchs/mardiv.htm*. The data series for divorce rates from 1998 on are not comparable with earlier years, because some states are omitted.
3. Moffitt (1992) provides graphical evidence suggesting that the growth in cash and noncash benefits over this period may explain the growth in the caseload. Particularly important is the growth in noncash benefits provided by the Food Stamp and Medicaid programs, which were introduced in the 1960s. However, the econometric evidence presented in Moffitt (1987) suggests that at most one-third of the caseload growth can be explained by increases in AFDC and food stamp benefits.
4. The six states that did not receive a waiver approval during this period were Alaska, Kentucky, New Mexico, Nevada, and Rhode Island. New Mexico applied for a waiver during this period but the application was withdrawn. Nevada's application was still pending when PRWORA was signed into law in August 1996 (Harvey, Camasso, and Jagannathan 2000).
5. Because of the complexities of the various waivers approved and implemented during the 1992 to 1996 period, different sources sometimes pro-

vide conflicting summaries of the timing of the waivers and their features. In the discussion and tables that follow, we rely on information compiled by the U.S. Department of Health and Human Services (see DHHS 1997; Crouse 1999).

6. Under AFDC, there was a $90 work expense disregard. In addition, for the first four months of earnings, the $30-and-a-third rule applied. From months five to twelve, only the $30 disregard applied, and no earnings were disregarded thereafter.

7. In addition to sanctions associated with nonparticipation in required work or related activities, waivers were also approved to impose sanctions for other behavior, such as quitting a job or refusing a job offer.

8. For additional details on PRWORA's provisions, see Committee on Ways and Means (2000).

9. This "maintenance of effort rule" could be increased if states failed to meet required work participation targets.

10. The policies recorded in Table 2.8 generally apply to the largest segment of the caseload in each state. Several states have implemented more than one program, with policies that vary for the different groups of recipients. In many cases, the state TANF policies summarized are more complex than what can be easily conveyed in the table. Interested readers should consult Rowe and Roberts (2004) for additional details regarding the policies shown in Table 2.8, as well as other TANF policies not covered in the table.

11. Exceptions to this rule can be made by the states for up to 20 percent of the caseload.

12. See Rowe and Roberts (2004) for additional detail on these and other state TANF policies.

13. Hotz and Scholz (2003) provide a detailed description of the EITC and a review of research into its effects.

14. Regarding public health programs, see Gruber (2003), LoSasso and Buchmueller (2002), and Aizer and Grogger (2003). Regarding the minimum wage, see U.S. Department of Labor (2003).

15. All of the data reported in this section are drawn from either DHHS (2001b) or Bavier (2001).

3. An Economic Model

1. As is common in the welfare incentives literature, we abstract from the broader tax and transfer system of which the welfare program is a part.

2. Furthermore, some consumers who remain just above the new break-even point may reduce their hours (and earnings) in order to qualify for benefits (Blank, Card, and Robins 2000). While predicted changes in welfare use, welfare payments, employment, earnings, and income for this group would be the same as those for the third group we consider, empirical estimates suggest that few consumers behave in this manner (Moffitt 1992).

3. A work requirement stipulating hours much in excess of h_2 would cause the recipient to become income-ineligible for aid.

4. In the context of the model, the recipient would never choose to satisfy the work-related activity mandate via unpaid activities if she could work instead. If her market productivity were less than the minimum wage, or if there were other rigidities in the labor market, she might not be able to find work. Recipients also may choose unpaid activities over work if the future payoff to such activities (for example, training) exceeded the opportunity cost of working. Finally, they may choose unpaid activities over work if the disutility of such activities is less than the disutility of working, contrary to our assumption.

5. The remainder of this section draws heavily on Grogger and Michalopoulos (1999). In addition to the assumptions stated above, they assume that consumers cannot borrow or save, which they argue is reasonable for low-income populations.

6. Lawrance (1991) estimates that $\rho = .84$ among poor families, as compared to .89 among well-off families.

7. For simplicity, we have omitted work requirements from the diagram, but the same general approach can be used to analyze the effects of time limits in conjunction with work requirements.

4. Methodological Issues

1. For a discussion of random assignment in the social science context, see Burtless (1995) and Heckman and Smith (1995).

2. In practice, studies usually report more efficient results which use regression methods partially to control for the remaining (random) differences between the two groups.

3. On the DHHS experience with waivers, see Harvey, Camasso and Jagannathan (2000).

4. Under certain conditions PRWORA allowed states to continue section 1115 waivers that were in effect as of August 1996. A few states continued longer-term follow-up analyses for evaluations that were in place prior to PRWORA's passage, but such evaluations became increasingly difficult given the need to maintain a control group subject to the old AFDC rules. In some states, their TANF plans provisions differed from those under their approved waivers, so the policy environment affecting the treatment group also changed.

5. See Meyers, Glaser, and MacDonald (1998) on financial incentive changes as part of California's Work Pays Experiment. Harvey, Camasso, and Jagannathan (2000) note that at least some control group subjects in the section 1115 waiver demonstration studies believed they were subject to time limits, a family cap, or one of the other state welfare waiver provisions being evaluated. Similarly, Miller et al. (2000, table B.1) report that many

members of MFIP's treatment and control groups thought they were subject to time limits, even though MFIP did not involve time limits.

6. This approach involves implicit assumptions that the effects of such variables are linear and additive. If these assumptions are incorrect, or the observed variable (for example, the unemployment rate) inadequately represents the potentially confounding factor (for example, the economy), then regression techniques may yield invalid estimates of the effects of reform.

7. Strictly speaking, the model in equation (4.1) applies to regressions estimated from household-level micro data. However, the models estimated from state-level aggregate data that are common in the welfare reform literature can be derived from equation (4.1) by averaging across households within cells defined by state and year. The approaches to control for policy endogeneity discussed below pertain to aggregated models as well.

8. The idiosyncratic unobservables v_{ist} represent deviations from state-year mean unobservables, and as such are uncorrelated with R_{st} by construction.

9. On the difference-in-difference methodology, see Meyer (1995). See also the discussion in Moffitt and Ver Ploeg (1999). Since the difference-in-difference terminology is sometimes applied to a model without regressions such as Z_{st} and X_{ist}, we use the term generalized difference-in-difference to refer to the model that includes such regressions.

10. Because data from multiple states are necessary to implement the difference-in-difference procedure, we omit from our study analyses based on data from single states, including Figlio and Ziliak (1999) and Klerman and Haider (2000).

11. Some states initially implemented their policy changes in only a portion of the state, which further complicates efforts to characterize the states' policies.

12. When the new policy was introduced within a calendar year, the dummy variable is usually replaced by a variable measuring the fraction of the year during which the new policy was in place.

13. One study suggests that as many as 540,000 recipients may have received full-family sanctions between 1997 and 1999 (Goldberg and Schott 2000). However, that study fails to account for families that would have left welfare anyway. Thus it probably overstates the net effect of sanctions on the welfare caseload.

14. We include only those studies that approximate the types of policies implemented under TANF. As a result, we exclude some evaluations that consider specialized reforms such as those that focus on service delivery for teen parents (for example, the Learning, Earning, and Parenting program, the New Chance program, and the Teen Parent Demonstration program), child support policies (for example, the New York Child Assistance Program), or specialized service delivery (for example, the Postemployment Services Demonstration program). Furthermore, we exclude some of the earlier welfare-to-work experiments that predate the 1988 Family Support Act (for example, San Diego's Saturation Work Initiative Model; the early GAIN

experiments in several California counties). We also exclude Project Independence, which was Florida's initial JOBS program. It was the precursor to Florida's Family Transition Program (FTP), which we do include.

15. There have been no experimental evaluations of TANF-based reforms.

16. Many of the experiments also report results for other subgroups of the study population, defined by educational attainment, employment history, or other measures of disadvantage. For a summary of subgroup findings from these studies, see Grogger, Karoly, and Klerman (2002).

17. For this reason, we do not focus on the five-year follow-up results for Indiana's reform, since the policies facing the treatment group changed (and hence the cohorts analyzed changed) midway through the experiment (Beecroft et al. 2003).

18. Control-group crossover is an issue with the long-term (five-year) results of FIP reported in Fraker et al. (2002). Hence, we focus on the short-term impacts for Iowa.

19. Just as we do not consider the results from experimental studies for population subgroups, we do not consider observational studies that focus primarily on more narrow population groups. For example, see Borjas (2001a) and Kaestner and Kaushal (forthcoming) for analyses of immigrant outcomes under welfare reform.

20. See, for example, Hsiao (1986).

21. For the Arkansas and New Jersey family cap demonstrations listed in panel E of Table 4.6, we note that although the impact analyses provide some results for welfare utilization, and employment and earnings, we do not discuss these findings in Chapters 5 or 6, respectively. Instead, since the main focus of these demonstrations is the impact on fertility, we only discuss these experiments in terms of their impact on this outcome in Chapter 8. Likewise, the impact analyses for the two parental responsibility demonstrations (PPI and PIP) are really only relevant for Chapter 9 on child outcomes.

5. Welfare Use and Welfare Payments

1. All monetary amounts from the SSP evaluations in the figures and text in this chapter and the chapters that follow have been translated into U.S. dollars using a conversion rate of $0.75 U.S. to $1 Canadian.

2. Members of the treatment groups were subject to some other policy changes as well, such as extended transitional child care and health insurance in the case of WRP or, in the case of MFIP, a food stamp cash-out. Because the MFIP treatment group received its food stamp benefits in the form of cash, the MFIP welfare use measure is an indicator of whether the participant received cash aid (welfare benefits plus cashed-out food stamp benefits) in the case of the treatment group, or whether the participant received cash aid (welfare) or food stamp benefits in the case of the control group.

3. As discussed in Chapter 3, the SSP Applicants program involved single parents who started new welfare spells during the program's random assign-

ment period, but who only became eligible for supplemental payments after remaining on welfare for one year.

4. More precisely, most of these studies used modified dummies, defined as the fraction of the year during which the policy was in place. Some studies used authorization dates rather than implementation dates to construct these variables, although this seems to have had little effect on the results.

5. For the observational studies, we indicate only whether the estimates are significant at the 10 percent level or better. For some of the estimates that were transformed for presentation purposes, it is difficult to assign a more precise level of confidence. In the case of Ziliak et al. (2000), the figures represent the sum of several coefficients for which a standard error cannot be computed. Some of the underlying regression coefficients were significant, although others were not, and in several cases, the sum involved significant coefficients of the opposite sign.

6. Three other analyses could be classified as early-generation studies under our definition (Gittleman, 2001; Hofferth, Stanhope, and Harris 2000, 2002). These studies analyze data from the PSID, which is a relatively small survey. Moreover, they analyze welfare entries and exits rather than welfare use. Welfare entry is a much rarer event than welfare use; the sample sizes available to study welfare exit are quite small, since they are limited to welfare recipients. These problems greatly exacerbate the collinearity issue that confronts all of the early-generation studies. In fact, these three studies yielded results whose signs, magnitudes, and significance levels made them appear to be quite unreliable. As a result, we have omitted them from our review.

7. Of all the experiments involving time limits that were discussed in Chapter 4, only these two provide the detailed quarter-by-quarter impact estimates that we use to estimate the mechanical effects of time limits.

8. We do not have the information required to construct a standard error for the difference-in-difference estimate; hence the statistical significance of the mechanical effects of time limits based on these two studies is not known.

9. Of course, the further into the future one goes in defining the post–time limit period, the less sure one can be that the difference-in-difference estimator isolates the mechanical effect of the time limit. For example, the impacts of Jobs First and FTP begin to fade a bit after roughly quarter 12, which clearly cannot be attributed to the mechanical effects of the time limit.

10. Results from Mueser et al. (2000) show the opposite pattern. They study welfare exits and entries using aggregate administrative data from five urban counties. They report that waivers had essentially no effect on welfare entries but sizable effects on welfare exits. They report that TANF had significant effects on both entries and exits, but smaller effects on exits than waivers. It is possible that the discrepancy between Mueser et al. (2000) and studies based on nationwide data are due to the limited geographic coverage of the Mueser et al. (2000) data set.

11. Schoeni and Blank (2000) do not present the unemployment coefficients from their regression models.

12. O'Neill and Hill (2001) do not present the unemployment coefficients from their models, but they can be inferred from the estimates that they provide regarding the proportion of the decline in the welfare participation rate that is explained by the unemployment rate.

6. Employment, Labor Supply, and Earnings

1. Evidence on hours of work would enable one to draw this conclusion more directly.

2. This is consistent with evidence from Hotz, Imbens, and Klerman (2000). They analyze longer-term data from the GAIN program, and find that the gap between work-oriented programs and skills-oriented programs fades over time.

3. A five-year follow-up for the subset of New Hope families with children aged one to ten at the time of random assignment shows a similar result (Huston et al. 2003).

4. The decline in FTP's impact on employment (and earnings) during the latter part of the follow-up period stems from increases in employment among the control group rather than decreases among the treatment group. D. Bloom, Kemple et al. (2000, 73) speculate that the control group may have been motivated to find work in the fourth year of the follow-up by publicity over Florida's impending TANF program, even though members of the control group were technically exempt from both FTP and TANF.

7. Income and Poverty

1. See, for example, Citro and Michael (1995) for a proposed modification to the official poverty measure that takes this approach.

2. The lack of correspondence with the official U.S. poverty measure is not necessarily problematic, given the concerns with the validity of that measure; see Citro and Michael (1995). The lack of comparability across studies, however, is of greater concern.

3. These time intervals are designed to capture the period prior to waivers; the initial welfare waiver period when the EITC also began to expand; the more active waiver period leading up to TANF when the EITC also continued to expand; and the post-TANF period.

4. Winship and Jencks (2002) use data from the Food Security Supplement to the 1995–1999 Current Population Surveys to examine differences in food security for single and married mothers over the period. Controlling for other factors, all food security measures improved for both groups from 1995 to 1997, but the changes were often larger for single mothers. Winship and Jencks interpret their results as indicating that single mothers were at

least as well off, if not better off, after welfare reform. Borjas (2001a) also uses data from the CPS (for 1994 to 1998) to examine the differential impact on food insecurity for immigrants in states that did and did not extend state-funded assistance to immigrants after PRWORA eliminated, for some groups of immigrants, eligibility for TANF and food stamps (specifically affecting nonrefugee, noncitizen households that arrived in the United States after 1996). Triple-difference models are estimated for affected and unaffected immigrant groups, in more and less generous states, for pre- versus post-PRWORA years, but Borjas does not consider the impact of welfare waivers, of TANF as a bundle, or of specific reform policies. His results show that food insecurity increased the most between 1994 and 1998 among those immigrants affected by the PRWORA changes in eligibility and living in states that did not extend state funding to cover them.

5. For the MFIP-IO sample for which both administrative and survey data on combined income (earnings plus welfare, including the food stamp cashout) are available, the mean survey report of combined income for the AFDC (control) group exceeds the administrative data mean for combined income, while the reverse is true for the MFIP-IO (treatment) group (Miller et al. 2000, table 4.6). Thus the impact estimate (treatment-control difference) for monthly combined income is $109 ($p < .05$) based on the administrative data versus $12 based on the survey data. There is almost no difference between the treatment and control groups in the mean value of the other income sources (for example, earnings of other household members, child support, other income) collected in the survey data.

6. With the exception of Riverside LFA, survey-based measures of recipient combined income from the NEWWS experiments yield impacts that have the same sign as the measures based on administrative data and that are similar in magnitude (not shown). In the case of Riverside LFA, the monthly income impact is positive ($19 per month) but insignificant, although the poverty impact estimate is negative (-6.3 percentage points, $p < .01$).

7. For the 11 NEWWS programs, the impacts for household income are often larger and/or the opposite sign compared with the narrower measure of recipient combined income. However, the sample sizes for the survey-based household income measures are considerably smaller than what is available using administrative data, which probably explains why none of the impacts is statistically significant.

8. In contrast to the significant income impact reported in Figure 7.1 at the thirty-six-month SSP follow-up when the earnings supplement was coming to an end, there was no difference in total family income for the treatment and control groups at the time of the fifty-four-month SSP follow-up (Michalopoulos et al. 2002). This is consistent with the long-term convergence in employment and earnings for this program discussed in Chapter 6.

9. In Grogger's specification, the main effect of any reform (waivers or TANF) applies only to women whose youngest child is less than one. For these

women, the interaction term between any reform and age of youngest child is zero.

10. Although the unemployment rate is included in the model of income estimated by Moffitt (1999) and the models of income and the poverty rate estimated by Schoeni and Blank (2000), the coefficient is not reported in either study; therefore it is not possible to calculate the effect of a change in the unemployment rate on the dependent variable.

8. Family Structure

1. Under the AFDC Unemployed Parent (AFDC-UP) program, the "100-hour rule" required that, in addition to being financially eligible for benefits, the primary wage-earner could work no more than 100 hours per month. The work history requirement required that a family also show that the primary wage-earner had earned at least $50 in at least six of the last thirteen calendar quarters or had been eligible for unemployment compensation during the past year.

2. In terms of welfare for two-parent families, this is a simplification of the AFDC/TANF rules. Under the AFDC-UP program, welfare was potentially available to two-parent families only when there was substantial previous labor market experience (six of the last thirteen quarters, but less than 100 hours of work in the current month). This condition made it unlikely that teens or young two-parent families would qualify. Under TANF, the work history requirement and 100-hour rule have been eliminated in many states, making it somewhat easier for two-parent families to qualify for welfare. However, our simplification is not an irrelevant one. Even when married couples are eligible for welfare, if a woman on welfare marries a man working full time at or slightly above the minimum wage, the family will usually be income ineligible for welfare.

3. It is theoretically possible for a family cap to induce more women to choose marriage rather than nonmarital childbearing such that total fertility would rise. This effect seems extremely unlikely.

4. As discussed below, observational studies of fertility have access to birth certificate data from vital statistics. Like administrative data, birth certificate data are available for the entire population (not just a sample), in every time period, and without recall bias. However, no experimental study has matched participant data to individual-level birth certificate records.

5. Individual-level vital statistics data on marriage are only available though 1995, making them less useful for evaluations of welfare reform beyond the waiver period.

6. To date, New Hope provides results on marriage from the five-year follow-up only for the subsample of families with children ages one to ten at the time of random assignment. For this subsample, there was no effect of New Hope on marriage in aggregate, or for the subgroups employed full time

at random assignment and not employed full time at random assignment (Huston et al. 2003).

7. In Canada, couples who live together for at least one year and are not legally married are considered common-law partners, with rights that are akin to marriage (Michalopoulos et al. 2000).

8. We do not include Ellwood's (2000) study of the effect of the EITC, welfare reform, and the strong economy on marriage and living arrangements, because he does not adopt the difference-in-difference methodology outlined in Chapter 4. Rather he examines changes in marriage and cohabitation between 1986 and 1999 for different population subgroups, and concludes that these factors combined had little effect on marriage behavior. He does not estimate a separate effect of welfare reform. We also do not consider a study by Kaestner and Kaushal (forthcoming), because their main focus is on outcomes for immigrants and we have excluded such studies of population subgroups. They find no effect of TANF on marriage decisions for foreign-born citizens but some evidence of a decrease in marriage propensity for foreign-born noncitizens.

9. Bitler, Gelbach, and Hoynes (2002) replicate their analysis on subsamples of black women in central cities, Hispanic women, and dropout women (as well as similarly defined subsamples of children). They find considerable heterogeneity in the impact of reform on these subgroups. For example, there is an 8-percentage-point (or 100 percent) increase in black central city children living with neither parent, along with a 13-percentage-point (or 21 percent) decline in living with unmarried parents for this group of children.

10. The estimated effect for TANF on divorce is also significant at the 10 percent level in a model that omits state-specific time trends (but retains state and year fixed effects).

11. At the five-year follow-up, the outcome measure is slightly different: the proportion of women having a new baby present in the household. This measure captures not only own fertility but also adoption.

12. The AAWDP outcome measure is the number of births rather than the percentage having a child (the measure used in all the other studies). In Figure 8.3, we have plotted the impact estimate (difference in mean number of births) multiplied by 100. Since most women who have a child have only one during the follow-up interval, the average number of births multiplied by 100 is approximately the same as the percentage of women having at least one birth.

13. In addition, a small number of cases (21, well under 1 percent of the control cases) were informed that they were subject to the family cap when they were not.

14. As we noted in Chapter 4, however, such analyses based on cross-state administrative data are difficult to implement due to differences across state data systems.

15. The full difference-in-difference-in-difference specification would include

not merely state and year fixed effects, but a fixed effect for every state-year combination.

9. Child Outcomes

1. Other recent syntheses of the relationship between child outcomes and welfare reform include Hamilton, Freedman, and McGroder (2000), D. Bloom and Michalopoulos (2001), Duncan and Chase-Lansdale (2001), Michalopoulos and Berlin (2001), Morris et al. (2001), and Zaslow et al. (2002). Compared with these efforts, our review encompasses a broader range of both experimental and observational studies. For some of the experimental studies, we draw on results based on longer-term follow-up.

2. This modeling framework does not delve into the sociological and psychological literatures, which offer additional theories about the ways in which parental behaviors and other environmental factors interact to produce child well-being.

3. In this chapter, "leisure" refers to activities other than work for pay or household work. This definition is closer to the vernacular meaning of the term than the definition employed in Chapter 3, which included household work—in particular child rearing—as part of leisure.

4. Haider, Jacknowitz, and Schoeni (2003) use aggregate state-level data on rates of breast-feeding from 1990 to 2000 to estimate the impact of various features of state work requirements under waivers and TANF on breast-feeding rates. They find that the most stringent work requirements that apply to women with infants have significantly reduced the prevalence of breast-feeding six months after birth for all mothers and for women on WIC (Special Supplemental Nutrition Program for Women, Infants, and Children). Since the incidence of breast-feeding is a more indirect measure of child well-being, we do not include their study in our review of observational studies.

5. A test is reliable if an individual has similar scores on repeated applications of the test. A valid test is one that measures what it purports to measure.

6. The Indiana evaluation provides results on child outcomes five years after randomization. By that time, however, the policies facing the treatment group had changed from those reported in Table 4.5, essentially converting the Basic Track into the Placement Track (Beecroft, Cahill, and Goodson 2002; Beecroft et al. 2003). As a result, the treatment group in the child-outcomes analysis differs from the samples used for analysis of the outcomes assessed two years after randomization covered in earlier chapters. Likewise, in Iowa, the child-outcomes analysis occurred five years after randomization, which was seventeen to twenty-nine months after the control group faced the reform policies (applied in the spring of 1997) (Fraker et al. 2002). Since there are no short-term child outcome results for these two studies that measure the effect of the original welfare reforms, we do not discuss

these two studies in this chapter. The broader conclusions that we draw in this chapter would not be changed, however, if we were to consider these two studies as well.

7. In the case of the SSP experiments, child outcomes are reported for only the primary study.

8. These domains overlap to some extent; some outcomes could be easily classified in more than one of the domains we have defined. For example, school suspensions could be a behavior problem or a school outcome. We have classified it as the former, but we recognize that others might place it in the latter category. For our purposes, the goal was to be consistent rather than rigid in defining these broad outcome domains.

9. Appendix Table A.7 records the child-outcome measures for each study by domain, the direction and statistical significance of each impact, and the effect size when it is available.

10. Given the differences in the follow-up periods, ranging from one to five years, children in the same age strata at the time of follow-up may have been "exposed" to welfare reform for differing lengths of time. In other words, their ages at random assignment will not necessarily be the same.

11. The effect size is a standardized measure of impact and is defined as the program impact (treatment minus control group difference) divided by the standard deviation of the outcome for treatment and control groups combined. In Appendix Table A.7, we report the absolute value of the effect size for those studies that report it.

12. Some measures are available for all children. Impacts for the full MFIP for adolescents aged 13 and above, in addition to those for the focal children aged 5 to 12, are discussed below.

13. For some outcomes, reports were made by both parents and children; other outcomes were collected from parents only or children only. When results are available from both parent and child reports, we record impacts for the parent result in Figure 9.1. Unless otherwise noted, the parent and child impact results were very similar.

14. There was no statistically significant difference in the child report of average school-subject achievement and in general health status. Both measures were reported by those aged 10–11 only. For both of these indicators, the favorable impact measured in the parental reports is strongest for children aged 6–8, suggesting that the difference in parent and child reports results from a lower impact among the older children in this age range.

15. New Hope also offered a generous child care subsidy for children up to age 13. The increased use of formal child care centers and after-school programs may explain some of the favorable impacts on child outcomes for this program.

16. The stated sanction was $25 per month, but compensatory policies in food stamps and housing vouchers effectively reduced the sanction to $10.

17. Recall that in Delaware, the control group was enrolled in ABC eighteen

months after the initial randomization. Thus by the second year of follow-up, some controls had received the treatment for up to six months. Also, by year 3 a substantial proportion of the treatment group had begun to hit their twenty-four-month time limits (but limits were reached by none of those in the treatment group, whose clocks started eighteen months later).

18. We do not discuss results based on a survey of the teachers of a subset of the focal children.

19. Our results are more complex than what has been portrayed in some other surveys, in part because we include a more comprehensive set of studies and consider a wider range of measures. Nevertheless, our conclusions are broadly consistent with the other reviews cited at the outset of the chapter.

10. Theory, Evidence, and Policy Trade-offs

1. For some outcomes, we omitted classes of studies or individual studies because of methodological concerns discussed in the relevant chapters. For example, we omitted results from CWPDP because different analysts obtained different results regarding its impacts on employment. We omitted the results from early observational studies of the effects of specific reforms on welfare use for reasons discussed in Chapter 5. Appendix B provides additional detail about our approach for generating the summaries in this chapter, including which studies were classified into the policy rows of the matrices.

2. Appendix B discusses the treatment of outcomes in Chapters 7, 8, and 9 where multiple results are reported for the same experimental study corresponding to different measures of the outcome or measures for different follow-up periods. In general, these studies still contributed one result. The income and poverty results tallied in Figure 10.2 represent an exception, since some studies report results based on both administrative data (narrow measure) and survey data (broad measure) for the same group. In constructing Figure 10.2, we count each estimate reported in Figure 7.1 and Figure 7.2 as a separate result, for reasons that are discussed more fully in Appendix B. Despite the potential for double counting that this procedure represents, it did not greatly change the summary figure; the survey-based estimates were neither uniformly smaller nor greater than the estimates based on administrative data, and in some cases the two different estimates had the opposite sign.

3. Also included in the cell pertaining to the effects of mandatory work or related activities on welfare use are the observational studies by CEA (1999b), Rector and Youssef (1999), and MaCurdy, Mancuso, and O'Brien-Strain (2002).

4. More precisely, the significance of the results based on the nonexperimental analyses of Jobs First and FTP cannot be determined.

5. See Appendix B for a discussion of the approach to tallying the results from the experimental studies with results on child outcomes.

6. There is one exception to this generalization: a significant unfavorable effect for recipients in MFIP-IO and MFIP in the health domain, a measure of emergency room visits. The result may indicate less parental supervision or better access to health care.

7. New Hope produced significant favorable impacts on current use of special education and current enrollment in a gifted or talented program. Since the same study also finds a significant unfavorable impact for three other measures in the same domain (current average performance in school, current school performance is below average, and repeated a grade since random assignment), the result for the study is divided, with 0.5 in the favorable significant category and 0.5 in the unfavorable significant category.

8. See Eccles and Gootman (2002) for a review of youth development programs.

9. As discussed in Appendix B, the definition of a result, as applied to the observational studies, differs in Figure 10.5 from the definition used in the previous figures. Many observational studies report two estimates of the effect of reform as a bundle: one for waivers and one for TANF. In most such studies, both estimates have the same sign. In those cases, tallying both estimates seemed like double counting, so we tallied both estimates as a single result. We counted the result as significant if either of the estimates was significant (in most cases, both were). For the few studies that reported a negative estimate for waivers and a positive estimate for TANF (or vice versa), we tallied each estimate as a separate result.

10. Results for child outcomes are not tallied in Figure 10.5 since they are based exclusively on two random assignment studies. The bundle of reforms implemented in these two states is not very representative of the reforms implemented in other states in terms of the length of the time limit (two years or less in both cases) or the generosity of the financial work incentives (notably in Connecticut). Thus these two studies do not necessarily capture the distribution of outcomes for reform as a whole, nor do they capture entry effects. In the case of the other outcomes shown in Figure 10.5, additional random assignment studies are available and/or results are also available from observational studies.

Appendix A. Sources for Experimental Study Results

1. Many of these measures relate to the child's current status at the time of data collection (for example, health status), while others capture outcomes over a child's lifetime (for example, ever repeated a grade in school). Others ask about behavior or outcomes since random assignment. We have indicated whether a measure is cumulative ("ever") or measured since random assignment ("since RA"). Those not explicitly designated are assumed to relate to current status.

Appendix B. Methodology for Summary Figures in Chapter 10

1. The one exception involved the effects of time limits on labor supply. The effect was insignificant, but was insignificantly positive for families whose youngest child was two and insignificantly negative for families whose youngest child was three. We classified this result as negative, which is as arbitrary as the alternative.

References

Acs, Gregory, and Pamela Loprest. 2000. *Initial Synthesis Report of the Findings from ASPE's Leavers Grants: Report to the US Department of Human Services.* Washington, D.C.: The Urban Institute. December.

Acs, Gregor, and Sandi Nelson. 2001. " 'Honey I'm Home': Changes in Living Arrangements in the Late 1990s." Urban Institute, series B, no. B-38. June. Available at: *http://newfederalism.urban.org/html/series_b/b38/b38.html.*

Acs, Gregory, Katherin Ross Phillips, Caroline Ratcliffe, and Douglas Wissoker. 2001. "Comings and Goings: The Changing Dynamics of Welfare in the 1990s." Urban Institute. Manuscript.

Adams, John, and V. Joseph Hotz. 2001. "The Statistical Power of National Data to Evaluate Welfare Reform." In Robert A. Moffitt and Michele Ver Ploeg, eds., *Evaluating Welfare Reform in an Era of Transition,* 209–219. Panel on Data and Methods for Measuring the Effects of Changes in Social Welfare Programs. Washington, D.C.: National Academy Press, Committee on National Statistics, Committee on Behavioral and Social Sciences and Education, and the National Research Council.

Ahn, Jay, Shon Kraley, Debra Fogarty, Faith Lai, and Laurie Deppman. 2000. *A Study of Washington State's TANF Leavers and TANF Recipients: Welfare Reform and Findings from Administrative Data. Final Report.* Washington Department of Social and Health Services, Offices of Planning and Research, Economic Service Administration. February.

Aizer, Anna, and Jeffrey Grogger. 2003. "Parental Medicaid Expansions and Health Insurance Coverage." National Bureau of Economic Research Working Paper no. 9907. Cambridge, Mass. August.

Bane, Mary Jo, and David T. Ellwood. 1983. *The Dynamics of Dependence: The Routes to Self-Sufficiency.* Report to the U.S. Department of Health and Human Services. Cambridge, Mass.: Urban Systems Research and Engineering.

Bane, Mary Jo, and David Ellwood. 1994. *Welfare Realities: From Rhetoric to Reform.* Cambridge, Mass.: Harvard University Press.

Bartik, Timothy J., and Randall W. Eberts. 1999. "Examining the Effect of Industry Trends and Structure on Welfare Caseloads." In Sheldon H.

Danziger, ed., *Economic Conditions and Welfare Reform*, 119–157. Kalamazoo, Mich.: W. E. Upjohn Institute for Employment Research.

Bavier, Richard. 2001. "Welfare Reform Data from the Survey of Income and Program Participation." *Monthly Labor Review* 124 (July): 13–24.

Becerra, Rosina M., Vivian Lew, Michael N. Mitchell, and Hiromi Ono. 1998. *California Work Pays Demonstration Project: Report of First Forty-Two Months (Final Report)*. Los Angeles: School of Public Policy and Social Research, University of California, Los Angeles. October.

Becker, Gary S. 1965. "A Theory of the Allocation of Time." *Economic Journal* 75: 493–517.

———— 1968. "Crime and Punishment: An Economic Approach." *Journal of Political Economy* 76, no. 2 (March–April): 169–217.

———— 1981. *A Treatise on the Family*. Cambridge, Mass.: Harvard University Press.

Beecroft, Erik, Kevin Cahill, and Barbara D. Goodson. 2002. *The Impacts of Welfare Reform on Children: The Indiana Welfare Reform Evaluation*. Cambridge, Mass.: Abt Associates. June.

Beecroft, Erik, Wang Lee, David Long, Pamela A. Holcomb, Terri S. Thompson, Nancy Pindus, Carolyn O'Brien, and Jenny Bernstein. 2003. *The Indiana Welfare Reform: Five-Year Impacts, Implementation, Costs and Benefits*. Cambridge, Mass.: Abt Associates. September.

Bell, Stephen H. 2001. "Why Are Welfare Caseloads Falling?" Urban Institute Working Paper no. 01-02. Washington, D.C. March.

Berkowitz, Edward D. 1991. *America's Welfare State: From Roosevelt to Reagan*. Baltimore: Johns Hopkins University Press.

Bitler, Marianne, Jonah B. Gelbach, and Hilary W. Hoynes. 2002. "The Impact of Welfare Reform on Living Arrangements." National Bureau of Economic Research Working Paper no. 8784. Cambridge, Mass. February.

———— 2003. "What Mean Impacts Miss: Distributional Effects of Welfare Reform Experiments." National Bureau of Economic Research Working Paper no. 10121. November.

Bitler, Marianne, Jonah B. Gelbach, Hilary W. Hoynes, and Madeline Zavodny. 2004. "The Impact of Welfare Reform on Marriage and Divorce." *Demography* 41, no. 2: 213–236.

Blank, Rebecca M. 1989. "Analyzing the Length of Welfare Spells," *Journal of Public Economics* 39, no. 3 (August): 245–273.

———— 2001. "What Causes Public Assistance Caseloads to Grow?" *Journal of Human Resources* 36, no. 1 (Winter): 85–118.

———— 2002. "Evaluating Welfare Reform in the United States," *Journal of Economic Literature* 40, no. 4 (December): 1105–66.

Blank, Rebecca M., David Card, and Philip K. Robins. 2000. "Financial Incentives for Increasing Work and Income among Low-Income Families." In David E. Card and Rebecca M. Blank, eds., *Finding Jobs: Work and Welfare Reform*, 373–419. New York: Russell Sage Foundation.

Blank, Rebecca M., and Patricia Ruggles. 1996. "When Do Women Use AFDC and Food Stamps? The Dynamics of Eligibility versus Participation." *Journal of Human Resources* 31, no. 1 (Winter): 57–89.

Bloom, Dan, Mary Farrell, and Barbara Fink. 2002. *Time Limits: State Policies, Implementation, and Effects on Families*. New York: MDRC. July.

Bloom, Dan, Mary Farrell, James Kemple, and Nandita Verma. 1999. *The Family Transition Program: Implementation and Three-Year Impacts of Florida's Initial Time-Limited Welfare Program*. New York: MDRC. April.

Bloom, Dan, Richard Hendra, and Charles Michalopoulos. 2000. *Vermont's Welfare Restructuring Project: Key Findings from the Forty-Two-Month Client Survey*. New York: MDRC. June.

Bloom, Dan, James J. Kemple, Pamela Morris, Susan Scrivener, Nandita Verma, and Richard Hendra. 2000. *The Family Transition Program: Final Report on Florida's Initial Time-Limited Welfare Program*. New York: MDRC. December.

Bloom, Dan, Laura Melton, Charles Michalopoulos, Susan Scrivener, and Johanna Walter. 2000. *Jobs First: Implementation and Early Impacts of Connecticut's Welfare Reform Initiative*. New York: MDRC. February.

Bloom, Dan, and Charles Michalopoulos. 2001. *How Welfare and Work Policies Affect Employment and Income: A Synthesis of Research*. New York: MDRC. January.

Bloom, Dan, Charles Michalopoulos, Johanna Walter, and Patricia Auspos. 1998. *Implementation and Early Impacts of Vermont's Welfare Restructuring Project*. New York: MDRC. October.

Bloom, Dan, Susan Scrivener, Charles Michalopoulos, Pamela Morris, Richard Hendra, Diana Adams-Ciardullo, Johanna Walter, with Wanda Vargas. 2002. *Jobs First: Final Report on Connecticut's Welfare Reform Initiative*. New York: MDRC. February.

Bloom, Howard S., Carolyn J. Hill, and James Riccio. 2001. *Modeling the Performance of Welfare-to-Work Programs: The Effects of Program Management and Services, Economic Environment, and Client Characteristics*. New York: MDRC.

BLS. *See* U.S. Bureau of Labor Statistics.

Borjas, George J. 2001a. "Food Insecurity and Public Assistance." Joint Center for Poverty Research Working Paper no. 243. Chicago. May.

——— 2001b. "Welfare Reform and Immigration." In Rebecca M. Blank and Ron Haskins, eds., *The New World of Welfare*, 369–390. Washington, D.C.: Brookings Institution Press.

Bos, Johannes M., Aletha C. Huston, Robert C. Granger, Greg J. Duncan, Thomas W. Brock, and Vonnie C. McLoyd. 1999. *New Hope for People with Low Incomes: Two-Year Results of a Program to Reduce Poverty and Reform Welfare*. New York: MDRC. August.

Bos, Johannes M., and Wanda G. Vargas. 2001. "Maternal Employment and Changes in Adolescent Outcomes: Evidence from Two Evaluations of Programs to Promote Work." Draft paper prepared for the Biannual Research Conference of the Society for Research on Child Development, April.

Brooks-Gunn, Jeanne, Pamela Klebanov, Judith R. Smith, and Kyunghee Lee. 2001. "Effects of Combining Public Assistance and Employment on Mothers and Their Very Young Children," *Women and Health* 32, no. 3:179–210.

Burke, Vee, and Melinda Gish. 1998. *Welfare Reform: Work Trigger Time Limits, Exemptions, and Sanctions under TANF.* Congressional Research Service, 98-697 EPW. August 6.

Burtless, Gary. 1986. "The Work Response to a Guaranteed Income: A Survey of Experimental Evidence." In Alicia Munnell, ed., *Lessons from the Income Maintenance Experiments*, 22–59. Boston: Federal Reserve Bank of Boston.

——— 1995. "The Case for Randomized Field Trails in Economic and Policy Research." *Journal of Economic Perspectives* 92, no. 2 (Spring): 63–84.

Cain, Glen G. 1986. "The Income Maintenance Experiments and the Issues of Marital Stability and Family Composition." In Alicia Munnell, ed., *Lessons from the Income Maintenance Experiments*, 60–93. Boston: Federal Reserve Bank.

Camasso, Michael J., Carol Harvey, and Radha Jagannathan. 1996. *An Interim Report on the Impact of New Jersey's Family Development Program.* New Brunswick, N.J.: Public Affairs.

Camasso, Michael J., Carol Harvey, Radha Jagannathan, and Mark Killingsworth. 1998. *New Jersey's Family Development Program: Results on Program Impacts, Experimental Control Group Analysis.* Trenton, N.J.: New Jersey Department of Family Services. October.

Camasso, Michael J., Carol Harvey, Mark Killingsworth, and Radha Jagannathan. 1999. "New Jersey's Family Cap and Family Size Decisions: Some Findings From a 5-Year Evaluation." Manuscript. April.

Cancian, Maria, Robert Haveman, Thomas Kaplan, Daniel Meyer, and Barbara Wolfe. 1999a. "Work, Earnings, and Well-Being after Welfare: What Do We Know?" In Sheldon H. Danziger, ed., *Economic Conditions and Welfare Reform*, 161–186. Kalamazoo, Mich.: W. E. Upjohn Institute for Employment Research.

Cancian, Maria, Robert Haveman, Thomas Kaplan, and Barbara Wolfe. 1999b. *Post-Exit Earnings and Benefit Receipt among Those Who Left AFDC in Wisconsin.* University of Wisconsin–Madison. Madison, Wis.: Institute for Research on Poverty. January.

Cancian, Maria, Robert Haveman, Daniel R. Meyer, and Barbara Wolfe. 2000. *Before and After TANF: The Economic Well-Being of Women Leaving Welfare.* IRP Special Report no. 77. University of Wisconsin–Madison. Madison, Wis.: Institute for Research on Poverty. May.

CEA. *See* Council of Economic Advisers.

Center on Budget and Policy Priorities (CBPP). 2001. *State Time Limits.* Unpublished data.

Citro, Constance F., and Robert T. Michael, eds. 1995. *Measuring Poverty: A New Approach.* Washington, D.C.: National Academy of Sciences Press.

Clark-Kauffman, Elizabeth, Greg J. Duncan, and Pamela Morris. 2003. "How Welfare Policies Affect Child and Adolescent Achievement." *American Economic Review* 93, no. 2 (May): 299–303.

Committee on Ways and Means. *See* U.S. House, Committee on Ways and Means.

Coulton, Claudia, and Nandita Verma. 2000. *Employment and Return to Public Assistance among Single, Female-Headed Families Leaving AFDC in Third Quarter, 1996.* Washington, D.C.: Cuyahoga Work and Training, MDRC, and Case Western Reserve University. September.

Council of Economic Advisers (CEA). 1997. *Explaining the Decline in Welfare Receipt, 1993–1996.* Washington, D.C. May.

—— 1999a. *Economic Report of the President.* Washington, D.C.: Government Printing Office.

—— 1999b. *The Effects of Welfare Policy and the Economic Expansion on Welfare Caseloads: An Update.* Washington, D.C. August.

Crouse, Gil. 1999. *State Implementation of Major Changes to Welfare Policies 1992–1998.* Available at: *http://aspe.hhs.gov/hsp/Waiver-Policies99/Table_B.htm.*

Currie, Janet, and Jeffrey Grogger. 2002. "Medicaid Expansions and Welfare Contractions: Offsetting Effects on Prenatal Care and Infant Health?" *Journal of Health Economics* 21: 313–335.

DeMarzo, Peter M., Michael J. Fishman, and Kathleen M. Hagerty. 1998. "The Optimal Enforcement of Insider Trading Regulations." *Journal of Political Economy* 106, no. 3 (June): 602–632.

Department of Health and Human Services (DHHS). *See* U.S. Department of Health and Human Services.

Dickens, William T., Lawrence F. Katz, Kevin Lang, and Lawrence H. Summers. 1989. "Employee Crime and the Monitoring Puzzle," *Journal of Labor Economics* 7, no. 3 (July): 331–347.

Du, Jean, Debra Fogarty, Devin Hopps, and James Hu. 2000. *A Study of Washington State's TANF Leavers and TANF Recipients: Findings from the April–June 1999 Telephone Survey. Final Report.* Washington Department of Social and Health Services, Offices of Planning and Research, Economic Service Administration. February.

Duncan, Greg J., and Jeanne Brooks-Gunn, eds. 1997. *Consequences of Growing Up Poor.* New York: Russell Sage Foundation.

Duncan, Greg J., and P. Lindsay Chase-Lansdale. 2001. "Welfare Reform and Children's Well-Being." In Rebecca M. Blank and Ron Haskins, eds., *The New World of Welfare,* 391–417. Washington, D.C.: Brookings Institution Press.

Dupree, Allen, and Wendell Primus. 2001. "Declining Share of Children Lived with Single Mothers in the Late 1990s." Washington, D.C.: Center on Budget and Policy Priorities. Available at: *http://www.cbpp.org/6-15-01wel.pdf.*

Eccles, Jacquelynne, and Jennifer Appleton Gootman, eds. 2002. *Community*

Programs to Promote Youth Development. Washington, D.C.: National Academy Press.

Edin, Kathryn, and Laura Lein. 1997. *Making Ends Meet: How Single Mothers Survive Welfare and Low-Wage Work.* New York: Russell Sage Foundation.

Ellwood, David T. 1988. *Poor Support.* New York: Basic Books.

———— 2000. "The Impact of the Earned Income Tax Credit and Social Policy Reforms on Work, Marriage, and Living Arrangements." *National Tax Journal* 53, no. 4, pt. 2 (December): 1063–1106.

Fein, David J. 1999. *Will Welfare Reform Influence Marriage and Fertility?: Early Evidence from the ABC Demonstration,* Cambridge, Mass.: Abt Associates. June.

Fein, David J., Erik Beecroft, William L. Hamilton, Wang S. Lee, Pamela A. Holcomb, Terri S. Thompson, and Caroline E. Ratcliffe. 1998. *The Indiana Welfare Reform Evaluation: Program Implementation and Economic Impacts after Two Years.* Cambridge, Mass.: Abt Associates. November.

Fein, David J., and Jennifer Karweit. 1997. *The ABC Evaluation: The Early Economic Impacts of Delaware's A Better Chance Welfare Reform Program,* Cambridge, Mass.: Abt Associates. December.

Fein, David J., and Wang S. Lee. 2000. *The ABC Evaluation: Impacts of Welfare Reform on Child Maltreatment.* Cambridge, Mass.: Abt Associates. December.

Fein, David J., Wang S. Lee, and E. Christina Schofield. 1999. *The ABC Evaluation: Do Welfare Recipients' Children Have a School Attendance Problem?* Cambridge, Mass.: Abt Associates. August.

Fein, David J., David A. Long, Joy M. Behrens, and Wang S. Lee. 2001. *The ABC Evaluation: Turning the Corner: Delaware's A Better Chance Welfare Reform Program at Four Years.* Cambridge, Mass.: Abt Associates. January.

Figlio, David N., and James P. Ziliak. 1999. "Welfare Reform, the Business Cycle, and the Decline in AFDC Caseloads." In Sheldon H. Danziger, ed., *Economic Conditions and Welfare Reform,* 17–48. Kalamazoo, Mich.: W. E. Upjohn Institute for Employment Research.

Fink, Barbara, and Rebecca Widom. 2001. *Social Service Organizations and Welfare Reform.* New York: MDRC.

Fogarty, Debra, and Shon Kraley. 2000. *A Study of Washington State's TANF Leavers and TANF Recipients: Findings from Administrative Data and the Telephone Survey. Summary Report.* Washington Department of Social and Health Services, Offices of Planning and Research, Economic Service Administration. March.

Foster, E. M. 1999. *Amended Quarterly Progress Report: Outcomes for Single Parent Leavers by Cohort Quarter.* Georgia State University. April.

Fraker, Thomas M., and Jonathan E. Jacobson. 2000. *Iowa's Family Investment Program: Impacts During the First 3 1/2 Years of Welfare Reform.* Washington, D.C.: Mathematica Policy Research. May.

Fraker, Thomas M., Christine M. Ross, Rita A. Stapulonis, Robert B. Olsen, Martha D. Kovac, M. Robin Dion, and Anu Rangarajan. 2002. *The Evaluation of Welfare Reform in Iowa: Final Impact Report.* Washington, D.C.: Mathematica Policy Research. June.

Freedman, Steven, Daniel Friedlander, and James A. Riccio. 1993. *GAIN: Benefits, Costs, and Three-Year Impacts of a Welfare-to-Work Program.* New York: MDRC.

Freedman, Stephen, Daniel Friedlander, Gayle Hamilton, JoAnn Rock, Marisa Mitchell, Jodi Nudelman, Amanda Schweder, and Laura Storto. 2000. *National Evaluation of Welfare-to-Work Strategies: Evaluating Alternative Welfare-to-Work Approaches: Two-Year Impacts of Eleven Programs.* New York: MDRC, U.S. Department of Health and Human Services, and U.S. Department of Education. June.

Freedman, Stephen, Jean Tansey Knab, Lisa A. Gennetian, and David Navarro. 2000. *The Los Angeles Jobs-First GAIN Evaluation: Final Report on a Work First Program in a Major Urban Center.* New York: MDRC. June.

Gais, Thomas L., Richard P. Nathan, Irene Lurie, and Thomas Kaplan. 2001. "Implementation of the Personal Responsibility Act of 1996." In Rebecca M. Blank and Ron Haskins, eds., *The New World of Welfare,* 35–69. Washington, D.C.: Brookings Institution Press.

GAO. *See* U.S. General Accounting Office.

Garfinkel, Irwin, and Sara McLanahan. 1986. *Single Mothers and Their Children: A New American Dilemma.* Changing Domestic Priorities Series. Washington, D.C.: Urban Institute Press.

Gennetian, Lisa A., and Cynthia Miller. 2000. *Reforming Welfare and Rewarding Work: Final Report on the Minnesota Family Investment Program.* Vol. 2, *Effects on Children.* New York: MDRC. September.

Gilens, Martin. 1999. *Why Americans Hate Welfare: Race, Media, and the Politics of Antipoverty Policy.* Chicago: University of Chicago Press.

Gittleman, Maury. 2001. "Declining Caseloads: What Do the Dynamics of Welfare Participation Reveal?" *Industrial Relations* 40 (October): 537–570.

Gladden, Tricia, and Christopher Taber. 2000. "Wage Progression among Less-Skilled Workers." In David E. Card and Rebecca M. Blank, eds., *Finding Jobs: Work and Welfare Reform,* 160–192. New York: Russell Sage Foundation.

Goldberg, Heidi, and Liz Schott. 2000. *A Compliance-Oriented Approach to Sanctions in State and County TANF Programs.* Washington, D.C.: Center on Budget and Policy Priorities. October 1.

Gordon, Anne, and Roberto Agodini. 1999. *Early Impacts of the Virginia Independence Program: Final Report.* Princeton, N.J.: Mathematica Policy Research. November.

Greenberg, David, Robert Meyer, Charles Michalopoulos, and Michael Wiseman. 2001. *Modeling the Performance of Welfare-to-Work Programs: The Effects of Program Management and Services, Economic Environment, and Client Characteristics.* Institute for Research on Poverty Working Paper.

Greenberg, David H., Charles Michalopoulos, and Philip K. Robins. 2001. "A Meta-Analysis of Government Sponsored Training Programs." University of Maryland. September.

Groeneveld, Lyle P., Michael T. Hannan, and Nancy Tuma. 1983. "Marital Stability." In *Final Report of the Seattle/Denver Income Maintenance Experiment.* Vol. 1, *Design and Results.* Washington, D.C.: Government Printing Office.

Grogger, Jeffrey. 2002. "The Behavioral Effects of Welfare Time Limits." *American Economic Review* 92, no. 2 (May): 385–389.

——— 2003. "The Effects of Time Limits, the EITC, and Other Policy Changes on Welfare Use, Work, and Income among Female-Headed Families." *Review of Economics and Statistics* 85, no. 2 (May): 394–408.

——— 2004. "Time Limits and Welfare Use." *Journal of Human Resources* 39, no. 2 (Spring): 405–424.

Grogger, Jeffrey, Steven J. Haider, and Jacob Klerman. 2003. "Why Did the Welfare Rolls Fall during the 1990s? The Importance of Entry" *American Economic Review* 93, no. 2 (May): 288–292.

Grogger, Jeffrey, Lynn A. Karoly, and Jacob Alex Klerman. 2002. "Consequences of Welfare Reform: A Research Synthesis," RAND working draft. Santa Monica, Calif. June.

Grogger, Jeffrey, and Charles Michalopoulos. 1999. "Welfare Dynamics under Time Limits." National Bureau of Economic Research Working Paper no. 7353. Cambridge, Mass. September.

——— 2003. "Welfare Dynamics under Time Limits." *Journal of Political Economy* 111, no. 3 (June): 530–554.

Gruber, Jonathan. 2003. "Medicaid." In Robert A. Moffitt, ed., *Means-Tested Transfer Programs in the United States,* 15–78. Chicago: University of Chicago Press.

Guyer, Jocelyn. 2000. *Health Care after Welfare: An Update of Findings from State-Level Leaver Studies.* Washington, D.C.: Center on Budget and Policy Priorities. August.

Haider, Steven, Alison Jacknowitz, and Robert F. Schoeni. 2003. "The Impact of Welfare Work Requirements on Breastfeeding." *Demography* 40, no. 3 (August): 479–497.

Haider, Steven, Jacob Alex Klerman, and Elizabeth Roth. 2001. "The Relationship between the Economy and the Welfare Caseload: A Dynamic Approach." Manuscript. RAND, Santa Monica, Calif. April.

Haider, Steven, Robert F. Schoeni, Yuhua Bao, and Caroline Danielson. 2001. "Immigrants, Welfare Reform, and the Economy in the 1990s." RAND Working Paper DRU-2681.

Hamilton, Gayle, Stephen Freedman, Lisa Gennetian, Charles Michalopoulos et al. 2001. *National Evaluation of Welfare-to-Work Strategies: How Ef-*

fective Are Different Welfare-to-Work Approaches? Five-Year Adult and Child Impacts for Eleven Programs. New York: MDRC, U.S. Department of Health and Human Services, and U.S. Department of Education. December.

Hamilton, Gayle, Stephen Freedman, and Sharon M. McGroder. 2000. *Do Mandatory Welfare-to-Work Programs Affect the Well-Being of Children?: A Synthesis of Child Research Conducted as Part of the National Evaluation of Welfare-to-Work Strategies.* New York: MDRC, U.S. Department of Health and Human Services, and U.S. Department of Education. June.

Harvey, Carol, Michael J. Camasso, and Radha Jagannathan. 2000. "Evaluating Welfare Reform Waivers under Section 1115." *Journal of Economic Perspectives* 14, no. 4 (Fall): 165–188.

Haskins, Ron. 2001. "Effects of Welfare Reform on Family Income and Poverty." In Rebecca M. Blank and Ron Haskins, eds., *The New World of Welfare,* 103–136. Washington, D.C.: Brookings Institution Press.

Haveman, Robert, and Barbara Wolfe. 1995. "The Determinants of Children's Attainments: A Review of Methods and Findings." *Journal of Economic Literature* 33 (December): 1829–78.

Heckman, James J., and Jeffrey A. Smith. 1995. "Assessing the Case for Social Experiments." *Journal of Economic Perspectives* 92, no. 2 (Spring): 85–110.

Heckman, James J., Jeffrey A. Smith, and Christopher Taber. 1998. "Accounting for Drop-Outs in Evaluations of Social Programs," *Review of Economics and Statistics* 80, no. 1 (February): 1–14.

Heclo, Hugh. 2001. "The Politics of Welfare Reform." In Rebecca M. Blank and Ron Haskins, eds., *The New World of Welfare,* 169–200. Washington, D.C.: Brookings Institution Press.

Hendra, Richard, and Charles Michalopoulos. 1999. *Forty-Two-Month Impacts of Vermont's Welfare Restructuring Project.* New York: MDRC. September.

Hendra, Richard, Charles Michalopoulos, and Dan Bloom. 2001. *Three-Year Impacts of Connecticut's Jobs First Welfare Reform Initiative.* New York: MDRC. April.

Hofferth, Sandra L., Stephen Stanhope, and Kathleen Mullan Harris. 2000. "Remaining off Welfare in the 1990s: The Influence of Public Policy and Economic Conditions." Institute for Social Research, Ann Arbor, Mich. October.

——— 2002. "Exiting Welfare in the 1990s: Did Public Policy Influence Recipients' Behavior." *Population Research and Policy Review* 21, no. 5 (October): 433–472.

Horvath-Rose, Ann, and H. Elizabeth Peters. 2002. "Welfare Waivers and Non-Marital Childbearing." In Greg Duncan and P. Lindsay Chase-Lansdale, eds., *For Better and for Worse: Welfare Reform and the Well-*

Being of Children and Families, 222–245. New York: Russell Sage Foundation.

Hotz, V. Joseph, Guido W. Imbens, and Jacob A. Klerman. 2000. "The Long-Term Gains from GAIN: A Re-Analysis of the Impacts of the California GAIN Program." National Bureau of Economic Research Working Paper no. 8007. Cambridge, Mass. November.

Hotz, V. Joseph, Charles Mullin, and John Karl Scholz. 2001. "The Earned Income Tax Credit and Labor Market Participation of Families on Welfare." Manuscript.

——— 2002. "Welfare, Employment and Income: Evidence on the Effects of Benefit Reductions from California." *American Economic Review* 92, no. 2 (May).

Hotz, V. Joseph, and John Karl Scholz. 2003. "The Earned Income Tax Credit." In Robert A. Moffitt, ed., *Means-Tested Transfer Programs in the United States,* 141–197. Chicago: University of Chicago Press.

Hsiao, Cheng. 1986. *Analysis of Panel Data.* Cambridge: Cambridge University Press.

Hu, Wei-Yin. 2003. "Marriage and Economic Incentives: Evidence from a Welfare Experiment." *Journal of Human Resources* 38, no. 4 (Fall): 942–963.

Huang, Chien-Chung, Irwin Garfinkel, and Jane Waldfogel. 2000. "Child Support and Welfare Caseloads." Institute for Research on Poverty Discussion Paper 1218-00, Madison, Wis.

Hurst, Erik, and James P. Ziliak. 2001. "Welfare Reform and Household Saving." Manuscript. July.

Huston, Aletha, Cynthia Miller, Lashawn Richburg-Hayes, Greg J. Duncan, Carolyn A. Eldred, Thomas S. Weisner, Edward Lowe, Vonnie C. McLoyd, Danielle A. Crosby, Marika N. Ripke, and Cindy Redcross. 2003. *New Hope for Families and Children: Five-Year Results of a Program to Reduce Poverty and Reform Welfare.* New York: MDRC. June.

Isaacs, Julia B., and Matthew R. Lyon. 2000. *A Cross-State Examination of Families Leaving Welfare: Findings from the ASPE-Funded Leavers Studies.* Washington, D.C.: Division of Data and Technical Analysis, Office of the Assistant Secretary for Planning and Evaluation, Department of Health and Human Services, November 2000. Available at: *http://aspc.hhs.gov/hsp/leavers99/cross-state00/.*

Julnes, George, Anthony Halter, Steven Anderson, Lee Frost-Kumpf, Richard Schuldt, Francis Staskon, and Barbara Ferrara. 2000. *Illinois Study of Former TANF Clients: Final Report.* Springfield, Ill.: Institute for Public Affairs, University of Illinois at Springfield, and School of Social Work, University of Illinois at Urbana-Champaign. August.

Kaestner, Robert, and Neeray Kaushal. Forthcoming. "Immigrant and Native Responses to Welfare Reform." *Journal of Population Economics.*

Karoly, Lynn A., Peter W. Greenwood, Susan S. Everingham, Jill Houbé, M. Rebecca Kilburn, C. Peter Rydell, Matthew Sanders, and James Chiesa. 1998. *Investing in Our Children: What We Know and Don't Know about the Costs and Benefits of Early Childhood Interventions.* MR-898. Santa Monica, Calif.: RAND Corporation.

Kaushal, Neeray, and Robert Kaestner. 2001. "From Welfare to Work: Has Welfare Reform Worked?" *Journal of Policy Analysis and Management* 20, no. 4: 699–719.

Kearney, Melissa Schettini. 2002. "Is There an Effect of Incremental Welfare Benefits on Fertility Behavior? A Look at the Family Cap." National Bureau of Economic Research Working Paper no. 9093. Cambridge, Mass. August.

Kerpelman, Larry C., David B. Connell, and Walter J. Gunn. 2000. "Effect of a Monetary Sanction on Immunization Rates of Recipients of Aid to Families with Dependent Children." *Journal of the American Medical Association* 284, no. 1 (July): 53–59.

Klerman, Jacob A., and Steven Haider. 2000. "A Stock-Flow Analysis of the Welfare Caseload: Insights from California Economic Conditions." RAND Corporation, Santa Monica, Calif. March.

Kornfeld, Robert, Laura Peck, Diane Porcari, John Straubinger, Zachary Johnson, and Clementina Cabral. 1999. *Evaluation of the Arizona EMPOWER Welfare Reform Demonstration: Impact Study Interim Report.* Cambridge, Mass.: Abt Associates. May.

Lawrance, Emily C. 1991. "Poverty and the Rate of Time Preference: Evidence from Panel Data." *Journal of Political Economy* 99, no. 1 (February): 54–77.

Levine, Phillip B. 2002. "The Impact of Social Policy and Economic Activity throughout the Fertility Decision Tree." National Bureau of Economic Research Working Paper no. 9021. Cambridge, Mass. June.

Levine, Phillip B., and Diane M. Whitmore. 1998. "The Impact of Welfare Reform on the AFDC Caseload." *National Tax Association Proceedings— 1997.* Washington, D.C.: National Tax Association.

Loeb, Susana, and Mary Corcoran. 2001. "Welfare, Work Experience, and Economic Self-Sufficiency." *Journal of Policy Analysis and Management* 20 (Winter): 1–20.

Loprest, Pamela. 1999. "Families Who Left Welfare: Who Are They and How Are They Doing?" Urban Institute Discussion Paper no. 99–02. Washington, D.C.

——— 2000. *How Are Families Who Left Welfare Doing over Time? A Comparison of Two Cohorts of Welfare Leavers.* Washington, D.C.: Urban Institute.

——— 2001. "How Are Families That Left Welfare Doing? A Comparison of Early and Recent Welfare Leavers." Urban Institute, series B, no. B-36. Washington, D.C. April.

Loprest, Pamela, and Gregory Acs. 2000. *The Status of TANF Leavers in the District of Columbia: Interim Report.* Urban Institute, Washington, D.C. February.

LoSasso, Anthony T., and Thomas C. Buchmueller. 2002. "The Effect of the

State Children's Health Insurance Program on Health Insurance Coverage." National Bureau of Economic Research Working Paper no. 9405. Cambridge, Mass. December.

MaCurdy, Thomas, David Mancuso, and Margaret O'Brien-Strain. 2002. *Does California's Welfare Policy Explain the Slower Decline of Its Caseload?* San Francisco: Public Policy Institute of California. January.

Magnuson, Katherine A., and Sharon M. McGroder. 2002. "The Effect of Increasing Welfare Mother's Education on Their Young Children's Academic Problems and School Readiness." Joint Center for Poverty Research Working Paper no. 280. Chicago. February.

Martin, Joyce A., Melissa M. Park, and Paul D. Sutton. 2002. *Births: Preliminary Data for 2001*. National Vital Statistics Reports, vol. 50, no. 10. National Center for Health Statistics, Hyattsville, Md. Available at: *www.cdc.gov/nchs/data/nvsr/nvsr50/nvsr50_10.pdf*. June 6.

Mayer, Susan E. 1997. *What Money Can't Buy: Family Income and Children's Life Chances*. Cambridge, Mass.: Harvard University Press.

McGroder, S., M. Zaslow, K. Moore, and S. LeMenestrel. 2000. *National Evaluation of Welfare-to-Work Strategies: Impacts on Young Children and Their Families Two Years after Enrollment: Findings from the Child Outcomes Study*. Washington, D.C.: U.S. Dept of Health and Human Services, Administration for Children and Families, Office of the Assistant Secretary for Planning and Evaluation, U.S. Dept of Education, Office of the Under Secretary, and Office of Vocational and Adult Education.

Mead, Lawrence M. 1999. "The Decline of Welfare in Wisconsin." *Journal of Public Administration Research and Theory* 9, no. 4: 597–622.

——— 2000. "Caseload Change: An Exploratory Study." *Journal of Policy Analysis and Management* 19, no. 3.

——— 2001. "Governmental Quality and Welfare Reform." Department of Politics, New York University. Manuscript.

Meyer, Bruce. 1995. "Natural and Quasi-Experiments in Economics." *Journal of Business and Economic Statistics* 13, no. 2 (April): 151–161.

Meyer, Bruce D., and Dan T. Rosenbaum. 2000. "Making Single Mothers Work: Recent Tax and Welfare Policy and Its Effects." Joint Center for Poverty Research Working Paper no. 152. Chicago. January.

——— 2001. "Welfare, the Earned Income Tax Credit, and the Labor Supply of Single Mothers." *Quarterly Journal of Economics* 116 (August): 1063–1114.

Meyer, Bruce D., and James X. Sullivan. 2003. "Measuring the Well-Being of the Poor Using Income and Consumption." *Journal of Human Resources* 38, supp.: 1180–1220.

——— 2004. "The Effects of Welfare and Tax Reform: The Material Well-Being of Single Mothers in the 1980s and 1990s." *Journal of Public Economics* 88, nos. 7–8 (July): 1387–1420.

Meyers, Marcia K., Bonnie Glaser, and Karin MacDonald. 1998. "On the

Front Lines of Welfare Delivery: Are Workers Implementing Policy Reforms?" *Journal of Policy Analysis and Management* 17, no. 1: 1–22.

Michalopoulos, Charles, and Gordon Berlin. 2001. "Financial Work Incentives for Low-Wage Workers: Encouraging Work, Reducing Poverty, and Benefiting Families." In Bruce Meyer and Greg Duncan, eds., *The Incentives of Government Programs and the Well-Being of Families,* chap. 4, pp. 1–16. Chicago: Joint Center for Poverty Research.

Michalopoulos, Charles, David E. Card, Lisa A. Gennetian, Kristen Harknett, and Philip K. Robins. 2000. *The Self-Sufficiency Project at 36 Months: Effects of a Financial Work Incentive on Employment and Income.* Ottawa: Social Research and Demonstration Corporation. June.

Michalopoulos, Charles, Phillip K. Robins, and David E. Card. 1999. *When Financial Incentives Pay for Themselves: Early Findings from the Self-Sufficiency Project's Applicant Study.* Ottawa: Social Research and Demonstration Corporation. May.

Michalopoulos, Charles, and Christine Schwartz, with Diana Adams-Ciardullo. 2000. *What Works Best for Whom: Impacts of 20 Welfare-to-Work Programs by Subgroup.* New York: MDRC, U.S. Department of Health and Human Services, and U.S. Department of Education. August.

Michalopoulos, Charles, Doug Tattrie, Cynthia Miller, Philip K. Robins, Pamela Morris, David Gyarmati, Cindy Redcross, Kelly Foley, and Reuben Ford. 2002. *Making Work Pay: Final Report on the Self-Sufficiency Project for Long-Term Welfare Reecipients.* Ottawa: Social Research and Demonstration Corporation. July.

Midwest Research Institute. 2000. *Chapter 1—Employment and Earnings of Former AFDC Recipients in Missouri, Chapter 2—Household Income and Poverty, Chapter 3—The Continuing Use of Assistance by Former Missouri AFDC Recipients, and Chapter 4—Insecurity Among Former AFDC Recipients.* Interim Reports for the Missouri Department of Social Services. June.

Miller, Cynthia, Virginia Knox, Patricia Auspos, Jo Anna Hunter-Manns, and Alan Orenstein. 1997. *Making Welfare Work and Work Pay: Implementation and 18-Month Impacts of the Minnesota Family Investment Program.* New York: MDRC. September.

Miller, Cynthia, Virginia Knox, Lisa A. Gennetian, Martey Dodoo, Jo Anna Hunter, and Cindy Redcross. 2000. *Reforming Welfare and Rewarding Work: Final Report on the Minnesota Family Investment Program.* Vol. 1, *Effects on Adults.* New York: MDRC. September.

Minkovitz, Cynthia, Elizabeth Holt, Nancy Hughart, William Hou, Larry Thomas, Eugene Dini, and Bernard Guyer. 1999. "The Effect of Parental Monetary Sanctions on the Vaccination Status of Young Children." *Archives of Pediatric Adolescent Medicine* 153. December.

Moffitt, Robert A. 1983. "An Economic Model of Welfare Stigma." *American Economic Review* 73, no. 5. (December): 1023–35.

———— 1987. "Historical Growth in Participation in Aid to Families with Dependent Children: Was There a Structural Shift?" *Journal of Post Keynsian Economics* 9 (Spring): 347–363.

———— 1992. "Incentive Effects of the U.S. Welfare System: A Review." *Journal of Economic Literature* 30 (March): 1–61.

———— 1999. "The Effect of Pre-PRWORA Waivers on AFDC Caseloads and Female Earnings, Income, and Labor Force Behavior." In Sheldon H. Danziger, ed., *Economic Conditions and Welfare Reform*, 91–118. Kalamazoo, Mich.: W. E. Upjohn Institute for Employment Research.

Moffitt, Robert A., and Michele Ver Ploeg, eds. 1999. *Data and Methodological Issues for Tracking Former Welfare Recipients: A Workshop Summary.* Panel on Data and Methods for Measuring the Effects of Changes in Social Welfare Programs, Committee on National Statistics, National Research Council. Washington, D.C.: National Academy Press.

Moffitt, Robert A., and Michele Ver Ploeg. 2001. *Evaluating Welfare Reform in an Era of Transition.* Panel on Data and Methods for Measuring the Effects of Changes in Social Welfare Programs, Committee on National Statistics, National Research Council. Washington, D.C.: National Academy Press.

Morris, Pamela A., Aletha C. Huston, Greg J. Duncan, Danielle A. Crosby, and Johannes Bos. 2001. *How Welfare and Work Policies Affect Children: A Synthesis of Research.* New York: MDRC. March.

Morris, Pamela, and Charles Michalopoulos. 2000. *The Self-Sufficiency Project at 36 Months: Effects on Children of a Program that Increased Parental Employment and Income.* Ottawa: Social Research and Demonstration Corporation. June.

Moses, Anne, and D. C. Macuso. 1999. *Examining Circumstances of Individuals and Families Who Leave TANF: Assessing the Validity of Administrative Data.* SPHERE Institute. Burlingame, Calif. May.

Mueser, Peter R., Julie L. Hotchkiss, Christopher T. King, Philip S. Rokicki, and David W. Stevens. 2000. "The Welfare Caseload, Economic Growth and Welfare-to-Work Policies: An Analysis of Five Urban Areas." University of Missouri. Columbia, Mo. July. Available at: *web.missouri.edu/ ~econwww/WP/WP2000/WP0005_Mueser.pdf.*

Murray, Charles. 1984. *Losing Ground: American Social Policy, 1950–1980.* New York: Basic Books.

Nathan, Richard P., and Thomas L. Gais. 1999. "Implementing the Personal Responsibility Act of 1996: A First Look." Federalism Research Group, Nelson A. Rockefeller Institute of Government, New York.

Nickell, Stephen. 1981. "Biases in Dynamic Models with Fixed Effects." *Econometrica* 49 (November): 1417–26.

O'Neill, June E. 2003. "The Gender Gap in Wages, Circa 2000." *American Economic Review* 93 (May): 309–314.

O'Neill, June E., and M. Anne Hill. 2001. *Gaining Ground? Measuring the*

Impact of Welfare Reform on Welfare and Work. Manhattan Institute for Policy Research Civic Report no. 17. New York. July.

Pavetti, LaDonna, and Dan Bloom. 2001. "State Sanctions and Time Limits." In Rebecca M. Blank and Ron Haskins, eds., *The New World of Welfare*, 245–269. Washington, D.C.: Brookings Institution Press.

Paxson, Christina, and Jane Waldfogel. 1999. "Parental Resources and Child Abuse and Neglect." *American Economic Review* 89, no. 2 (May): 239–244.

——— 2003. "Welfare Reforms, Family Resources, and Child Maltreatment." *Journal of Policy Analysis and Management* 22, no. 1 (Winter): 85–113.

Piven, Frances Fox, and Richard Cloward. 1971. *Regulating the Poor*. New York: Vintage Books.

Primus, Wendell, L. Rawlings, K. Larin, and K. Porter. 1999. *The Initial Impacts of Welfare Reform on the Incomes of Single Mother Families*. Washington, D.C.: Center on Budget and Policy Priorities.

Quets, Gail, Phillip K. Robins, Elsie C. Pan, Charles Michalopoulos, and David Card. 1999. *Does SSP Plus Increase Employment?: The Effect of Adding Services to the Self-Sufficiency Project's Financial Incentives*. Ottawa: Social Research and Demonstration Corporation. May.

Quint, Janet, Kathryn Edin, Maria Buck, Barbara Fink, Yolanda Padilla, Olis Simmons-Hewitt, and Mary Valmont. 1999. *Big Cities and Welfare Reform: Early Implementation and Ethnographic Findings from the Project on Devolution and Urban Change*. New York: MDRC.

Rector, Robert E., and Sarah E. Youssef. 1999. "The Determinants of Welfare Caseload Decline." Heritage Foundation Paper no. CDA99-04. May.

Rockefeller Institute, New York State Office of Temporary and Disability Assistance, and the New York State Department of Labor. 1999. *After Welfare: A Study of Work and Benefit Use After Case Closing*. Revised Interim Report. December.

Rosenbaum, Dan T. 2000. "Taxes, the Earned Income Tax Credit, and Marital Status." Joint Center for Poverty Research Working Paper no. 177. Chicago. August.

Rowe, Gretchen, and Tracy Roberts. 2004. *Welfare Rules Databook: State Policies as of July 2000*. Washington, D.C.: Urban Institute.

Ryan, S., M. Theilbar, S. Choi, J. Qu, M. Deng, and L. Ellebracht. 1999. *Preliminary Outcomes for 1996 Fourth Quarter AFDC Leavers: Revised Interim Report*. University of Missouri–Columbia. September.

Sandfort, Jodi. 1999. "The Structural Impediments to Human Service Collaboration: Examining Welfare Reform at the Front Lines." *Social Service Review* 73, no. 3: 324–339.

Schoeni, Robert F., and Rebecca M. Blank. 2000. "What Has Welfare Reform Accomplished? Impacts on Welfare Participation, Employment, Income, Poverty, and Family Structure." National Bureau of Economic Research Working Paper no. 7627. March.

Scott, Ellen K., Kathryn Edin, Andrew S. London, and Joan Maya Mazelis. 2001. "My Children Come First: Welfare-Reliant Women's Post-TANF Views of Work-Family Tradeoffs, Neighborhoods, and Marriage." In Greg J. Duncan and P. Lindsay Chase-Lansdale, eds., *For Better and For Worse: Welfare Reform and the Well-Being of Children and Families,* 132–153. New York: Russell Sage Foundation.

Scott, Ellen K., Andrew S. London, and Kathryn Edin. 2001. "Looking to the Future: Welfare-Reliant Women Talk about Their Job Aspirations in the Context of Welfare Reform." *Journal of Social Issues* 56, no. 4: 727–746.

Turturro, Carolyn, Brent Benda, and Howard Turney. 1997. *Arkansas Welfare Waiver Demonstration Project. Final Report.* Little Rock: University of Arkansas at Little Rock, School of Social Work. June.

U.S. Bureau of the Census. 1960. *Persons by Family Characteristics.* 1960 Census of the Population, PC(2)-4. Washington, D.C.: U.S. Census Bureau.

——— 1994. *Marital Status and Living Arrangements: March 1994.* Current Population Reports. Washington, D.C.: U.S. Census Bureau.

——— 1995. *Statistical Abstract of the United States, 1995.* Washington, D.C.: U.S. Government Printing Office.

——— 2001a. *Historical Poverty Tables, 2001.* Available at: *http://www. census.gov/hhes/poverty/histpov/hstpov1.html.*

——— 2001b. *Living Arrangements of Children under 18 Years Old: 1960 to Present.* June 29. Available at: *http://www.census.gov/population/ socdemo/hh-fam/tabCH-1.pdf.*

U.S. Bureau of Labor Statistics (BLS). 1989. *Employment and Wages Annual Averages.* Washington, D.C.: U.S. Government Printing Office.

——— 2002. *Labor Force Statistics from the Current Population Survey.* Available at: *http://www.bls.gov/cps/home.htm.*

U.S. Department of Health and Human Services (DHHS). 1985. *Report to Congress on Out-of-Wedlock Childbearing.* September.

——— 1997. *Setting the Baseline: A Report on State Welfare Waivers.* June. Available at: *http://aspe.hhs.gov/hsp/isp/waiver2/title.htm.*

——— 2000. *Temporary Assistance for Needy Families (TANF Program): Third Annual Report to Congress.* August. Available at: *http:// www.acf.hhs.gov/programs/ofa/opreweb/annual3.pdf.*

——— 2001a. *Status Report on Research on the Outcomes of Welfare Reform.* Washington, D.C.: Office of the Assistant Secretary for Planning and Evaluation, Administration for Children and Families. Available at: *http:// aspe.hhs.gov/hsp/welf-ref-outcomes01/index.htm.* July.

——— 2001b. *Total Number of Families, Temporary Assistance for Needy Families.* Washington, D.C.: Administration for Children and Families. Available at: *http://www.acf.dhhs.gov/news/families.htm.*

——— 2003. *Temporary Assistance for Needy Families (TANF) Program: Fifth Annual Report to Congress.* February. Available at: *http:// www.acf.dhhs.gov/programs/ofa/annualreport5/.*

U.S. Department of Labor. 2003. *History of the Minimum Wage, 2003.* Available at: *http://www.dol.gov/esa/minwage/coverage.htm.*

U.S. General Accounting Office. 2000. *Welfare Reform: State Sanction Policies and Number of Families Affected.* GAO/HEHS-00-44. Washington, D.C.: U.S. General Accounting Office. March.

U.S. House. Committee on Ways and Means. Various years. *Green Book.* Washington, D.C.: Government Printing Office.

U.S. National Center for Health Statistics. 2002. *Births: Final Data for 2000.* National Vital Statistics Reports. February 12.

Vandell, D. L., and K. M. Pierce. 2003. "Child Care Quality and Children's Success at School." In Arthur J. Reynolds, Herbert J. Walberg, and Margaret C. Wang, ed., *Early Childhood Programs for a New Century,* 115–139. New York: Child Welfare League of America.

Vandell, D. L., and L. Shumow. 1999. "After-School Child Care Programs." *The Future of Children* 9, no. 2: 64–80.

Vandell, D. L. and B. Wolfe. 2000. *Child Care Quality: Does It Matter and Does It Need to be Improved?* Washington, D.C.: Office of the Assistant Secretary for Planning and Evaluation, Department of Health and Human Services.

Verma, Nandita, and B. Goldman. 2000. *Los Angeles County Post-TANF Tracking Project: Quarterly Progress Report.* New York: MDRC. January.

Wallace, Geoffrey, and Rebecca M. Blank. 1999. "What Goes Up Must Come Down?: Explaining Recent Changes in Public Assistance Caseloads." In Sheldon H. Danziger, ed., *Economic Conditions and Welfare Reform,* 49–89. Kalamazoo, Mich.: W. E. Upjohn Institute for Employment Research.

Weaver, R. Kent. 2000. *Ending Welfare as We Know It.* Washington, D.C.: Brookings Institution Press.

Werner, Alan, and Robert Kornfeld. 1997. *The Evaluation of 'To Strengthen Michigan Families': Final Impact Report.* Cambridge, Mass.: Abt Associates. September.

Westra, Karen, and John Routley. 1999. *Arizona Cash Assistance Exit Study: Cases Exiting Fourth Quarter 1996.* Arizona Department of Economic Security. July.

———— 2000. *Arizona Cash Assistance Exit Study: First Quarter 1998 Final Report.* Washington, D.C.: Arizona Department of Economic Security, U.S. Department of Health and Human Services. January.

Wilson, William Julius, and Kathryn Neckerman. 1986. "Poverty and Family Structure: The Widening Gap between Evidence and Policy Issues." In Sheldon H. Danziger and Daniel H. Weinberg, eds., *Fighting Poverty: What Works and What Doesn't,* 232–259. Cambridge, Mass.: Harvard University Press.

Winship, Scott, and Christopher Jencks. 2002. "Changes in Food Security after Welfare Reform: Can We Identify a Policy Effect?" Working draft. March.

Zabel, Jeffrey, Saul Schwartz, and Stephen Donald. 2004. "An Econometric Analysis of the Impact of the Self-Sufficiency Project on Unemployment and Employment Durations." Tufts University Department of Economics. Manuscript. February.

Zaslow, Martha J., Kristin A. Moore, Jennifer L. Brooks, Pamela A. Morris et al. 2002. "Experimental Studies of Welfare Reform and Children." *The Future of Children* 12, no. 1 (Winter/Spring): 79–95.

Ziliak, James P., and David N. Figlio. 2000. "Geographic Differences in AFDC and Food Stamp Caseloads in the Welfare Reform Era." Joint Center for Poverty Research Working Paper no. 180. Chicago. June.

Ziliak, James P., David N. Figlio, Elizabeth E. Davis, and Laura S. Connolly. 2000. "Accounting for the Decline in AFDC Caseloads: Welfare Reform or the Economy?" *Journal of Human Resources* 35, no. 3 (January): 570–586.

Index